Beardo

"The Miracle of Creation"

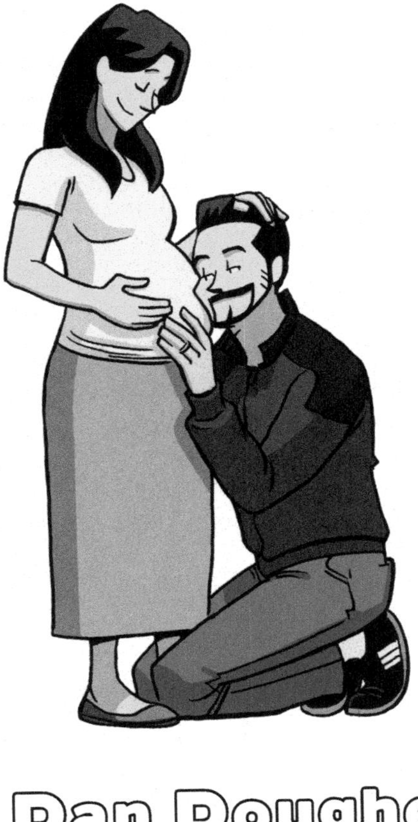

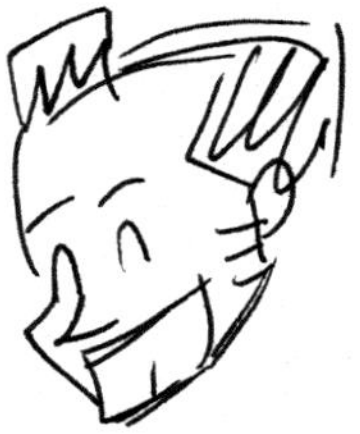

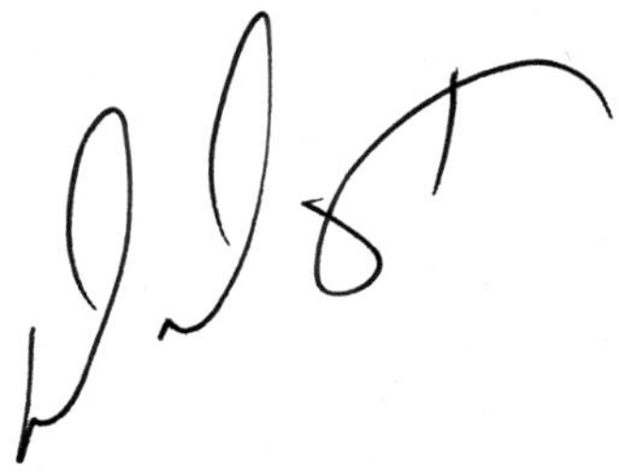

By Dan Dougherty

Written, illustrated, and executed by Dan Dougherty

Additional coloring by Milena Deneno

Beardo™: Volume 5: The Miracle of Creation

Produced in conjunction with

ComicMix Pro Services
304 Main Avenue Suite 194
Norwalk CT 06851
http://www.comicmix.com/pro-services/

BEARDO is a trademark of Dan Dougherty.

ISBN 978-1-939888-49-5

To Sweet Pea

HANDS OFF MY BEARDO!
Possessive praise for panel perfection
by Jay P. Fosgitt

Finally! A Comic strip for ME!

Me, as in someone who doesn't work in an office while wearing a crooked tie.

Me, as in someone who doesn't hate Mondays, but loves lasagna and communicates in thought balloons.

Me, as in someone who doesn't philosophize about golf, doesn't have an overbearing boss/wife/mother-in-law, who doesn't have a brood of precocious, quipping kids, or a million other comic strip tropes that I can't relate to.

What Dan Dougherty has crafted here with "Beardo" is an epic tale viewed through a mundane lens, where our hero balances day-to-day life with a career as a cartoonist,

and all the awkward, unglamorous, and yet somehow exotic realities of our profession that fuel the fantasy we cartoonists create.

Like I said, a comic strip for me.

That's not to say I can relate to every aspect of the comic. I am not married, and don't have a baby. I was never in a band, and never worked with a writing partner. And I imagine some readers, who have no prior knowledge or experience about the world of a professional cartoonist, have even fewer things to relate to here than I have.

Now, hold your pitchforks and Frankenstein rakes and back away from the windmill, "Beardo" fans. I'm getting to the "but"...

BUT—the playfully appealing lines of Dan's art, the delightful, original and hilarious execution of his gags, and the heart...my goodness, the heart....that Dan instills in his characters negates any concerns about relatability. There's so much to love here, and such pure joy that radiates off Dan's work, that his readers' appreciation is a given—written in the stars, foretold by prophets, and one of the few sure bets found in the rigged game of life.

Am I gilding a lily a bit here? Maybe. I'm pretty passionate about "Beardo". One might even say a little possessive. Like I said, it's a comic strip for ME.

But turn the page. I'm happy to share it with you, too....

—Jay P. Fosgitt

Jay P. Fosgitt is the creator of BODIE TROLL, and DEAD DUCK AND ZOMBIE CHICK (Source Point Press). He is an artist on the MY LITTLE PONY comics, and has done other artwork for IDW, Marvel, Image, Boom, Archie, Hasbro, Rue Morgue Magazine, and Andrew McMeel Publishing, among others.

Jay is a member of the National Cartoonists Society, and you can find him online at www.jayfosgitt.com.

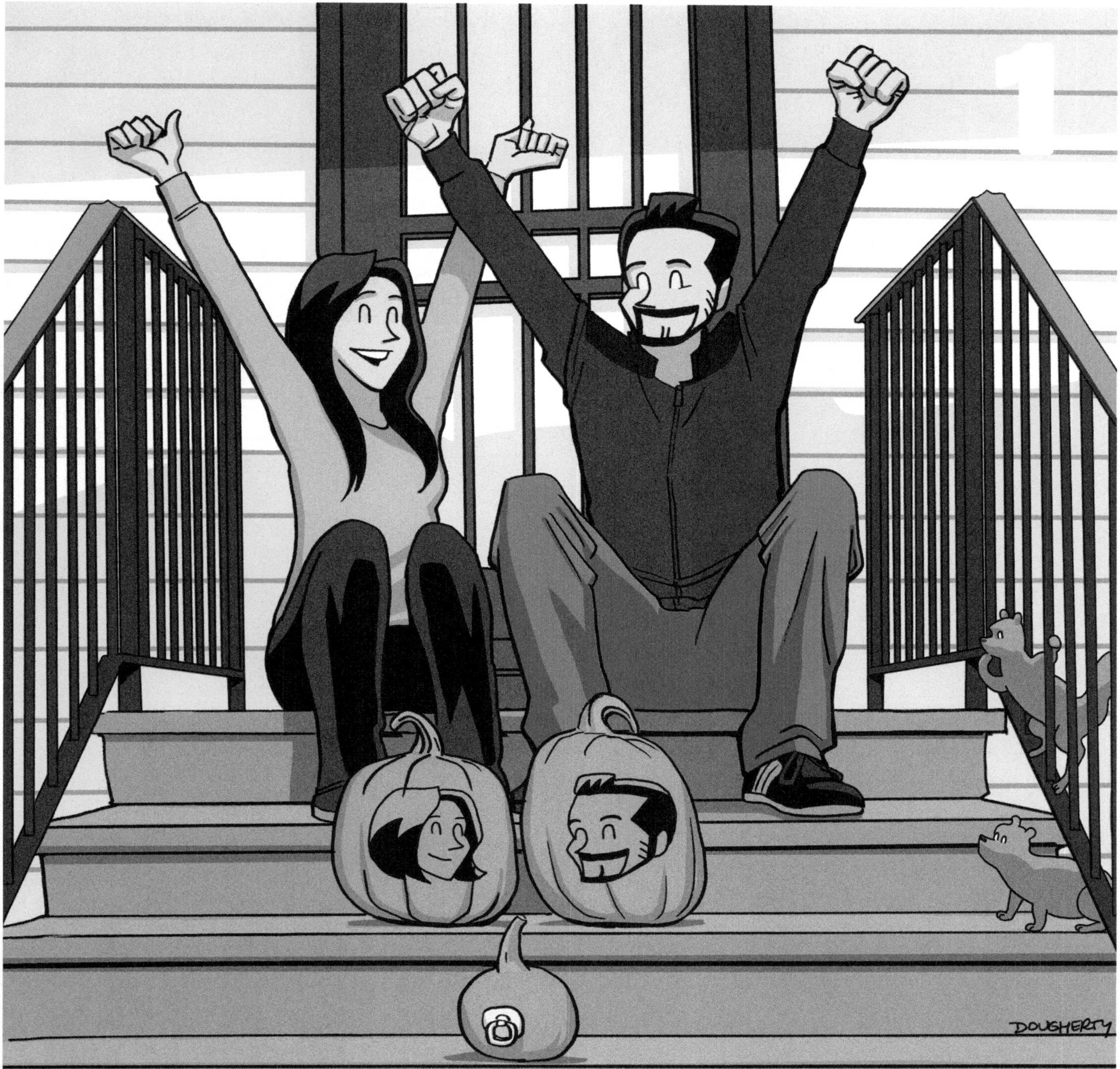
1
DOUGHERTY

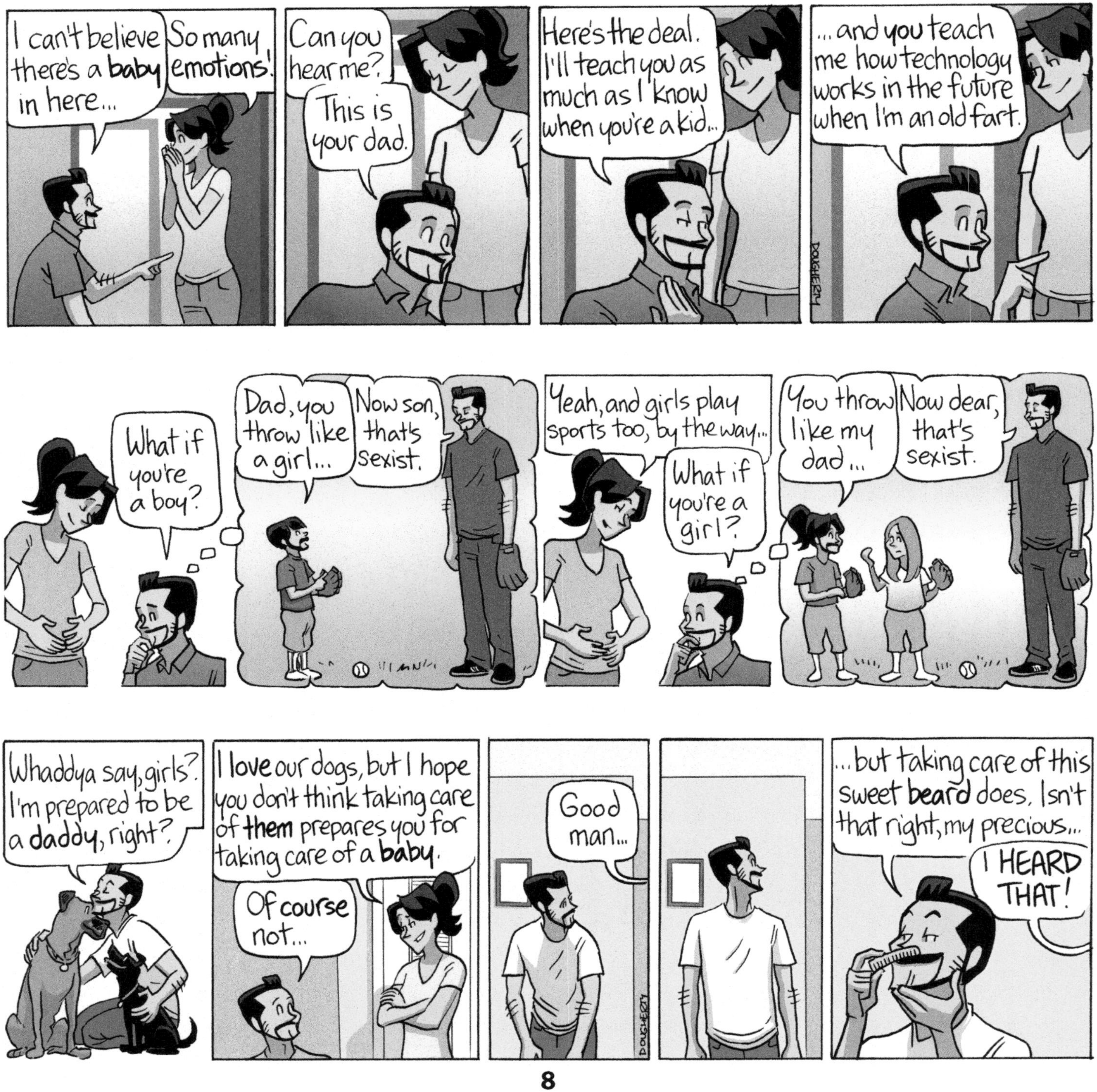
I can't believe there's a **baby** in here...
So many **emotions**!
Can you hear me?
This is your dad.
Here's the deal. I'll teach you as much as I know when you're a kid...
DOUGHERTY
...and **you** teach me how technology works in the future when I'm an old fart.
What if you're a boy?
Dad, you throw like a girl...
Now son, that's sexist.
Yeah, and girls play sports too, by the way...
What if you're a girl?
You throw like my dad...
Now dear, that's sexist.
Whaddya say, girls? I'm prepared to be a **daddy**, right?
I **love** our dogs, but I hope you don't think taking care of **them** prepares you for taking care of a **baby**.
Of **course** not...
Good man...
DOUGHERTY
...but taking care of this sweet **beard** does. Isn't that right, my precious...
I HEARD THAT!

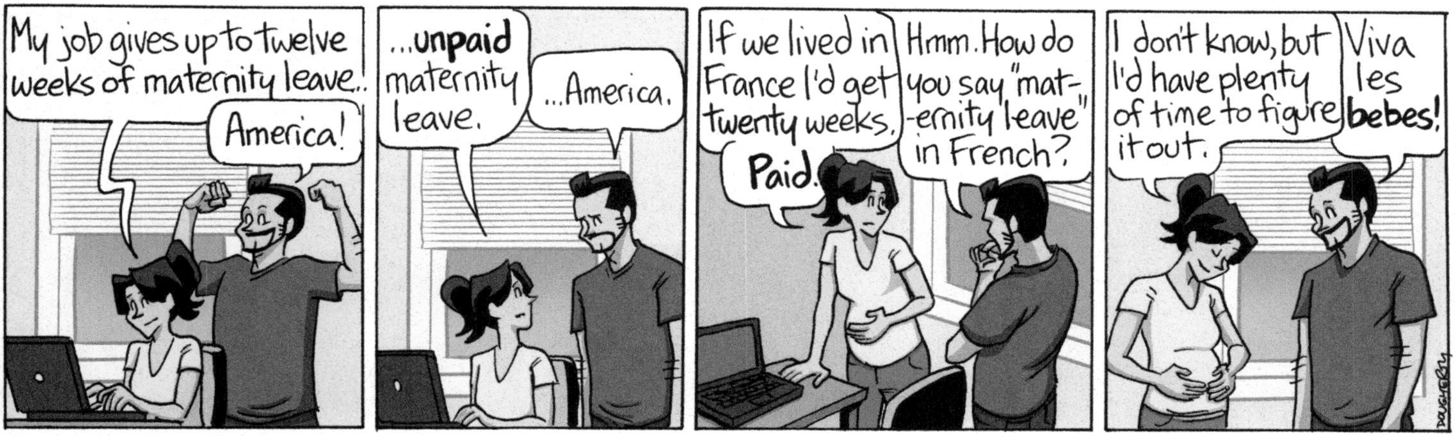
My job gives up to twelve weeks of maternity leave...
America!
...unpaid maternity leave.
...America.
If we lived in France I'd get twenty weeks.
Paid.
Hmm. How do you say "mat-ernity leave" in French?
I don't know, but I'd have plenty of time to figure it out.
Viva les bebes!

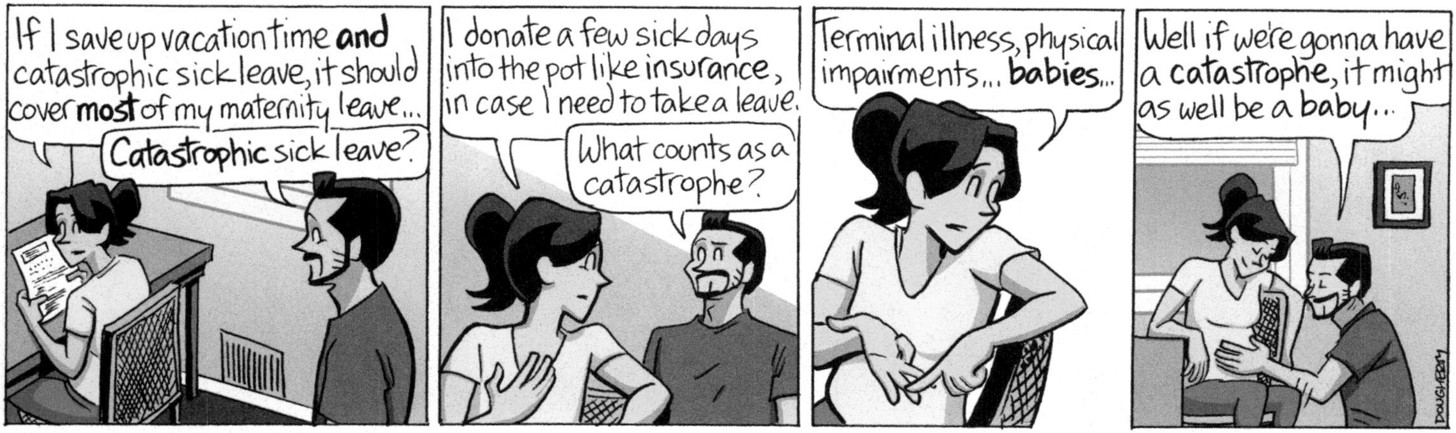
If I save up vacation time and catastrophic sick leave, it should cover most of my maternity leave...
Catastrophic sick leave?
I donate a few sick days into the pot like insurance, in case I need to take a leave.
What counts as a catastrophe?
Terminal illness, physical impairments... babies...
Well if we're gonna have a catastrophe, it might as well be a baby...

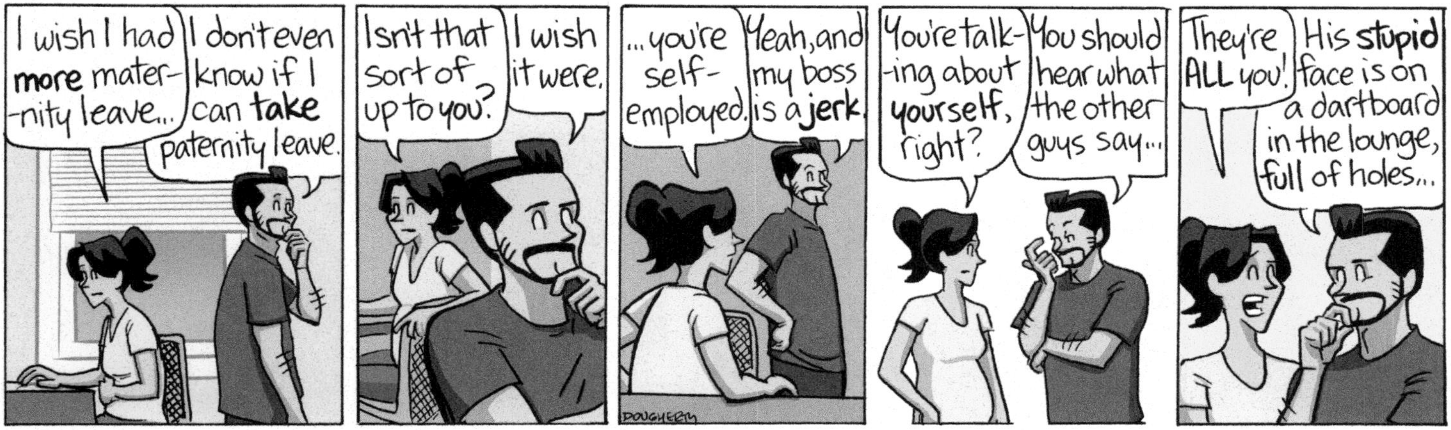
I wish I had more mater-nity leave...
I don't even know if I can take paternity leave.
Isn't that sort of up to you?
I wish it were.
...you're self-employed.
Yeah, and my boss is a jerk.
You're talk-ing about yourself, right?
You should hear what the other guys say...
They're ALL you!
His stupid face is on a dartboard in the lounge, full of holes...

Let the self-employed staff meeting come to **order**!

First on the agenda: picking the self-employee of the month.

Normally **I** pick the winner, but in an effort to be fair we set up this **ballot box**.

SELF EMPLOYEE BALLOTS

It's about time...

It's nice to know upper management is listening.

ADVERTISING
LOGOS
SYNERGY
FUTURE

Finally, the **voice** of the people will be heard!

Okay, all the votes are in. Let's see what we have...

SELF EMPLO BALLOTS

One for "me"...

SELF EMPLO BALLOTS

...one for "myself"...

SELF EMPLOYEE BALLOTS

...and one for "I." Unbelievable! It's a three way tie!

SELF EMPLOYEE BALLOTS

It isn't easy being the deciding vote. Some real solid candidates here...

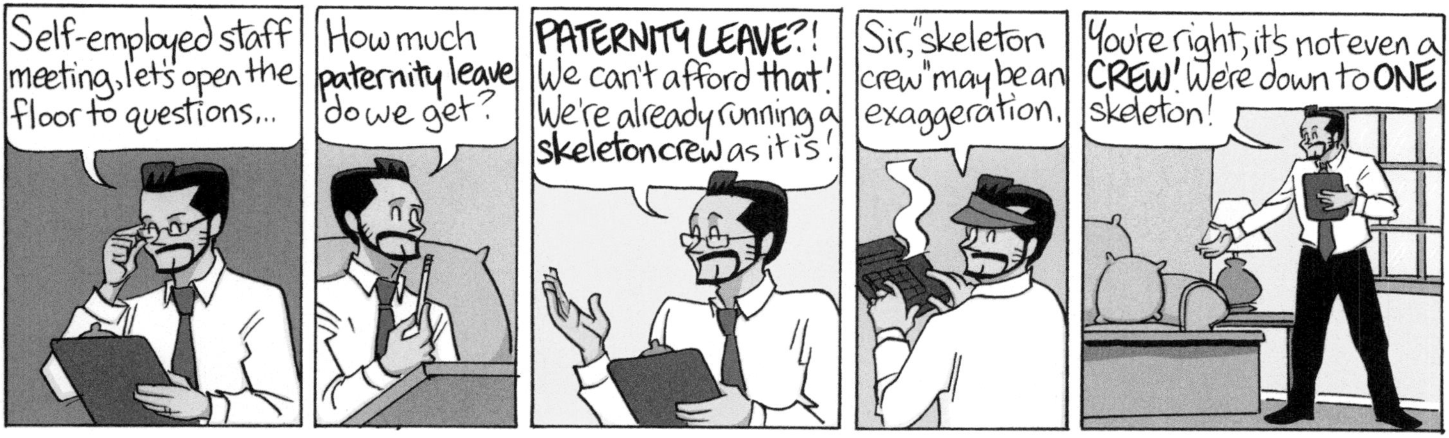
Self-employed staff meeting, let's open the floor to questions...
How much paternity leave do we get?
PATERNITY LEAVE?! We can't afford that! We're already running a skeleton crew as it is!
Sir, "skeleton crew" may be an exaggeration.
You're right, it's not even a CREW! We're down to ONE skeleton!

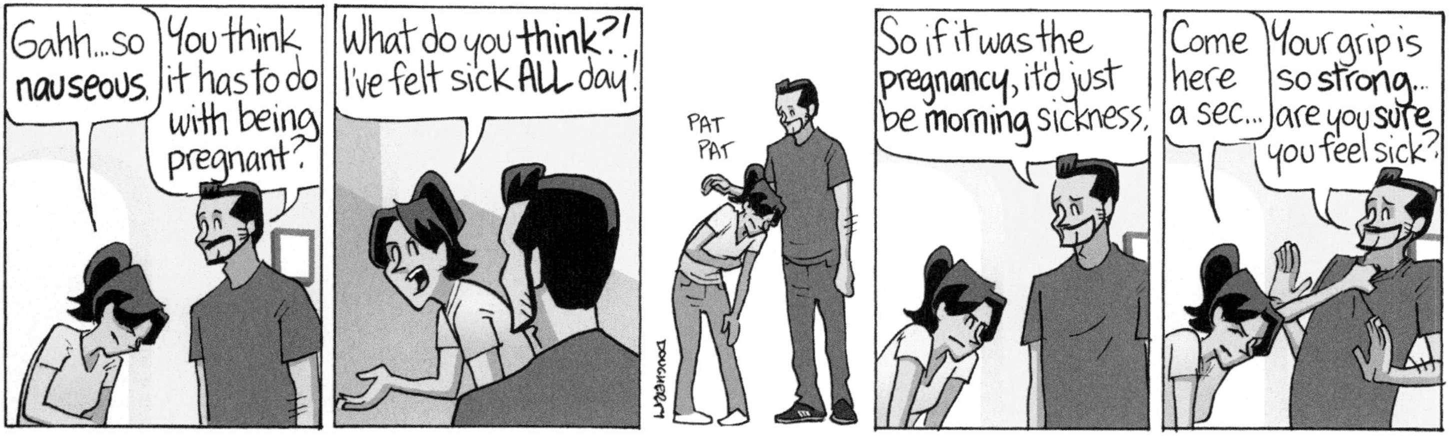
Gahh... so nauseous.
You think it has to do with being pregnant?
What do you think?! I've felt sick ALL day!
PAT PAT
So if it was the pregnancy, it'd just be morning sickness.
Come here a sec...
Your grip is so strong... are you sure you feel sick?

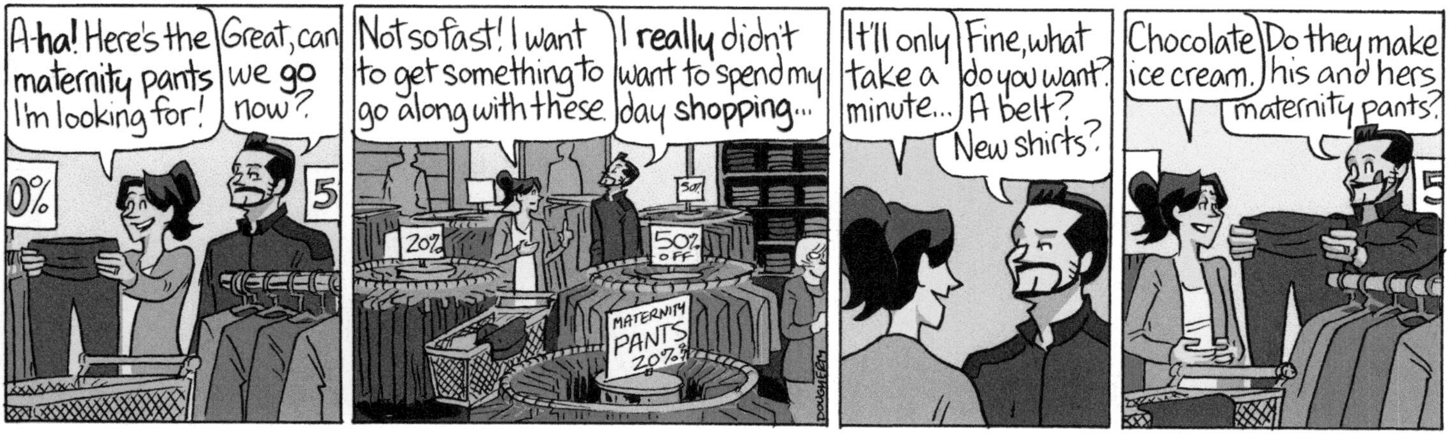
A-ha! Here's the maternity pants I'm looking for!
Great, can we go now?
Not so fast! I want to get something to go along with these.
I really didn't want to spend my day shopping...
20%
50% OFF
MATERNITY PANTS 20%
It'll only take a minute...
Fine, what do you want? A belt? New shirts?
Chocolate ice cream.
Do they make his and hers maternity pants?

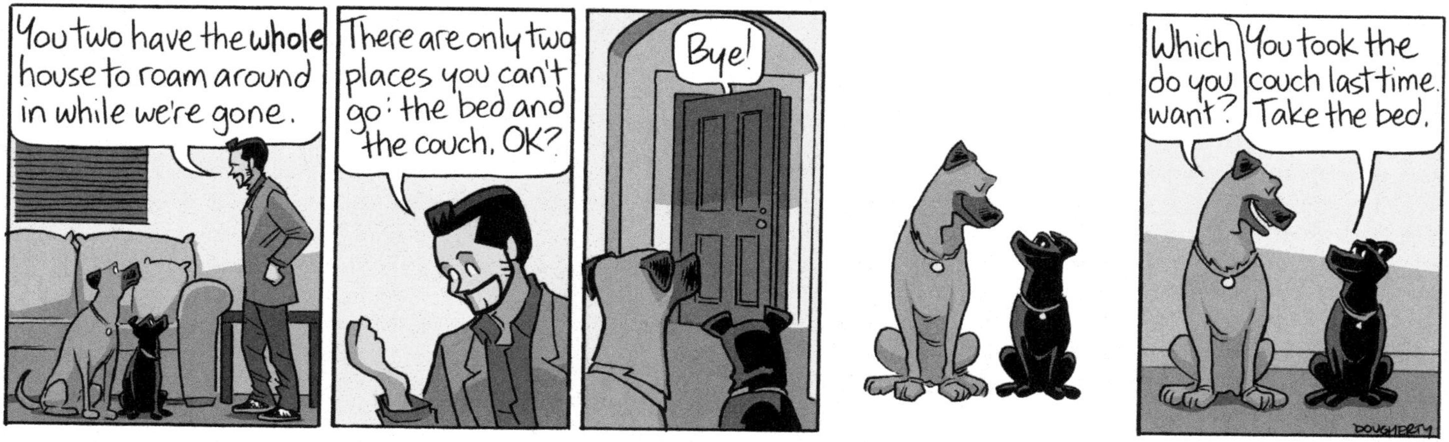
You two have the **whole** house to roam around in while we're gone.
There are only two places you can't go: the bed and the couch, OK?
Bye!
Which do you want?
You took the couch last time. Take the bed.
DOUGHERTY

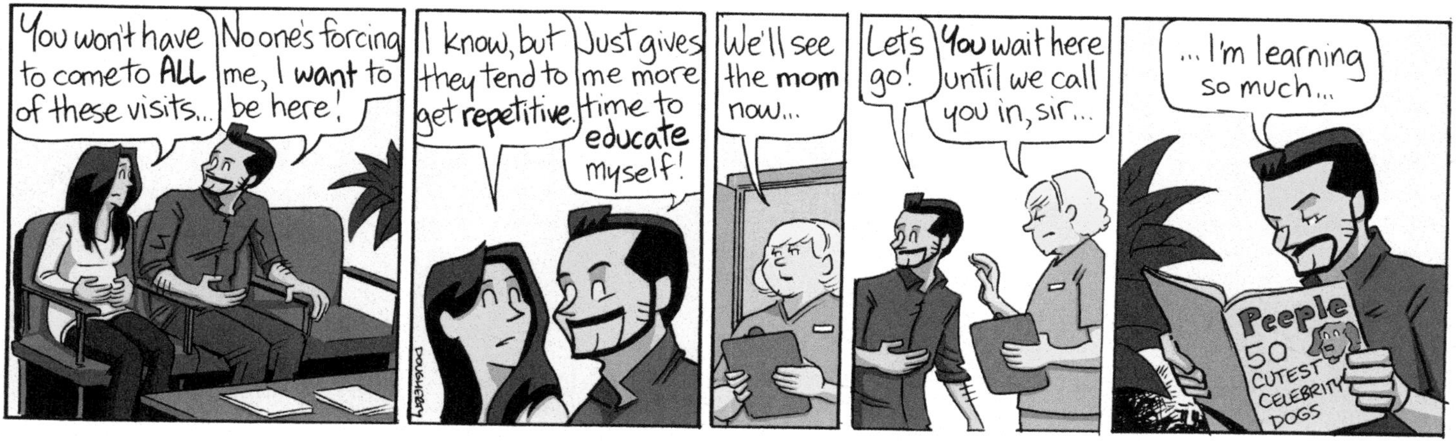
You won't have to come to **ALL** of these visits...
No one's forcing me, I **want** to be here!
I know, but they tend to get **repetitive**.
Just gives me more time to **educate** myself!
DOUGHERTY
We'll see the **mom** now...
Let's go!
You wait here until we call you in, sir...
... I'm learning so much...
Peeple
50 CUTEST CELEBRITY DOGS

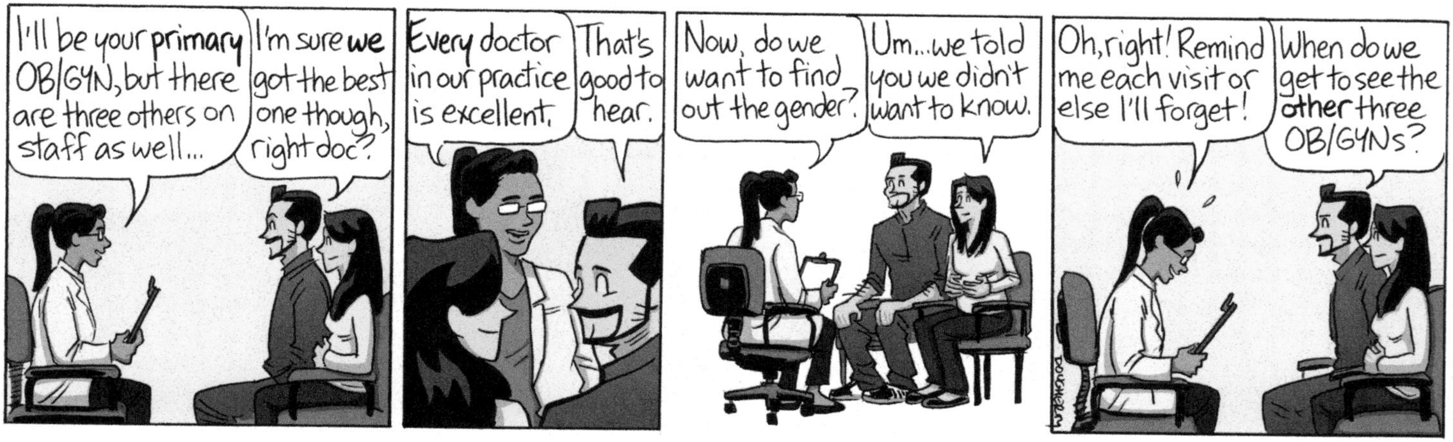
I'll be your **primary** OB/GYN, but there are three others on staff as well...
I'm sure **we** got the best one though, right doc?
Every doctor in our practice is excellent.
That's good to hear.
Now, do we want to find out the gender?
Um...we told you we didn't want to know.
DOUGHERTY
Oh, right! Remind me each visit or else I'll forget!
When do we get to see the **other** three OB/GYNs?

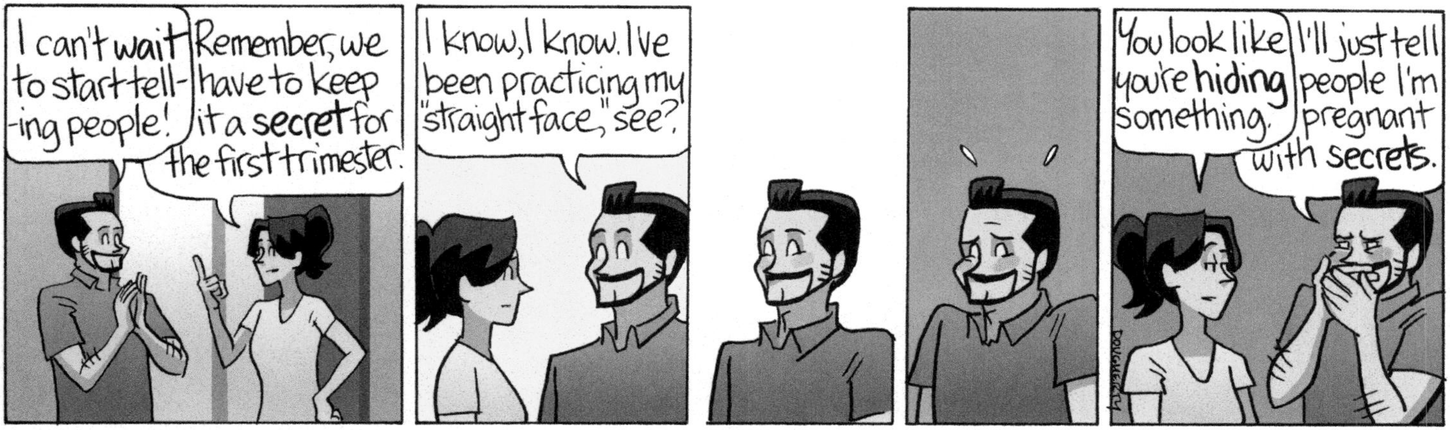
I can't wait to start tell-ing people!
Remember, we have to keep it a secret for the first trimester.
I know, I know. I've been practicing my "straight face," see?
You look like you're hiding something.
I'll just tell people I'm pregnant with secrets.

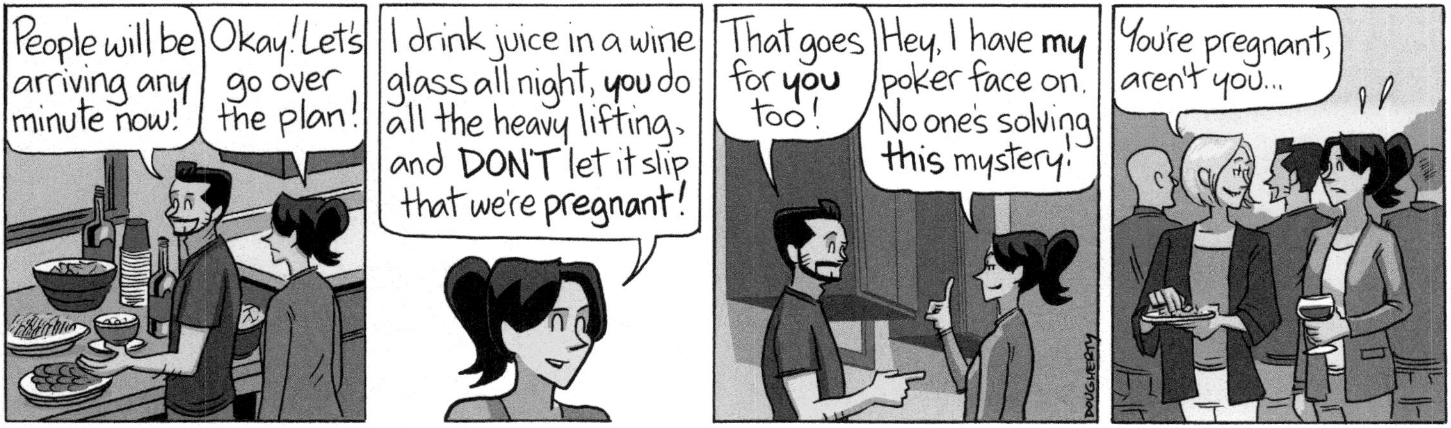
People will be arriving any minute now!
Okay! Let's go over the plan!
I drink juice in a wine glass all night, you do all the heavy lifting, and DON'T let it slip that we're pregnant!
That goes for you too!
Hey, I have my poker face on. No one's solving this mystery!
You're pregnant, aren't you...

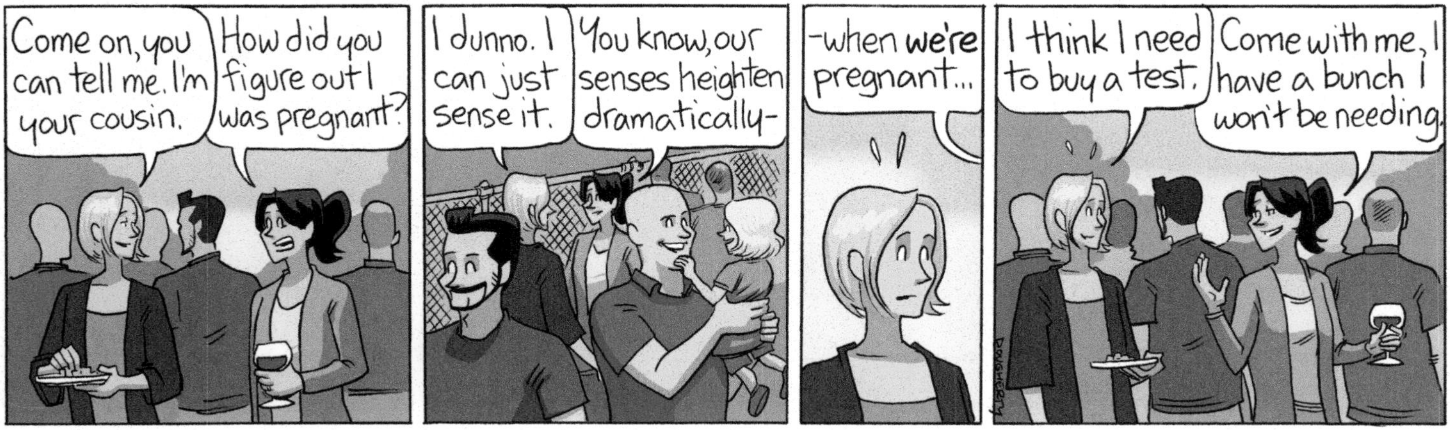
Come on, you can tell me. I'm your cousin.
How did you figure out I was pregnant?
I dunno. I can just sense it.
You know, our senses heighten dramatically-
-when we're pregnant...
I think I need to buy a test.
Come with me, I have a bunch I won't be needing.

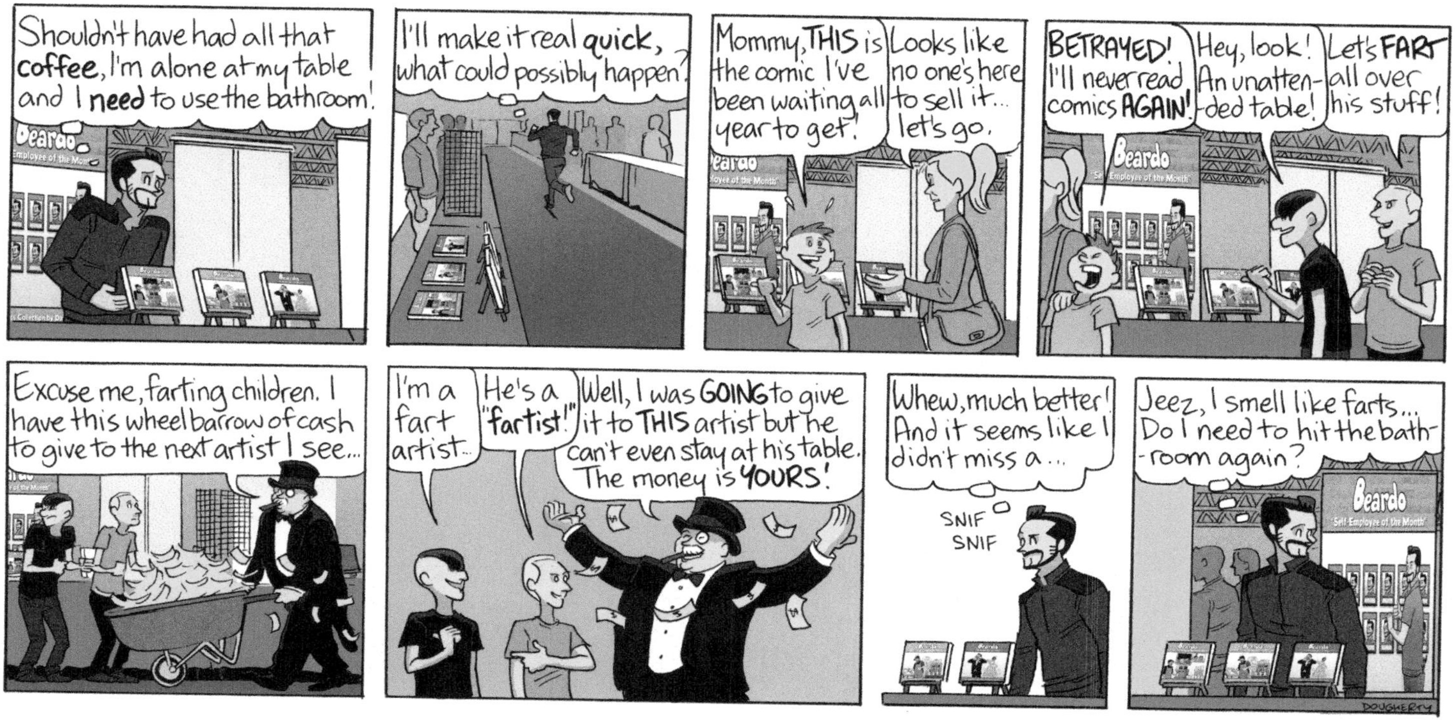
Shouldn't have had all that **coffee**, I'm alone at my table and I **need** to use the bathroom!
Beardo
Employee of the Month
I'll make it real **quick**, what could possibly happen?
Mommy, **THIS** is the comic I've been waiting all year to get!
Looks like no one's here to sell it... let's go.
BETRAYED! I'll never read comics **AGAIN!**
Hey, look! An unattended table!
Let's **FART** all over his stuff!
Beardo
Self-Employee of the Month
Excuse me, farting children. I have this wheelbarrow of cash to give to the next artist I see...
I'm a fart artist...
He's a "**fartist!**"
Well, I was **GOING** to give it to **THIS** artist but he can't even stay at his table. The money is **YOURS**!
Whew, much better! And it seems like I didn't miss a...
SNIF
SNIF
Jeez, I smell like farts... Do I need to hit the bathroom again?
Beardo
Self-Employee of the Month
DOUGHERTY

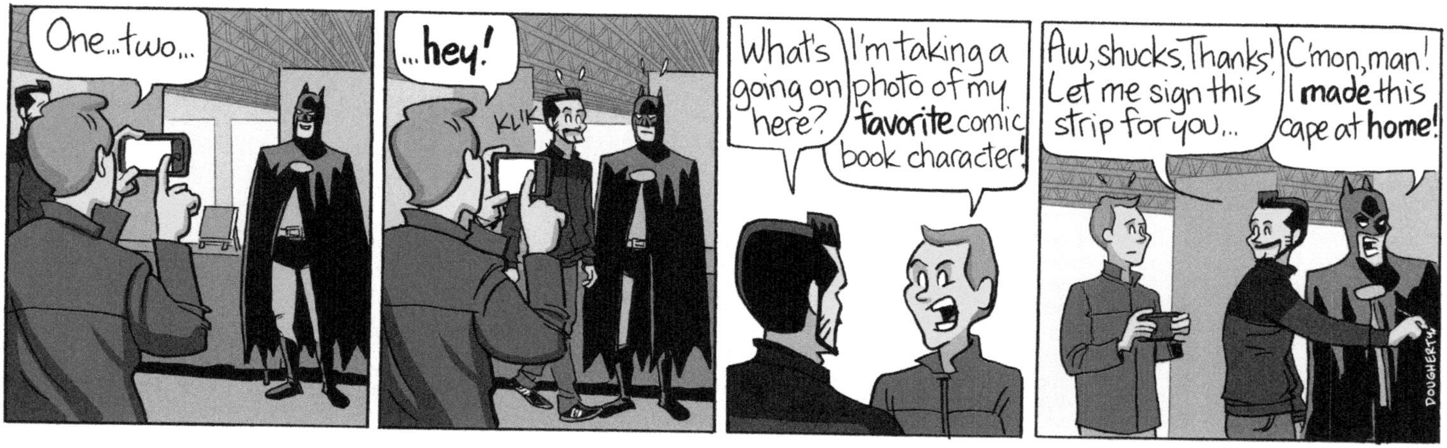
One... two...
...**hey!**
KLIK
What's going on here?
I'm taking a photo of my **favorite** comic book character!
Aw, shucks. Thanks! Let me sign this strip for you...
C'mon, man! I **made** this cape at **home**!
DOUGHERTY

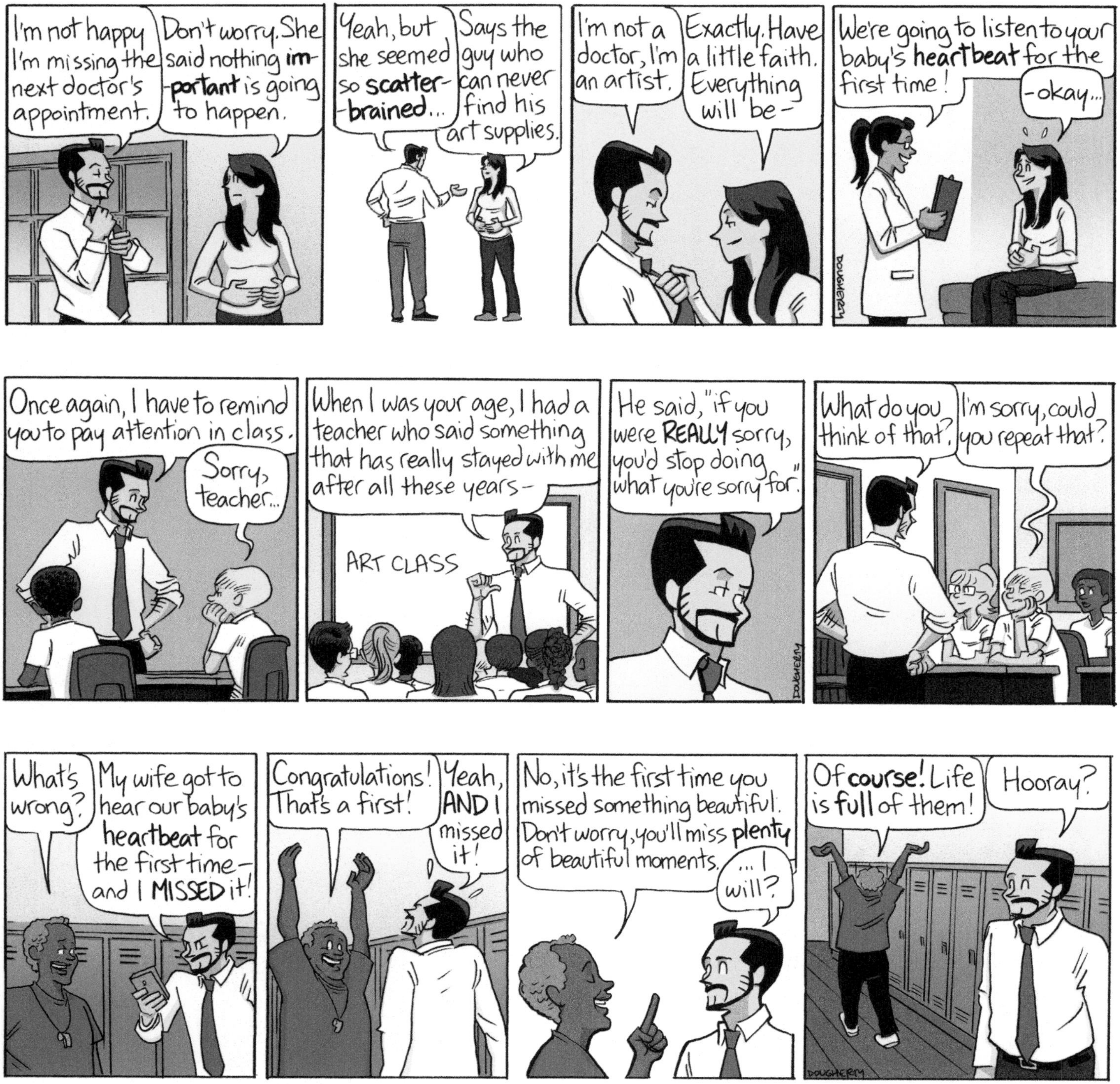
I'm not happy I'm missing the next doctor's appointment.
Don't worry. She said nothing **important** is going to happen.
Yeah, but she seemed so **scatter-brained**...
Says the guy who can never find his art supplies.
I'm not a doctor, I'm an artist.
Exactly. Have a little faith. Everything will be-
We're going to listen to your baby's **heartbeat** for the first time!
-okay...
Once again, I have to remind you to pay attention in class.
Sorry, teacher...
When I was your age, I had a teacher who said something that has really stayed with me after all these years-
ART CLASS
He said, "if you were **REALLY** sorry, you'd stop doing what you're sorry for."
What do you think of that?
I'm sorry, could you repeat that?
What's wrong?
My wife got to hear our baby's **heartbeat** for the first time- and I **MISSED** it!
Congratulations! That's a first!
Yeah, **AND** I missed it!
No, it's the first time you missed something beautiful. Don't worry, you'll miss **plenty** of beautiful moments.
...I will?
Of **course**! Life is **full** of them!
Hooray?

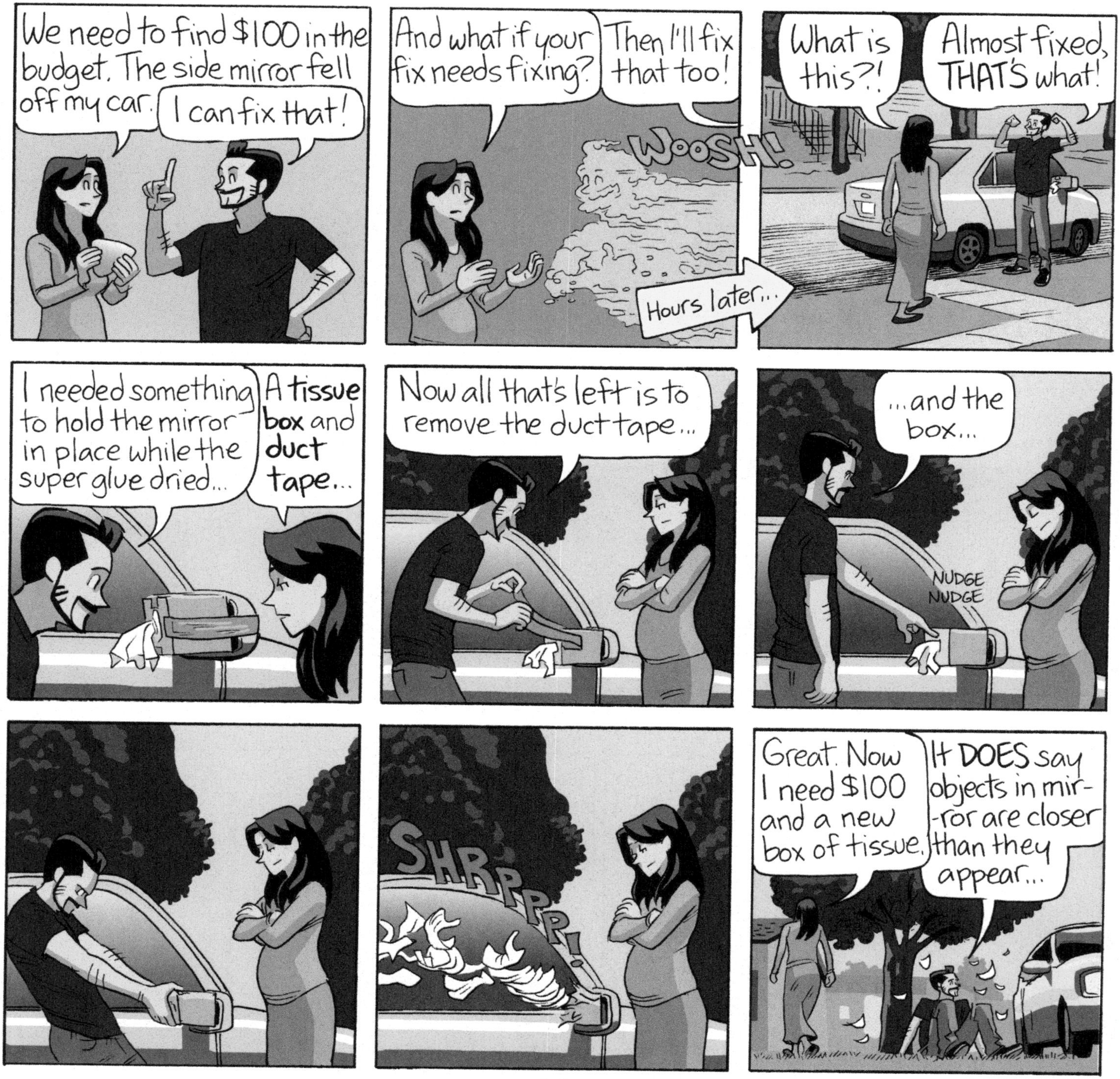
We need to find $100 in the budget. The side mirror fell off my car.
I can fix that!
And what if your fix needs fixing?
Then I'll fix that too!
WOOSH!
Hours later...
What is this?!
Almost fixed, THAT'S what!
I needed something to hold the mirror in place while the super glue dried...
A tissue box and duct tape...
Now all that's left is to remove the duct tape...
...and the box...
NUDGE NUDGE
SHRPPP!
Great. Now I need $100 and a new box of tissue.
It DOES say objects in mir- -ror are closer than they appear...

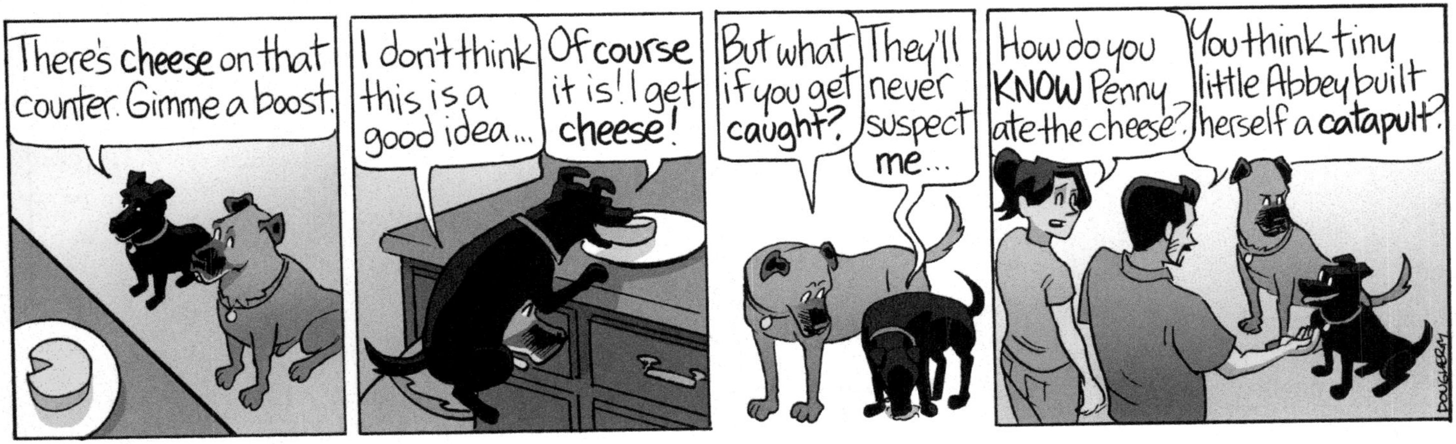
There's cheese on that counter. Gimme a boost.
I don't think this is a good idea...
Of course it is! I get cheese!
But what if you get caught?
They'll never suspect me...
How do you KNOW Penny ate the cheese?
You think tiny little Abbey built herself a catapult?
DOUGHERTY

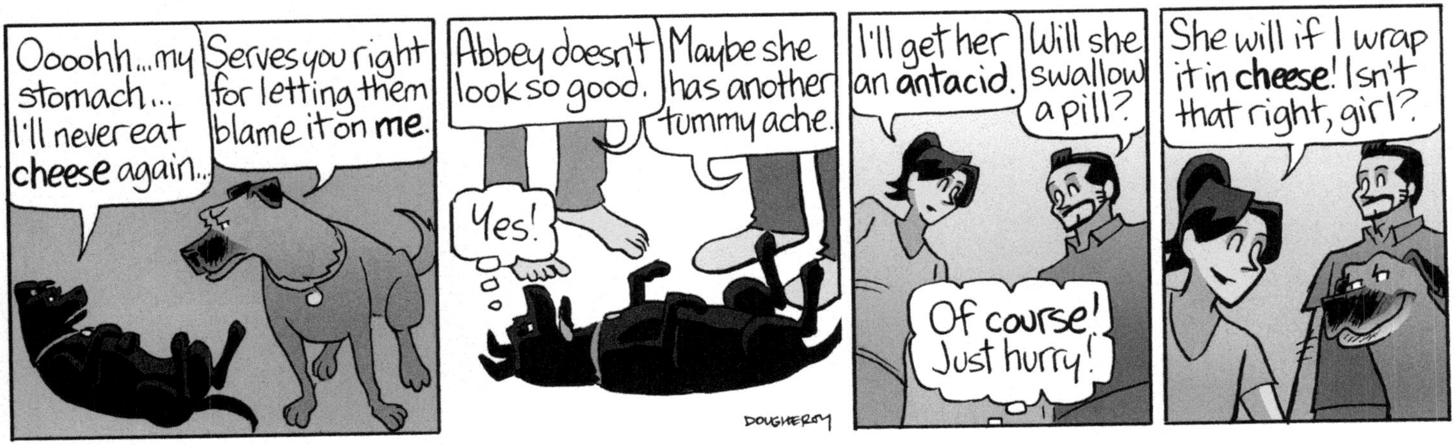
Oooohh...my stomach... I'll never eat cheese again...
Serves you right for letting them blame it on me.
Abbey doesn't look so good.
Maybe she has another tummy ache.
Yes!
DOUGHERTY
I'll get her an antacid.
Will she swallow a pill?
Of course! Just hurry!
She will if I wrap it in cheese! Isn't that right, girl?

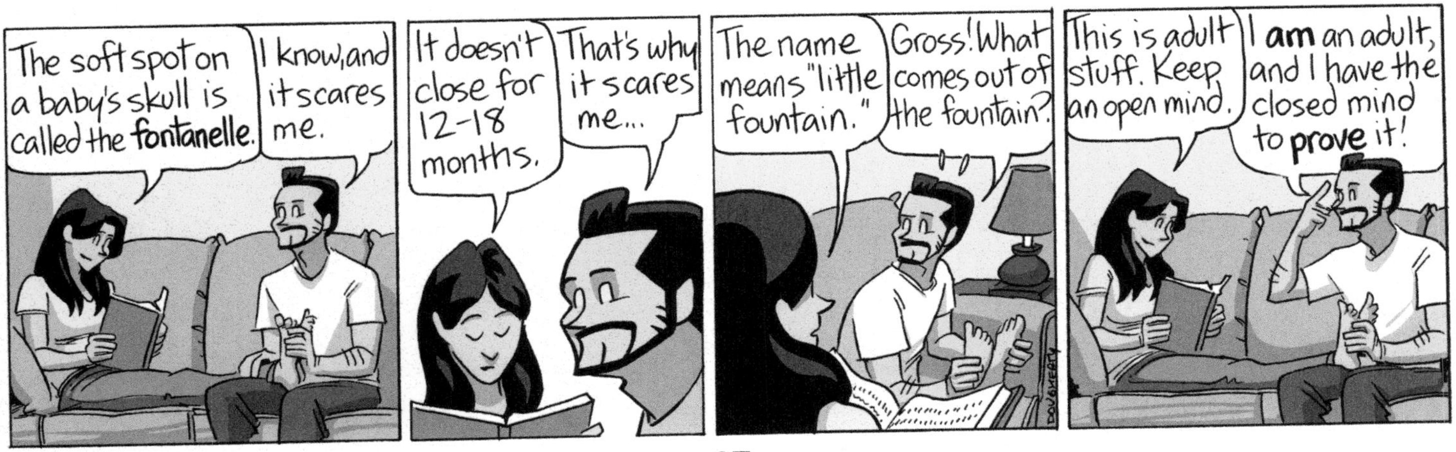
The soft spot on a baby's skull is called the fontanelle.
I know, and it scares me.
It doesn't close for 12-18 months.
That's why it scares me...
The name means "little fountain."
Gross! What comes out of the fountain?
DOUGHERTY
This is adult stuff. Keep an open mind.
I am an adult, and I have the closed mind to prove it!

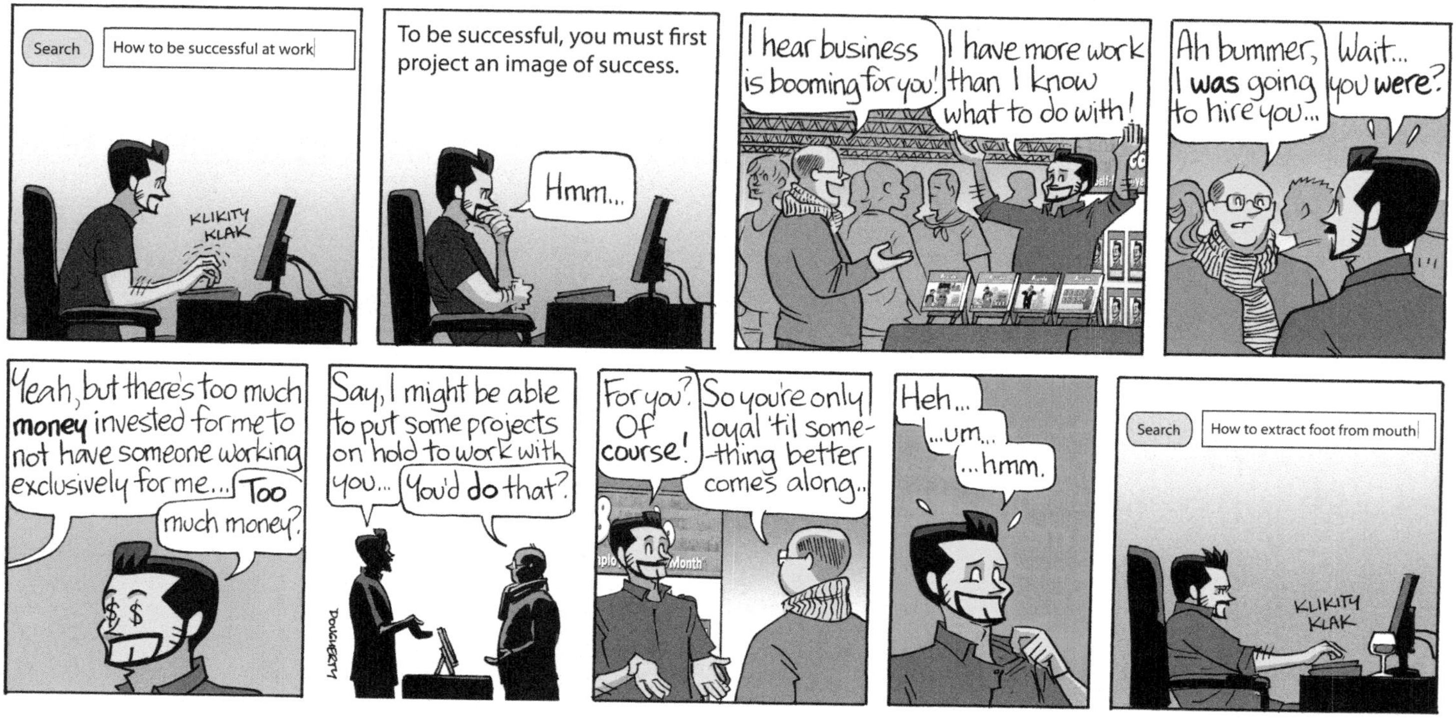
Search
How to be successful at work
KLIKITY KLAK
To be successful, you must first project an image of success.
Hmm...
I hear business is booming for you!
I have more work than I know what to do with!
Ah bummer, I **was** going to hire you...
Wait... you **were**?
Yeah, but there's too much **money** invested for me to not have someone working exclusively for me...
Too much money?
Say, I might be able to put some projects on hold to work with you...
You'd **do** that?
For you? Of **course**!
So you're only loyal 'til some-thing better comes along...
Heh...
...um...
...hmm.
Search
How to extract foot from mouth
KLIKITY KLAK

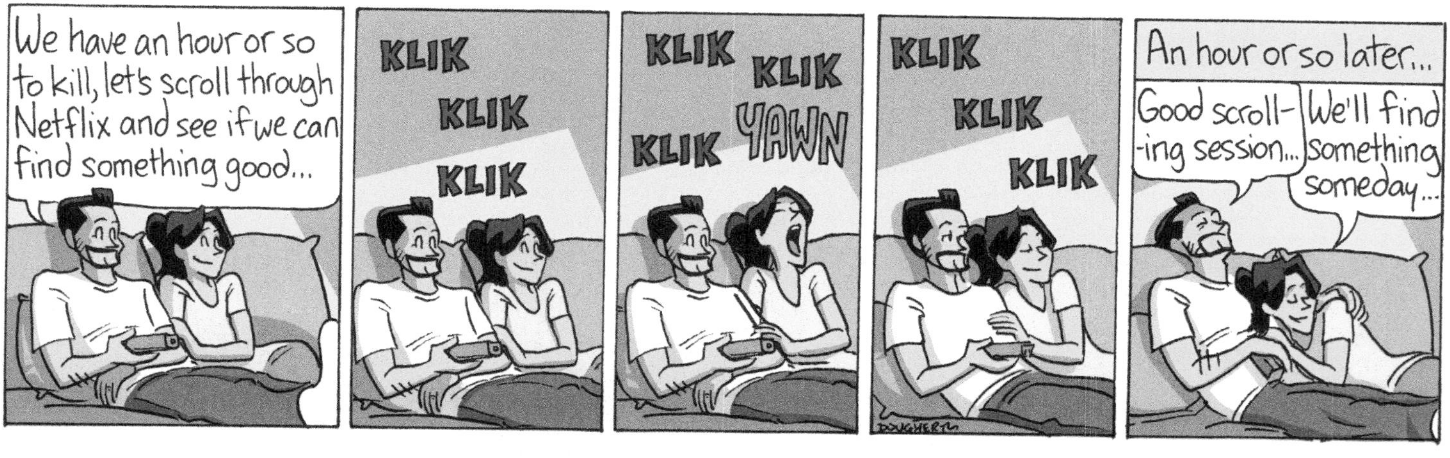
We have an hour or so to kill, let's scroll through Netflix and see if we can find something good...
KLIK
KLIK
KLIK
KLIK
KLIK
KLIK
YAWN
KLIK
KLIK
KLIK
An hour or so later...
Good scroll-ing session...
We'll find something someday...

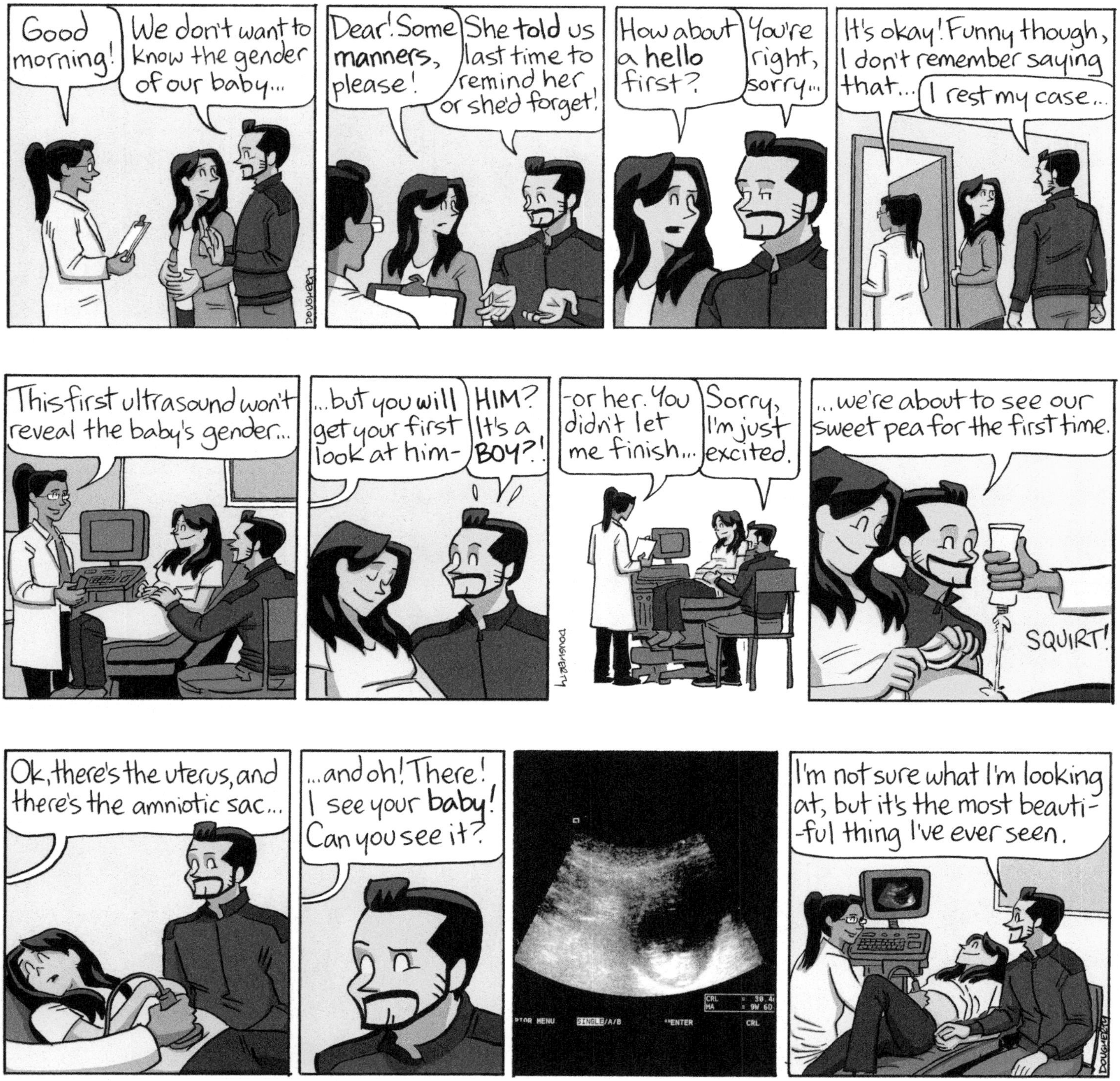
Good morning!
We don't want to know the gender of our baby...
Dear! Some **manners**, please!
She **told** us last time to remind her or she'd forget!
How about a **hello** first?
You're right, sorry...
It's okay! Funny though, I don't remember saying that...
I rest my case...
This first ultrasound won't reveal the baby's gender...
...but you **will** get your first look at him-
HIM? It's a BOY?!
-or her. You didn't let me finish...
Sorry, I'm just excited.
...we're about to see our sweet pea for the first time.
SQUIRT!
Ok, there's the uterus, and there's the amniotic sac...
...and oh! There! I see your **baby**! Can you see it?
I'm not sure what I'm looking at, but it's the most beauti--ful thing I've ever seen.

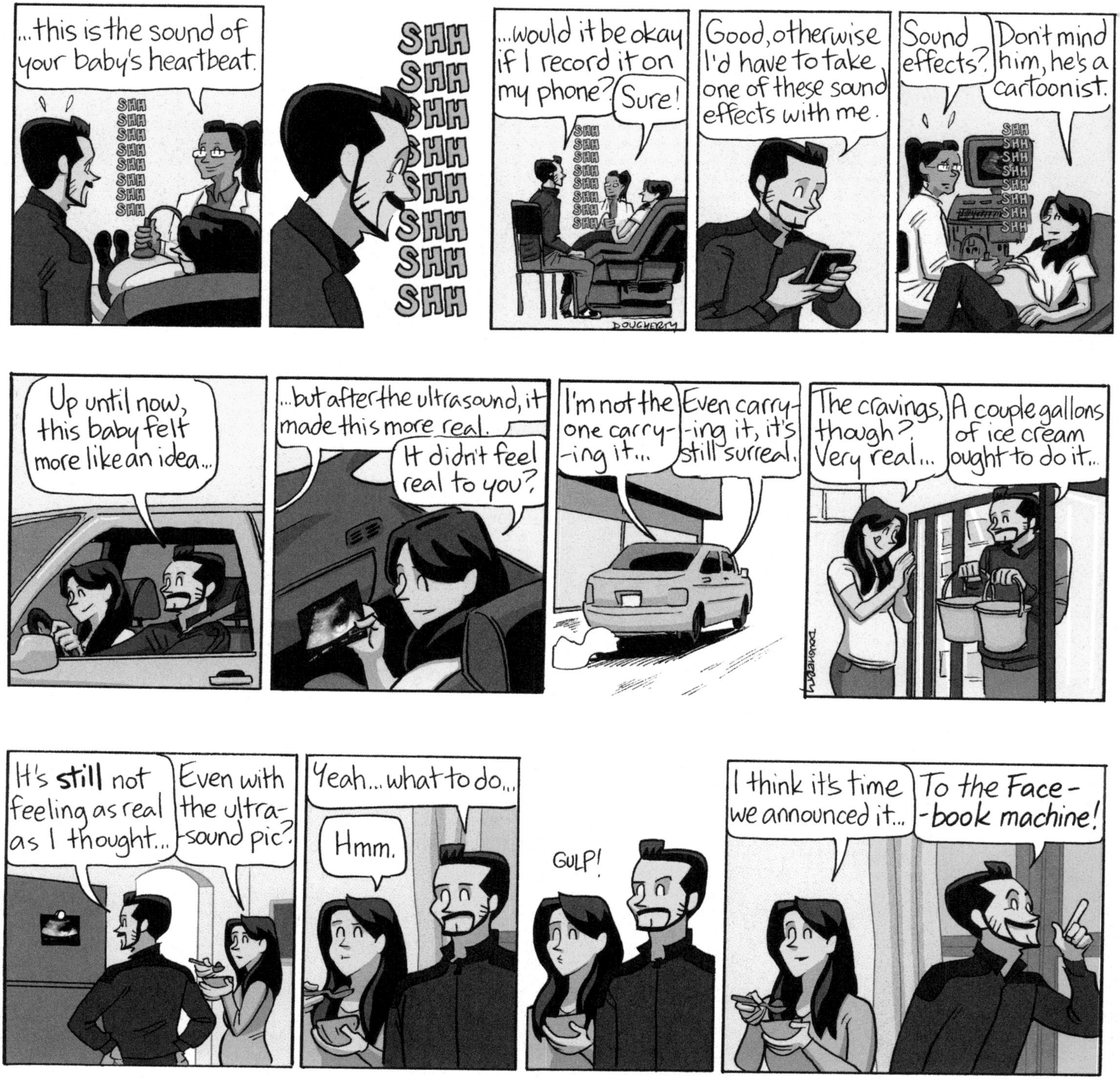
...this is the sound of your baby's heartbeat.
SHH SHH SHH SHH SHH SHH SHH SHH
SHH SHH SHH SHH SHH SHH SHH SHH
...would it be okay if I record it on my phone?
Sure!
SHH SHH SHH SHH SHH SHH SHH SHH
DOUGHERTY
Good, otherwise I'd have to take one of these sound effects with me.
Sound effects?
Don't mind him, he's a cartoonist.
SHH SHH SHH SHH SHH SHH SHH SHH
Up until now, this baby felt more like an idea...
...but after the ultrasound, it made this more real.
It didn't feel real to you?
I'm not the one carry-ing it...
Even carry-ing it, it's still surreal.
The cravings, though? Very real...
A couple gallons of ice cream ought to do it...
DOUGHERTY
It's **still** not feeling as real as I thought...
Even with the ultra-sound pic?
Yeah... what to do...
Hmm.
GULP!
I think it's time we announced it...
To the Face-book machine!

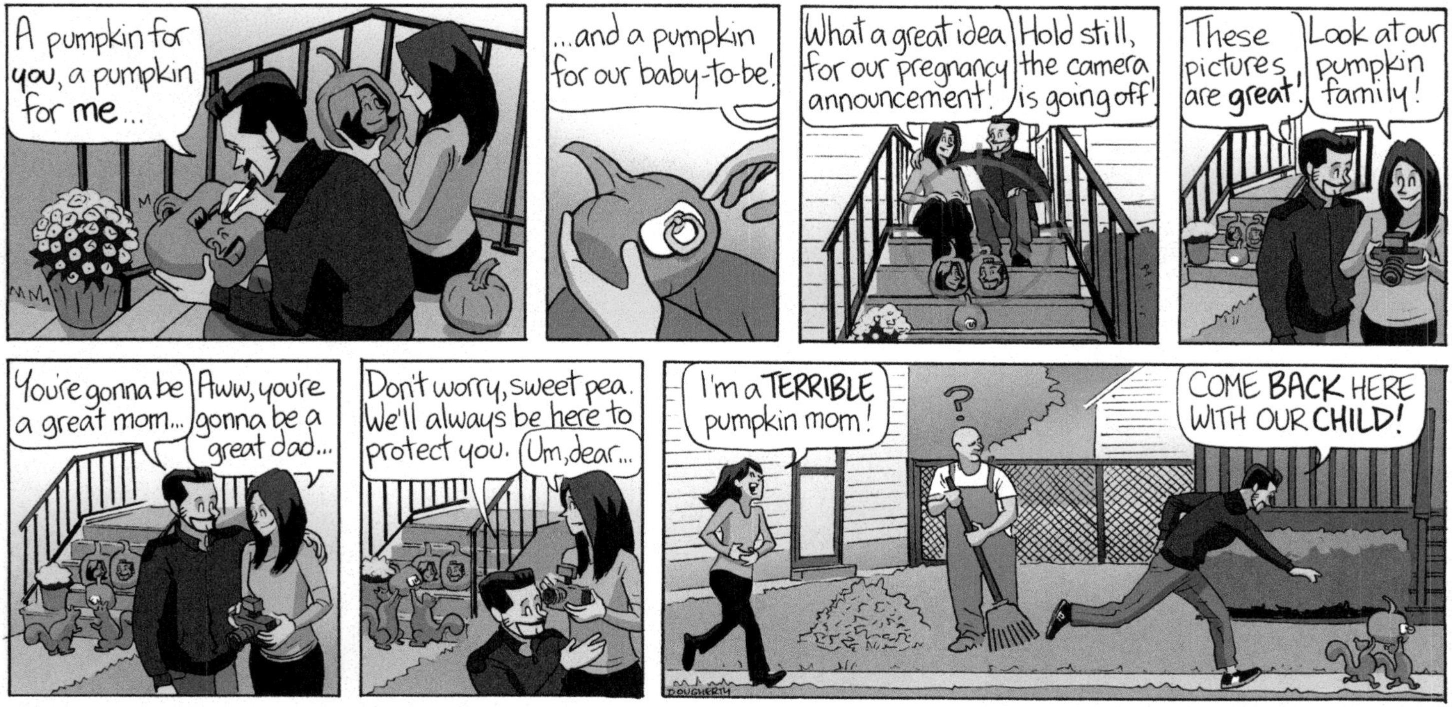
A pumpkin for **you**, a pumpkin for **me**...
...and a pumpkin for our baby-to-be!
What a great idea for our pregnancy announcement!
Hold still, the camera is going off!
These pictures are **great**!
Look at our pumpkin family!
You're gonna be a great mom...
Aww, you're gonna be a great dad...
Don't worry, sweet pea. We'll always be here to protect you.
Um, dear...
I'm a **TERRIBLE** pumpkin mom!
?
COME **BACK** HERE WITH OUR **CHILD**!
DOUGHERTY

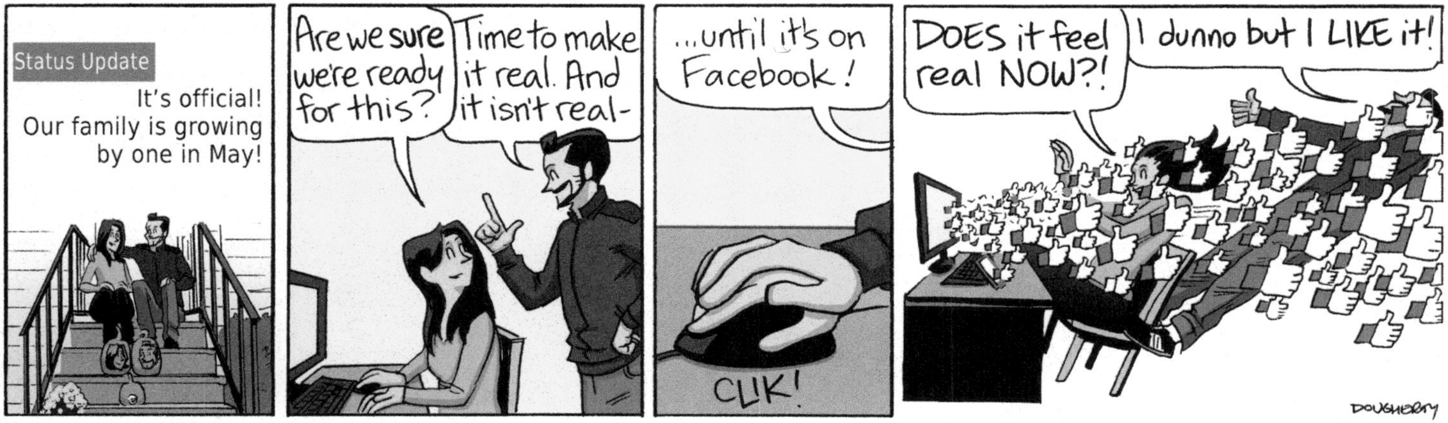
Status Update
It's official! Our family is growing by one in May!
Are we **sure** we're ready for this?
Time to make it real. And it isn't real-
...until it's on Facebook!
CLIK!
DOES it feel real NOW?!
I dunno but I LIKE it!
DOUGHERTY

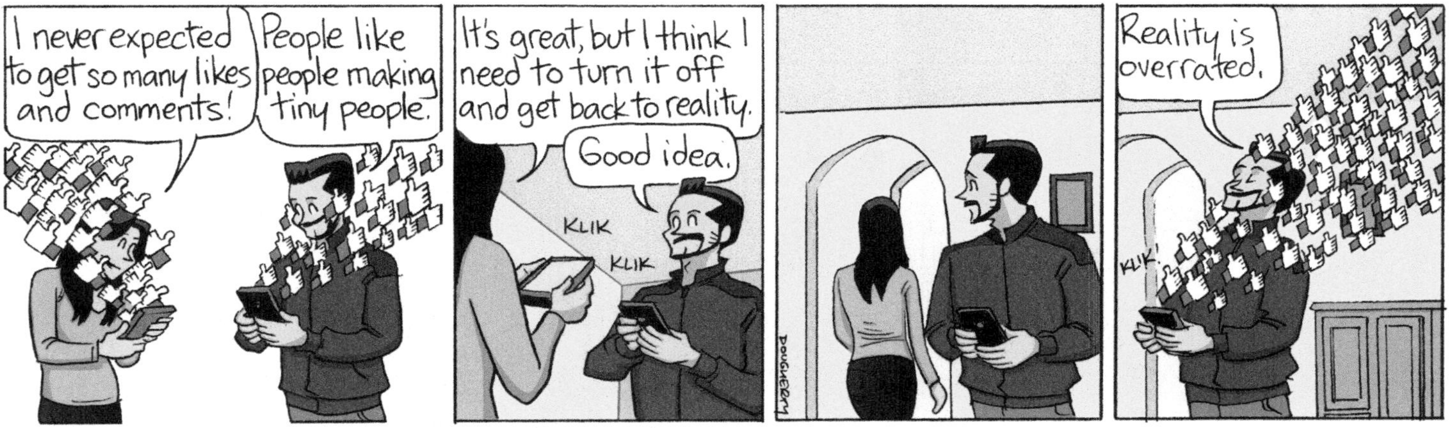
I never expected to get so many likes and comments!
People like people making tiny people.
It's great, but I think I need to turn it off and get back to reality.
Good idea.
KLIK
KLIK
Reality is overrated.
KLIK!
DOUGHERTY

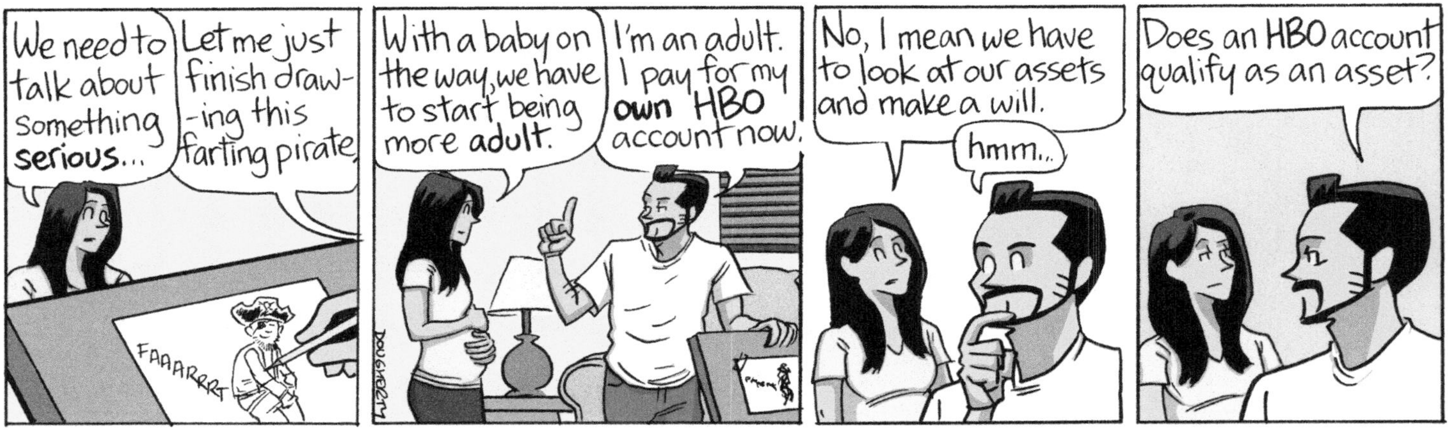
We need to talk about something **serious**...
Let me just finish draw-ing this farting pirate.
FAAARRRT
With a baby on the way, we have to start being more **adult**.
I'm an adult. I pay for my **own** HBO account now.
DOUGHERTY
No, I mean we have to look at our assets and make a will.
hmm...
Does an HBO account qualify as an asset?

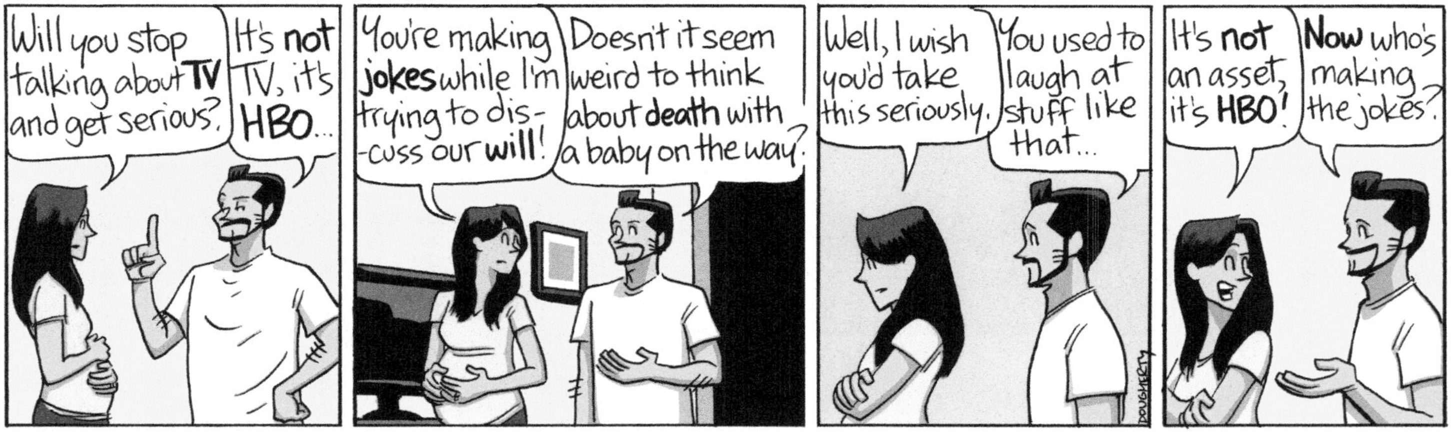
Will you stop talking about **TV** and get serious?
It's **not** TV, it's **HBO**...
You're making **jokes** while I'm trying to dis-cuss our **will**!
Doesn't it seem weird to think about **death** with a baby on the way?
Well, I wish you'd take this seriously.
You used to laugh at stuff like that...
It's **not** an asset, it's **HBO**!
Now who's making the jokes?
DOUGHERTY

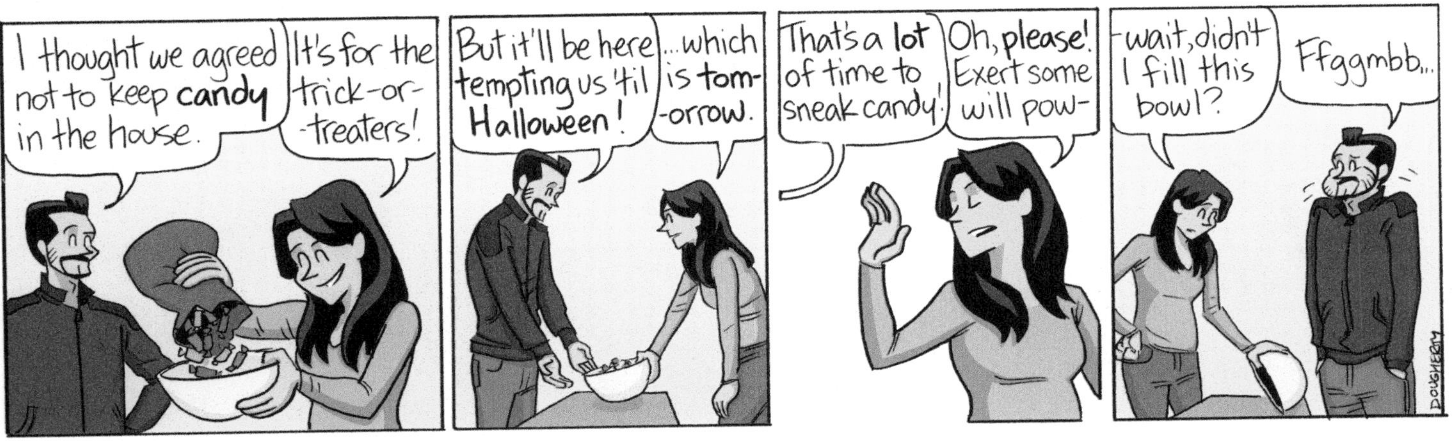

I thought we agreed not to keep **candy** in the house.
It's for the trick-or--treaters!
But it'll be here tempting us 'til **Halloween**!
...which is **tom--orrow**.
That's a **lot** of time to sneak candy!
Oh, **please**! Exert some will pow-
-wait, didn't I fill this bowl?
Ffggmbb...

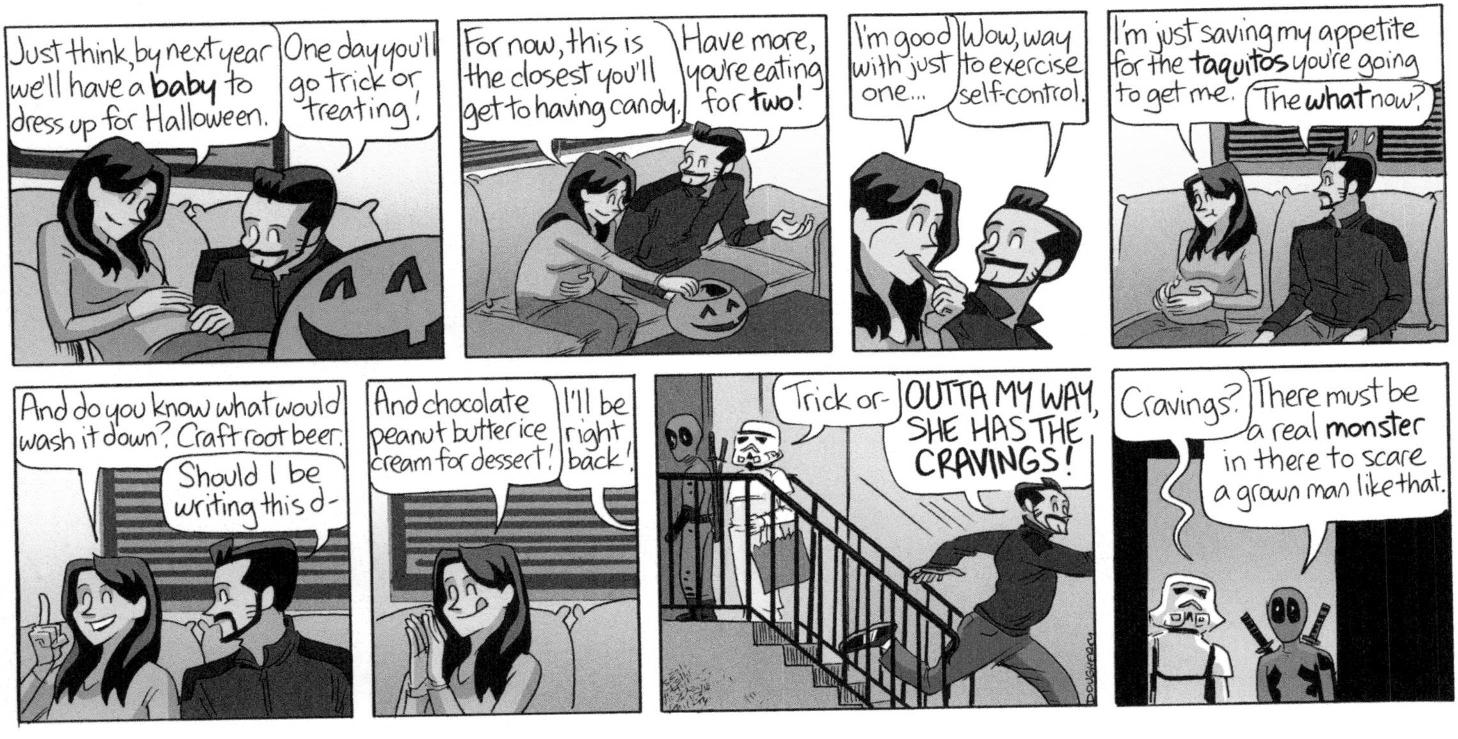

Just think, by next year we'll have a **baby** to dress up for Halloween.
One day you'll go trick or treating!
For now, this is the closest you'll get to having candy.
Have more, you're eating for **two**!
I'm good with just one...
Wow, way to exercise self-control.
I'm just saving my appetite for the **taquitos** you're going to get me.
The **what** now?
And do you know what would wash it down? Craft root beer.
Should I be writing this d-
And chocolate peanut butter ice cream for dessert!
I'll be right back!
Trick or-
OUTTA MY WAY, SHE HAS THE CRAVINGS!
Cravings?
There must be a real **monster** in there to scare a grown man like that.

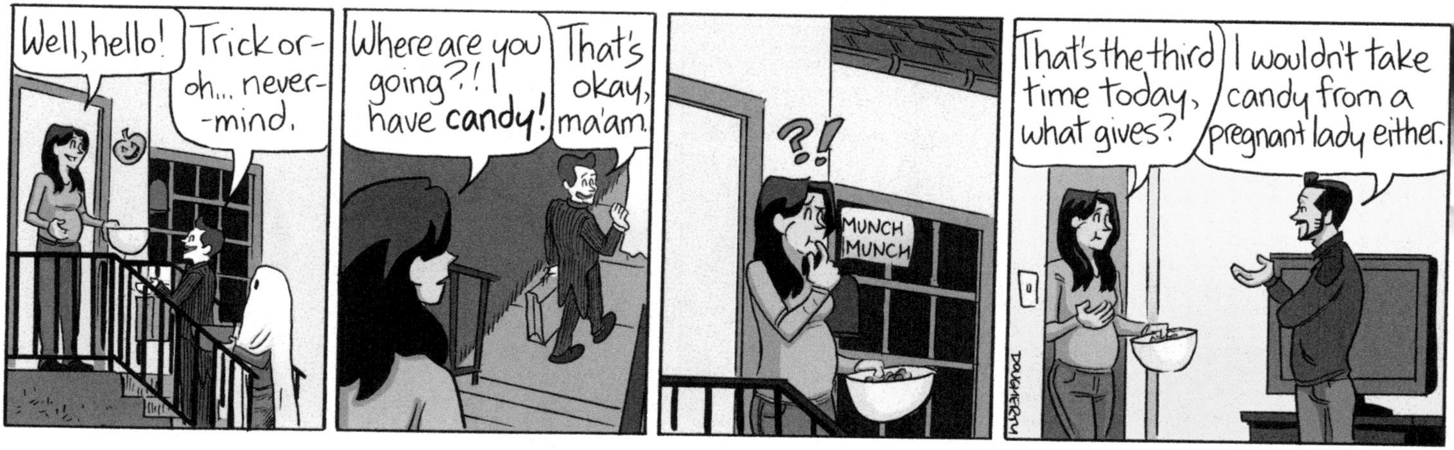
Well, hello!
Trick or- oh... never- -mind.
Where are you going?! I have candy!
That's okay, ma'am.
?!
MUNCH MUNCH
That's the third time today, what gives?
I wouldn't take candy from a pregnant lady either.
DOUGHERTY

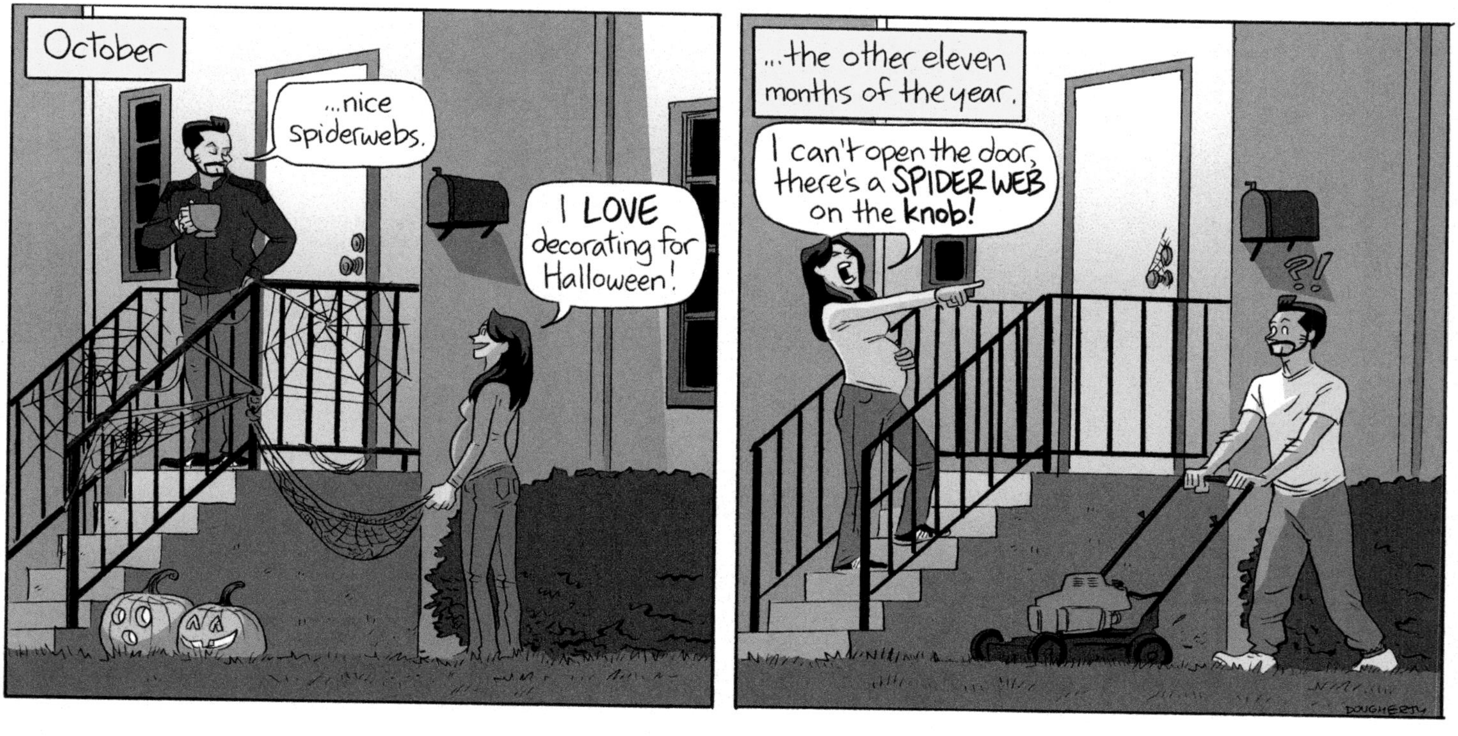
October
...nice spiderwebs.
I LOVE decorating for Halloween!
...the other eleven months of the year.
I can't open the door, there's a SPIDER WEB on the knob!
?!
DOUGHERTY

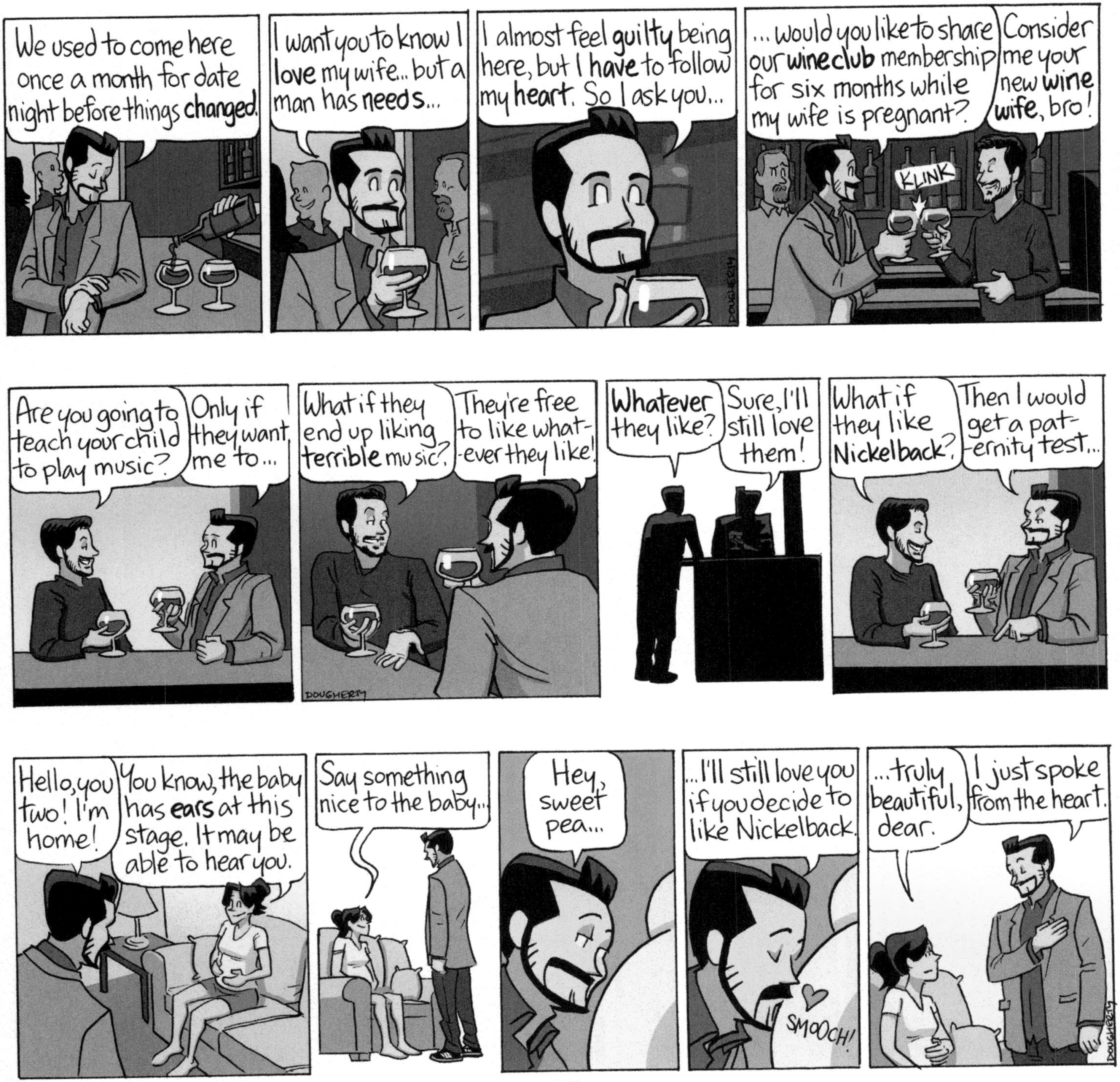
We used to come here once a month for date night before things **changed**.
I want you to know I **love** my wife... but a man has **needs**...
I almost feel **guilty** being here, but I **have** to follow my **heart**. So I ask you...
...would you like to share our **wine club** membership for six months while my wife is pregnant?
KLINK
Consider me your new **wine wife**, bro!
Are you going to teach your child to play music?
Only if they want me to...
What if they end up liking **terrible** music?
They're free to like whatever they like!
Whatever they like?
Sure, I'll still love them!
What if they like **Nickelback**?
Then I would get a paternity test...
Hello, you two! I'm home!
You know, the baby has **ears** at this stage. It may be able to hear you.
Say something nice to the baby...
Hey, sweet pea...
...I'll still love you if you decide to like Nickelback.
SMOOCH!
...truly beautiful, dear.
I just spoke from the heart.

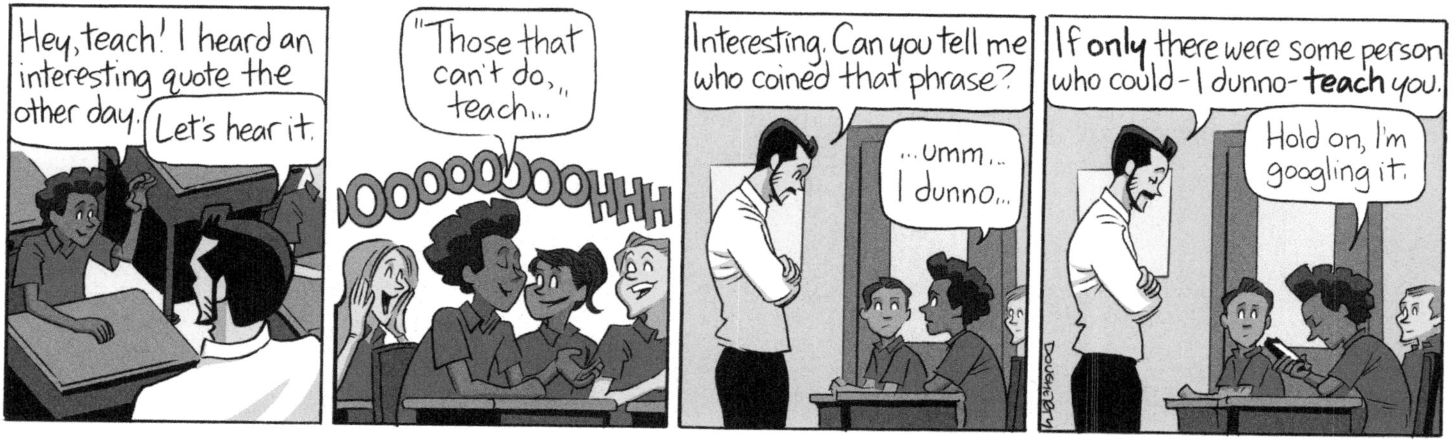
Hey, teach! I heard an interesting quote the other day.
Let's hear it.
"Those that can't do,,, teach...
OOOOOOOOOOHHH
Interesting. Can you tell me who coined that phrase?
...umm... I dunno...
If **only** there were some person who could - I dunno - **teach** you.
Hold on, I'm googling it.
DOUGHERTY

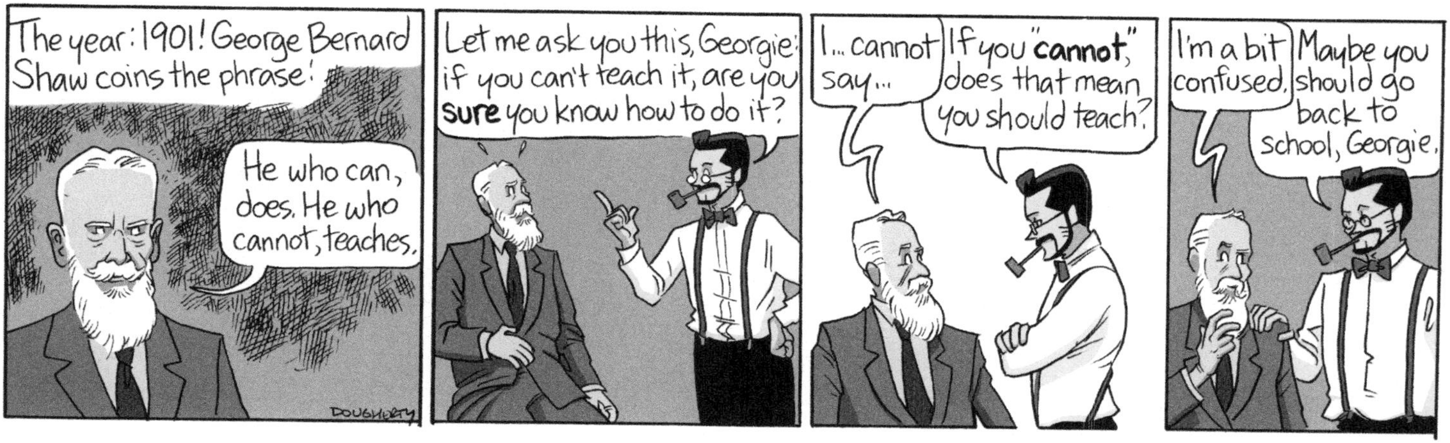
The year: 1901! George Bernard Shaw coins the phrase!
He who can, does. He who cannot, teaches.
DOUGHERTY
Let me ask you this, Georgie: if you can't teach it, are you **sure** you know how to do it?
I... cannot say...
If you "**cannot**," does that mean you should teach?
I'm a bit confused.
Maybe you should go back to school, Georgie.

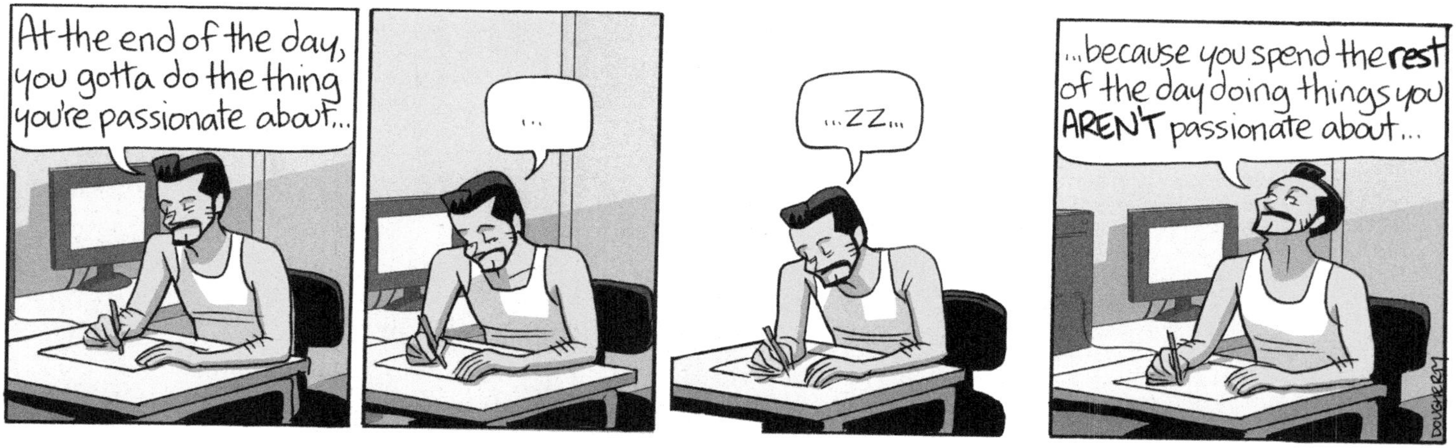
At the end of the day, you gotta do the thing you're passionate about...
...
...zz...
...because you spend the **rest** of the day doing things you **AREN'T** passionate about...
DOUGHERTY

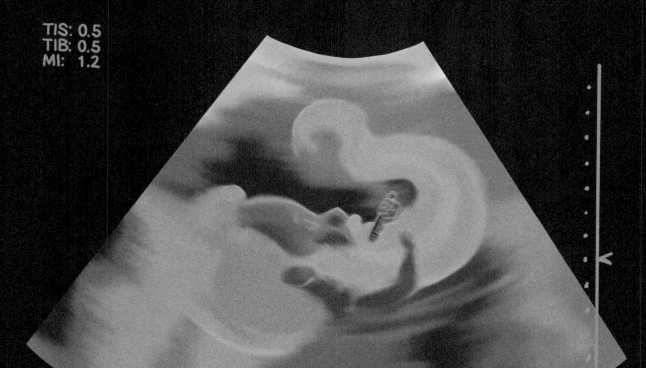

2

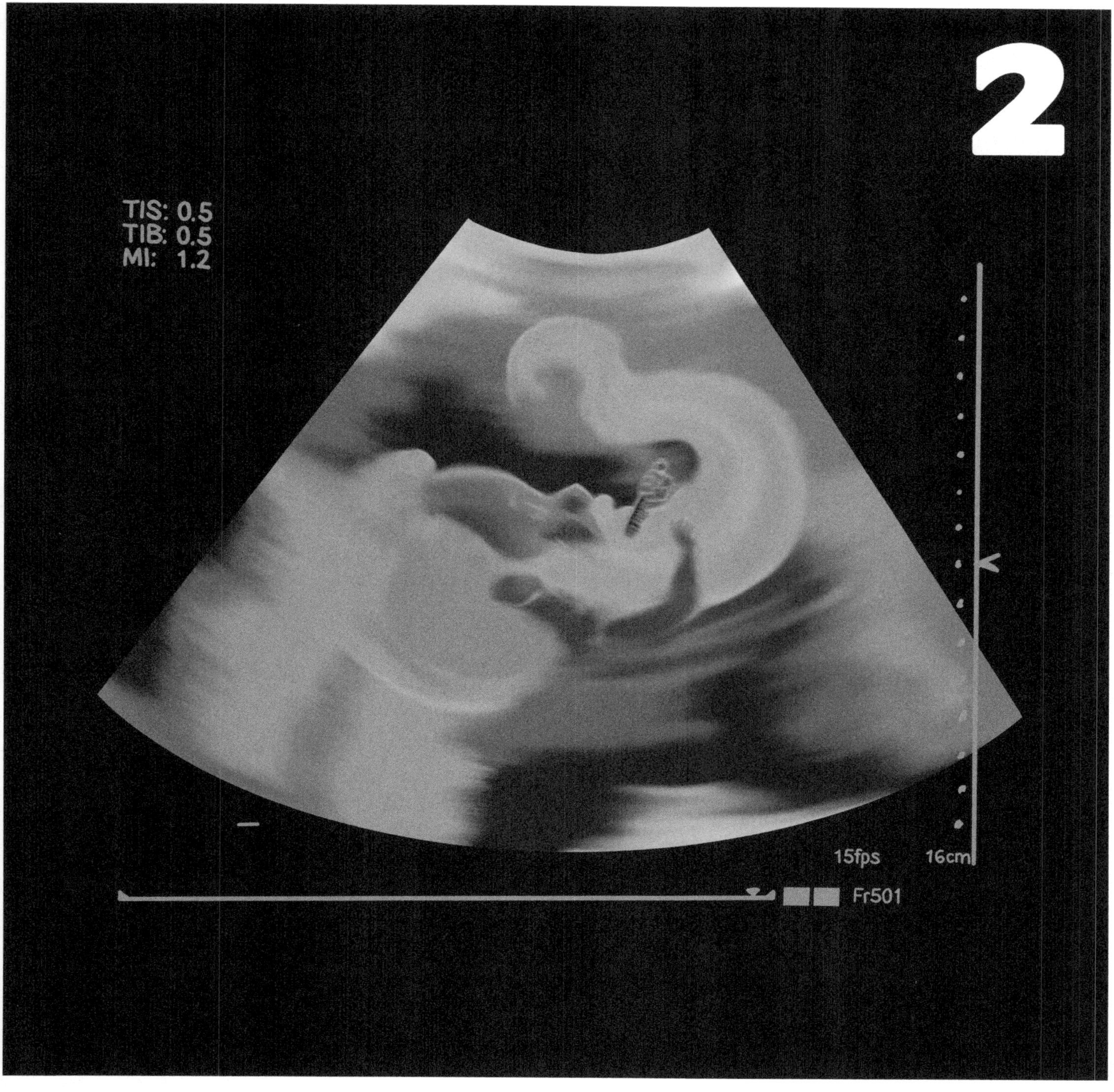

TIS: 0.5
TIB: 0.5
MI: 1.2

15fps

16cm

Fr501

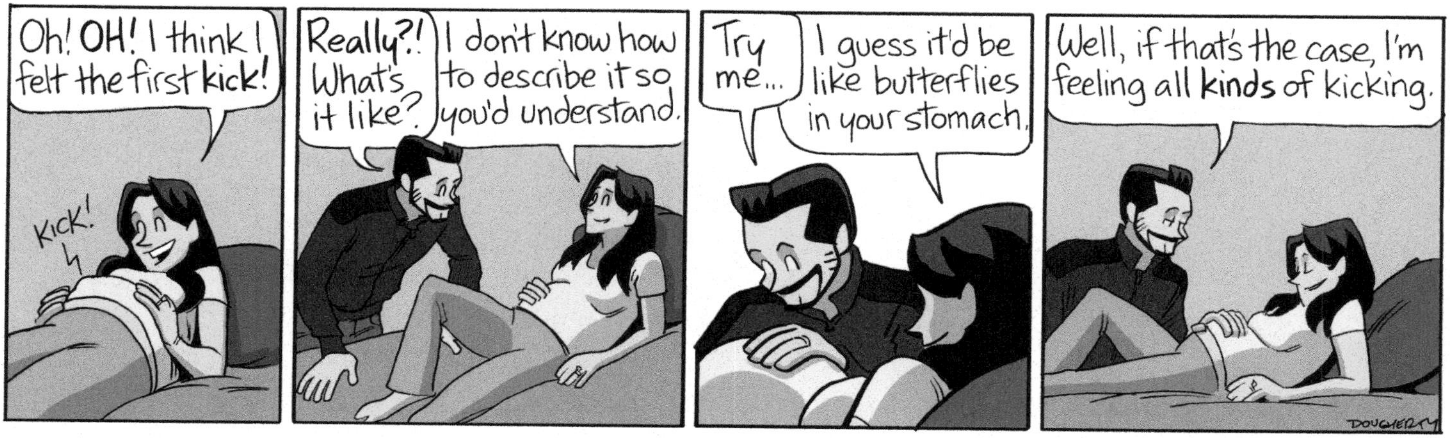
Oh! OH! I think I felt the first kick!
KICK!
Really?! What's it like?
I don't know how to describe it so you'd understand.
Try me...
I guess it'd be like butterflies in your stomach.
Well, if that's the case, I'm feeling all kinds of kicking.
DOUGHERTY

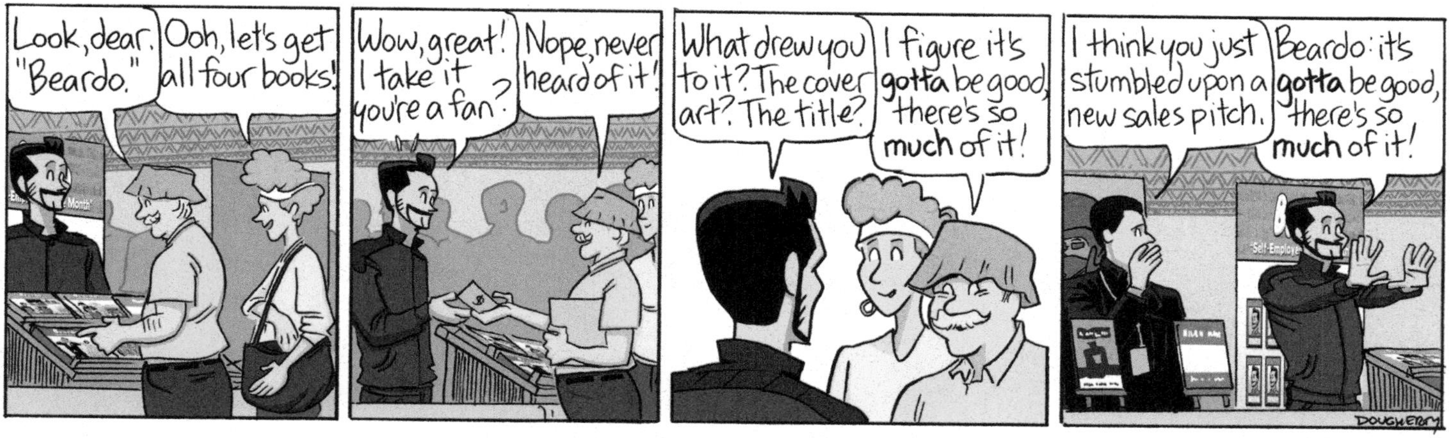
Look, dear. "Beardo."
Ooh, let's get all four books!
Wow, great! I take it you're a fan?
Nope, never heard of it!
What drew you to it? The cover art? The title?
I figure it's gotta be good, there's so much of it!
I think you just stumbled upon a new sales pitch.
Beardo: it's gotta be good, there's so much of it!
DOUGHERTY

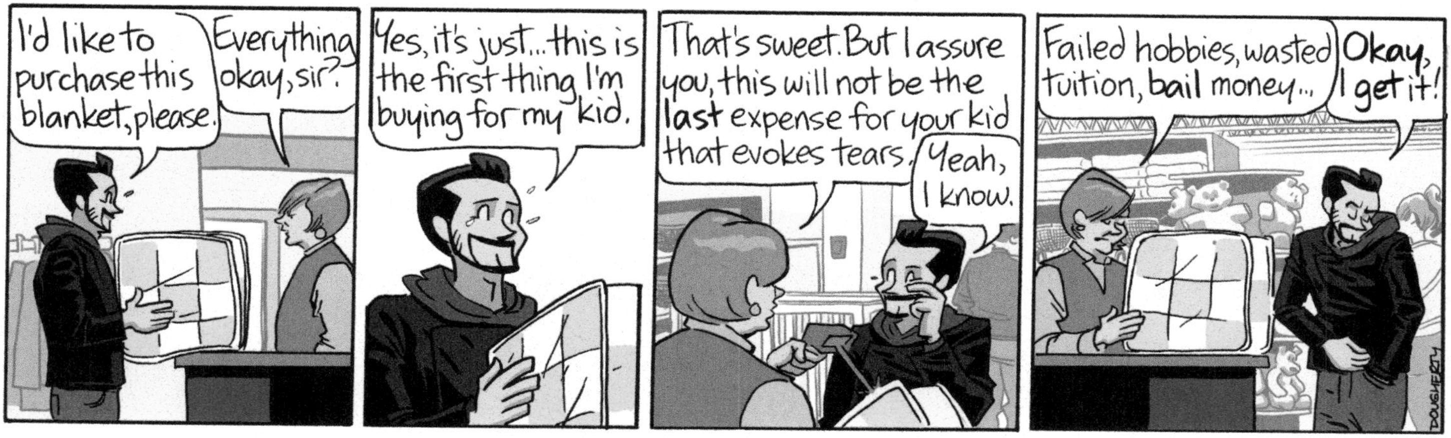
I'd like to purchase this blanket, please.
Everything okay, sir?
Yes, it's just... this is the first thing I'm buying for my kid.
That's sweet. But I assure you, this will not be the last expense for your kid that evokes tears.
Yeah, I know.
Failed hobbies, wasted tuition, bail money...
Okay, I get it!
DOUGHERTY

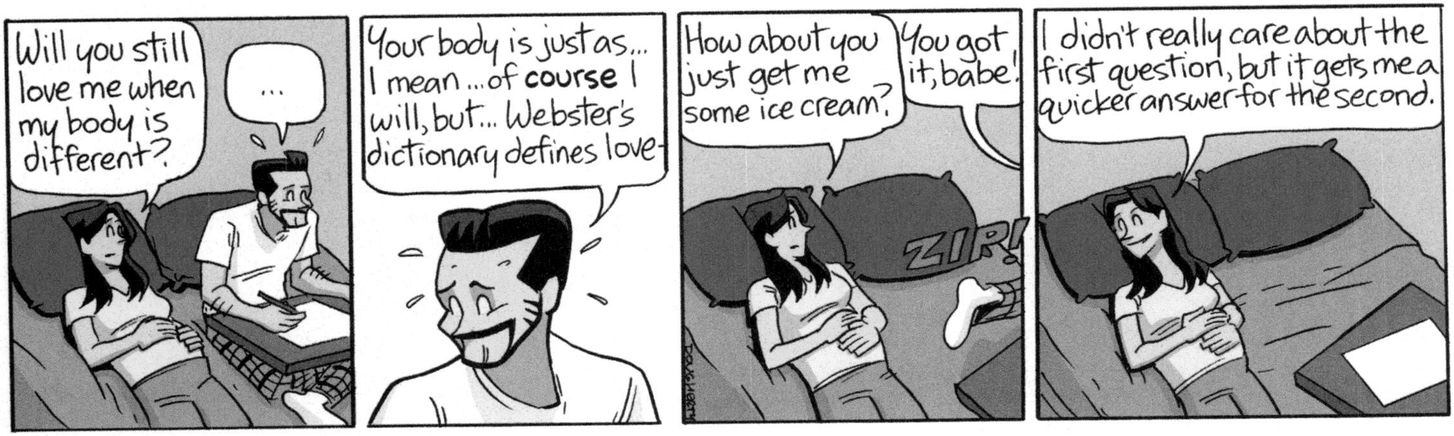

Will you still love me when my body is different?
...
Your body is just as... I mean ...of **course** I will, but... Webster's dictionary defines love-
How about you just get me some ice cream?
You got it, babe!
ZIP!
I didn't really care about the first question, but it gets me a quicker answer for the second.

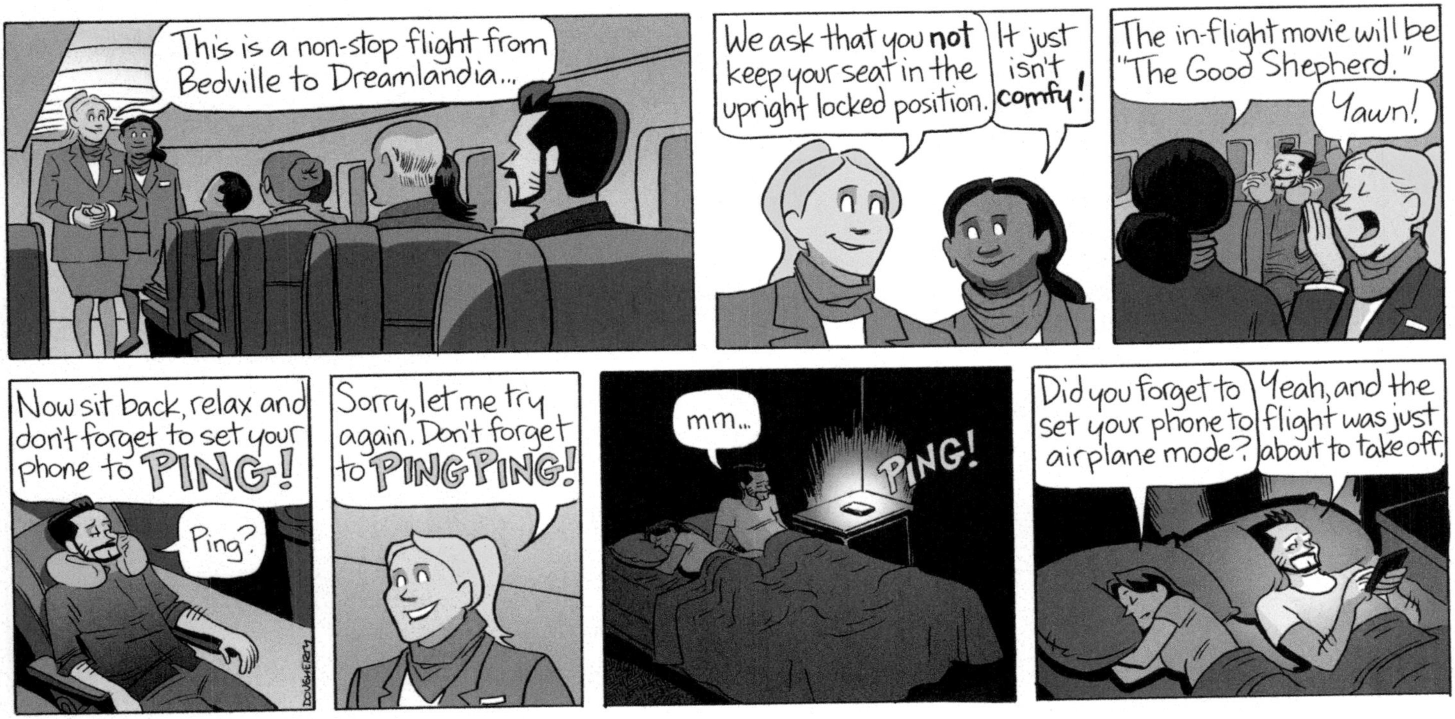

This is a non-stop flight from Bedville to Dreamlandia...
We ask that you **not** keep your seat in the upright locked position.
It just isn't **comfy**!
The in-flight movie will be "The Good Shepherd."
Yawn!
Now sit back, relax and don't forget to set your phone to PING!
Ping?
Sorry, let me try again. Don't forget to PING PING!
mm...
PING!
Did you forget to set your phone to airplane mode?
Yeah, and the flight was just about to take off.

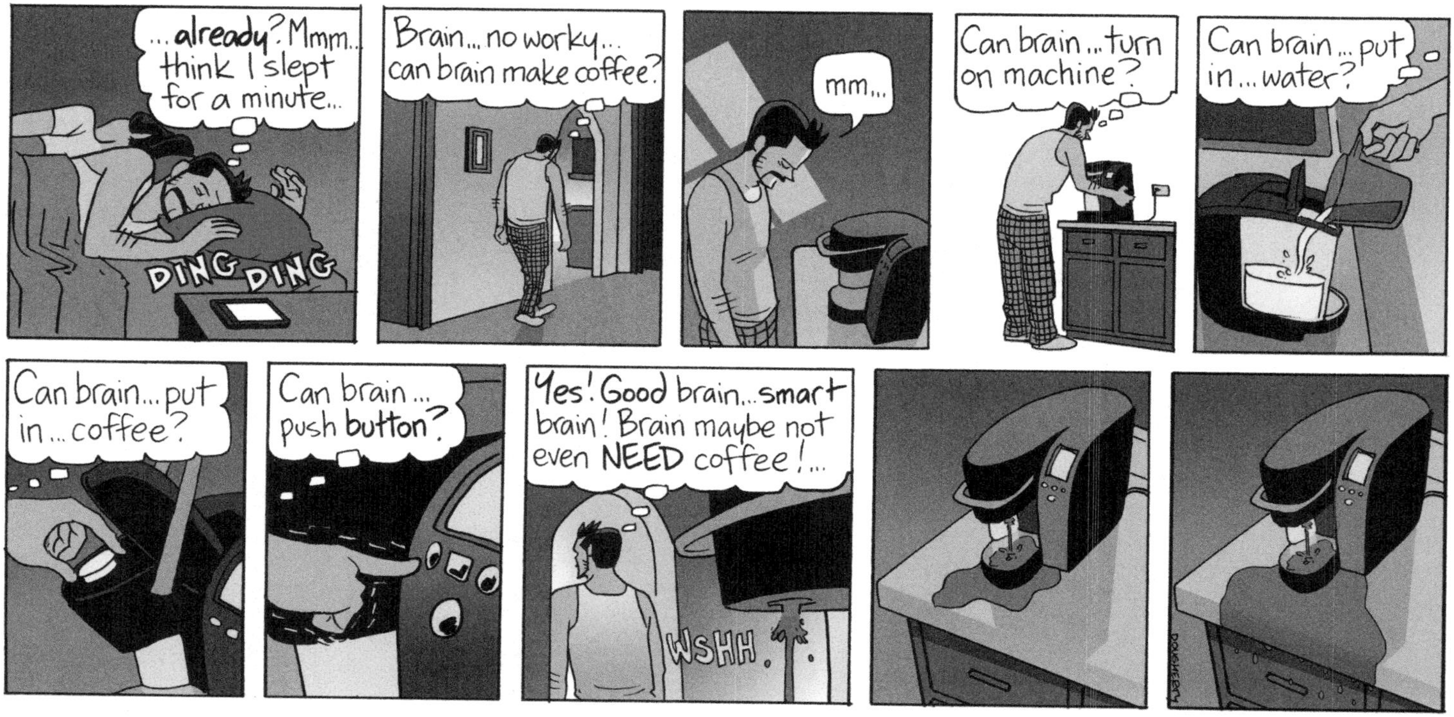
...already? Mmm... think I slept for a minute...
DING DING
Brain... no worky... can brain make coffee?
mm...
Can brain... turn on machine?
Can brain... put in... water?
Can brain... put in... coffee?
Can brain... push button?
Yes! Good brain... smart brain! Brain maybe not even NEED coffee!...
WSHH
DOUGHERTY

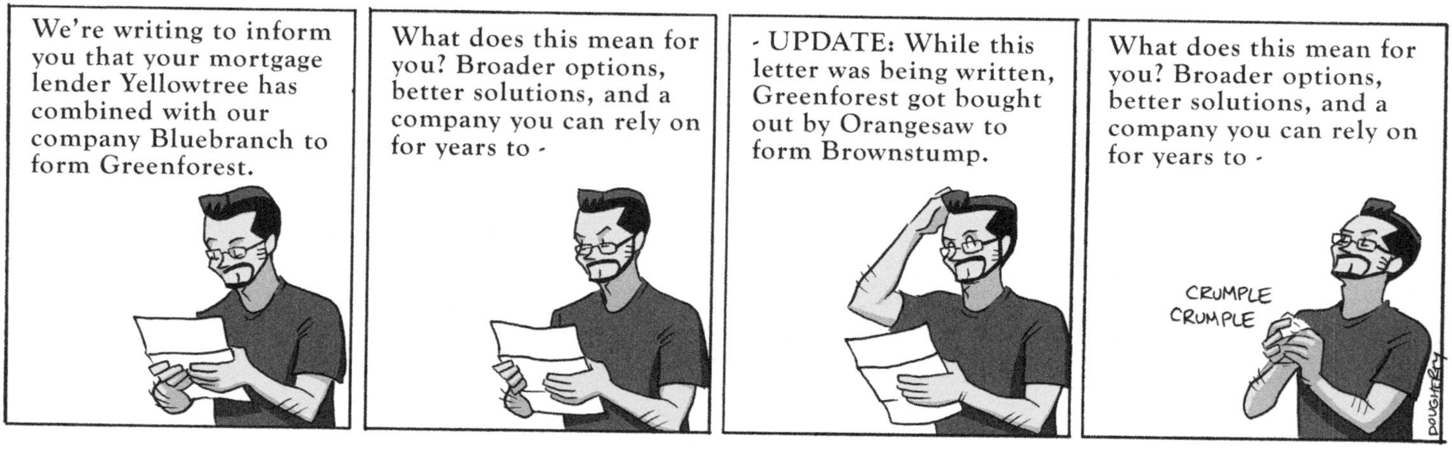
We're writing to inform you that your mortgage lender Yellowtree has combined with our company Bluebranch to form Greenforest.
What does this mean for you? Broader options, better solutions, and a company you can rely on for years to -
- UPDATE: While this letter was being written, Greenforest got bought out by Orangesaw to form Brownstump.
What does this mean for you? Broader options, better solutions, and a company you can rely on for years to -
CRUMPLE
CRUMPLE
DOUGHERTY

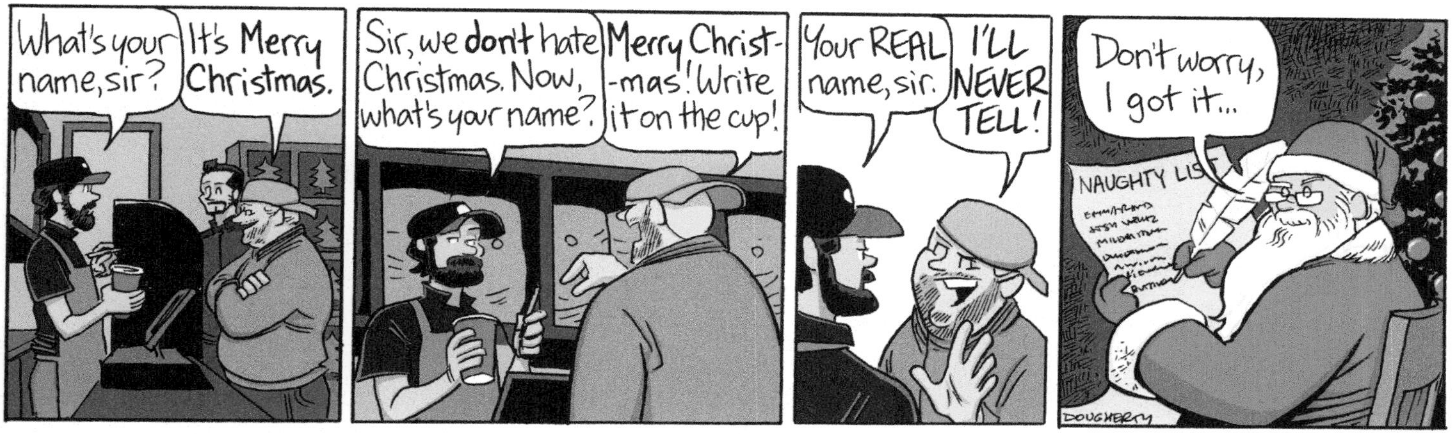
What's your name, sir?
It's Merry Christmas.
Sir, we **don't** hate Christmas. Now, what's your name?
Merry Christ-mas! Write it on the cup!
Your REAL name, sir.
I'LL NEVER TELL!
Don't worry, I got it...
NAUGHTY LIST
DOUGHERTY

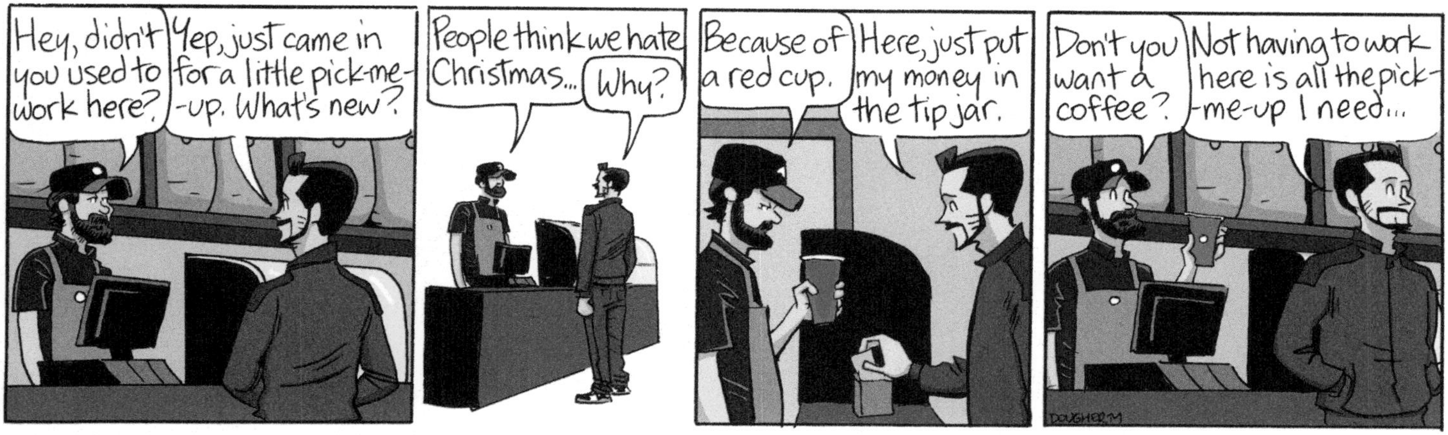
Hey, didn't you used to work here?
Yep, just came in for a little pick-me-up. What's new?
People think we hate Christmas...
Why?
Because of a red cup.
Here, just put my money in the tip jar.
Don't you want a coffee?
Not having to work here is all the pick-me-up I need...
DOUGHERTY

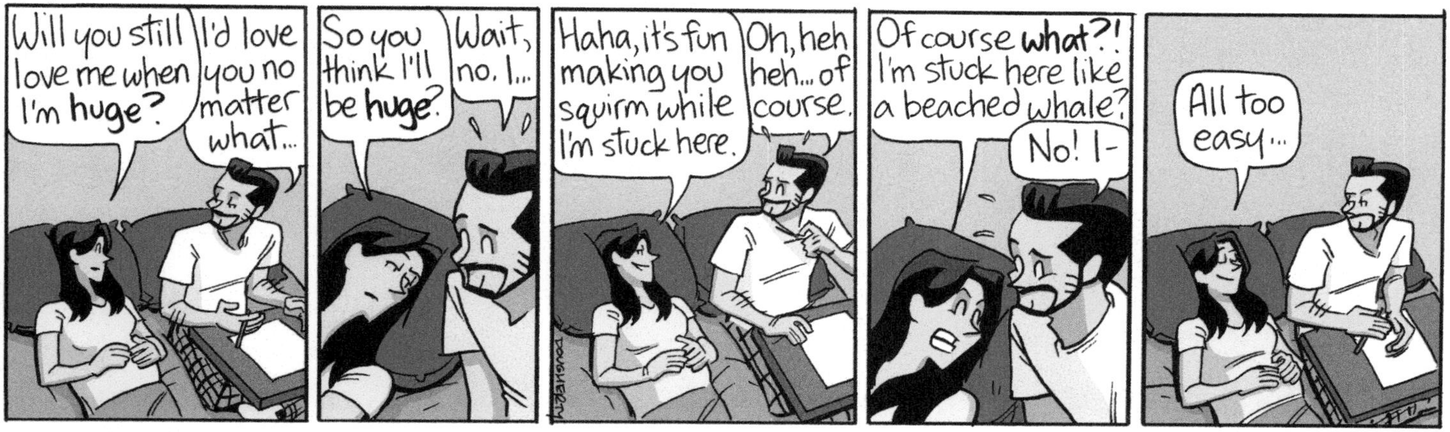
Will you still love me when I'm **huge**?
I'd love you no matter what...
So you think I'll be **huge**?
Wait, no. I...
Haha, it's fun making you squirm while I'm stuck here.
Oh, heh heh... of course.
Of course **what**?! I'm stuck here like a beached whale?
No! I-
All too easy...
DOUGHERTY

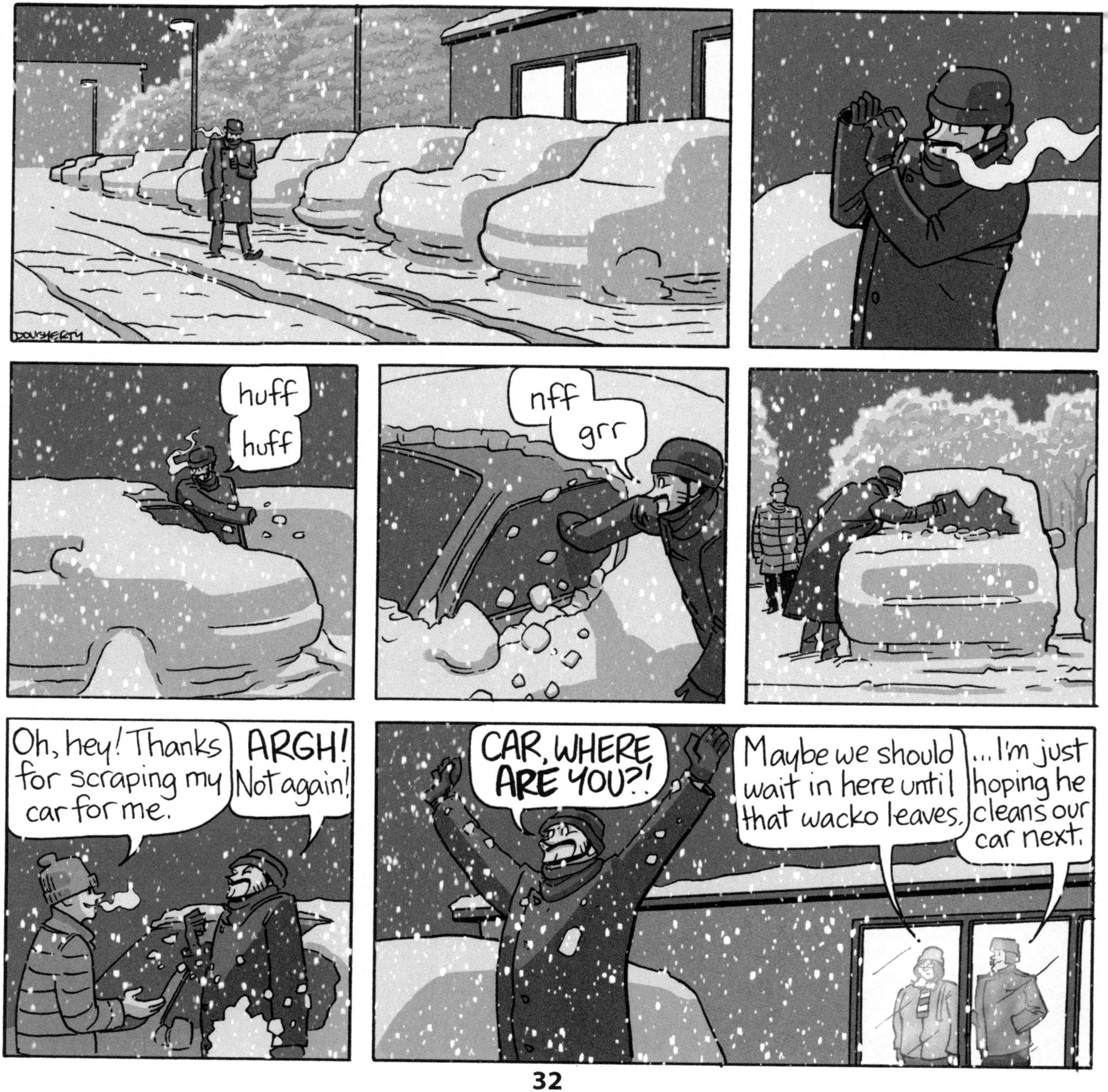
DOUGHERTY
huff
huff
nff
grr
Oh, hey! Thanks for scraping my car for me.
ARGH! Not again!
CAR, WHERE ARE YOU?!
Maybe we should wait in here until that wacko leaves.
...I'm just hoping he cleans our car next.

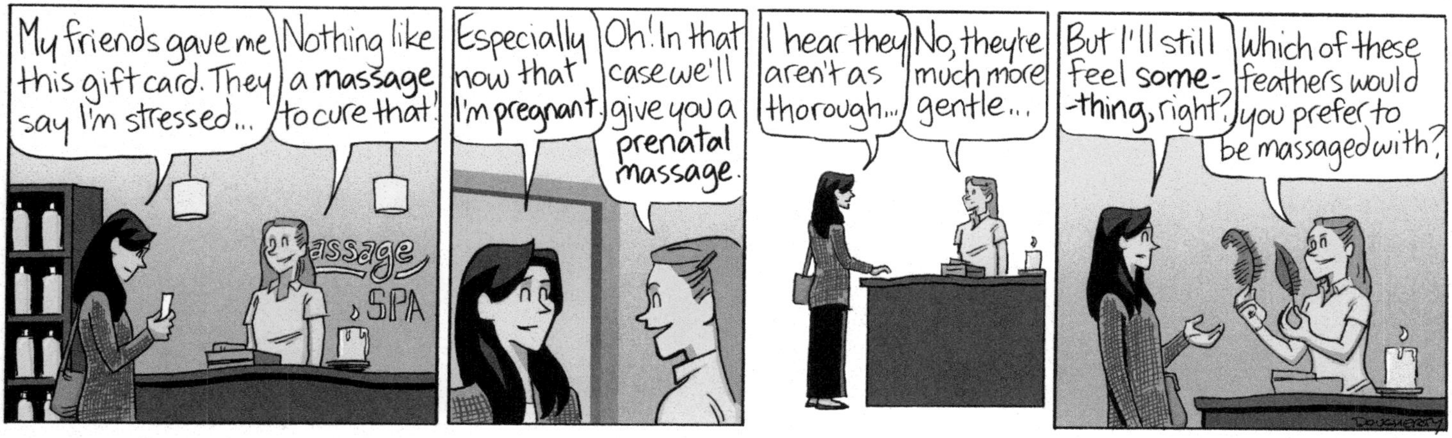
My friends gave me this gift card. They say I'm stressed...
Nothing like a **massage** to cure that!
Massage SPA
Especially now that I'm **pregnant**.
Oh! In that case we'll give you a **prenatal massage**.
I hear they aren't as thorough...
No, they're much more gentle...
But I'll still feel **some-thing**, right?
Which of these feathers would you prefer to be massaged with?
DOUGHERTY

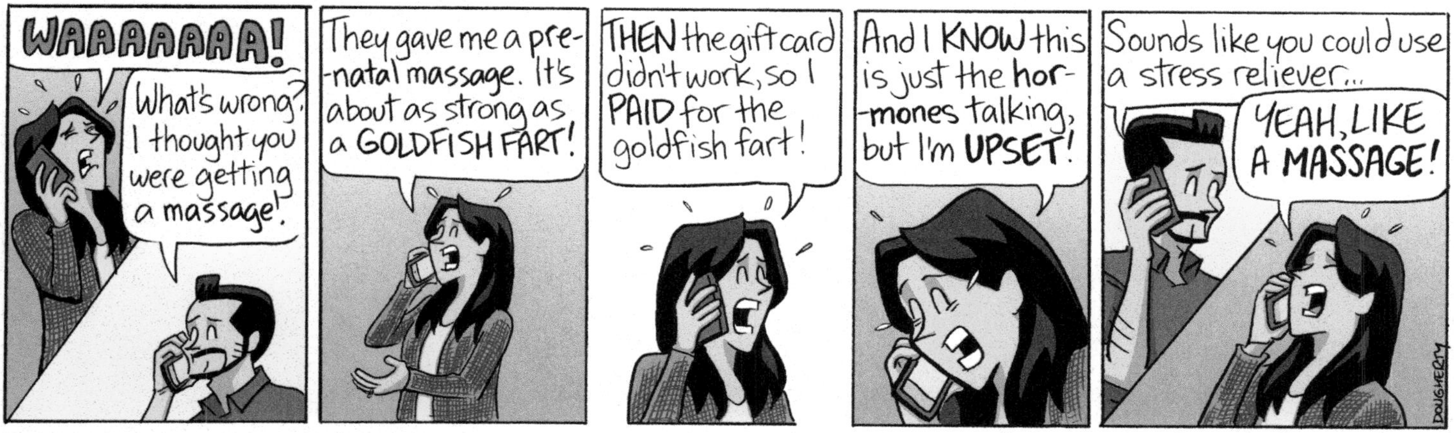
WAAAAAAA!
What's wrong? I thought you were getting a **massage**!
They gave me a **pre-natal massage**. It's about as strong as a **GOLDFISH FART**!
THEN the gift card didn't work, so I **PAID** for the goldfish fart!
And I **KNOW** this is just the **hor-mones** talking, but I'm **UPSET**!
Sounds like you could use a stress reliever...
YEAH, LIKE A **MASSAGE**!
DOUGHERTY

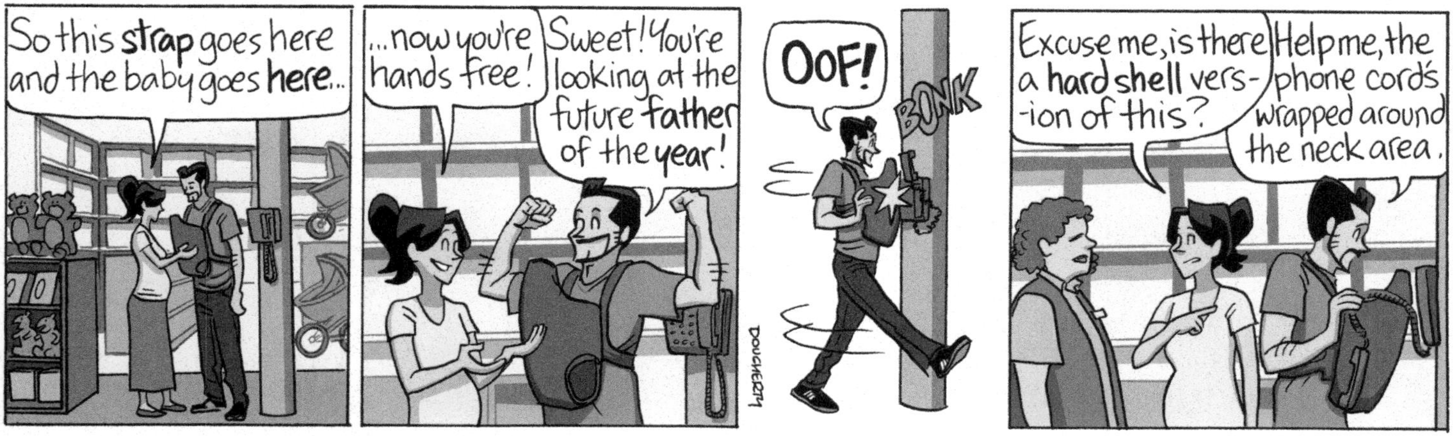
So this **strap** goes here and the baby goes **here**...
...now you're hands free!
Sweet! You're looking at the future **father** of the **year**!
DOUGHERTY
OOF!
BONK
Excuse me, is there a **hard shell** vers-ion of this?
Help me, the phone cord's wrapped around the neck area.

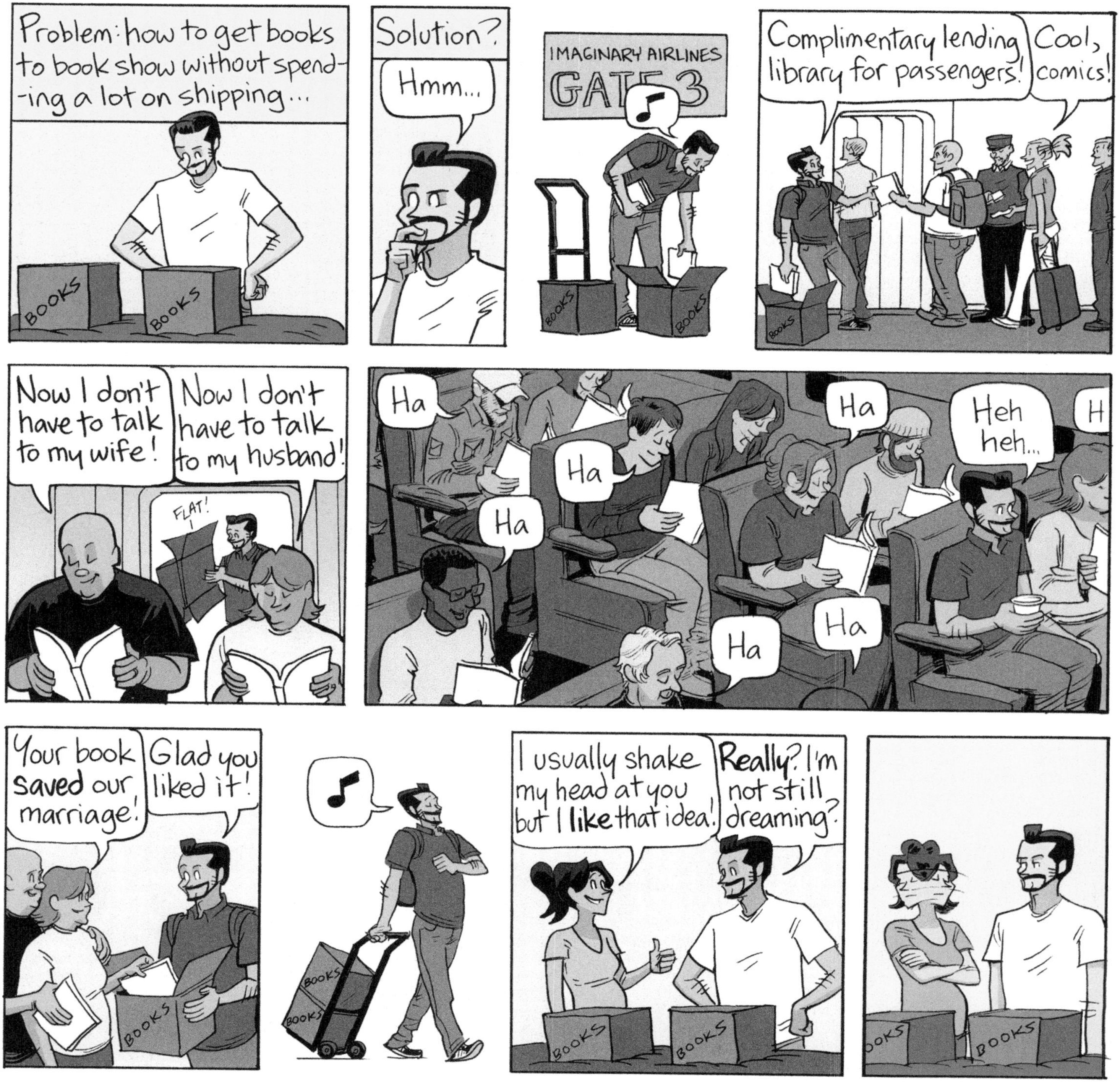
Problem: how to get books to book show without spend-ing a lot on shipping...
BOOKS
BOOKS
Solution?
Hmm...
IMAGINARY AIRLINES
GATE 3
BOOKS
BOOKS
Complimentary lending library for passengers!
Cool, comics!
BOOKS
Now I don't have to talk to my wife!
Now I don't have to talk to my husband!
FLAT!
Ha
Ha
Heh heh...
Ha
Ha
Ha
Ha
Your book saved our marriage!
Glad you liked it!
BOOKS
BOOKS
BOOKS
I usually shake my head at you but I like that idea!
Really? I'm not still dreaming?
BOOKS
BOOKS
BOOKS

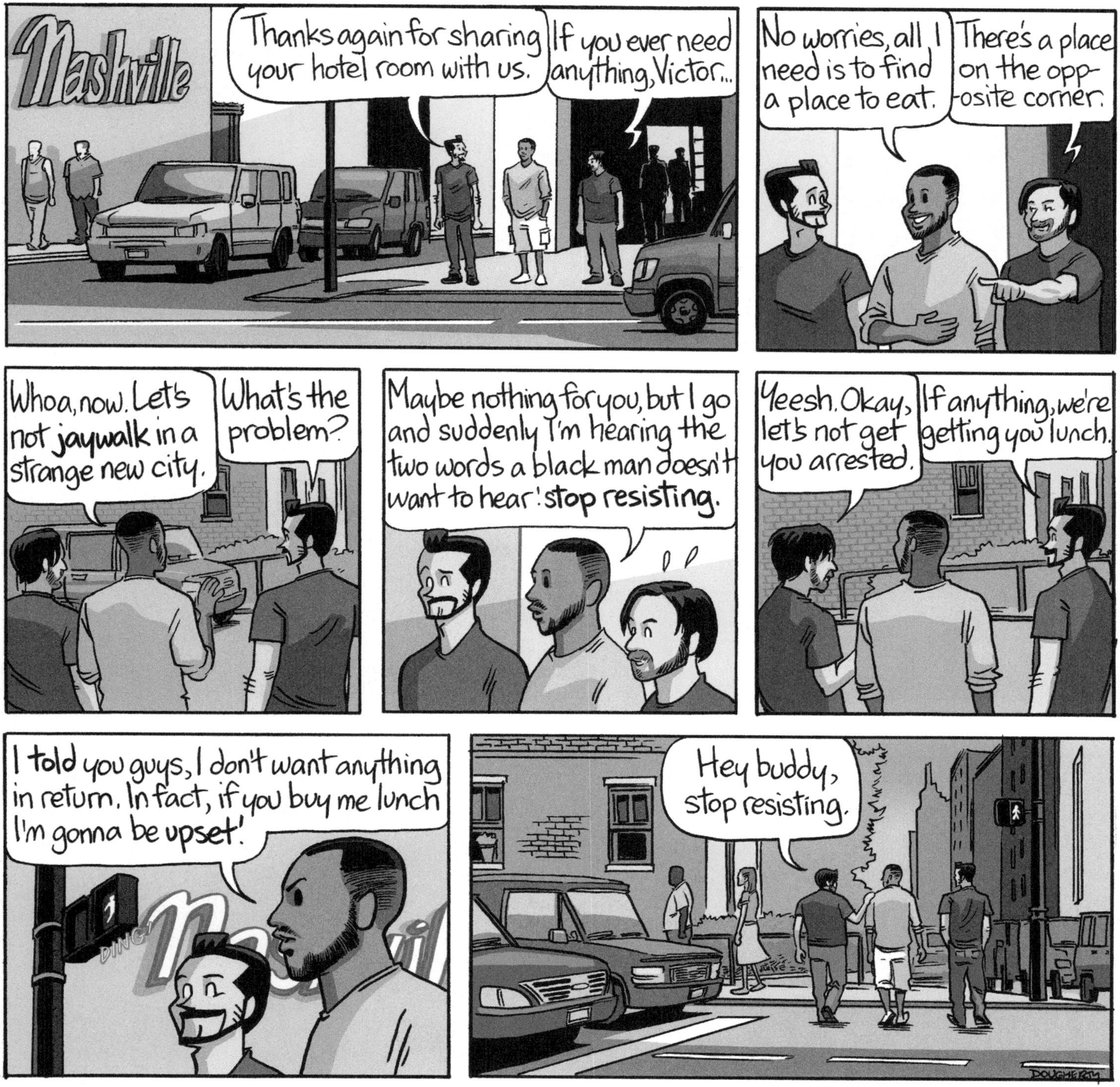
Nashville
Thanks again for sharing your hotel room with us.
If you ever need anything, Victor...
No worries, all I need is to find a place to eat.
There's a place on the opp-osite corner.
Whoa, now. Let's not **jaywalk** in a strange new city.
What's the problem?
Maybe nothing for you, but I go and suddenly I'm hearing the two words a black man doesn't want to hear: **stop resisting.**
Yeesh. Okay, let's not get you arrested.
If anything, we're getting you lunch.
I **told** you guys, I don't want anything in return. In fact, if you buy me lunch I'm gonna be **upset**!
DING!
Hey buddy, stop resisting.
DOUGHERTY

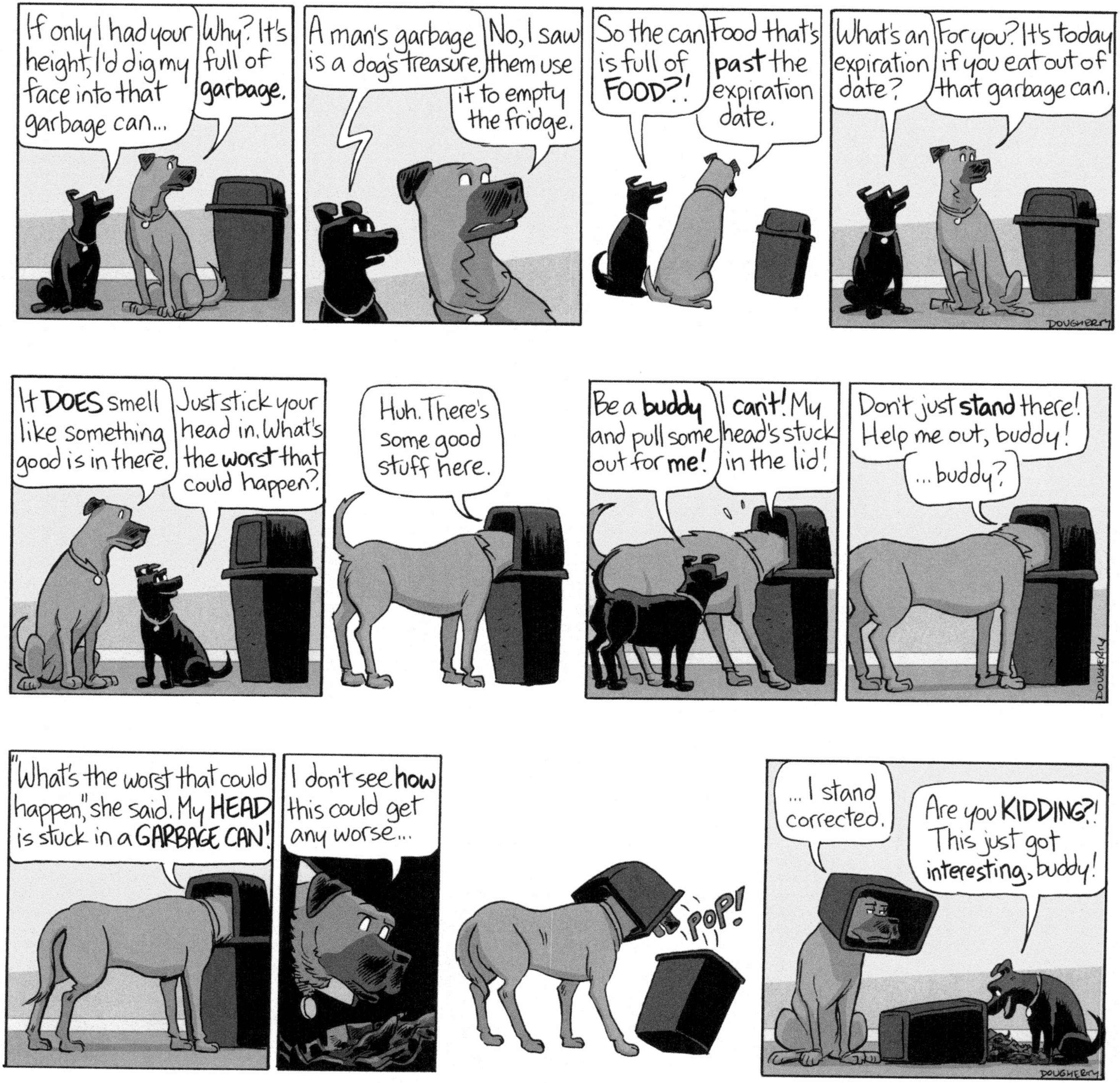
If only I had your height, I'd dig my face into that garbage can...
Why? It's full of **garbage.**
A man's garbage is a dog's treasure.
No, I saw them use it to empty the fridge.
So the can is full of FOOD?!
Food that's **past** the expiration date.
What's an expiration date?
For you? It's today if you eat out of that garbage can.
DOUGHERTY
It **DOES** smell like something good is in there.
Just stick your head in. What's the **worst** that could happen?
Huh. There's some good stuff here.
Be a **buddy** and pull some out for **me**!
I **can't**! My head's stuck in the lid!
Don't just **stand** there! Help me out, buddy!
... buddy?
DOUGHERTY
"What's the worst that could happen," she said. My **HEAD** is stuck in a **GARBAGE CAN**!
I don't see **how** this could get any worse...
POP!
... I stand corrected.
Are you **KIDDING?!** This just got **interesting**, buddy!
DOUGHERTY

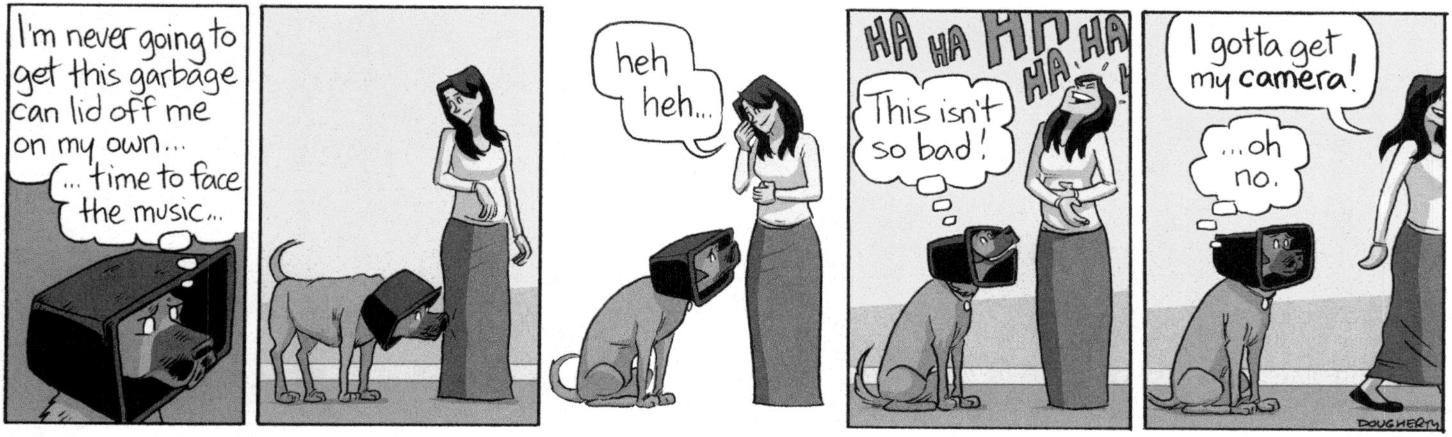
I'm never going to get this garbage can lid off me on my own...
... time to face the music...
heh heh...
HA HA HA HA HA HA
This isn't so bad!
I gotta get my **camera**!
...oh no.
DOUGHERTY

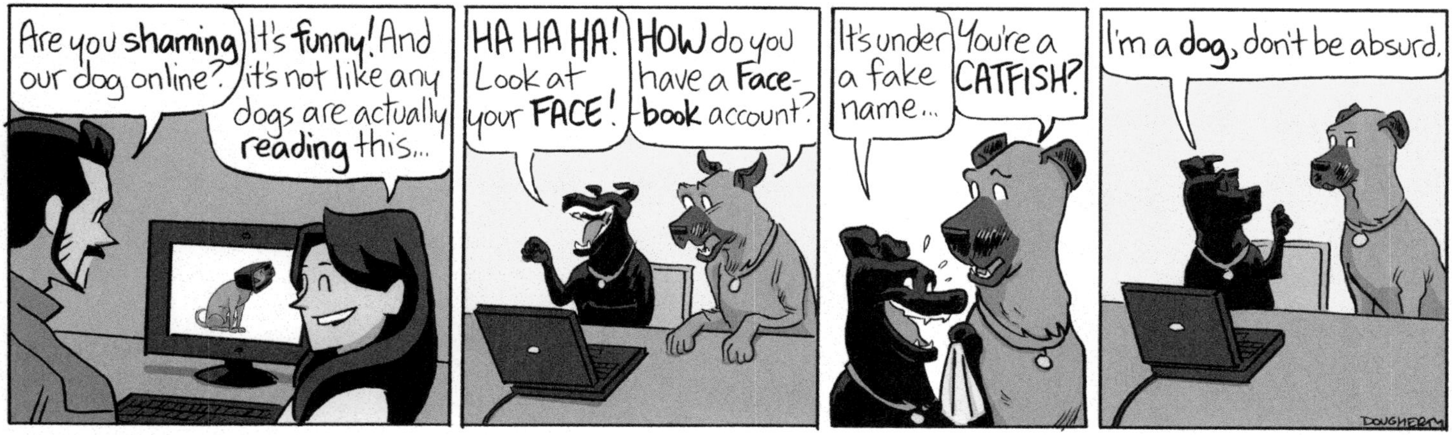
Are you **shaming** our dog online?
It's **funny**! And it's not like any dogs are actually **reading** this...
HA HA HA! Look at your **FACE**!
HOW do you have a **Face-book** account?
It's under a fake name...
You're a **CATFISH**?
I'm a **dog**, don't be absurd.
DOUGHERTY

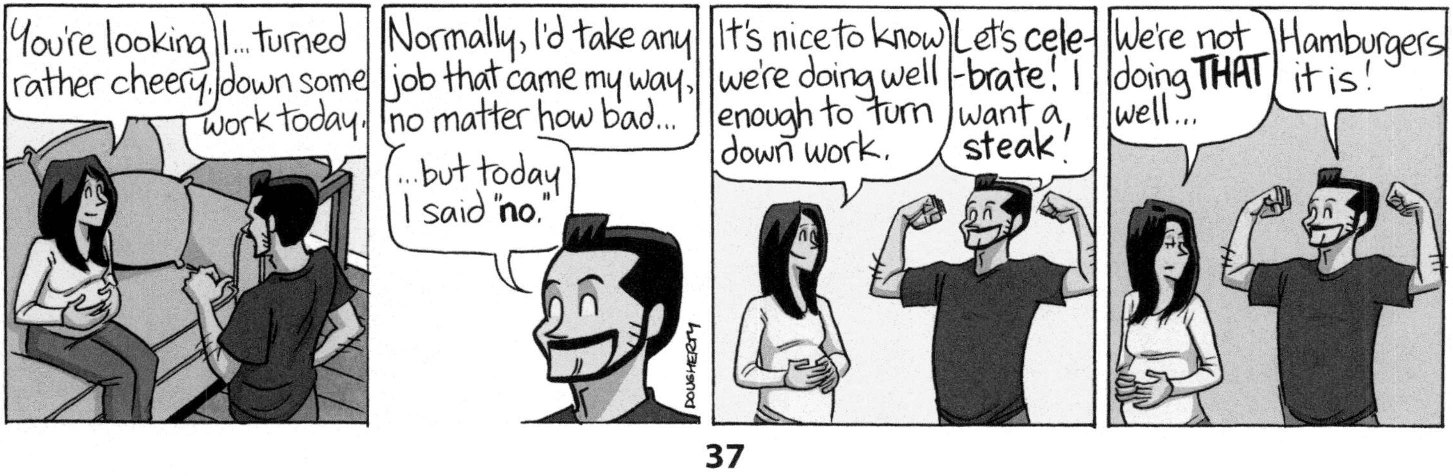
You're looking rather cheery.
I... turned down some work today.
Normally, I'd take any job that came my way, no matter how bad...
...but today I said "**no**."
DOUGHERTY
It's nice to know we're doing well enough to turn down work.
Let's **cele-brate**! I want a **steak**!
We're not doing **THAT** well...
Hamburgers it is!

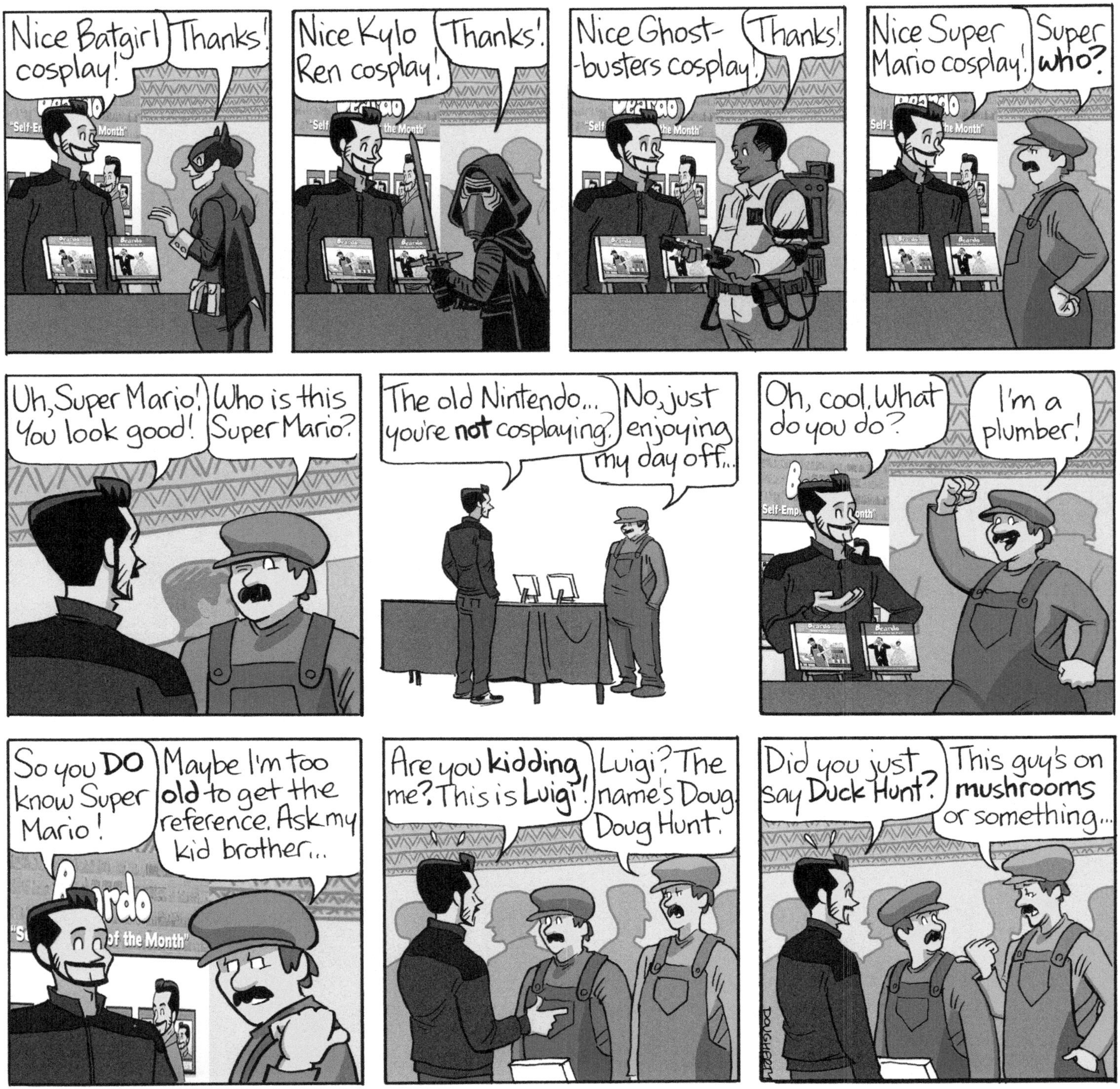
Nice Batgirl cosplay!
Thanks!
Nice Kylo Ren cosplay!
Thanks!
Nice Ghost--busters cosplay!
Thanks!
Nice Super Mario cosplay!
Super **who?**
Uh, Super Mario! You look good!
Who is this Super Mario?
The old Nintendo... you're **not** cosplaying?
No, just enjoying my day off...
Oh, cool. What do you do?
I'm a plumber!
So you **DO** know Super Mario!
Maybe I'm too **old** to get the reference. Ask my kid brother...
Are you **kidding** me? This is **Luigi**!
Luigi? The name's Doug. Doug Hunt.
Did you just say **Duck Hunt**?
This guy's on **mushrooms** or something...

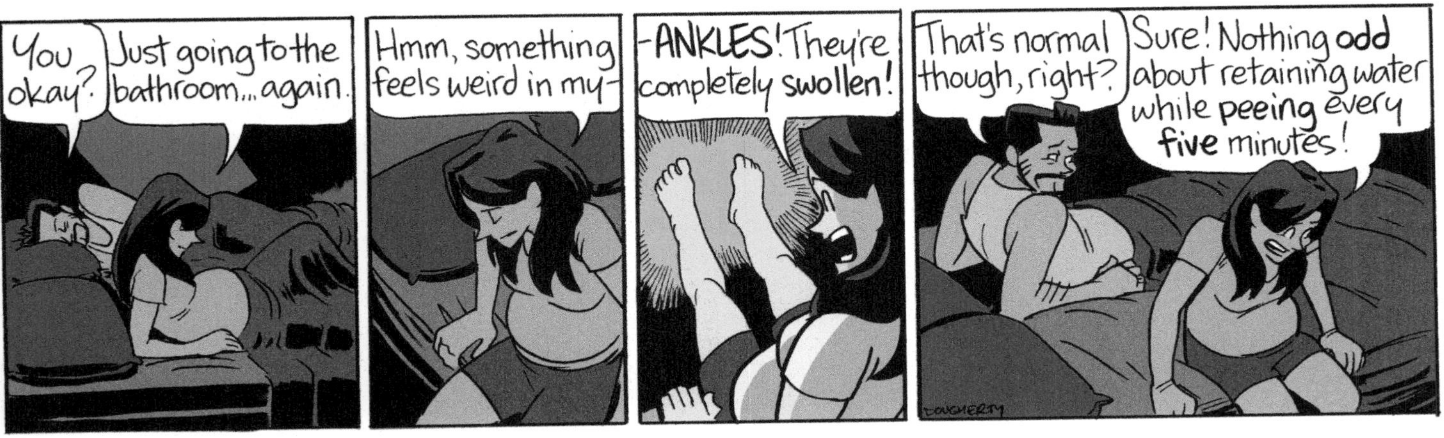
You okay?
Just going to the bathroom... again.
Hmm, something feels weird in my-
-ANKLES! They're completely swollen!
That's normal though, right?
Sure! Nothing odd about retaining water while peeing every five minutes!
DOUGHERTY

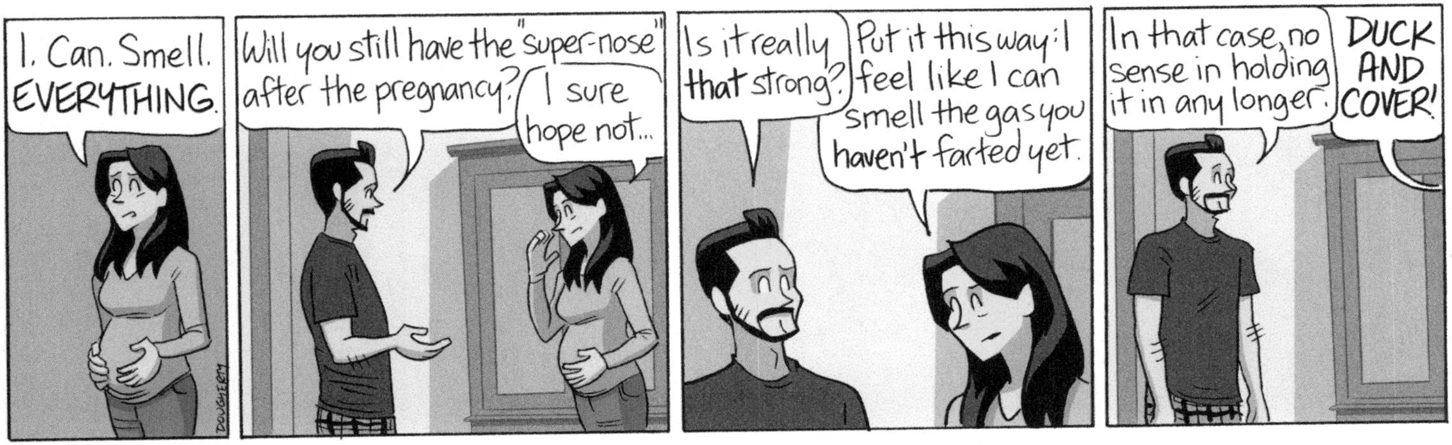
I. Can. Smell. EVERYTHING.
DOUGHERTY
Will you still have the "super-nose" after the pregnancy?
I sure hope not...
Is it really that strong?
Put it this way: I feel like I can smell the gas you haven't farted yet.
In that case, no sense in holding it in any longer.
DUCK AND COVER!

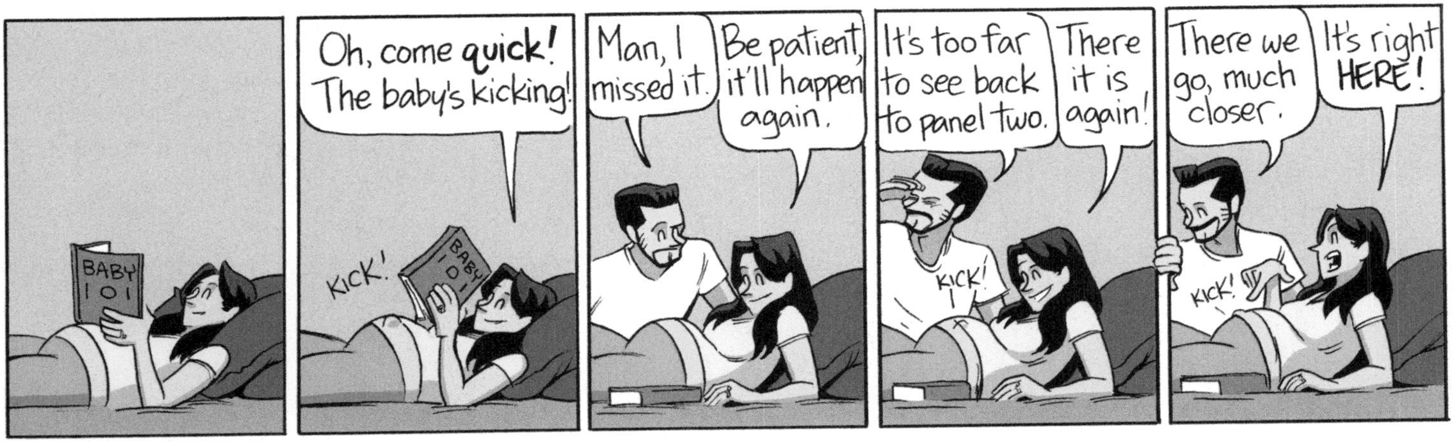
BABY 101
Oh, come quick! The baby's kicking!
KICK!
BABY 101
Man, I missed it.
Be patient, it'll happen again.
It's too far to see back to panel two.
There it is again!
KICK!
There we go, much closer.
It's right HERE!
KICK!

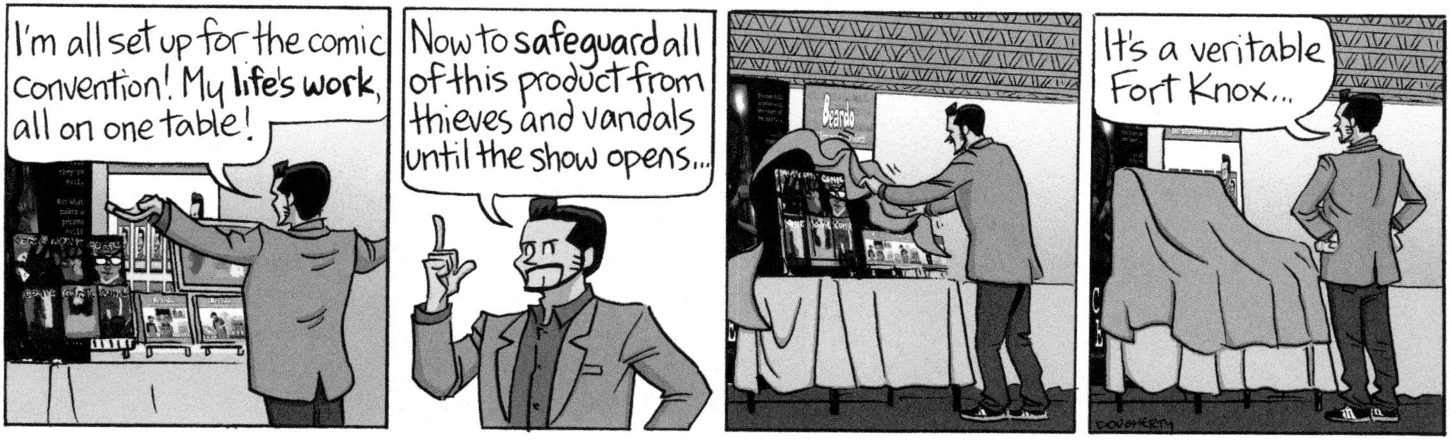
I'm all set up for the comic convention! My **life's work**, all on one table!
Now to **safeguard** all of this product from thieves and vandals until the show opens...
It's a veritable Fort Knox...
DOUGHERTY

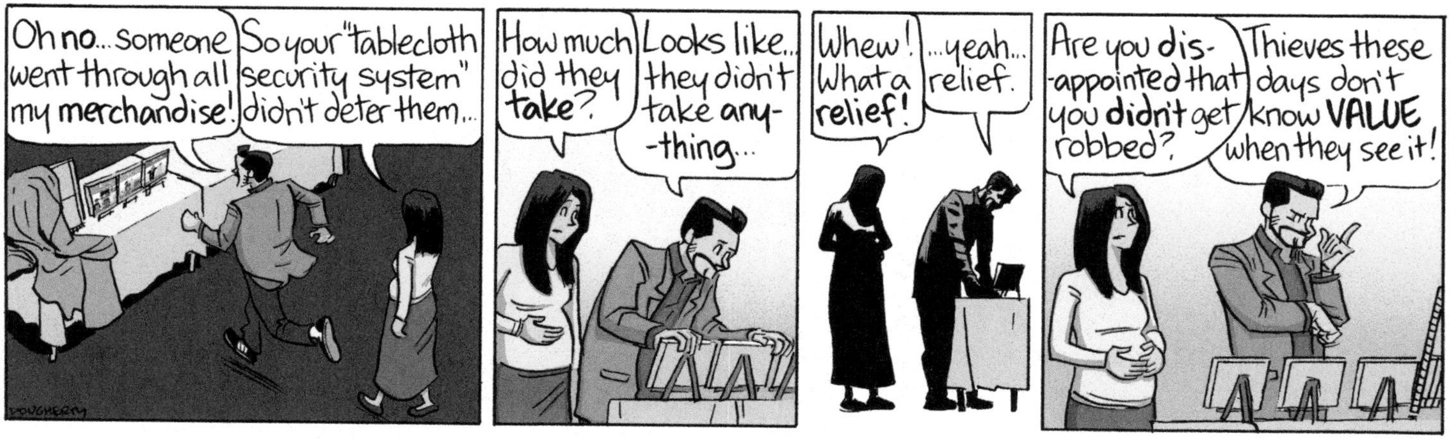
Oh **no**... someone went through all my **merchandise**!
So your "tablecloth security system" didn't deter them...
How much did they **take**?
Looks like... they didn't take **any-**
-thing...
Whew! What a **relief**!
...yeah... relief.
Are you **dis-**
-appointed that you **didn't** get robbed?
Thieves these days don't know **VALUE** when they see it!
DOUGHERTY

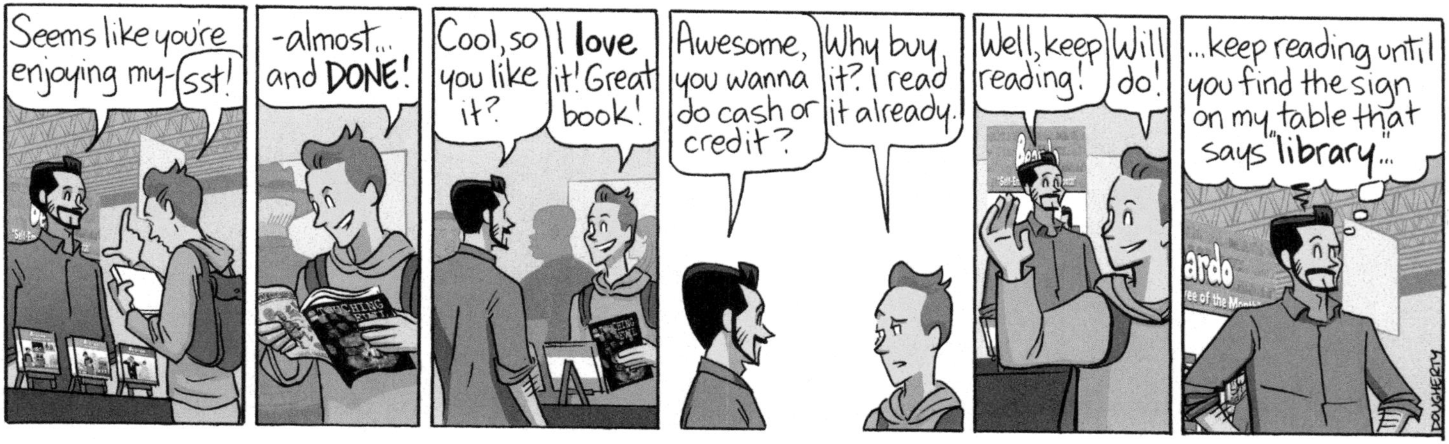
Seems like you're enjoying my-
sst!
-almost... and **DONE**!
Cool, so you like it?
I **love** it! Great book!
Awesome, you wanna do cash or credit?
Why buy it? I read it already.
Well, keep reading!
Will do!
...keep reading until you find the sign on my table that says "**library**"...
DOUGHERTY

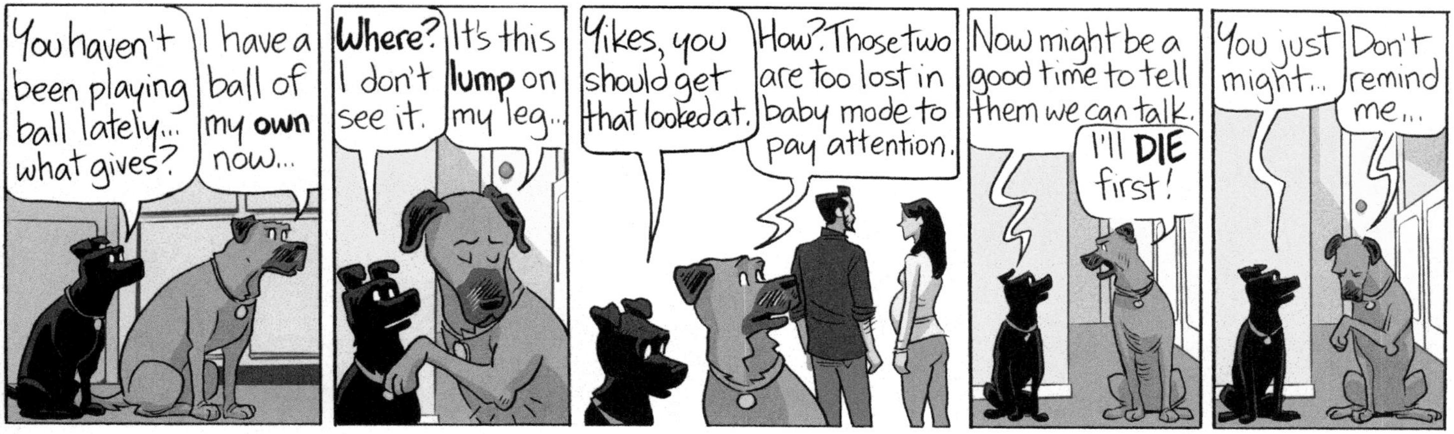
You haven't been playing ball lately... what gives?
I have a ball of my **own** now...
Where? I don't see it.
It's this **lump** on my leg...
Yikes, you should get that looked at.
How? Those two are too lost in baby mode to pay attention.
Now might be a good time to tell them we can talk.
I'll **DIE** first!
You just might...
Don't remind me...

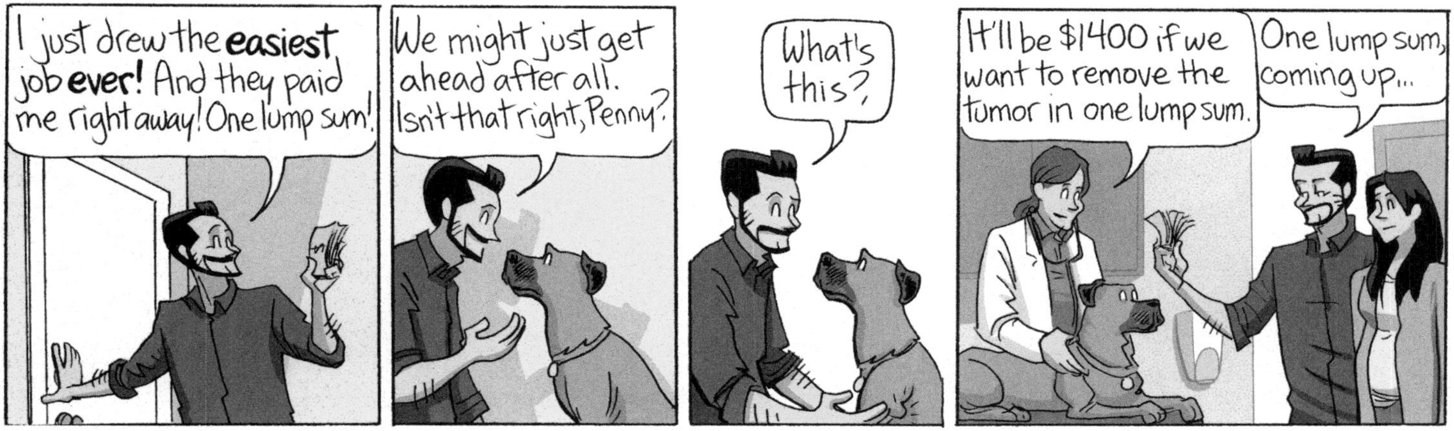
I just drew the **easiest** job **ever!** And they paid me right away! One lump sum!
We might just get ahead after all. Isn't that right, Penny?
What's this?
It'll be $1400 if we want to remove the tumor in one lump sum.
One lump sum, coming up...

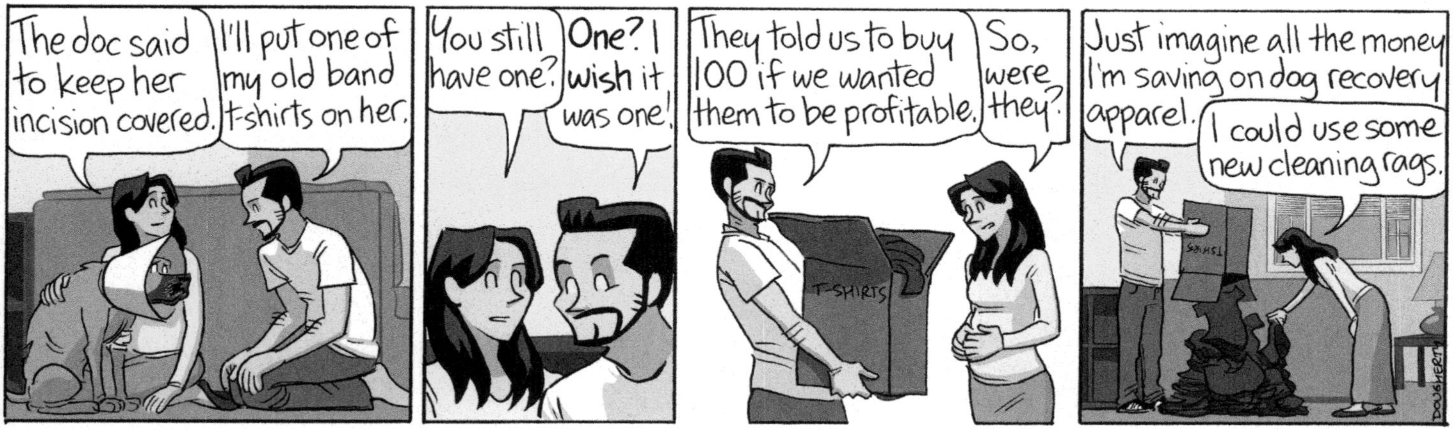
The doc said to keep her incision covered.
I'll put one of my old band t-shirts on her.
You still have one?
One? I **wish** it was one!
They told us to buy 100 if we wanted them to be profitable.
So, were they?
T-SHIRTS
Just imagine all the money I'm saving on dog recovery apparel.
I could use some new cleaning rags.

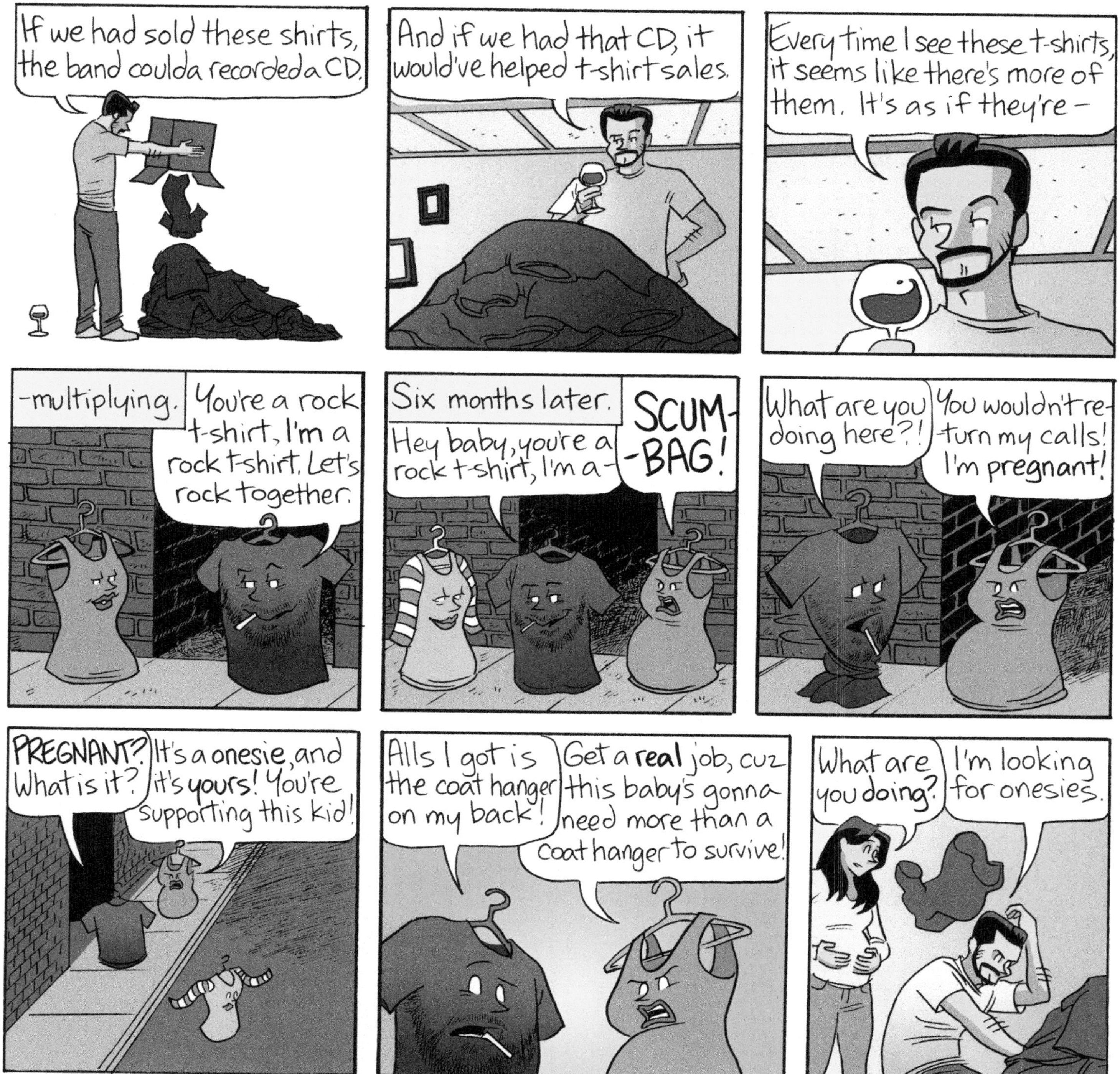
If we had sold these shirts, the band coulda recorded a CD.
And if we had that CD, it would've helped t-shirt sales.
Every time I see these t-shirts, it seems like there's more of them. It's as if they're -
-multiplying.
You're a rock t-shirt, I'm a rock t-shirt. Let's rock together.
Six months later.
Hey baby, you're a rock t-shirt, I'm a -
SCUM- -BAG!
What are you doing here?!
You wouldn't re-turn my calls! I'm pregnant!
PREGNANT?! What is it?
It's a onesie, and it's yours! You're supporting this kid!
Alls I got is the coat hanger on my back!
Get a real job, cuz this baby's gonna need more than a coat hanger to survive!
What are you doing?
I'm looking for onesies.

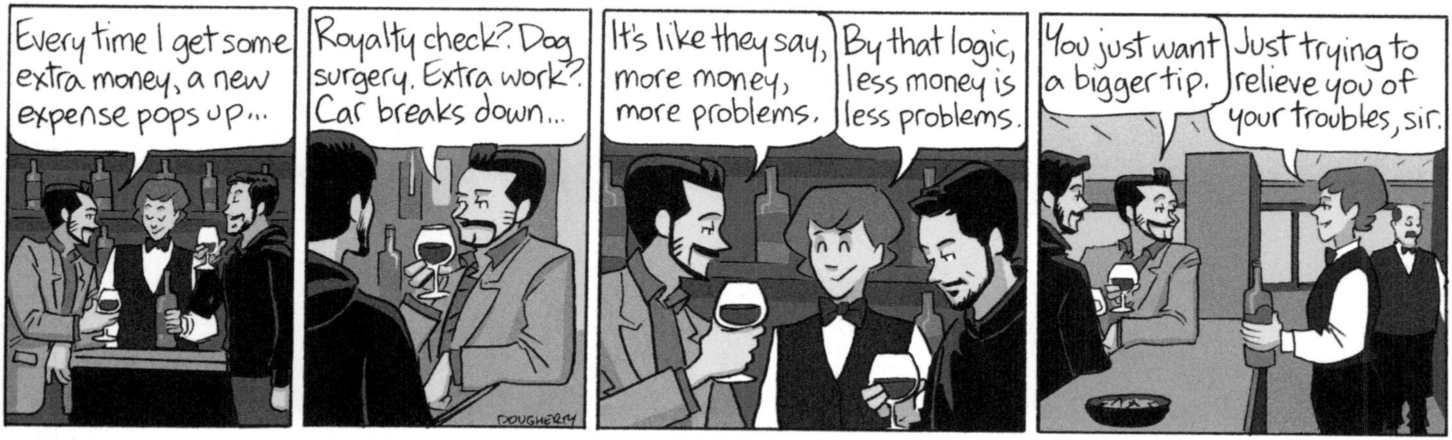
Every time I get some extra money, a new expense pops up...
Royalty check? Dog surgery. Extra work? Car breaks down...
DOUGHERTY
It's like they say, more money, more problems.
By that logic, less money is less problems.
You just want a bigger tip.
Just trying to relieve you of your troubles, sir.

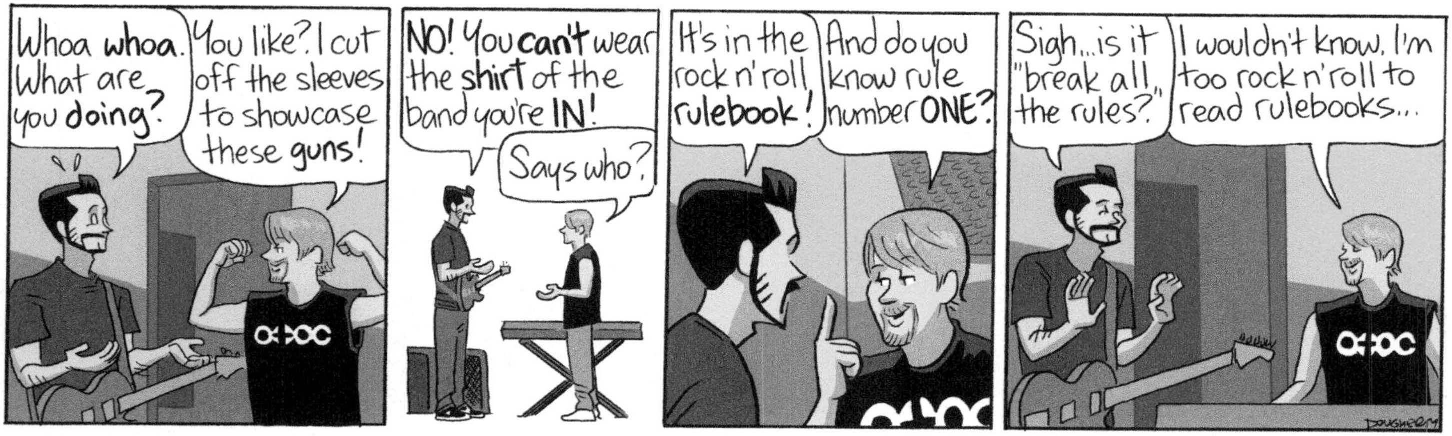
Whoa **whoa**. What are you **doing**?
You like? I cut off the sleeves to showcase these **guns**!
NO! You **can't** wear the **shirt** of the band you're **IN**!
Says who?
It's in the rock n' roll **rulebook**!
And do you know rule number **ONE**?
Sigh... is it "break all the rules?"
I wouldn't know. I'm too rock n' roll to read rulebooks...
DOUGHERTY

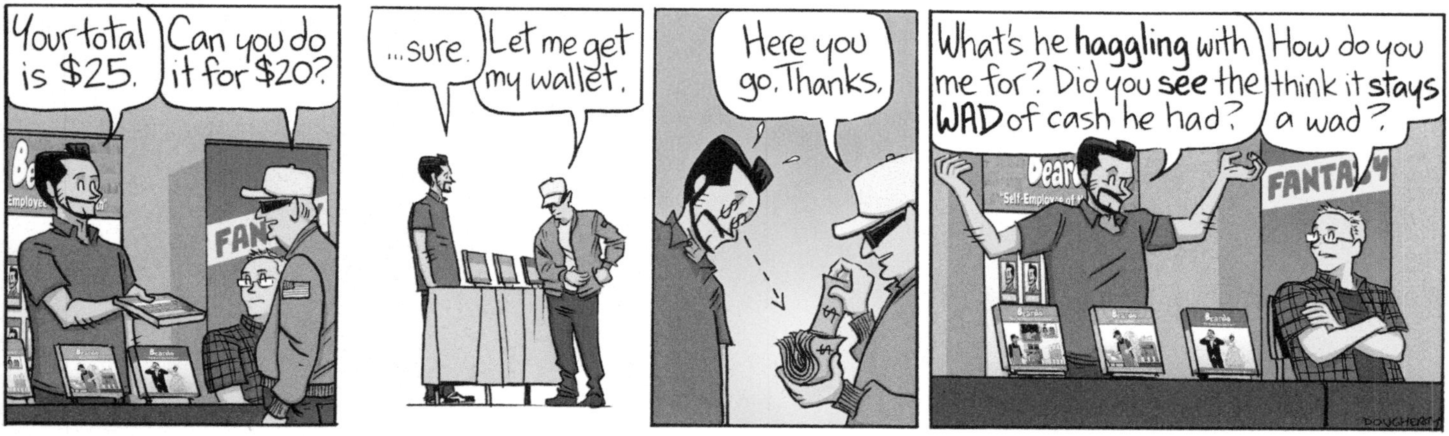
Your total is $25.
Can you do it for $20?
...sure.
Let me get my wallet.
Here you go. Thanks.
What's he **haggling** with me for? Did you **see** the **WAD** of cash he had?
How do you think it **stays** a wad?
DOUGHERTY

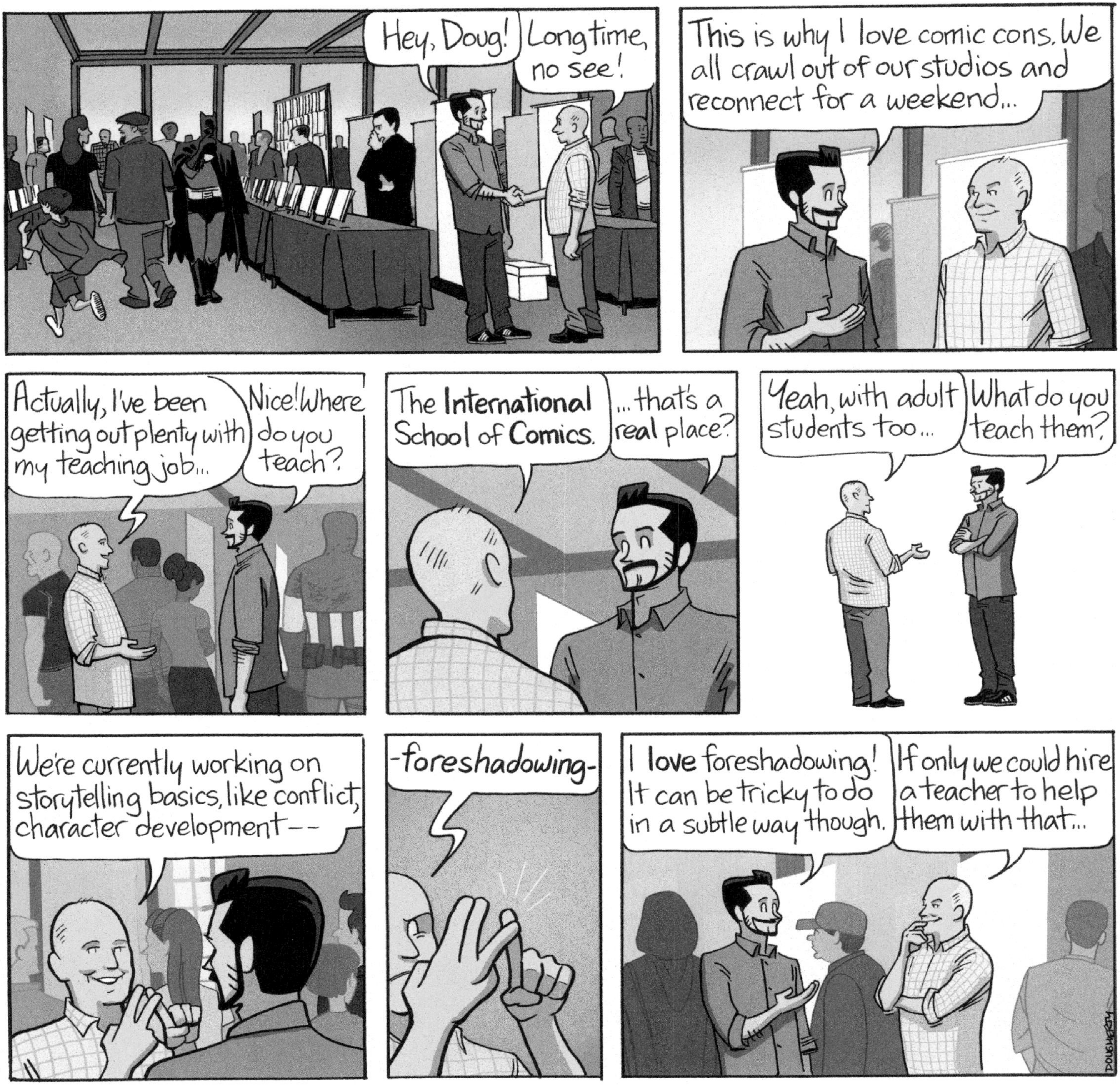
Hey, Doug!
Long time, no see!
This is why I love comic cons. We all crawl out of our studios and reconnect for a weekend...
Actually, I've been getting out plenty with my teaching job...
Nice! Where do you teach?
The **International** School of **Comics**.
...that's a **real** place?
Yeah, with adult students too...
What do you teach them?
We're currently working on storytelling basics, like conflict, character development--
-foreshadowing-
I **love** foreshadowing! It can be tricky to do in a subtle way though.
If only we could hire a teacher to help them with that...

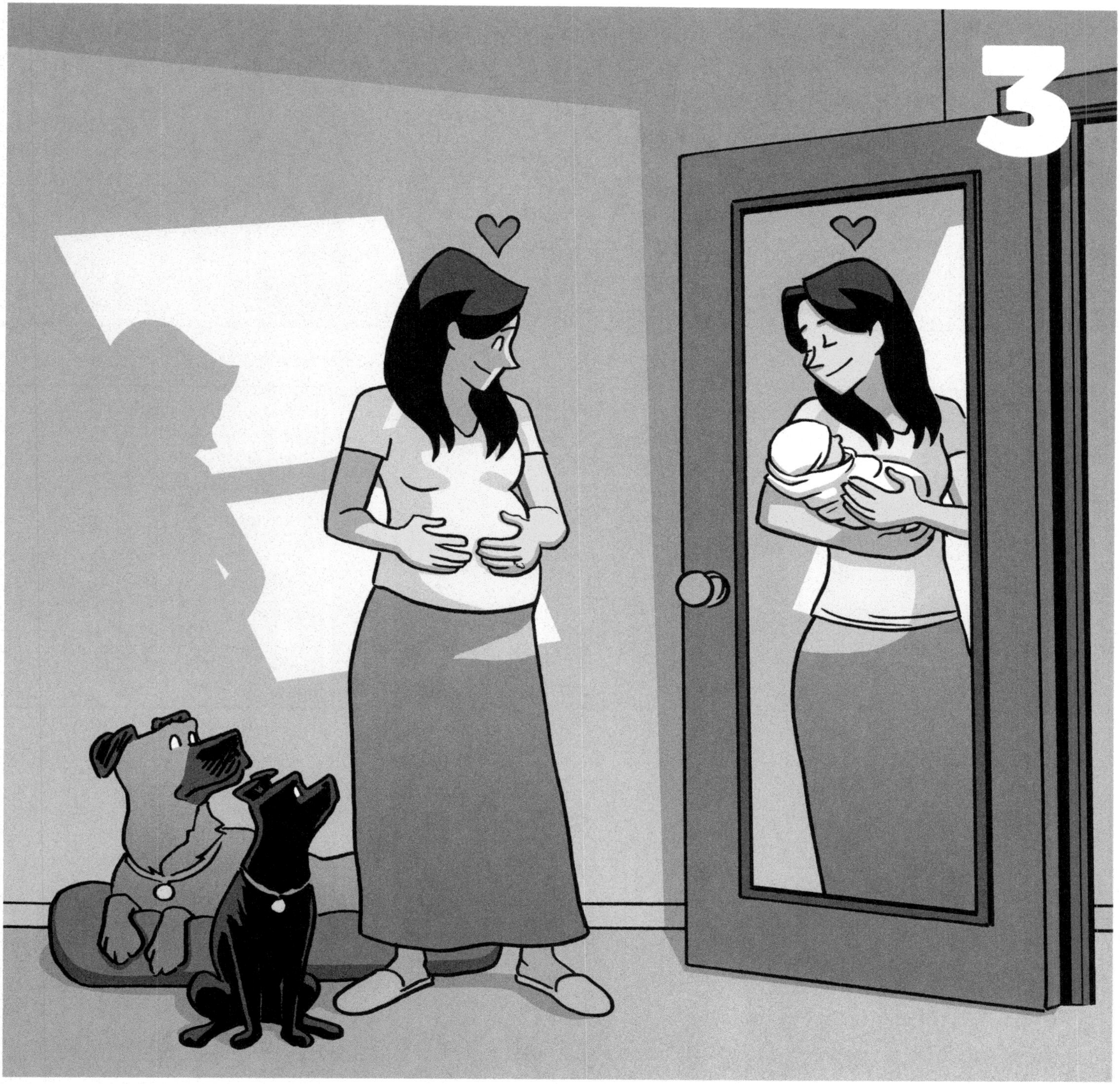
3

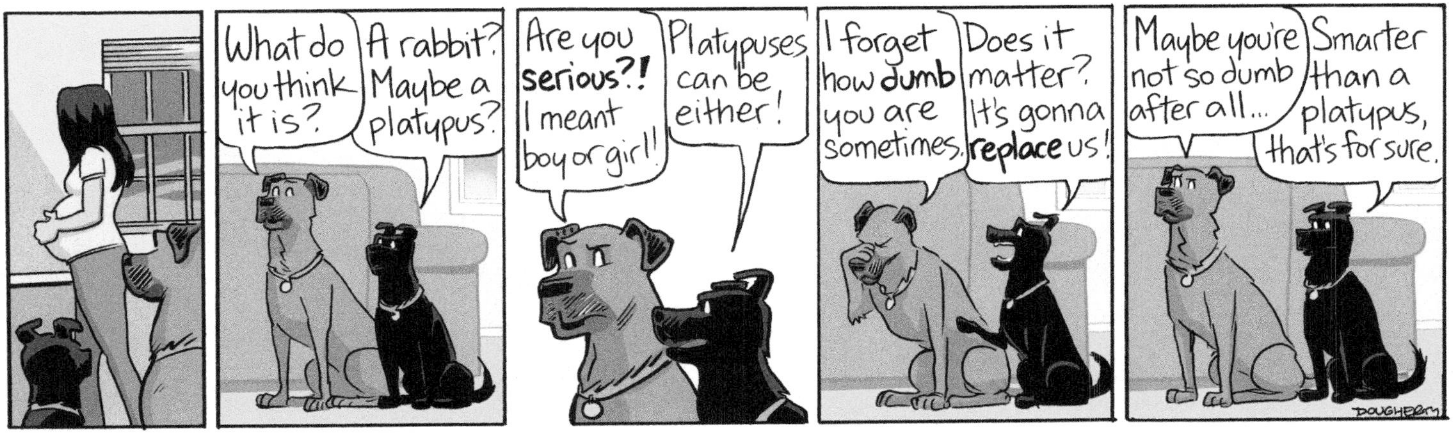
What do you think it is?
A rabbit? Maybe a platypus?
Are you **serious?!** I meant boy or girl!
Platypuses can be either!
I forget how **dumb** you are sometimes.
Does it matter? It's gonna **replace** us!
Maybe you're not so dumb after all...
Smarter than a platypus, that's for sure.
DOUGHERTY

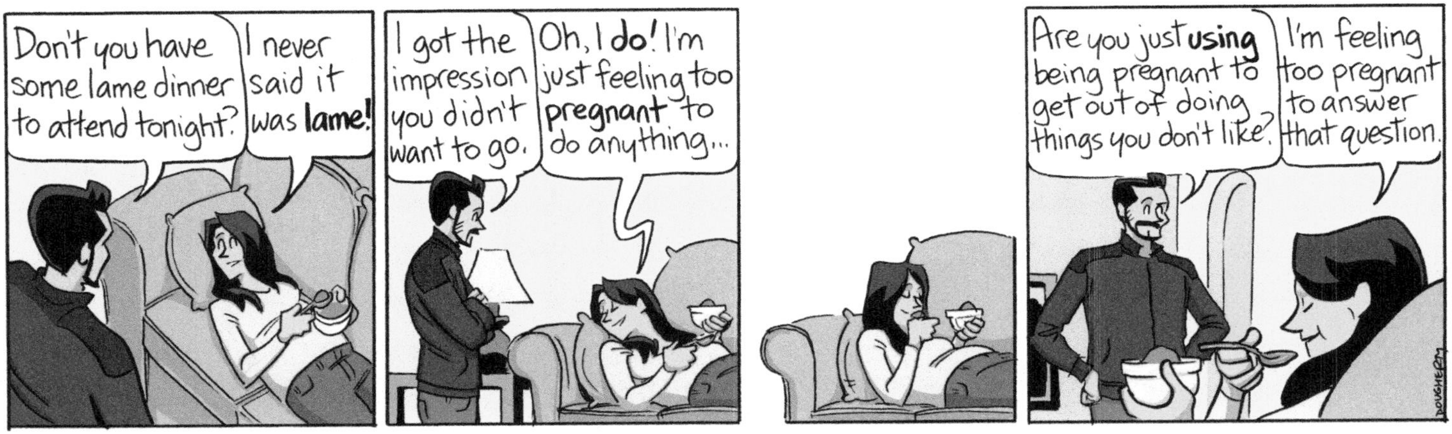
Don't you have some lame dinner to attend tonight?
I never said it was **lame!**
I got the impression you didn't want to go.
Oh, I **do!** I'm just feeling too **pregnant** to do anything...
Are you just **using** being pregnant to get out of doing things you don't like?
I'm feeling too pregnant to answer that question.
DOUGHERTY

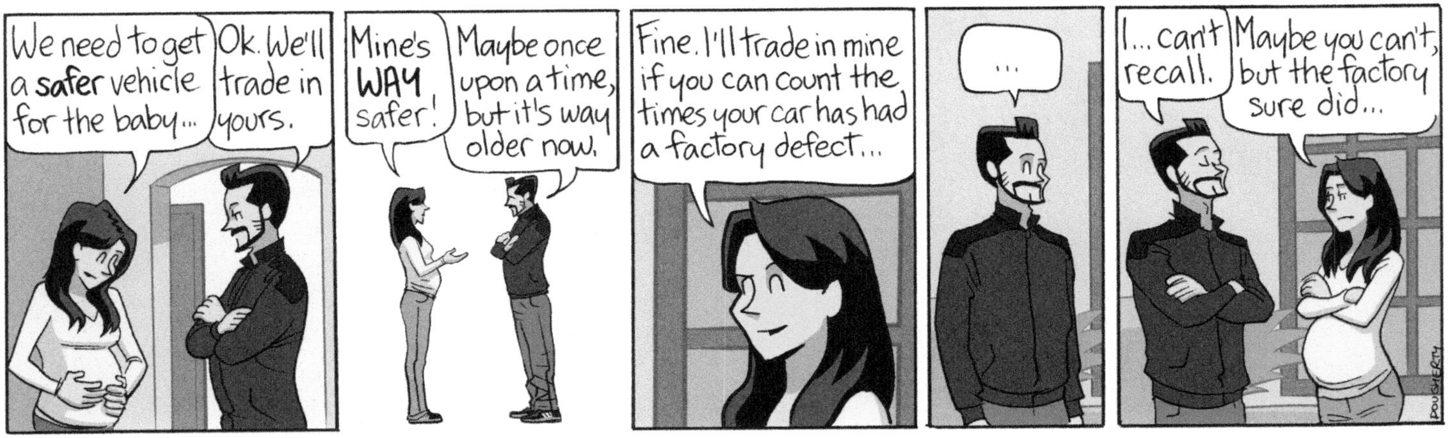
We need to get a **safer** vehicle for the baby...
Ok. We'll trade in yours.
Mine's **WAY** safer!
Maybe once upon a time, but it's way older now.
Fine. I'll trade in mine if you can count the times your car has had a factory defect...
...
I... can't recall.
Maybe you can't, but the factory sure did...
DOUGHERTY

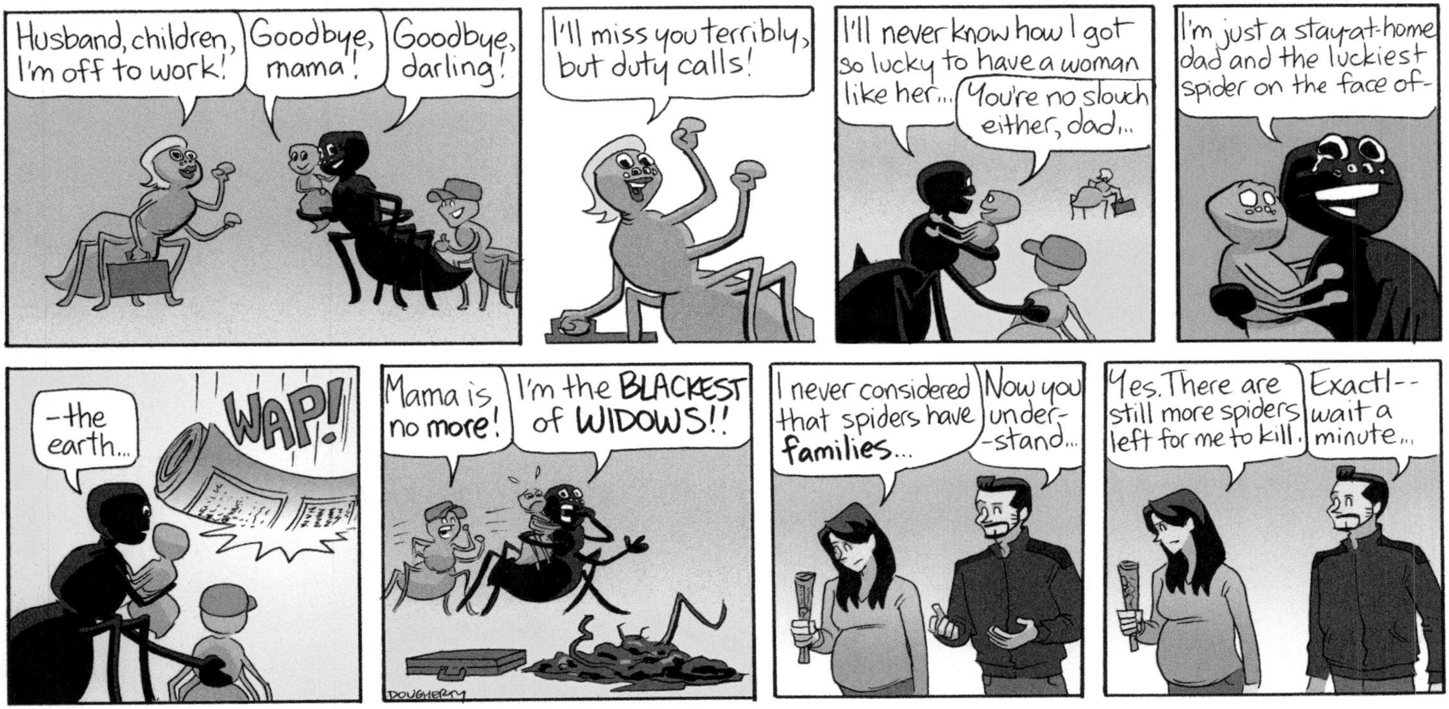
Husband, children, I'm off to work!
Goodbye, mama!
Goodbye, darling!
I'll miss you terribly, but duty calls!
I'll never know how I got so lucky to have a woman like her...
You're no slouch either, dad...
I'm just a stay-at-home dad and the luckiest spider on the face of-
-the earth...
WAP!
Mama is no more!
I'm the BLACKEST of WIDOWS!!
DOUGHERTY
I never considered that spiders have families...
Now you under- -stand...
Yes. There are still more spiders left for me to kill.
Exactl-- wait a minute...

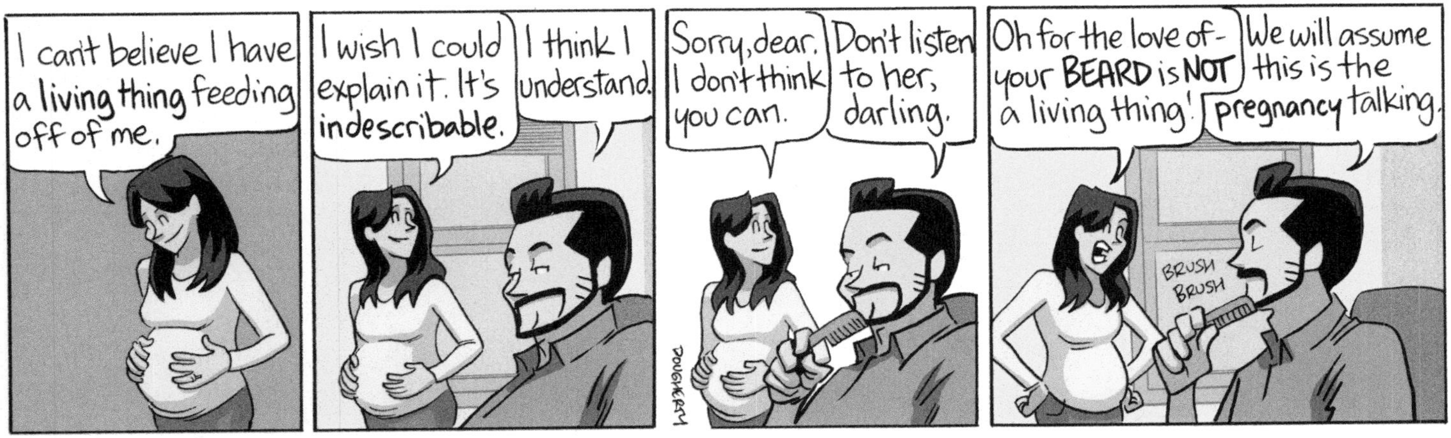
I can't believe I have a living thing feeding off of me.
I wish I could explain it. It's indescribable.
I think I understand.
Sorry, dear. I don't think you can.
Don't listen to her, darling.
DOUGHERTY
Oh for the love of- your BEARD is NOT a living thing!
We will assume this is the pregnancy talking.
BRUSH BRUSH

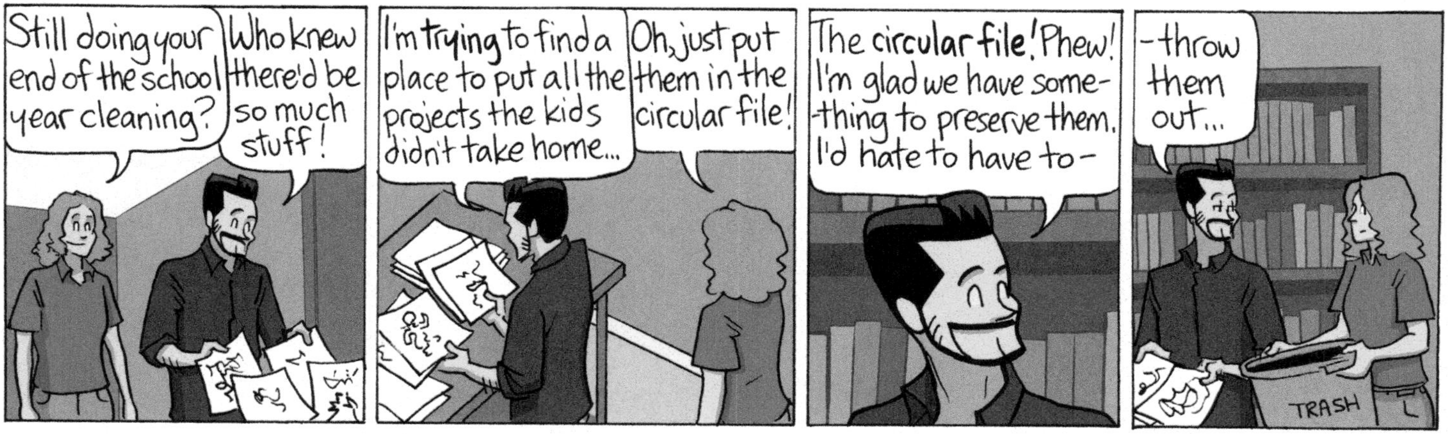
Still doing your end of the school year cleaning?
Who knew there'd be so much stuff!
I'm trying to find a place to put all the projects the kids didn't take home...
Oh, just put them in the circular file!
The circular file! Phew! I'm glad we have some-thing to preserve them. I'd hate to have to-
-throw them out...
TRASH

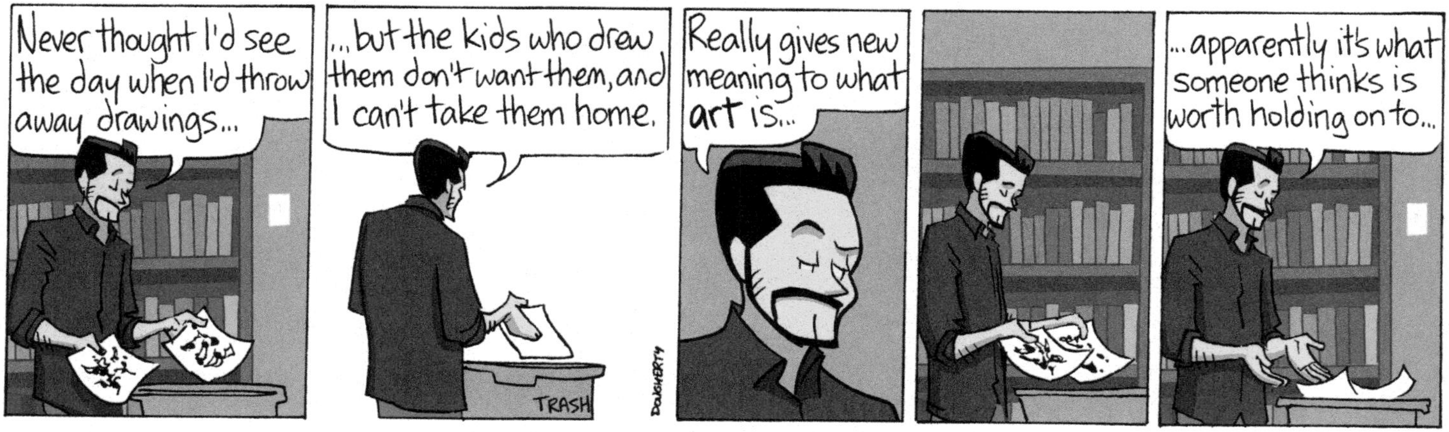
Never thought I'd see the day when I'd throw away drawings...
...but the kids who drew them don't want them, and I can't take them home.
TRASH
Really gives new meaning to what art is...
...apparently it's what someone thinks is worth holding on to...

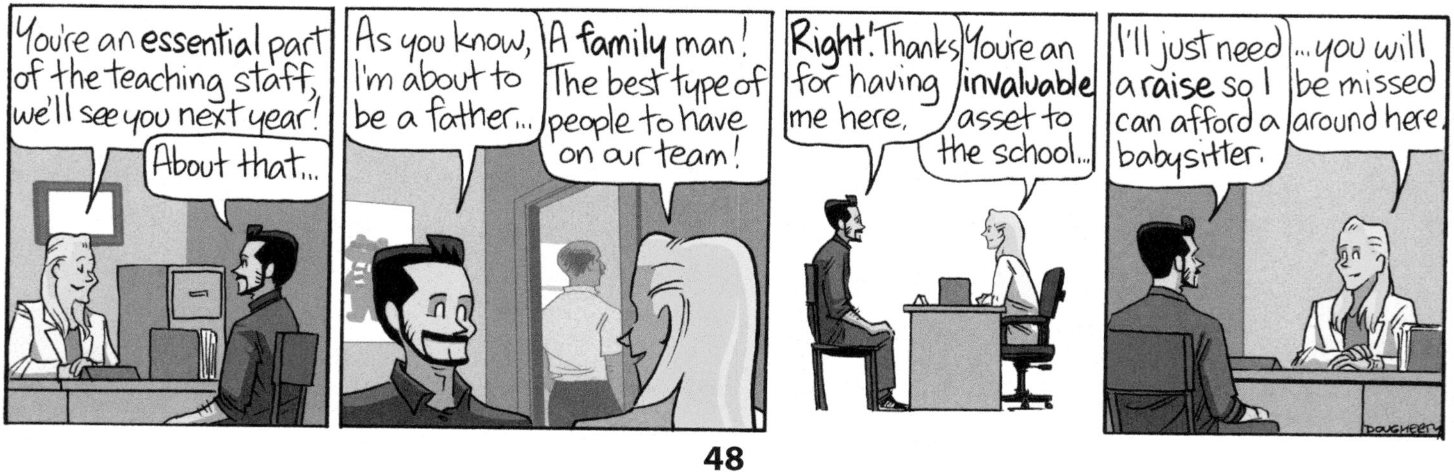
You're an essential part of the teaching staff, we'll see you next year!
About that...
As you know, I'm about to be a father...
A family man! The best type of people to have on our team!
Right! Thanks for having me here.
You're an invaluable asset to the school...
I'll just need a raise so I can afford a babysitter.
...you will be missed around here.

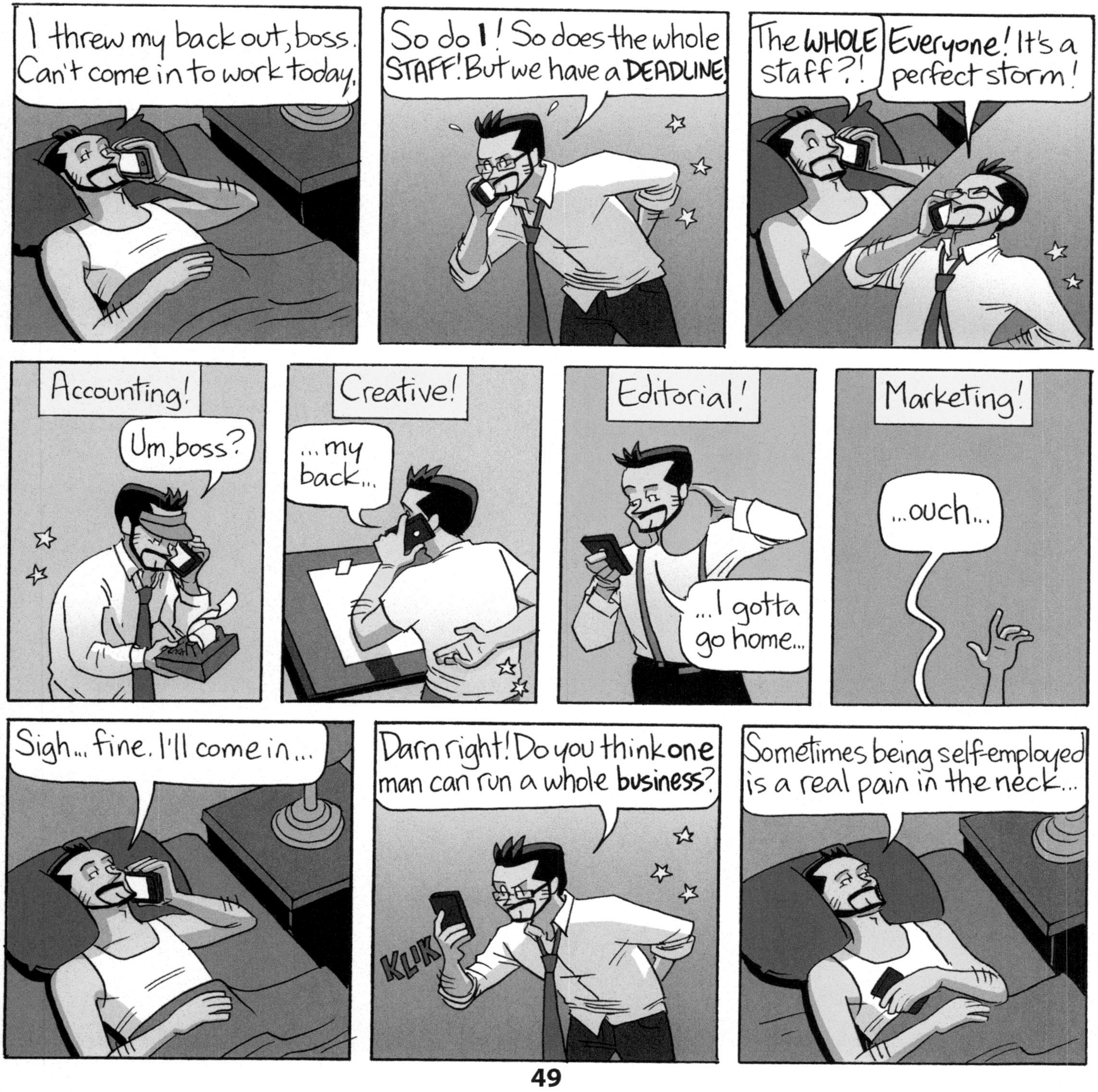
I threw my back out, boss. Can't come in to work today.
So do I! So does the whole STAFF! But we have a DEADLINE!
The WHOLE staff?!
Everyone! It's a perfect storm!
Accounting!
Um, boss?
Creative!
...my back...
Editorial!
...I gotta go home...
Marketing!
...ouch...
Sigh... fine. I'll come in...
Darn right! Do you think one man can run a whole business?
KLIK
Sometimes being self-employed is a real pain in the neck...

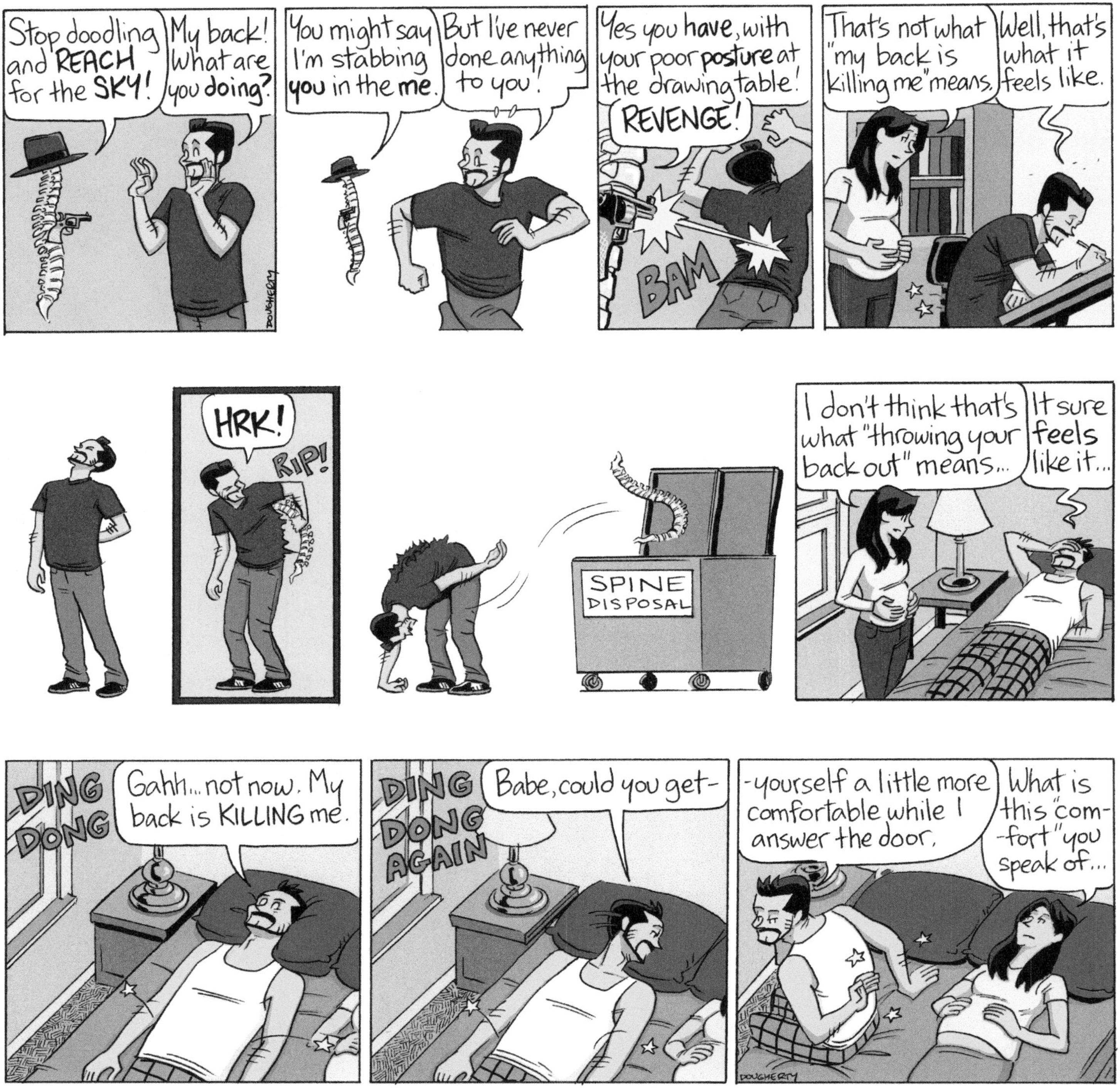
Stop doodling and REACH for the SKY!
My back! What are you doing?
DOUGHERTY
You might say I'm stabbing you in the me.
But I've never done anything to you!
Yes you have, with your poor posture at the drawing table!
REVENGE!
BAM
That's not what "my back is killing me" means.
Well, that's what it feels like.
HRK!
RIP!
SPINE DISPOSAL
I don't think that's what "throwing your back out" means...
It sure feels like it...
DING DONG
Gahh... not now. My back is KILLING me.
DING DONG AGAIN
Babe, could you get-
-yourself a little more comfortable while I answer the door.
What is this "com- -fort" you speak of...
DOUGHERTY

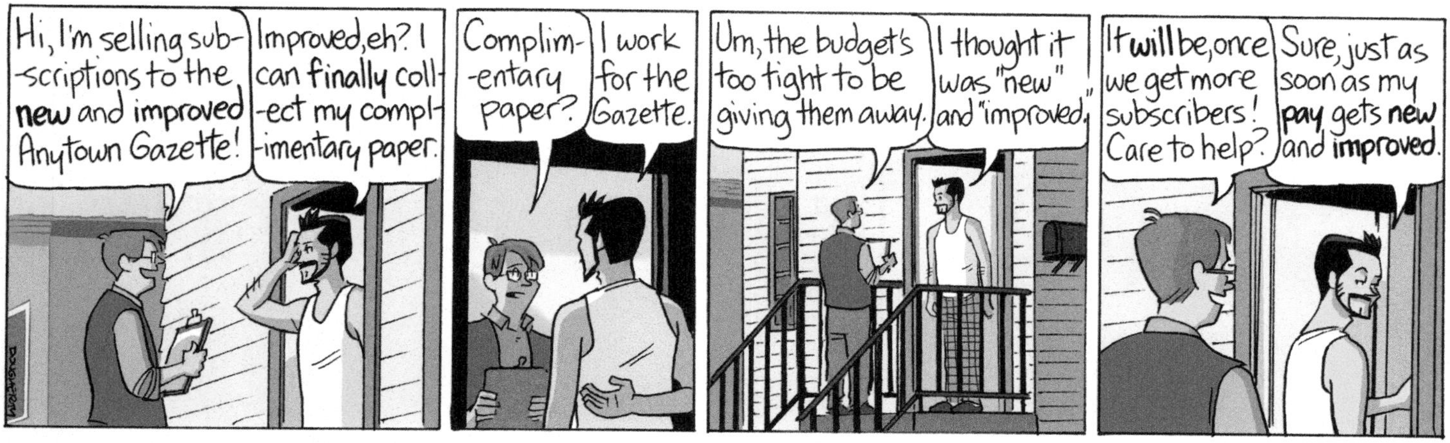
Hi, I'm selling sub-scriptions to the **new** and **improved** Anytown Gazette!
Improved, eh? I can **finally** coll-ect my compl-imentary paper.
Complim-entary paper?
I work for the Gazette.
Um, the budget's too tight to be giving them away.
I thought it was "new" and "improved."
It **will** be, once we get more subscribers! Care to help?
Sure, just as soon as my **pay** gets **new** and **improved**.

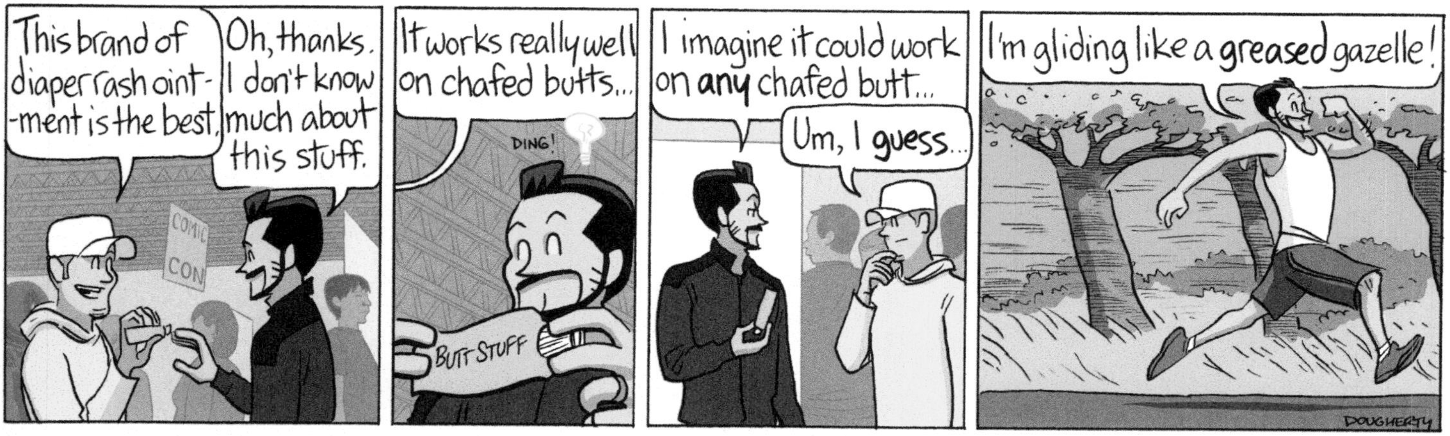
This brand of diaper rash oint-ment is the best,
Oh, thanks. I don't know much about this stuff.
COMIC CON
It works really well on chafed butts...
DING!
BUTT STUFF
I imagine it could work on **any** chafed butt...
Um, I **guess**...
I'm gliding like a **greased** gazelle!
DOUGHERTY

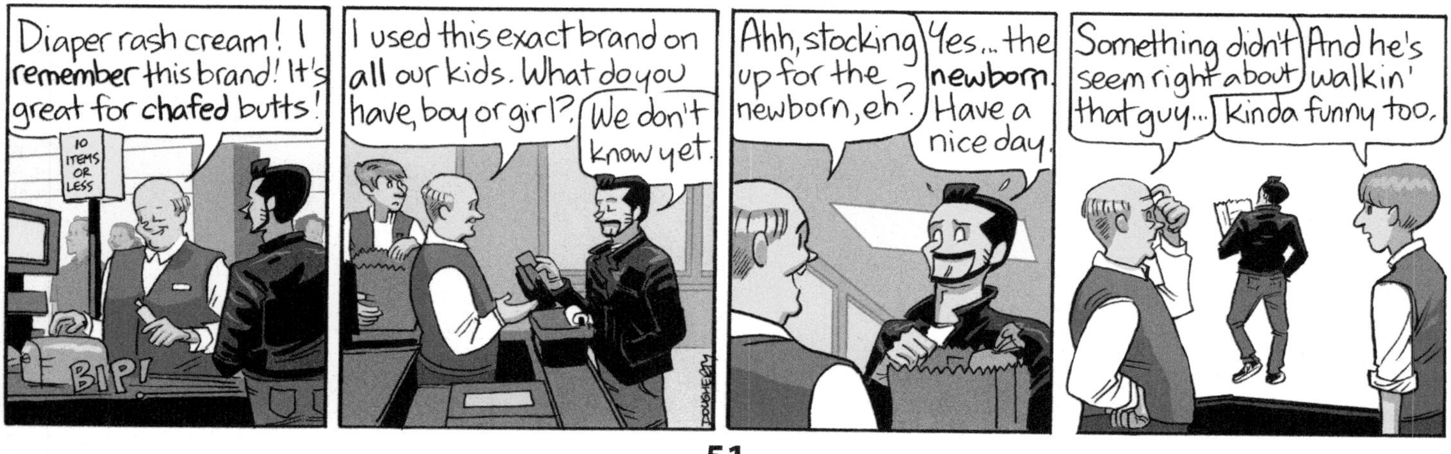
Diaper rash cream! I **remember** this brand! It's great for **chafed** butts!
10 ITEMS OR LESS
BIP!
I used this exact brand on **all** our kids. What do you have, boy or girl?
We don't know yet.
Ahh, stocking up for the newborn, eh?
Yes... the **newborn**. Have a nice day.
Something didn't seem right about that guy...
And he's walkin' kinda funny too.

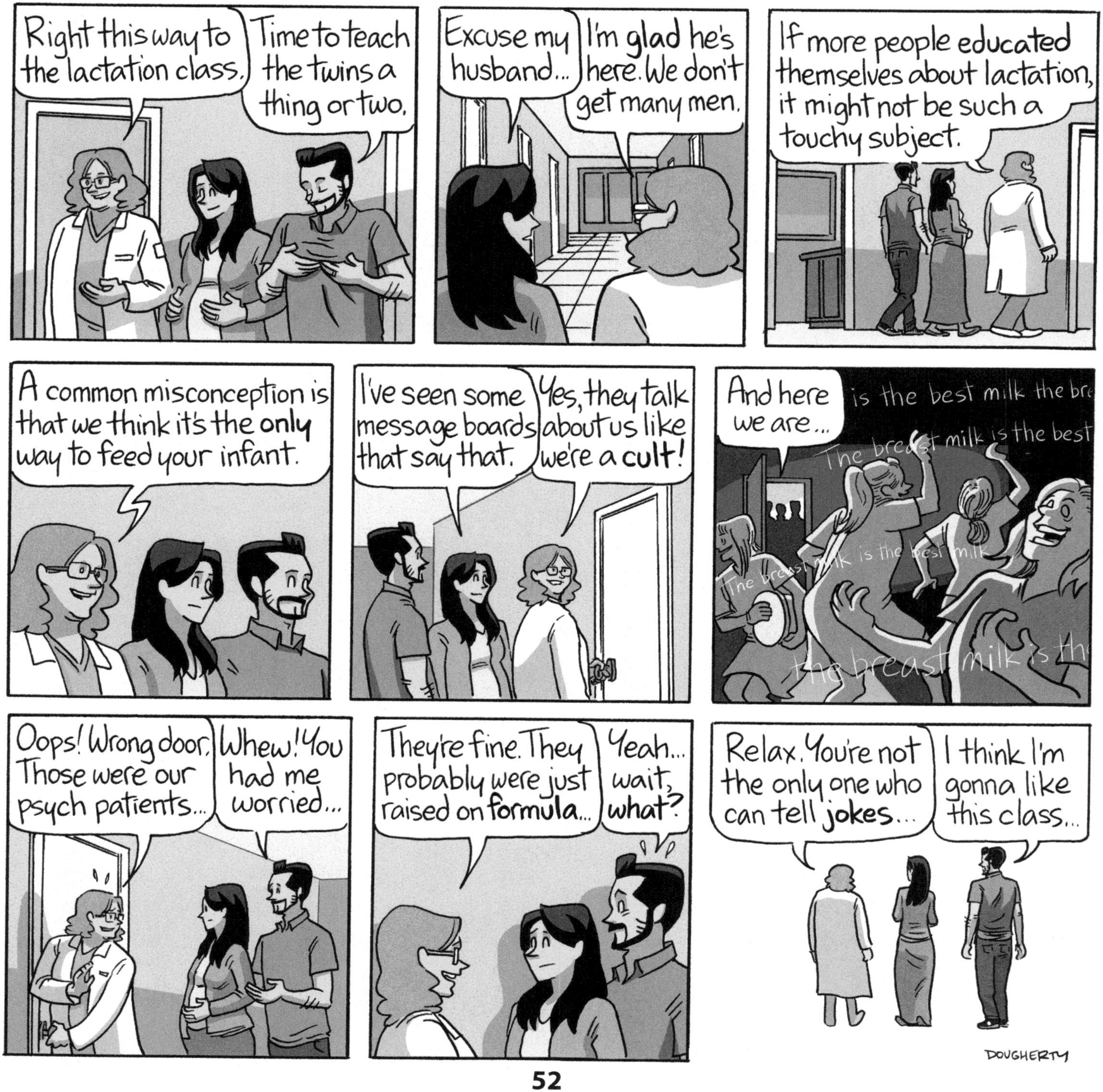
Right this way to the lactation class.
Time to teach the twins a thing or two.
Excuse my husband...
I'm glad he's here. We don't get many men.
If more people educated themselves about lactation, it might not be such a touchy subject.
A common misconception is that we think it's the **only** way to feed your infant.
I've seen some message boards that say that.
Yes, they talk about us like we're a **cult**!
And here we are...
The breast milk is the best milk
Oops! Wrong door. Those were our psych patients...
Whew! You had me worried...
They're fine. They probably were just raised on **formula**...
Yeah... wait, **what**?
Relax. You're not the only one who can tell **jokes**...
I think I'm gonna like this class...
DOUGHERTY

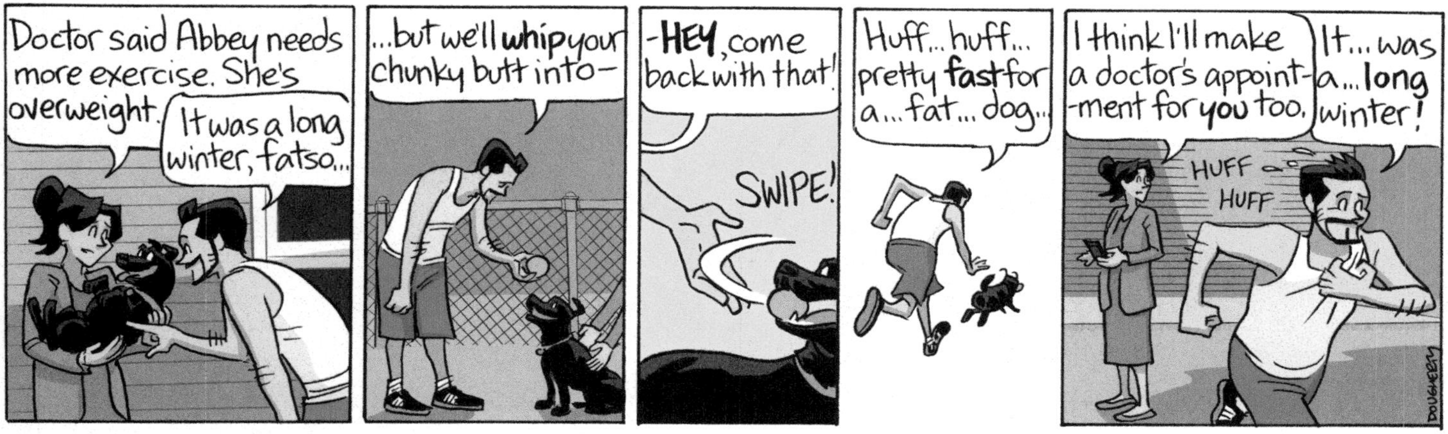
Doctor said Abbey needs more exercise. She's **overweight**.
It was a long winter, fatso...
...but we'll **whip** your chunky butt into–
–**HEY**, come back with that!
SWIPE!
Huff... huff... pretty **fast** for a... fat... dog...
I think I'll make a doctor's appoint- -ment for **you** too.
HUFF HUFF
It... was a... **long** winter!
DOUGHERTY

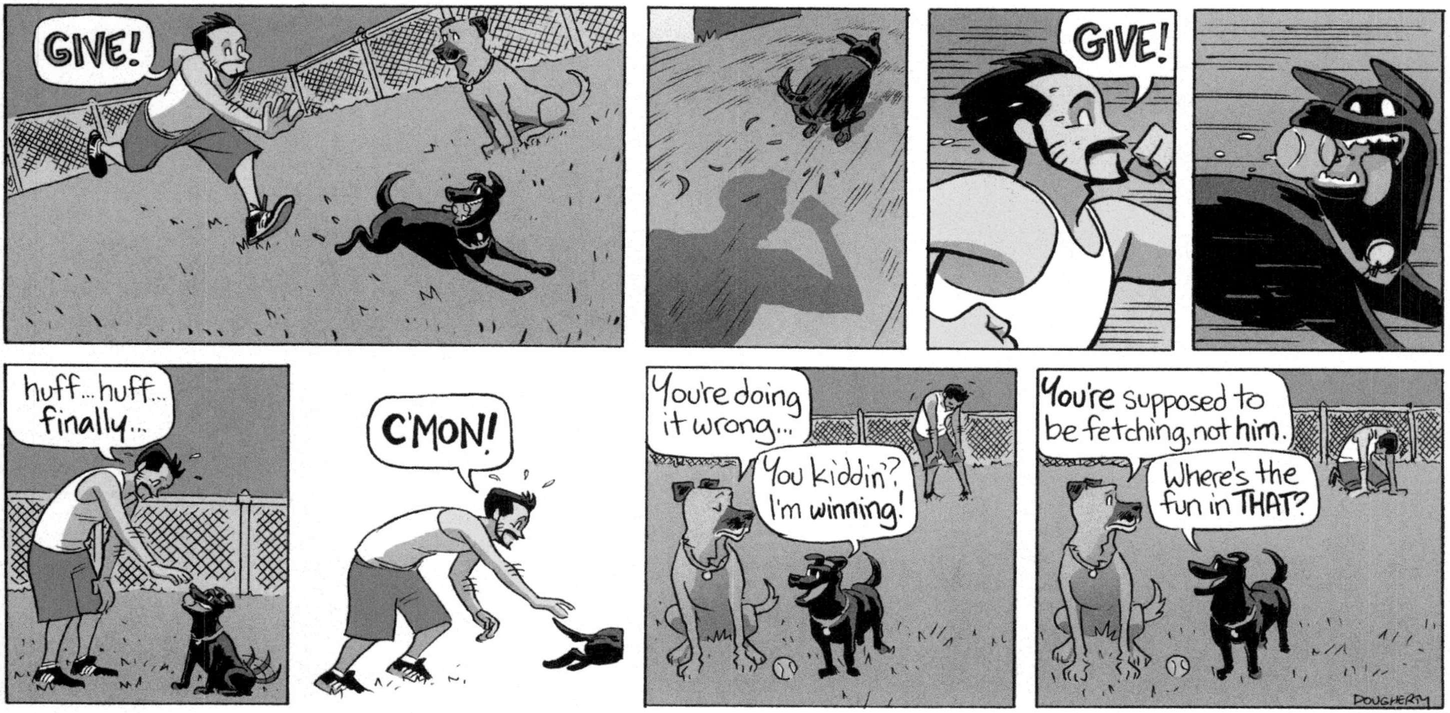
GIVE!
GIVE!
huff... huff... **finally**...
C'MON!
You're doing it wrong...
You kiddin'? I'm **winning**!
You're supposed to be fetching, not **him**.
Where's the fun in **THAT**?
DOUGHERTY

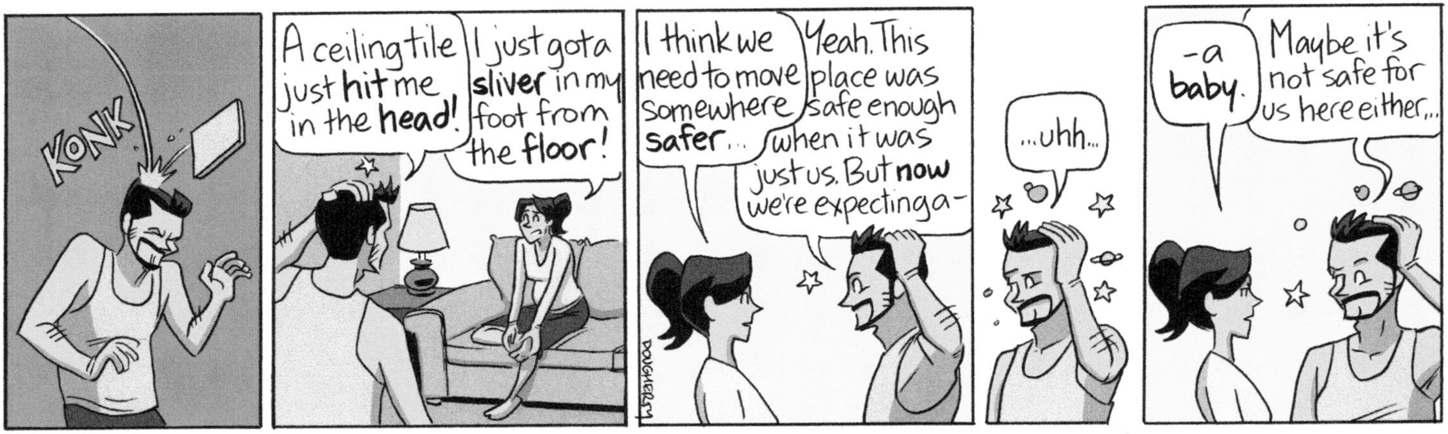
KONK
A ceiling tile just hit me in the head!
I just got a sliver in my foot from the floor!
I think we need to move somewhere safer...
Yeah. This place was safe enough when it was just us. But now we're expecting a-
...uhh...
-a baby.
Maybe it's not safe for us here either...

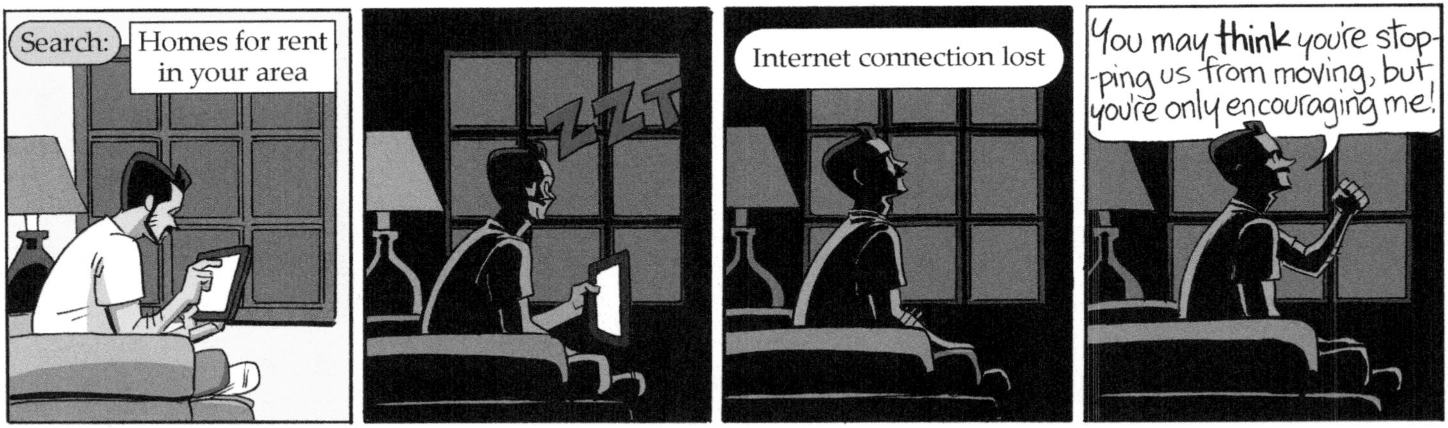
Search:
Homes for rent in your area
ZZZT
Internet connection lost
You may think you're stop-ping us from moving, but you're only encouraging me!

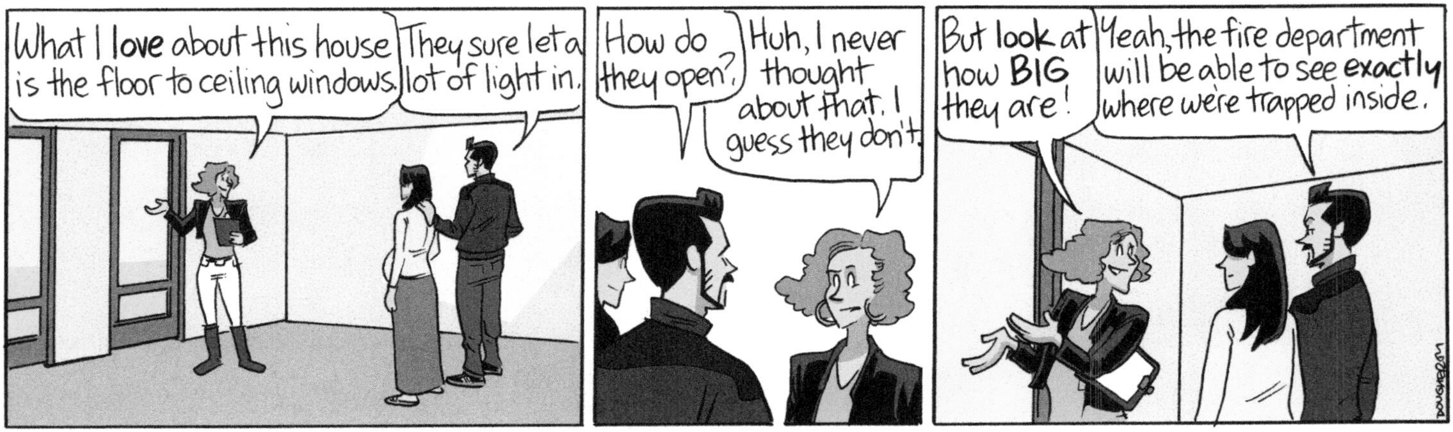
What I love about this house is the floor to ceiling windows.
They sure let a lot of light in.
How do they open?
Huh, I never thought about that. I guess they don't.
But look at how BIG they are!
Yeah, the fire department will be able to see exactly where we're trapped inside.

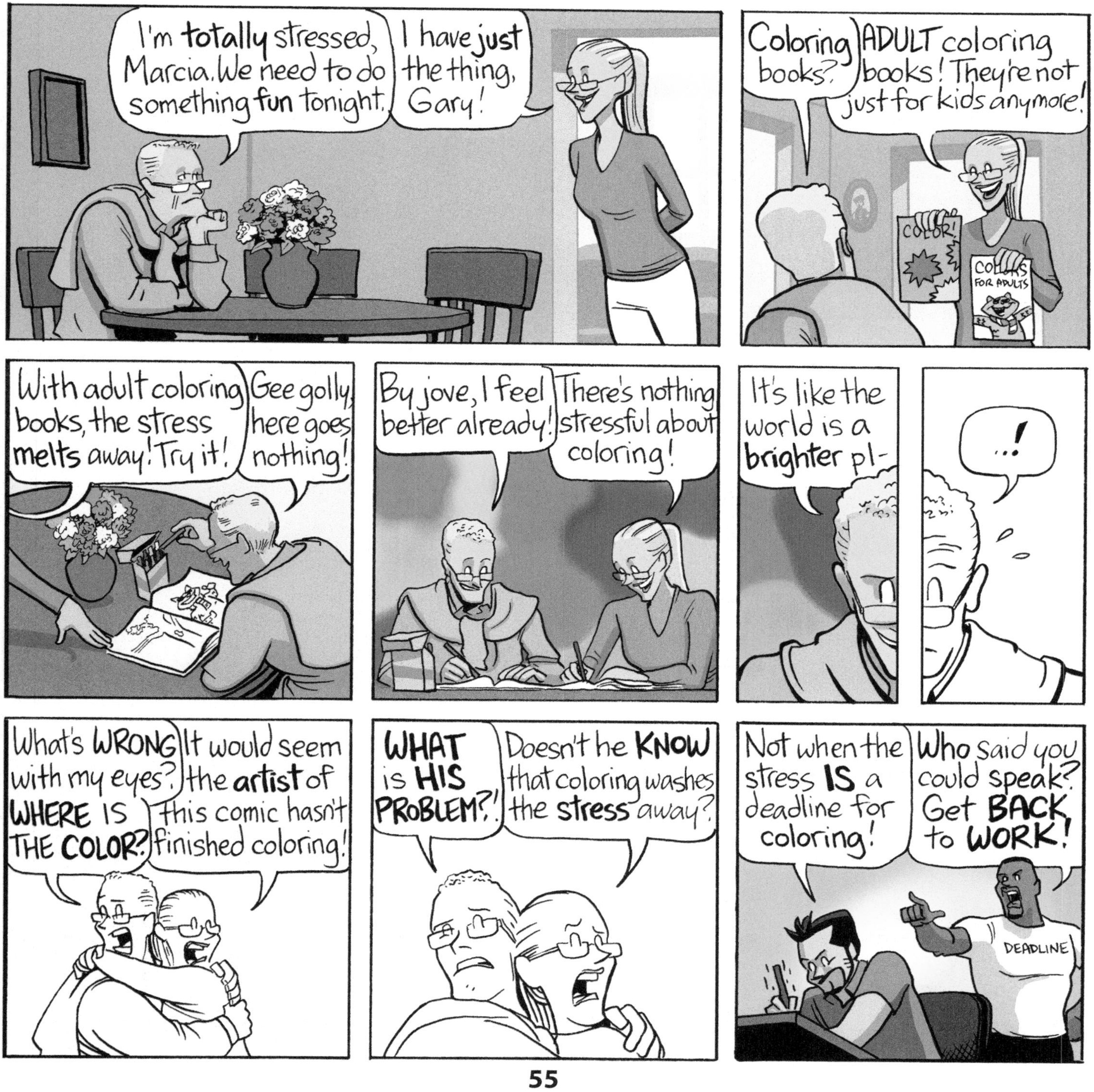
I'm **totally** stressed, Marcia. We need to do something **fun** tonight.
I have **just** the thing, Gary!
Coloring books?
ADULT coloring books! They're not just for kids anymore!
COLOR!
COLORS FOR ADULTS
With adult coloring books, the stress **melts** away! Try it!
Gee golly, here goes nothing!
By jove, I feel better already!
There's nothing stressful about coloring!
It's like the world is a **brighter** pl-
..!
What's **WRONG** with my eyes? **WHERE IS THE COLOR?**
It would seem the **artist** of this comic hasn't finished coloring!
WHAT is **HIS PROBLEM?!**
Doesn't he **KNOW** that coloring washes the **stress** away?
Not when the stress **IS** a deadline for coloring!
Who said you could speak? Get **BACK** to **WORK**!
DEADLINE

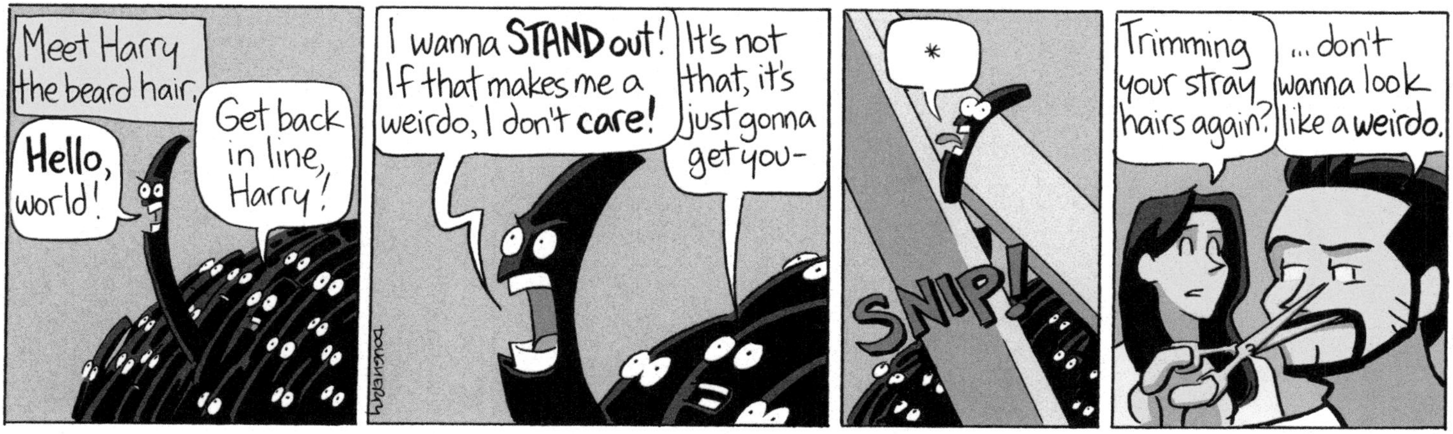
Meet Harry the beard hair.
Hello, world!
Get back in line, Harry!
I wanna STAND out! If that makes me a weirdo, I don't care!
It's not that, it's just gonna get you-
*
SNIP!
Trimming your stray hairs again?
...don't wanna look like a weirdo.

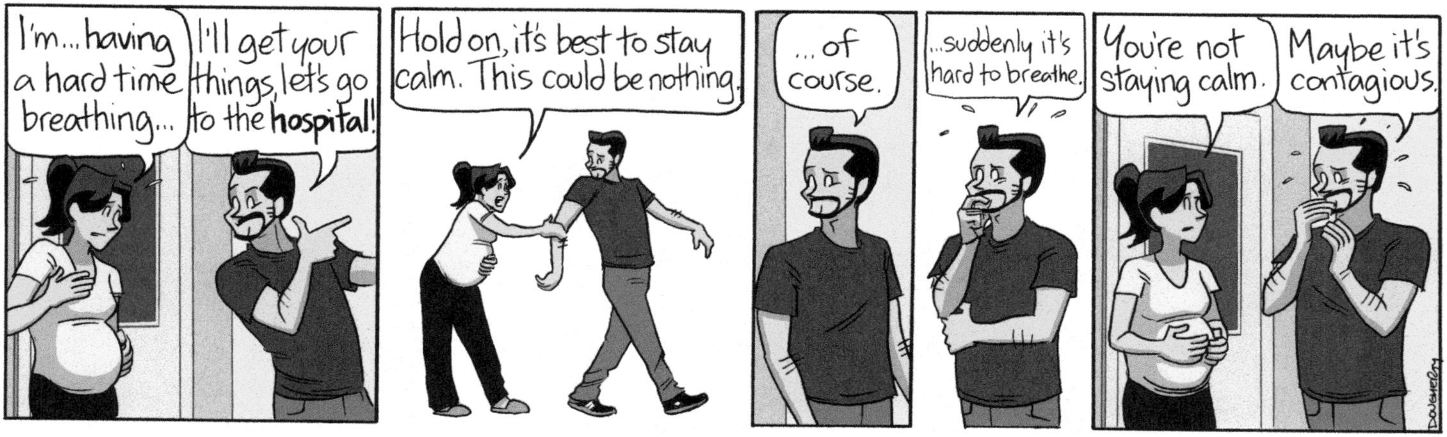
I'm... having a hard time breathing...
I'll get your things, let's go to the hospital!
Hold on, it's best to stay calm. This could be nothing.
...of course.
...suddenly it's hard to breathe.
You're not staying calm.
Maybe it's contagious.

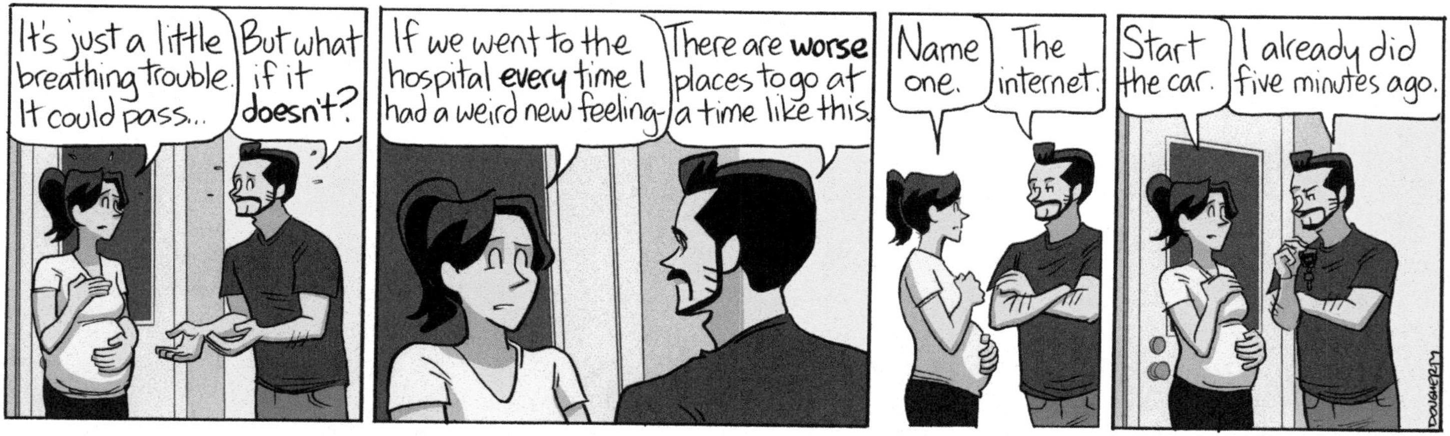
It's just a little breathing trouble. It could pass...
But what if it doesn't?
If we went to the hospital every time I had a weird new feeling-
There are worse places to go at a time like this.
Name one.
The internet.
Start the car.
I already did five minutes ago.

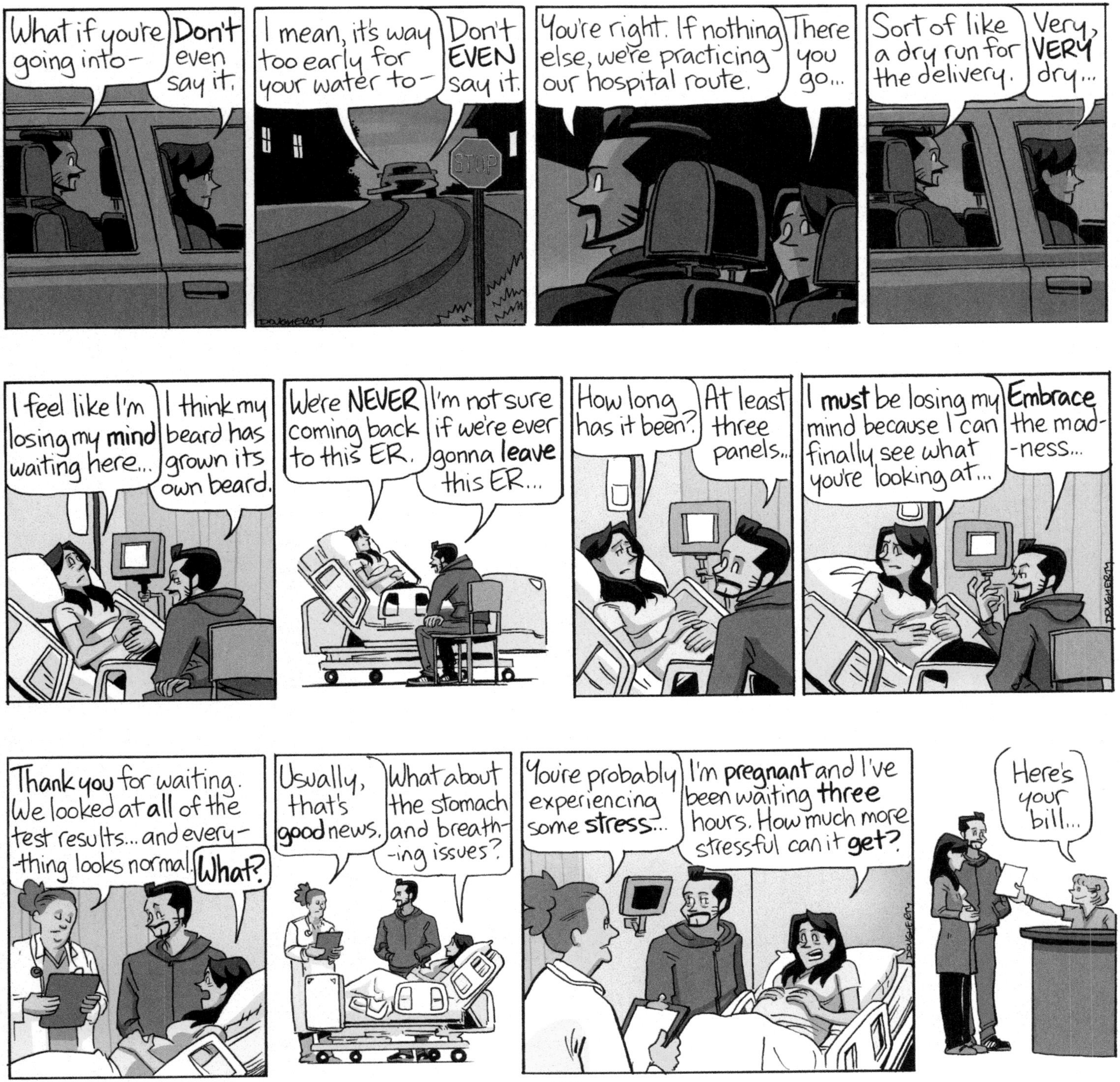
What if you're going into-
Don't even say it.
I mean, it's way too early for your water to-
Don't EVEN say it.
You're right. If nothing else, we're practicing our hospital route.
There you go...
Sort of like a dry run for the delivery.
Very, VERY dry...
I feel like I'm losing my mind waiting here...
I think my beard has grown its own beard.
We're NEVER coming back to this ER.
I'm not sure if we're ever gonna leave this ER...
How long has it been?
At least three panels...
I must be losing my mind because I can finally see what you're looking at...
Embrace the mad-ness...
Thank you for waiting. We looked at all of the test results... and every-thing looks normal!
What?
Usually, that's good news.
What about the stomach and breath-ing issues?
You're probably experiencing some stress...
I'm pregnant and I've been waiting three hours. How much more stressful can it get?
Here's your bill...

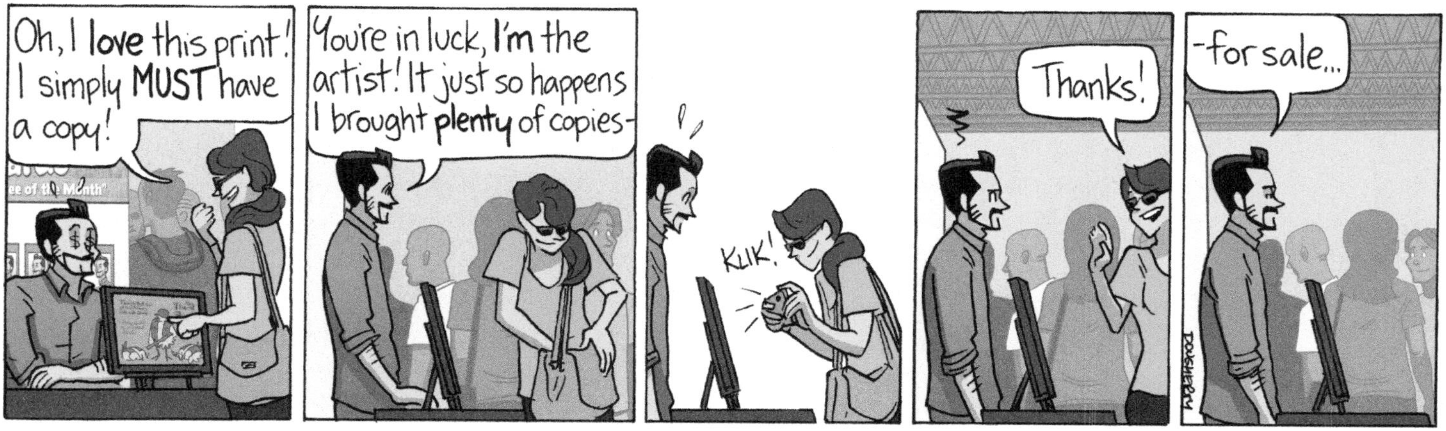
Oh, I **love** this print! I simply **MUST** have a copy!
You're in luck, **I'm** the artist! It just so happens I brought **plenty** of copies-
KLIK!
Thanks!
-for sale...

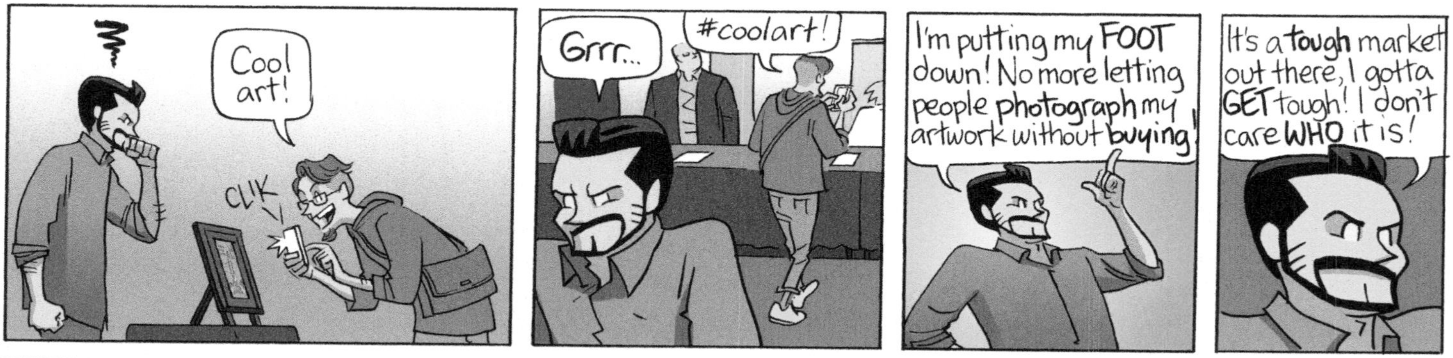
Cool art!
CLIK
Grrr...
#coolart!
I'm putting my **FOOT** down! No more letting people **photograph** my artwork without **buying**!
It's a **tough** market out there, I gotta **GET** tough! I don't care **WHO** it is!

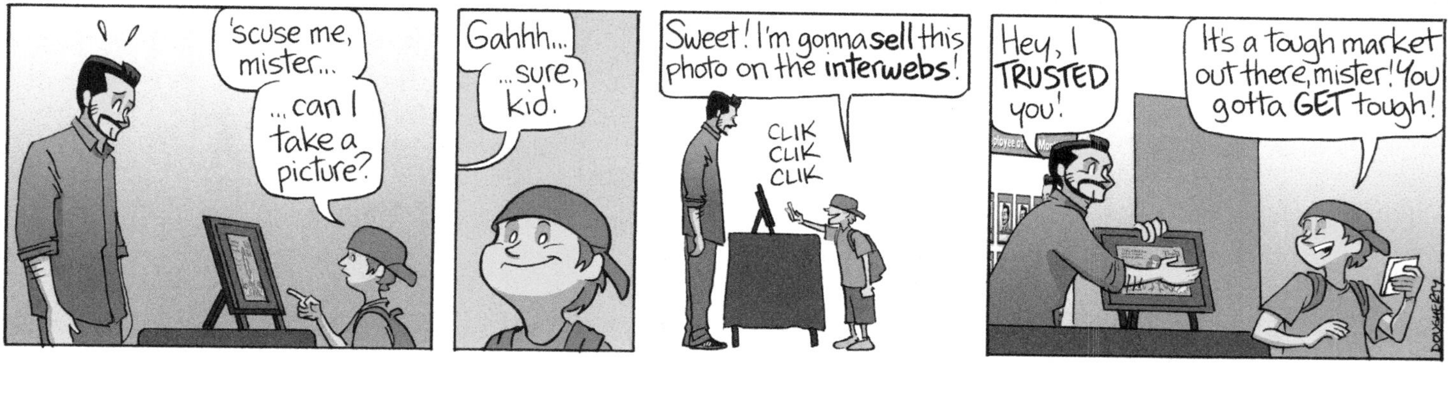
'scuse me, mister...
...can I take a picture?
Gahhh...
...sure, kid.
Sweet! I'm gonna **sell** this photo on the **interwebs**!
CLIK
CLIK
CLIK
Hey, I **TRUSTED** you!
It's a tough market out there, mister! You gotta **GET** tough!

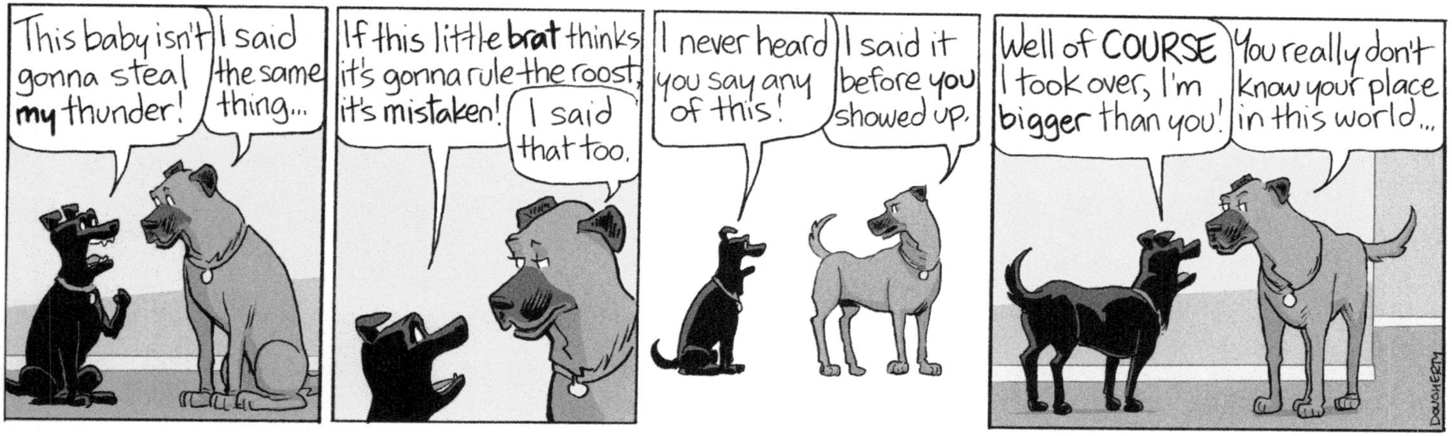
This baby isn't gonna steal **my** thunder!
I said the same thing...
If this little **brat** thinks it's gonna rule the roost, it's **mistaken**!
I said that too.
I never heard you say any of this!
I said it before **you** showed up.
Well of **COURSE** I took over, I'm **bigger** than you!
You really don't know your place in this world...
DOUGHERTY

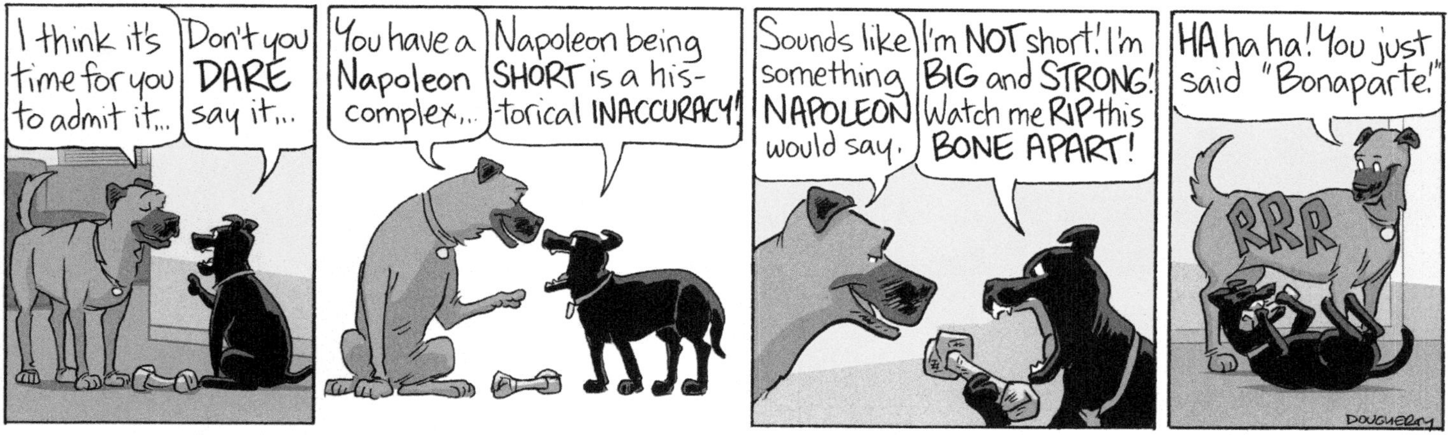
I think it's time for you to admit it...
Don't you **DARE** say it...
You have a **Napoleon** complex...
Napoleon being **SHORT** is a his-torical **INACCURACY**!
Sounds like something **NAPOLEON** would say.
I'm **NOT** short! I'm **BIG** and **STRONG**! Watch me **RIP** this **BONE APART**!
HA ha ha! You just said "Bonaparte."
RRR
DOUGHERTY

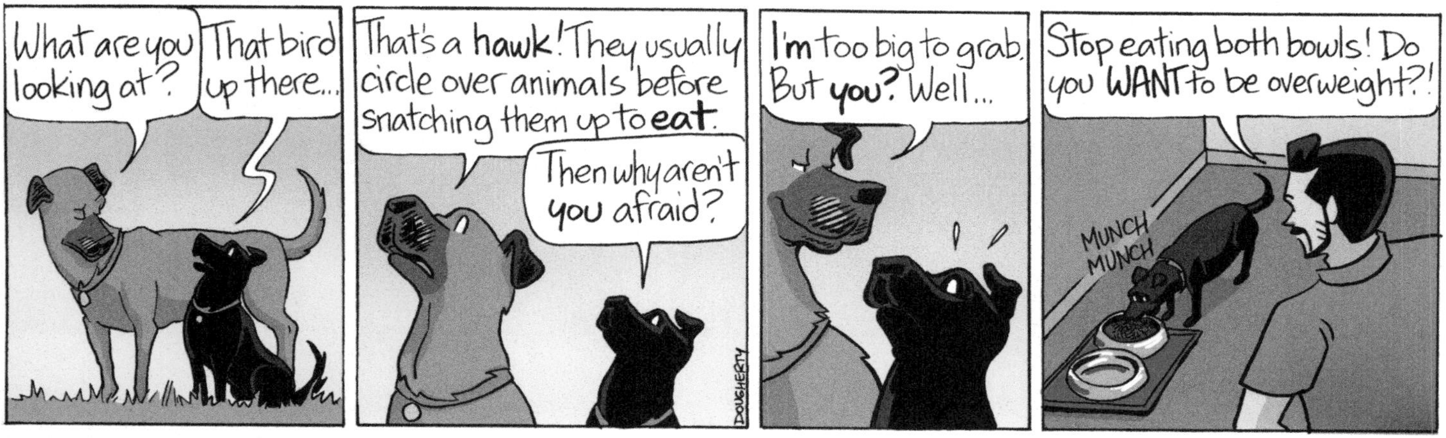
What are you looking at?
That bird up there...
That's a **hawk**! They usually circle over animals before snatching them up to **eat**.
Then why aren't **you** afraid?
DOUGHERTY
I'm too big to grab. But **you**? Well...
Stop eating both bowls! Do you **WANT** to be overweight?!
MUNCH MUNCH

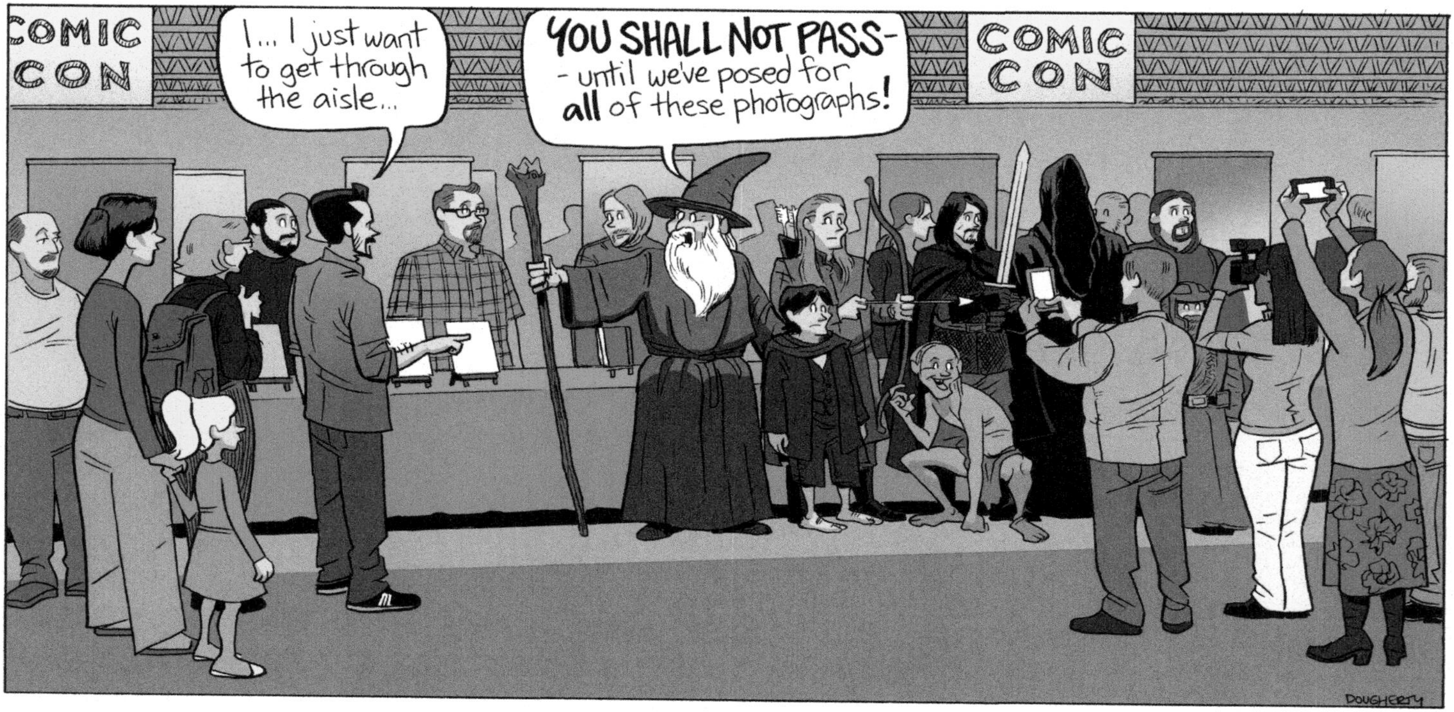
COMIC CON
I... I just want to get through the aisle...
YOU SHALL NOT PASS- - until we've posed for **all** of these photographs!
COMIC CON
DOUGHERTY

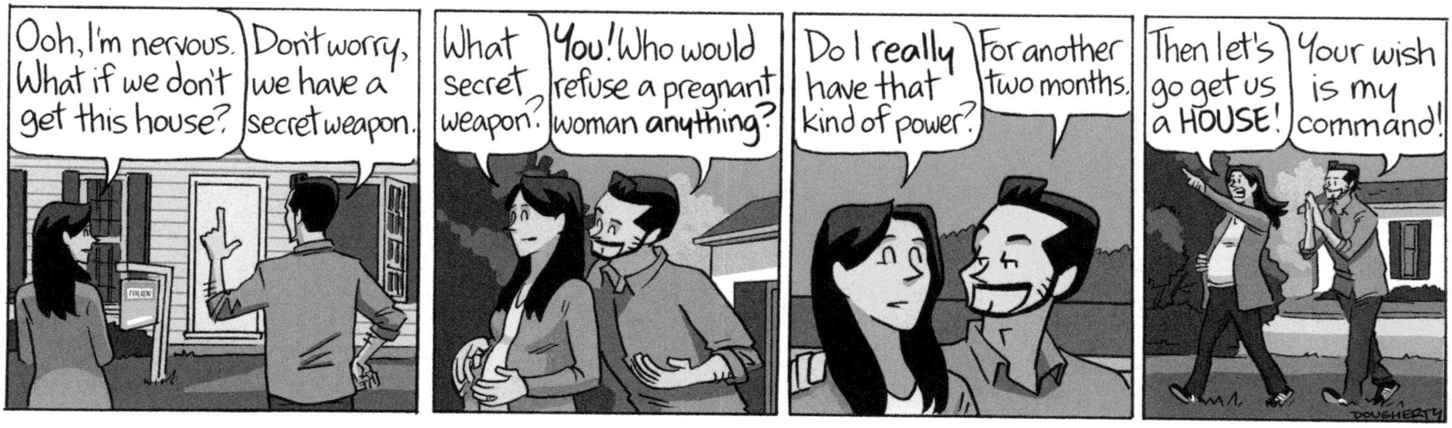
Ooh, I'm nervous. What if we don't get this house?
Don't worry, we have a secret weapon.
What secret weapon?
You! Who would refuse a pregnant woman **anything**?
Do I **really** have that kind of power?
For another two months.
Then let's go get us a **HOUSE**!
Your wish is my command!
DOUGHERTY

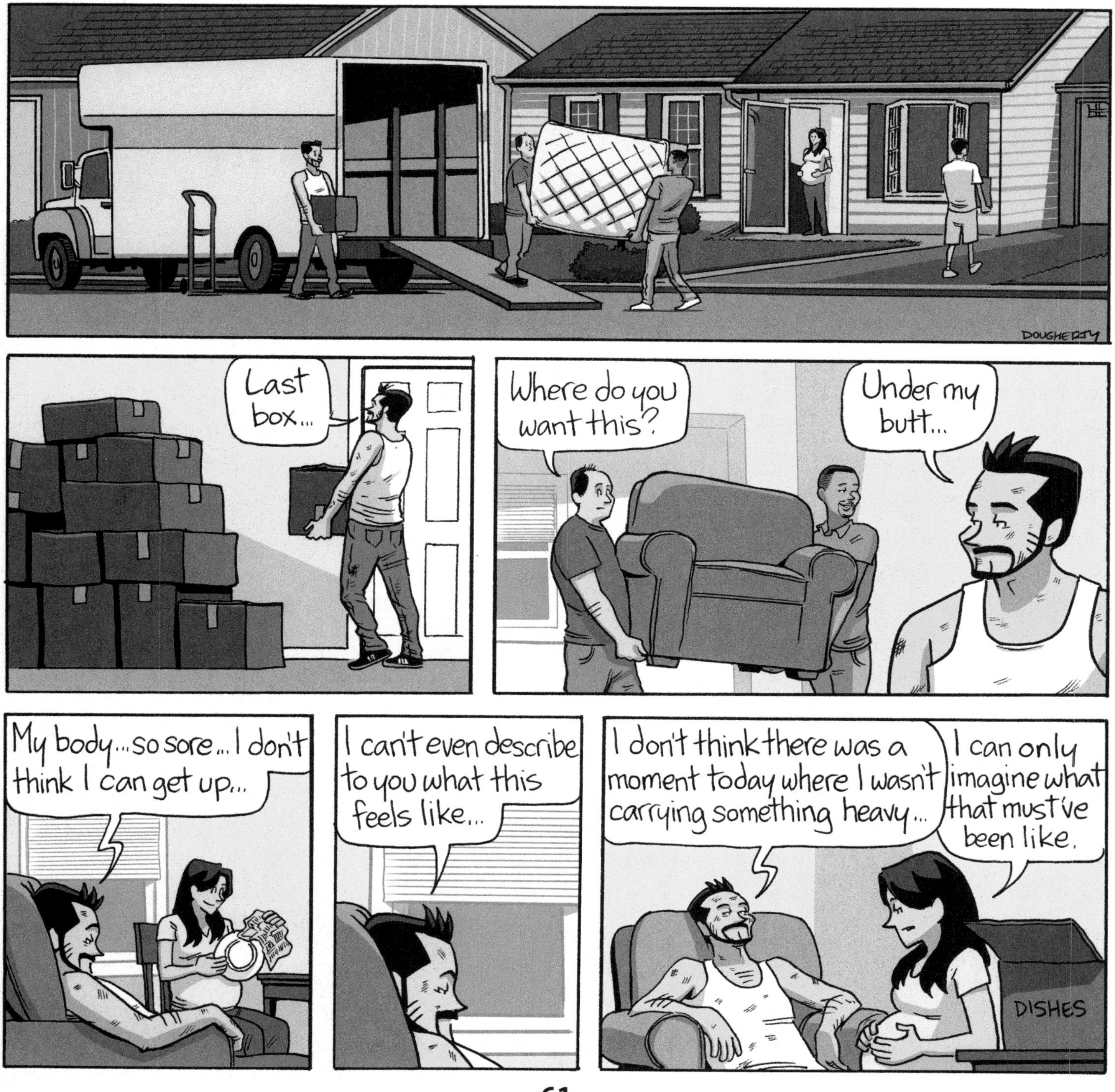
DOUGHERTY
Last box...
Where do you want this?
Under my butt...
My body...so sore...I don't think I can get up...
I can't even describe to you what this feels like...
I don't think there was a moment today where I wasn't carrying something heavy...
I can only imagine what that must've been like.
DISHES

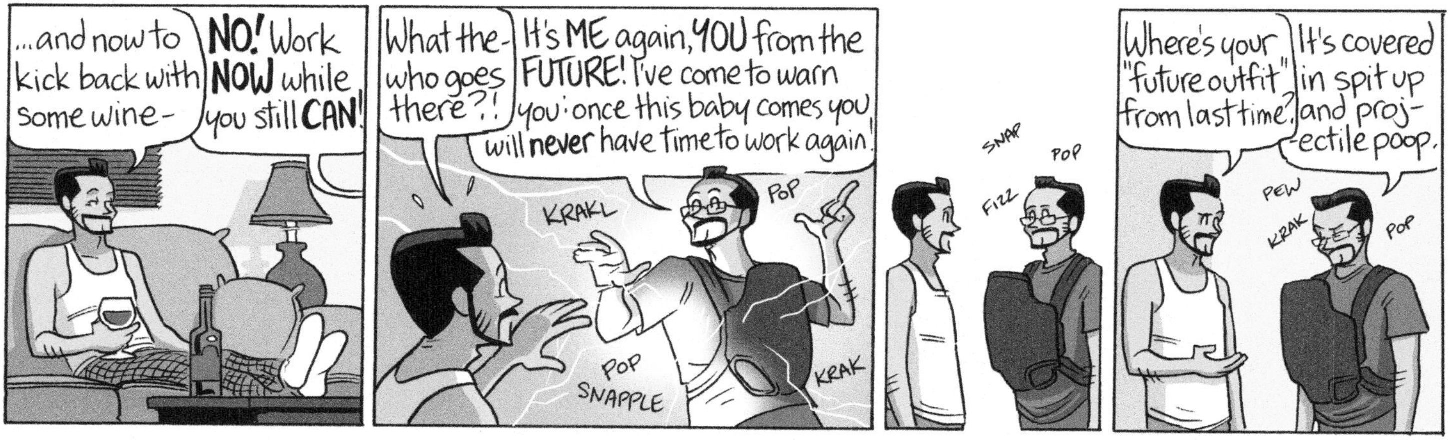
...and now to kick back with some wine-
NO! Work NOW while you still CAN!
What the- who goes there?!
It's ME again, YOU from the FUTURE! I've come to warn you: once this baby comes you will never have time to work again!
KRAKL
POP
POP
SNAPPLE
KRAK
SNAP
POP
FIZZ
Where's your "future outfit" from last time?
It's covered in spit up and proj- -ectile poop.
PEW
KRAK
POP

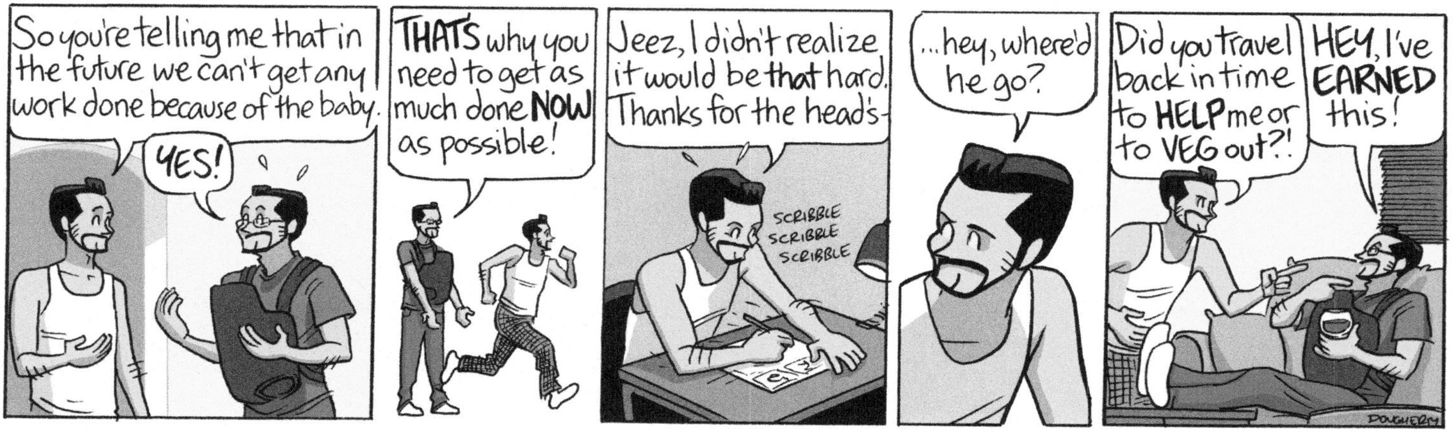
So you're telling me that in the future we can't get any work done because of the baby.
YES!
THAT'S why you need to get as much done NOW as possible!
Jeez, I didn't realize it would be that hard. Thanks for the head's-
SCRIBBLE
SCRIBBLE
SCRIBBLE
...hey, where'd he go?
Did you travel back in time to HELP me or to VEG out?!
HEY, I've EARNED this!
DOUGHERTY

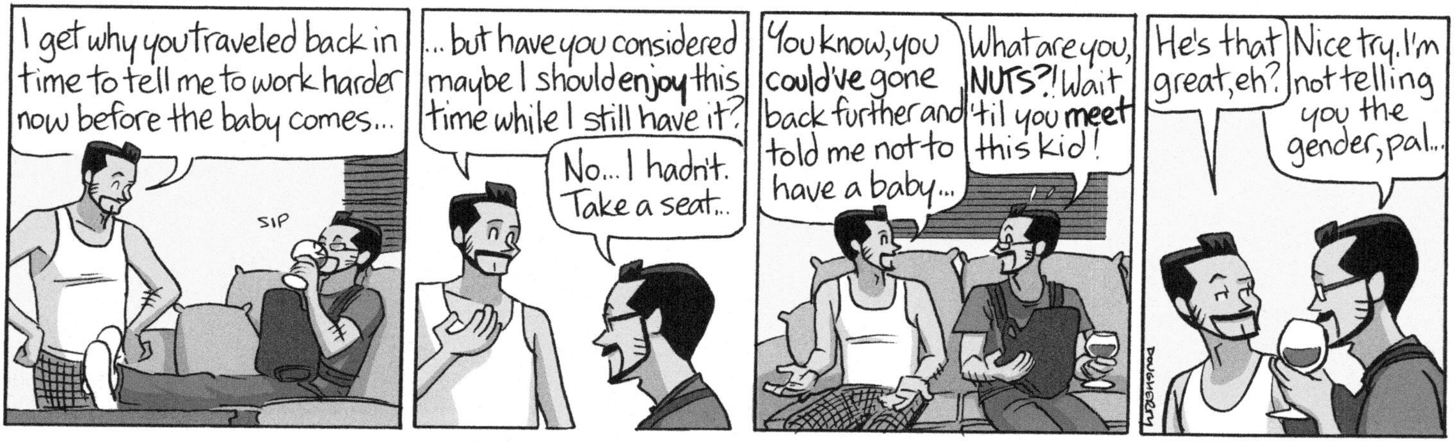
I get why you traveled back in time to tell me to work harder now before the baby comes...
SIP
...but have you considered maybe I should enjoy this time while I still have it?
No... I hadn't. Take a seat...
You know, you could've gone back further and told me not to have a baby...
What are you, NUTS?! Wait 'til you meet this kid!
He's that great, eh?
Nice try. I'm not telling you the gender, pal...

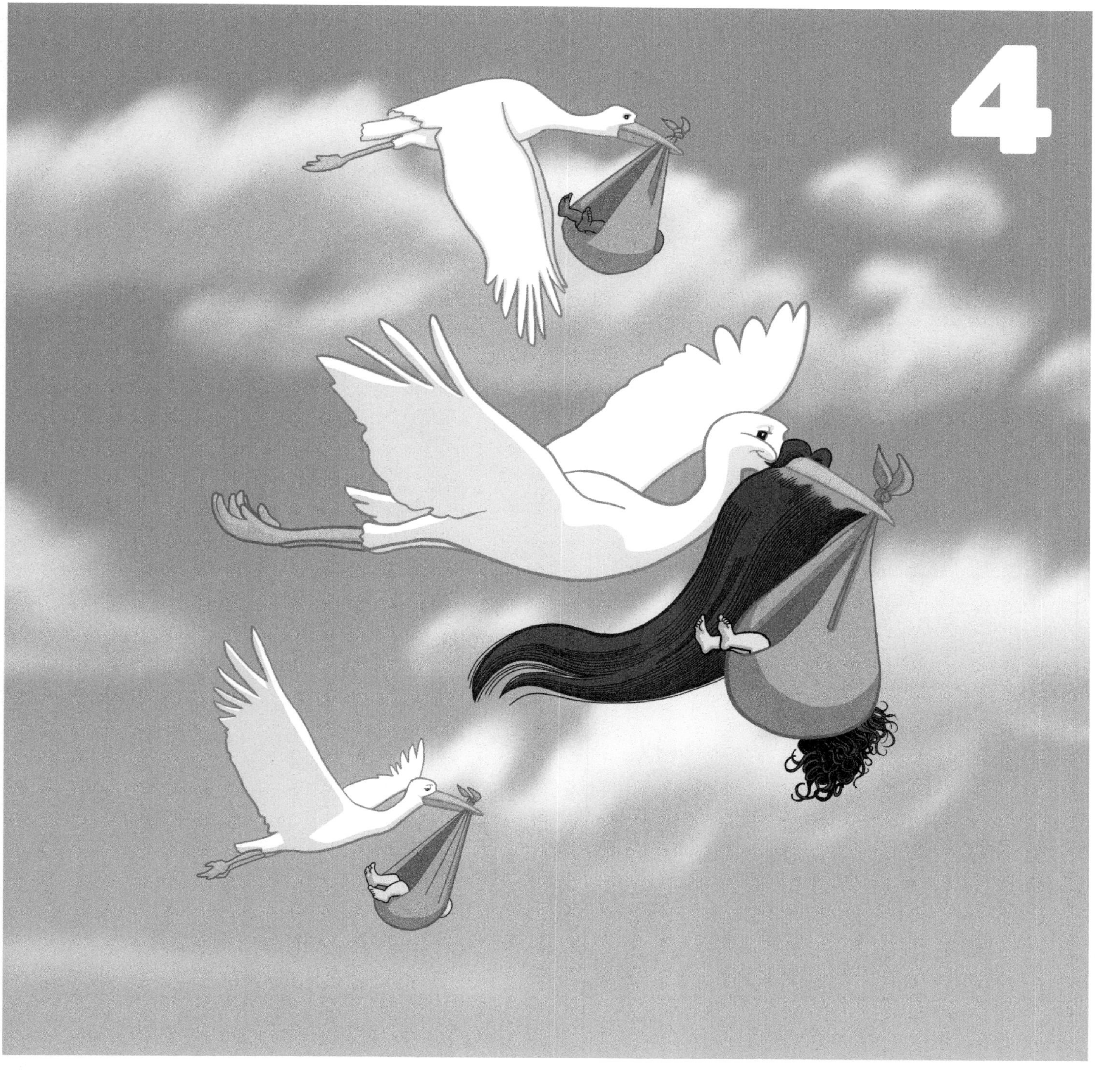
4

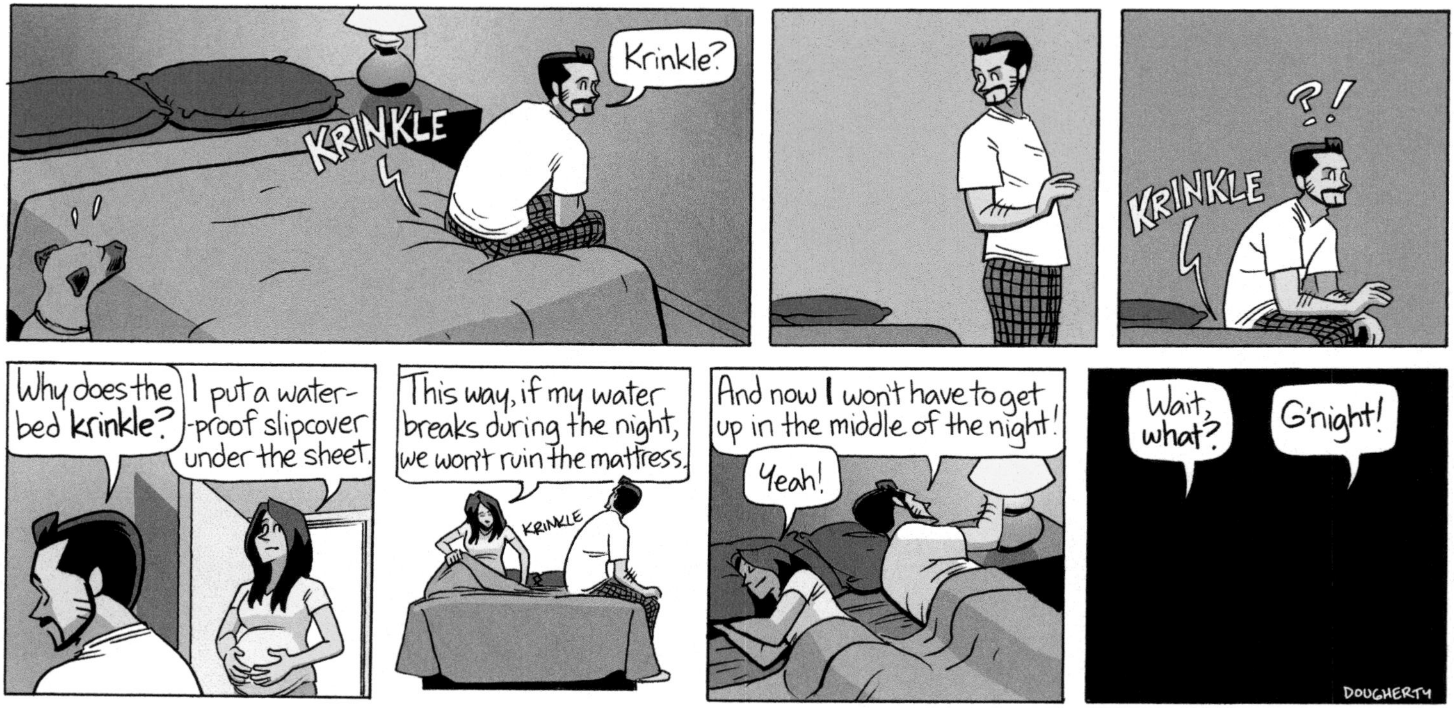
Krinkle?
KRINKLE
KRINKLE
?!
KRINKLE
Why does the bed **krinkle?**
I put a water-proof slipcover under the sheet.
This way, if my water breaks during the night, we won't ruin the mattress.
KRINKLE
And now **I** won't have to get up in the middle of the night!
Yeah!
Wait, **what?**
G'night!
DOUGHERTY

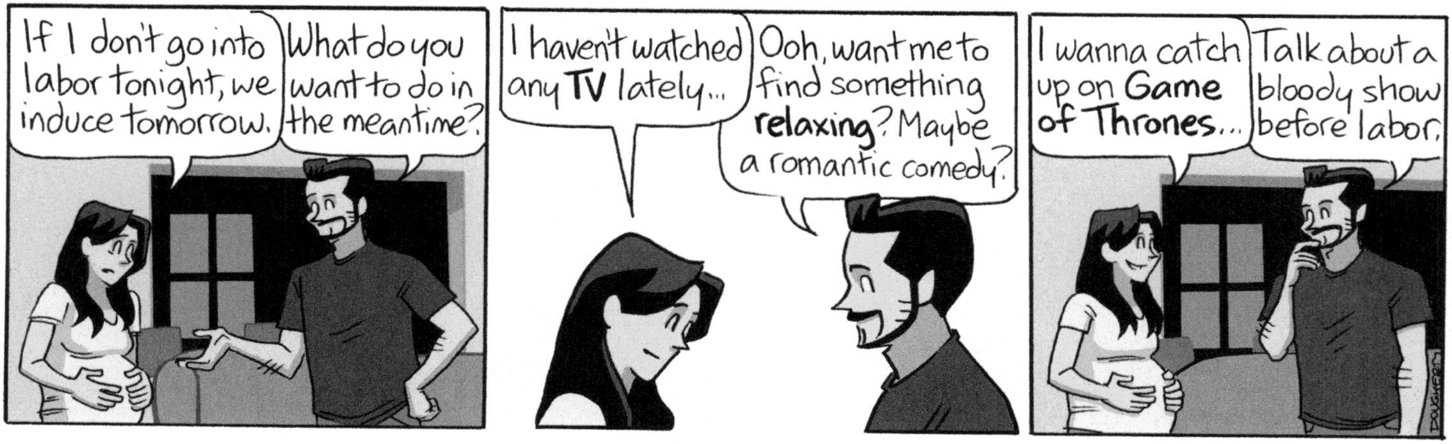
If I don't go into labor tonight, we induce tomorrow.
What do you want to do in the meantime?
I haven't watched any **TV** lately...
Ooh, want me to find something **relaxing**? Maybe a romantic comedy?
I wanna catch up on **Game of Thrones**...
Talk about a bloody show before labor.
DOUGHERTY

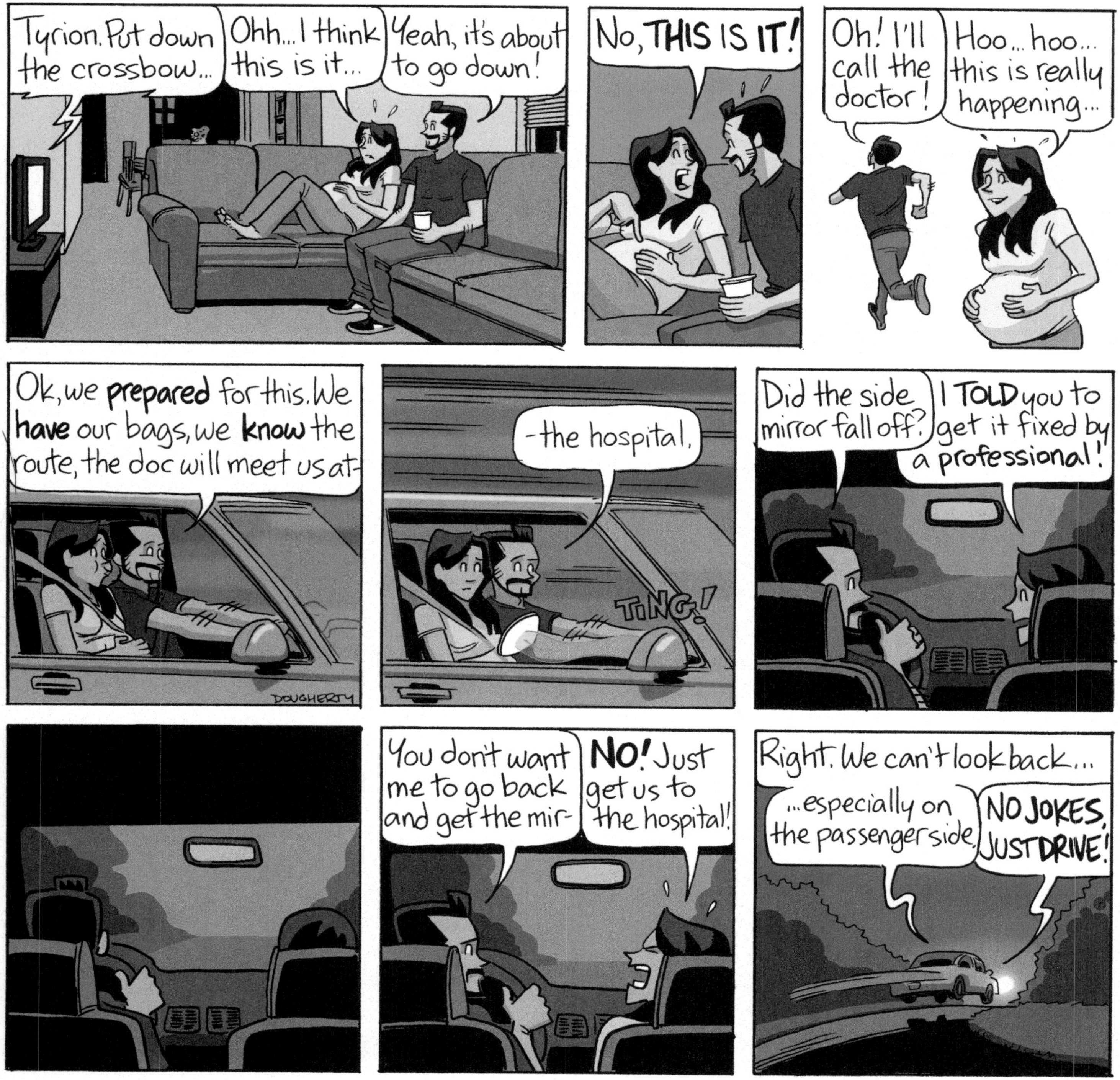
Tyrion. Put down the crossbow...
Ohh... I think this is it...
Yeah, it's about to go down!
No, THIS IS IT!
Oh! I'll call the doctor!
Hoo... hoo... this is really happening...
Ok, we prepared for this. We have our bags, we know the route, the doc will meet us at-
DOUGHERTY
-the hospital.
TING!
Did the side mirror fall off?
I TOLD you to get it fixed by a professional!
You don't want me to go back and get the mir-
NO! Just get us to the hospital!
Right. We can't look back...
...especially on the passenger side.
NO JOKES, JUST DRIVE!

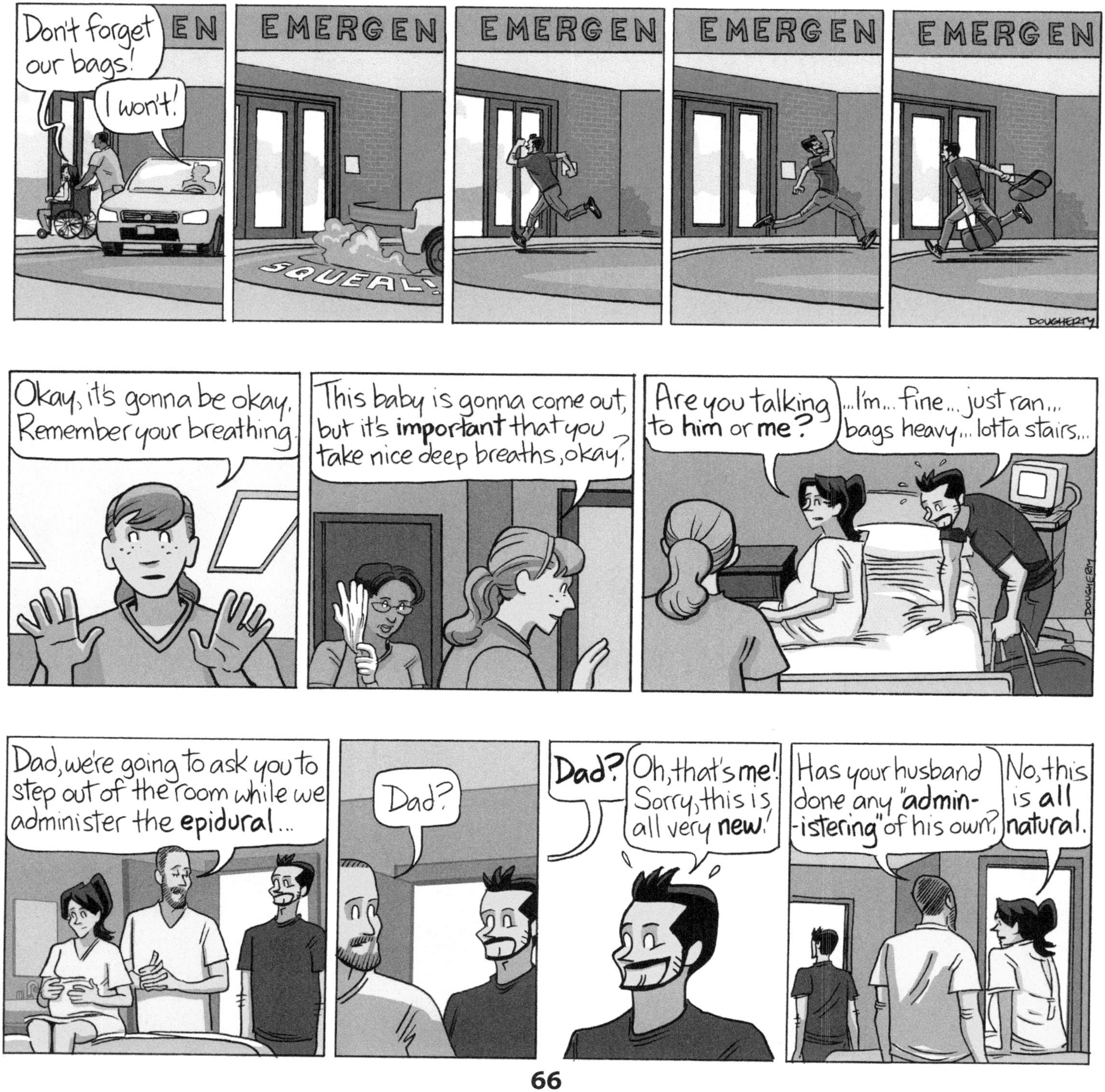
Don't forget our bags!
I won't!
EN
EMERGEN
SQUEAL!
EMERGEN
EMERGEN
EMERGEN
DOUGHERTY
Okay, it's gonna be okay. Remember your breathing.
This baby is gonna come out, but it's **important** that you take nice deep breaths, okay?
Are you talking to **him** or **me**?
...I'm... fine... just ran... bags heavy... lotta stairs...
DOUGHERTY
Dad, we're going to ask you to step out of the room while we administer the **epidural**...
Dad?
Dad?
Oh, that's **me**! Sorry, this is all very **new**!
Has your husband done any "**admin-istering**" of his own?
No, this is **all natural**.

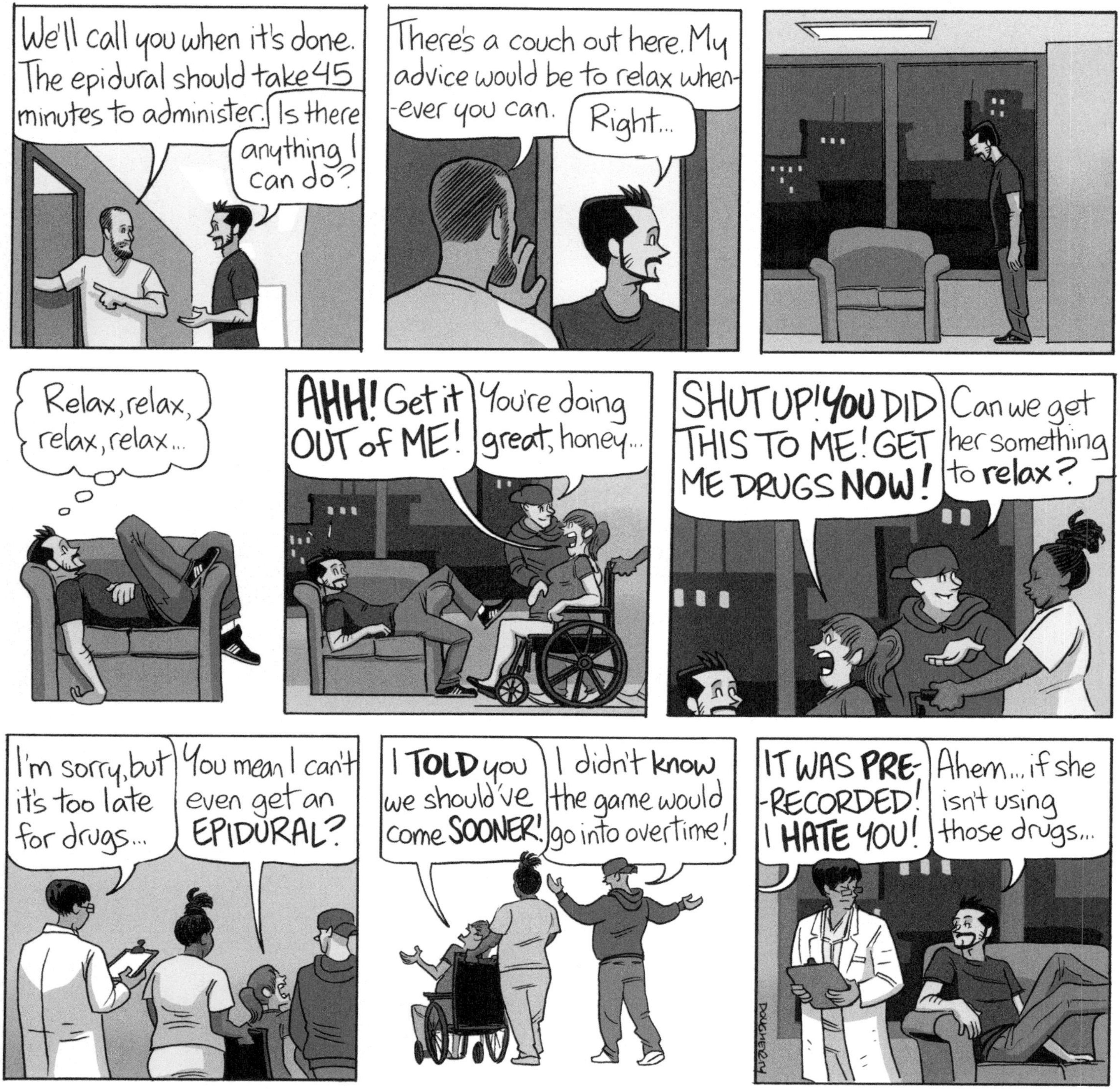
We'll call you when it's done. The epidural should take 45 minutes to administer.
Is there anything I can do?
There's a couch out here. My advice would be to relax when-ever you can.
Right...
Relax, relax, relax, relax...
AHH! Get it OUT of ME!
You're doing great, honey...
SHUT UP! YOU DID THIS TO ME! GET ME DRUGS NOW!
Can we get her something to relax?
I'm sorry, but it's too late for drugs...
You mean I can't even get an EPIDURAL?
I TOLD you we should've come SOONER!
I didn't know the game would go into overtime!
IT WAS PRE-RECORDED! I HATE YOU!
Ahem... if she isn't using those drugs...

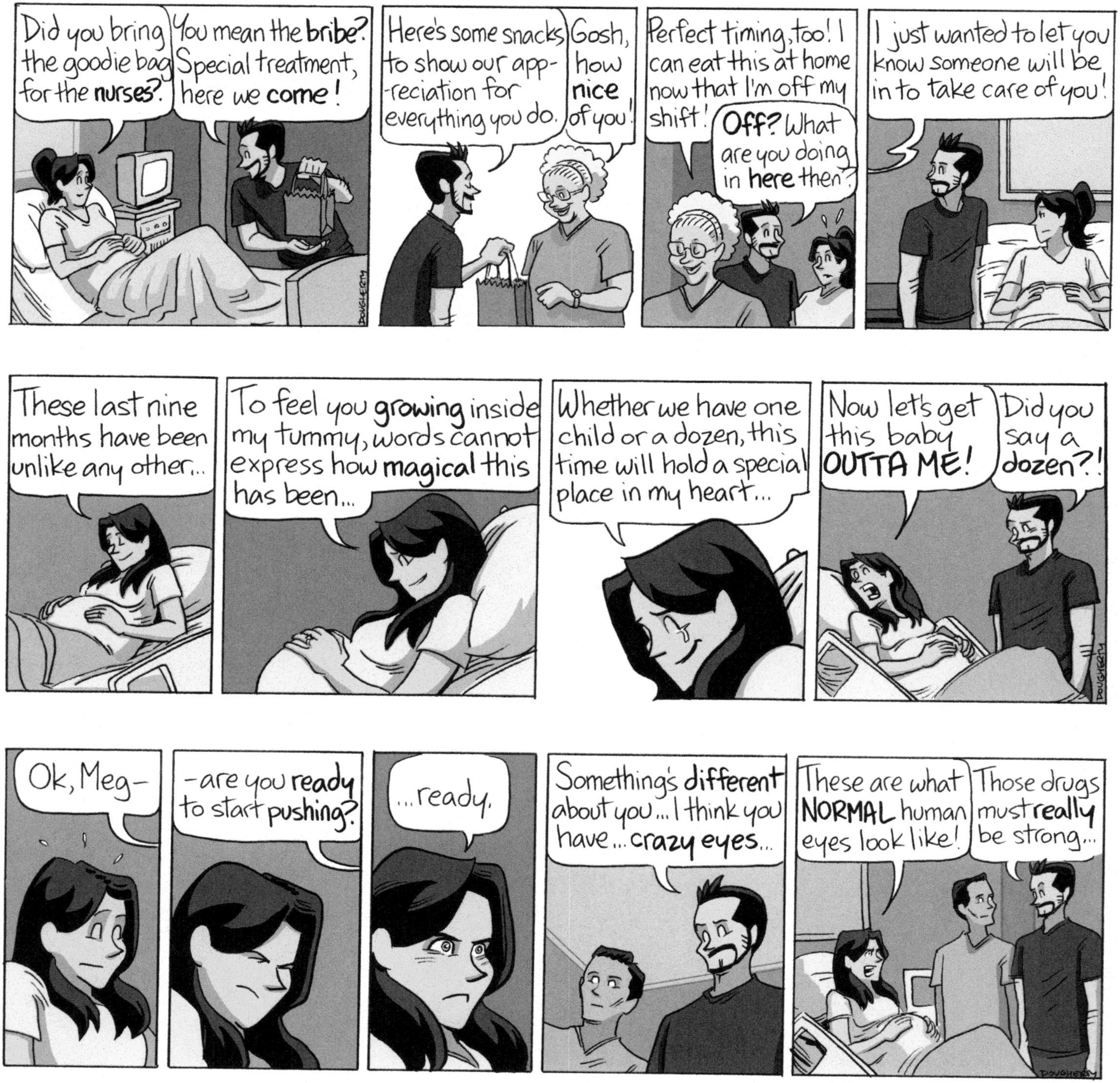

Did you bring the goodie bag for the **nurses**?
You mean the **bribe**? Special treatment, here we **come**!
Here's some snacks to show our app-reciation for everything you do.
Gosh, how **nice** of you!
Perfect timing, too! I can eat this at home now that I'm off my shift!
Off? What are you doing in **here** then?
I just wanted to let you know someone will be in to take care of you!
DOUGHERTY
These last nine months have been unlike any other...
To feel you **growing** inside my tummy, words cannot express how **magical** this has been...
Whether we have one child or a dozen, this time will hold a special place in my heart...
Now let's get this baby **OUTTA ME**!
Did you say a **dozen**?!
DOUGHERTY
Ok, Meg–
–are you **ready** to start **pushing**?
...ready.
Something's **different** about you... I think you have... **crazy eyes**...
These are what **NORMAL** human eyes look like!
Those drugs must **really** be strong...
DOUGHERTY

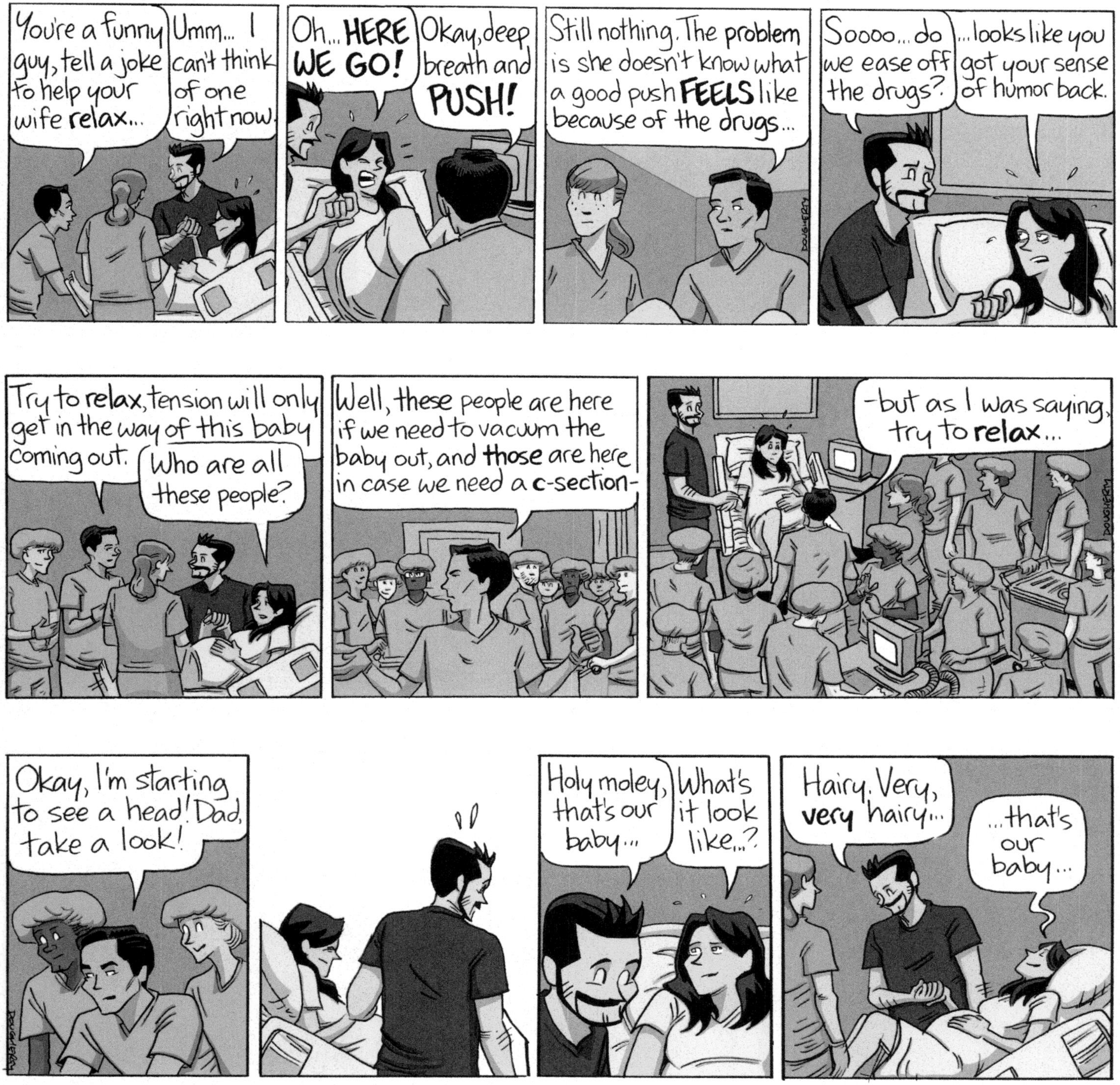
You're a funny guy, tell a joke to help your wife relax...
Umm... I can't think of one right now.
Oh... HERE WE GO!
Okay, deep breath and PUSH!
Still nothing. The problem is she doesn't know what a good push FEELS like because of the drugs...
Soooo... do we ease off the drugs?
...looks like you got your sense of humor back.
Try to relax, tension will only get in the way of this baby coming out.
Who are all these people?
Well, these people are here if we need to vacuum the baby out, and those are here in case we need a c-section-
-but as I was saying, try to relax...
Okay, I'm starting to see a head! Dad, take a look!
Holy moley, that's our baby...
What's it look like...?
Hairy. Very, very hairy...
...that's our baby...

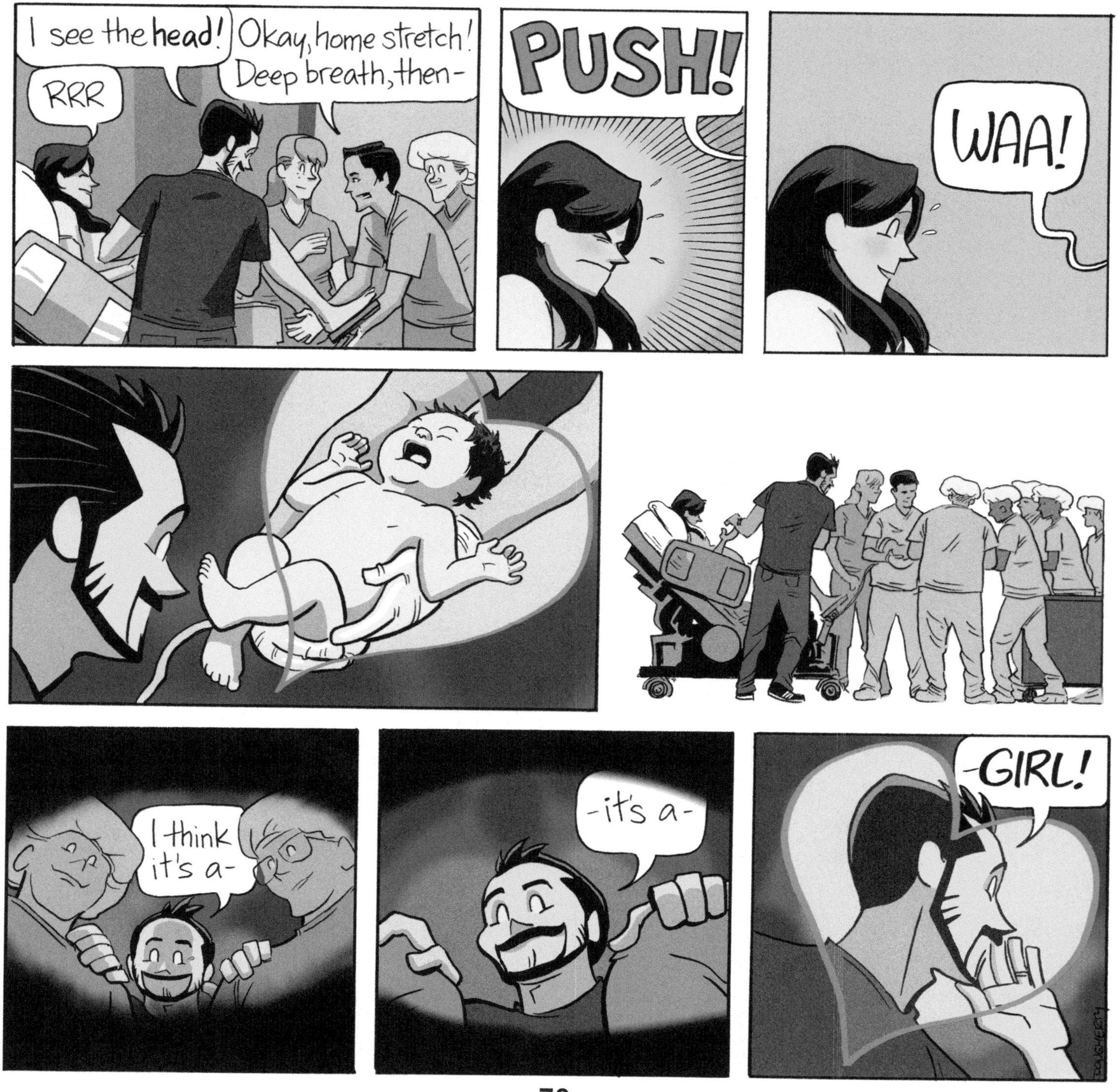

I see the head!
RRR
Okay, home stretch! Deep breath, then-
PUSH!
WAA!
I think it's a-
-it's a-
-GIRL!

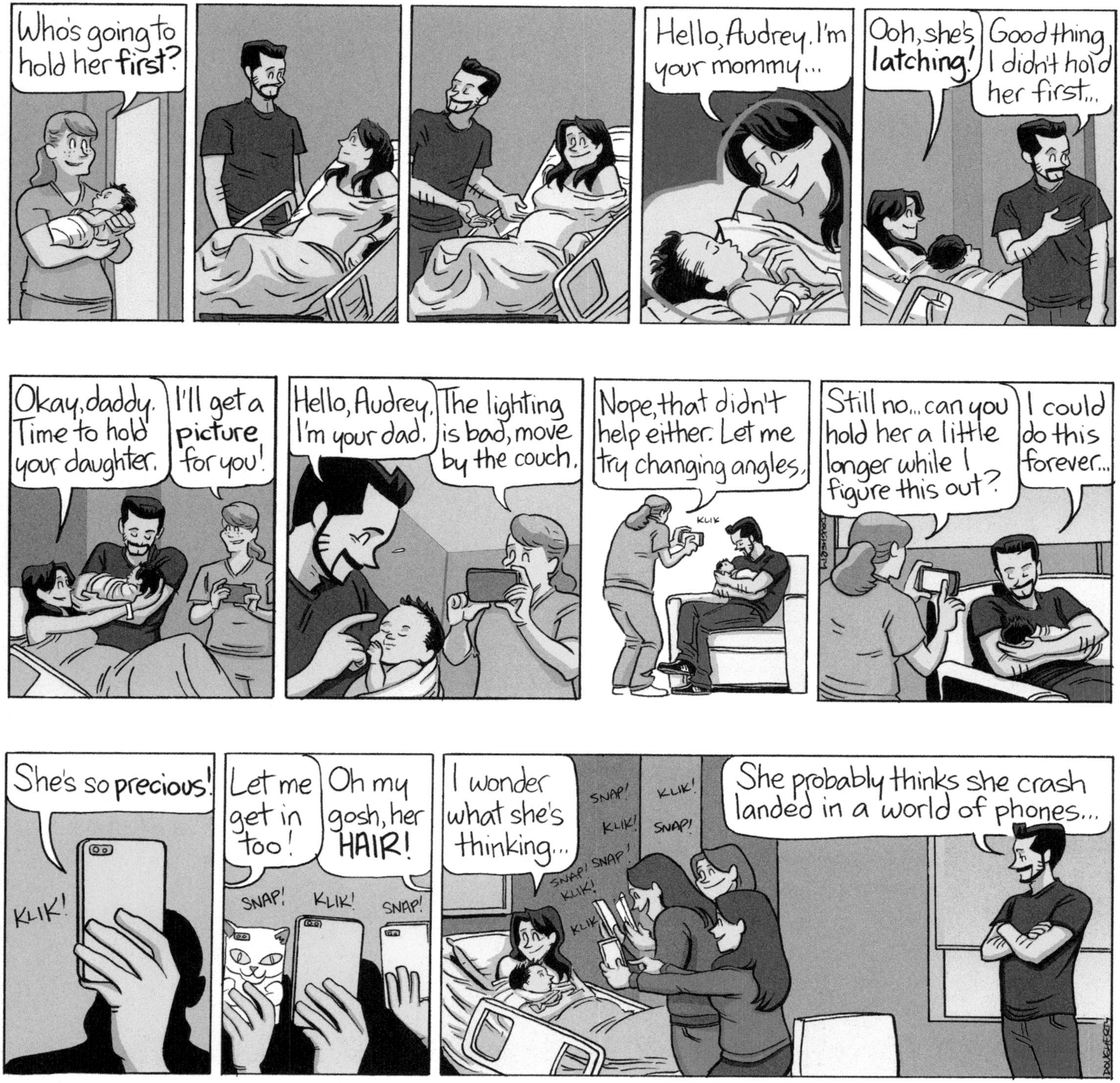
Who's going to hold her first?
Hello, Audrey. I'm your mommy...
Ooh, she's latching!
Good thing I didn't hold her first...
Okay, daddy. Time to hold your daughter.
I'll get a picture for you!
Hello, Audrey, I'm your dad.
The lighting is bad, move by the couch.
Nope, that didn't help either. Let me try changing angles,
KLIK
Still no... can you hold her a little longer while I figure this out?
I could do this forever...
She's so precious!
KLIK!
Let me get in too!
Oh my gosh, her HAIR!
SNAP!
KLIK!
SNAP!
I wonder what she's thinking...
SNAP!
KLIK!
KLIK!
SNAP!
SNAP! SNAP!
KLIK!
KLIK
She probably thinks she crash landed in a world of phones...

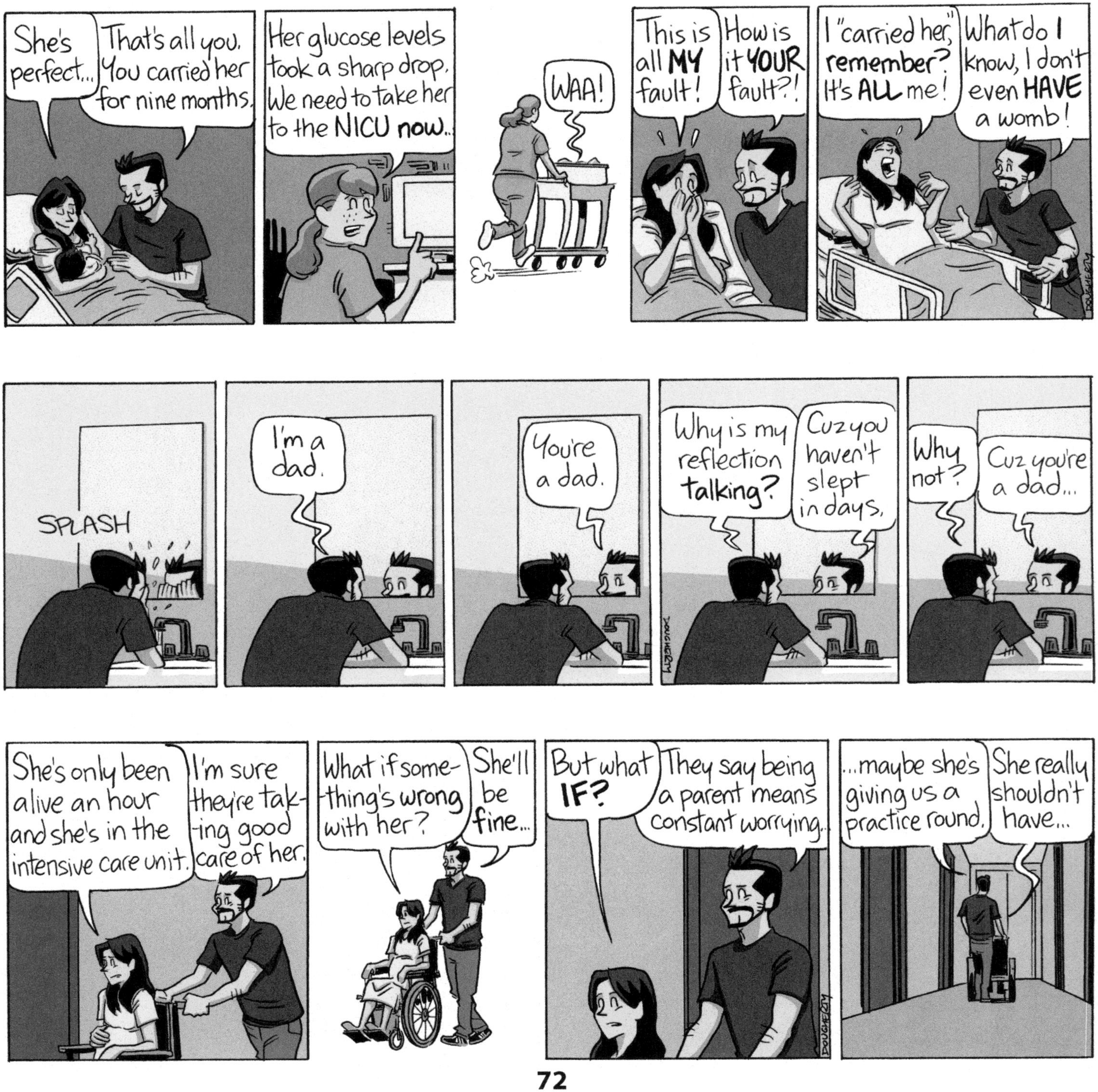

She's perfect...
That's all you. You carried her for nine months.
Her glucose levels took a sharp drop. We need to take her to the NICU now...
WAA!
This is all MY fault!
How is it YOUR fault?!
I "carried her," remember? It's ALL me!
What do I know, I don't even HAVE a womb!
SPLASH
I'm a dad.
You're a dad.
Why is my reflection talking?
Cuz you haven't slept in days.
Why not?
Cuz you're a dad...
She's only been alive an hour and she's in the intensive care unit.
I'm sure they're tak-ing good care of her.
What if some-thing's wrong with her?
She'll be fine...
But what IF?
They say being a parent means constant worrying...
...maybe she's giving us a practice round.
She really shouldn't have...

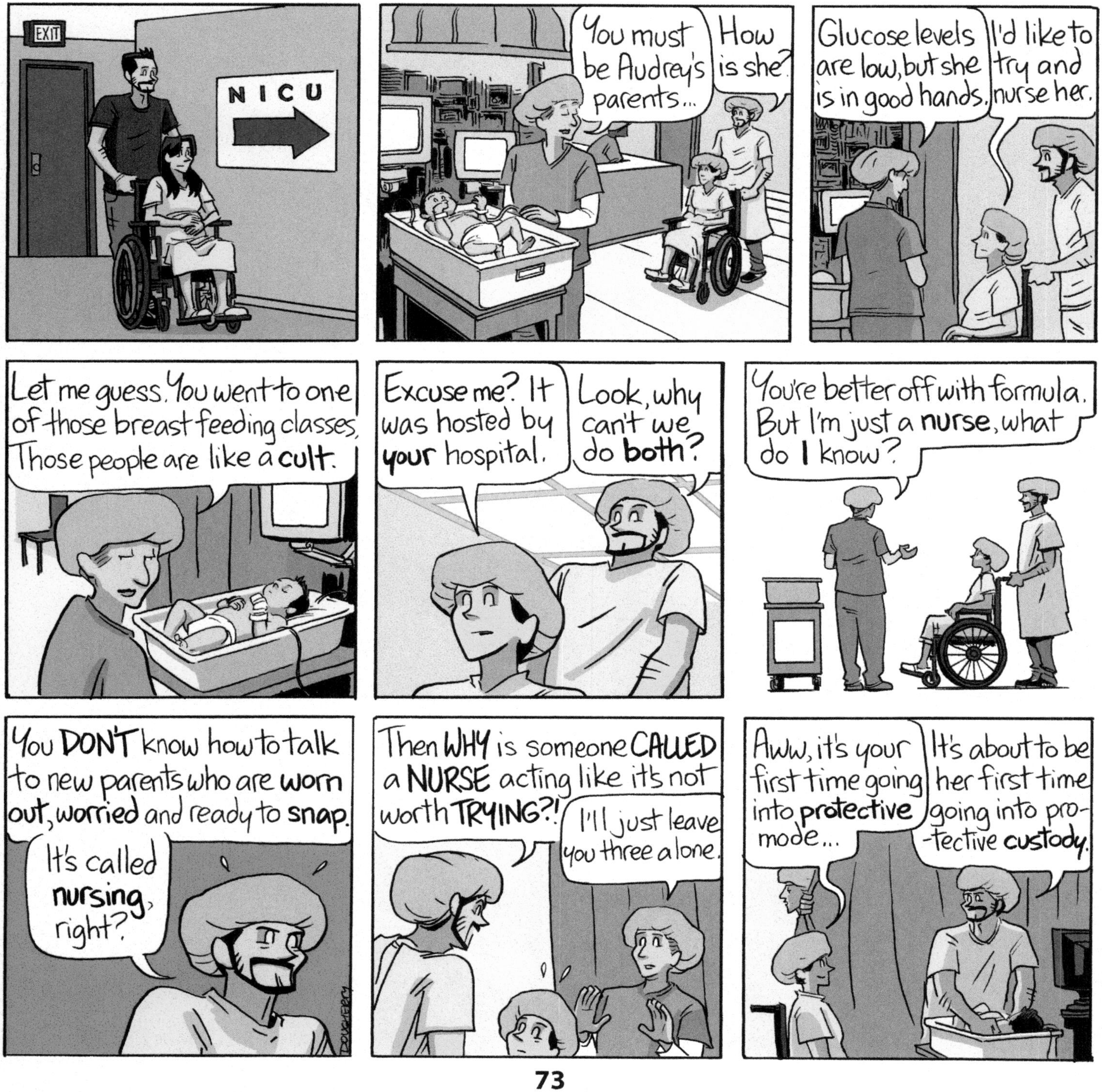
EXIT
NICU
You must be Audrey's parents...
How is she?
Glucose levels are low, but she is in good hands.
I'd like to try and nurse her.
Let me guess. You went to one of those breast feeding classes. Those people are like a **cult**.
Excuse me? It was hosted by **your** hospital.
Look, why can't we do **both**?
You're better off with formula. But I'm just a **nurse**, what do **I** know?
You **DON'T** know how to talk to new parents who are **worn out**, **worried** and ready to **snap**.
It's called **nursing**, right?
Then **WHY** is someone **CALLED** a **NURSE** acting like it's not worth **TRYING**?!
I'll just leave you three alone.
Aww, it's your first time going into **protective** mode...
It's about to be her first time going into pro-tective **custody**.

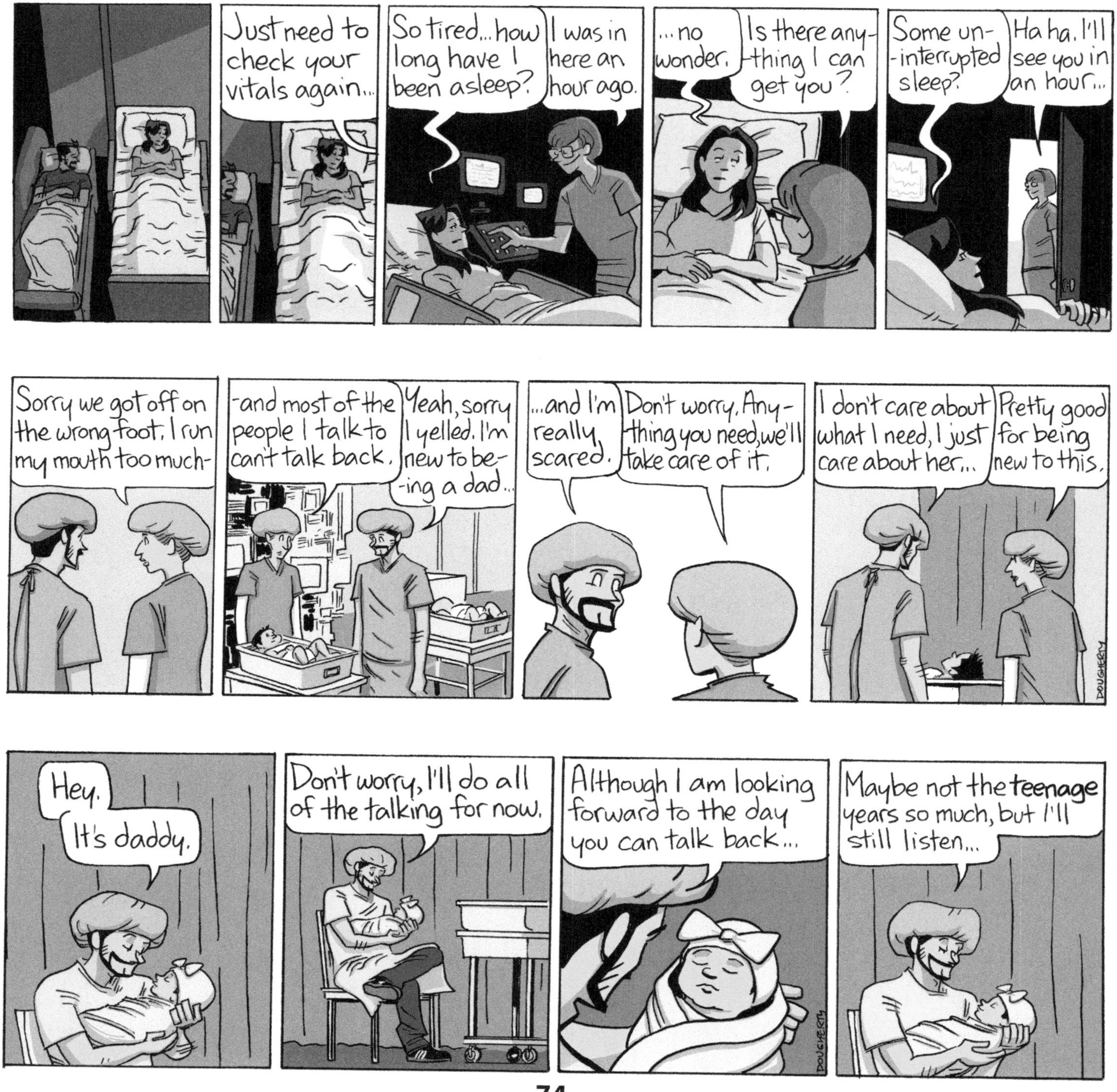
Just need to check your vitals again...
So tired... how long have I been asleep?
I was in here an hour ago.
...no wonder.
Is there anything I can get you?
Some uninterrupted sleep?
Ha ha. I'll see you in an hour...
Sorry we got off on the wrong foot. I run my mouth too much-
-and most of the people I talk to can't talk back.
Yeah, sorry I yelled. I'm new to being a dad...
...and I'm really scared.
Don't worry. Anything you need, we'll take care of it.
I don't care about what I need, I just care about her...
Pretty good for being new to this.
DOUGHERTY
Hey.
It's daddy.
Don't worry, I'll do all of the talking for now.
Although I am looking forward to the day you can talk back...
DOUGHERTY
Maybe not the teenage years so much, but I'll still listen...

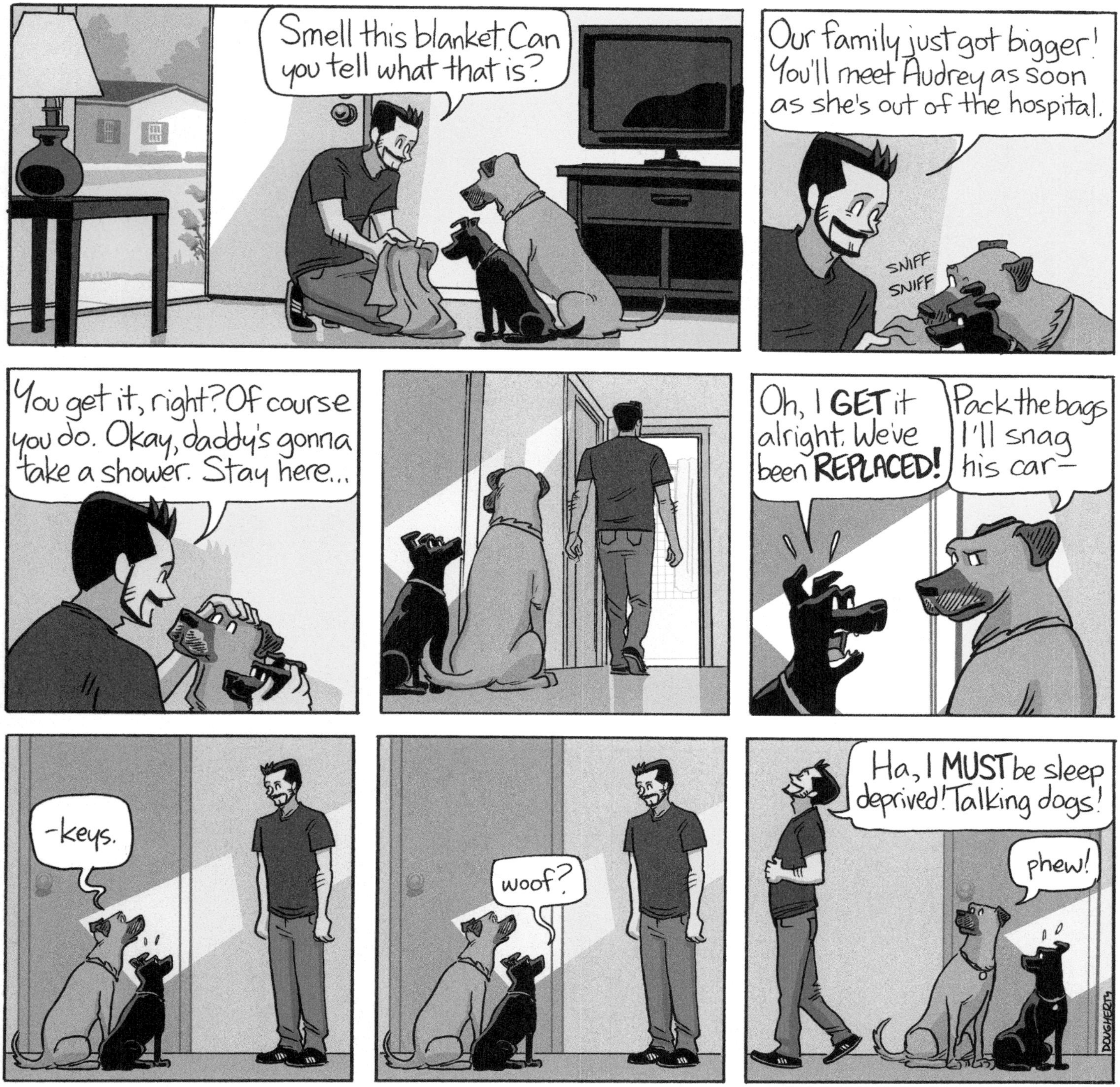
Smell this blanket. Can you tell what that is?
Our family just got bigger! You'll meet Audrey as soon as she's out of the hospital.
SNIFF
SNIFF
You get it, right? Of course you do. Okay, daddy's gonna take a shower. Stay here...
Oh, I GET it alright. We've been REPLACED!
Pack the bags I'll snag his car—
-keys.
woof?
Ha, I MUST be sleep deprived! Talking dogs!
phew!
DOUGHERTY

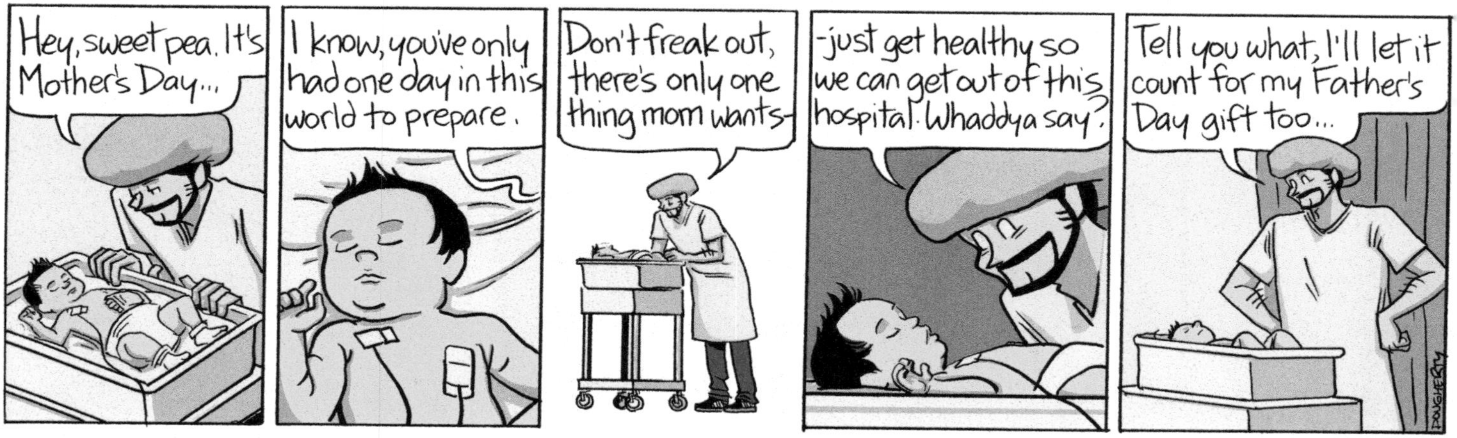
Hey, sweet pea. It's Mother's Day...
I know, you've only had one day in this world to prepare.
Don't freak out, there's only one thing mom wants-
-just get healthy so we can get out of this hospital. Whaddya say?
Tell you what, I'll let it count for my Father's Day gift too...
DOUGHERTY

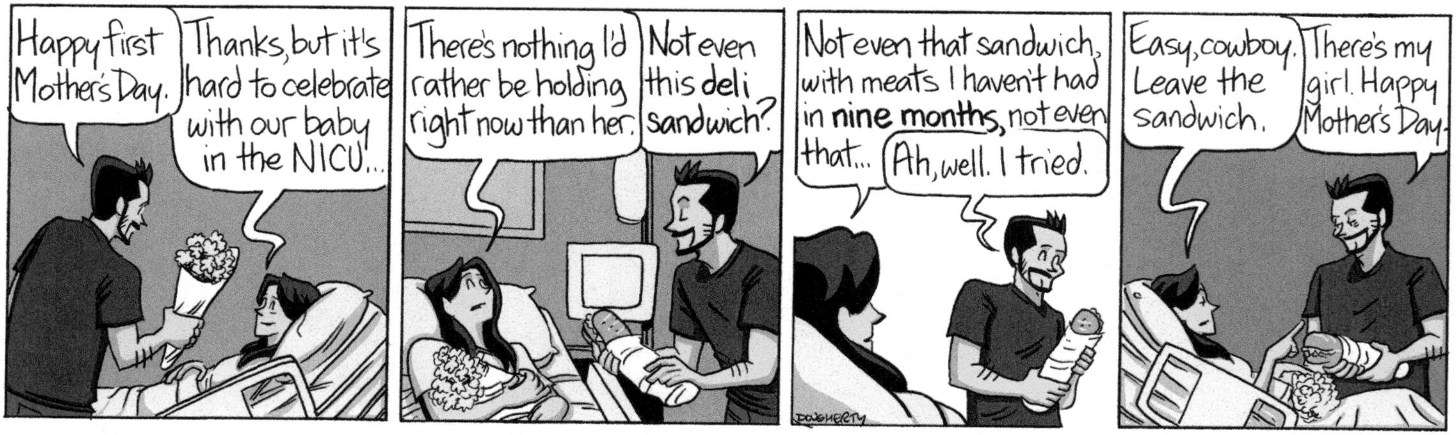
Happy first Mother's Day.
Thanks, but it's hard to celebrate with our baby in the NICU...
There's nothing I'd rather be holding right now than her.
Not even this **deli sandwich**?
Not even that sandwich, with meats I haven't had in **nine months,** not even that...
Ah, well. I tried.
Easy, cowboy. Leave the sandwich.
There's my girl. Happy Mother's Day-
DOUGHERTY

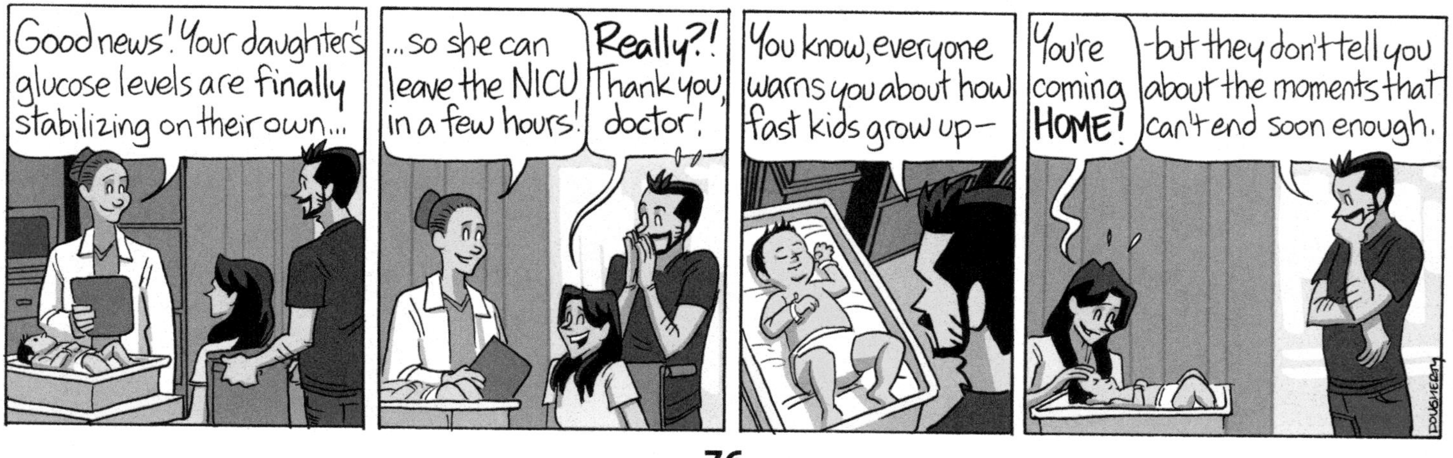
Good news! Your daughter's glucose levels are **finally** stabilizing on their own...
...so she can leave the NICU in a few hours!
Really?! Thank you, doctor!
You know, everyone warns you about how fast kids grow up-
You're coming **HOME!**
-but they don't tell you about the moments that can't end soon enough.
DOUGHERTY

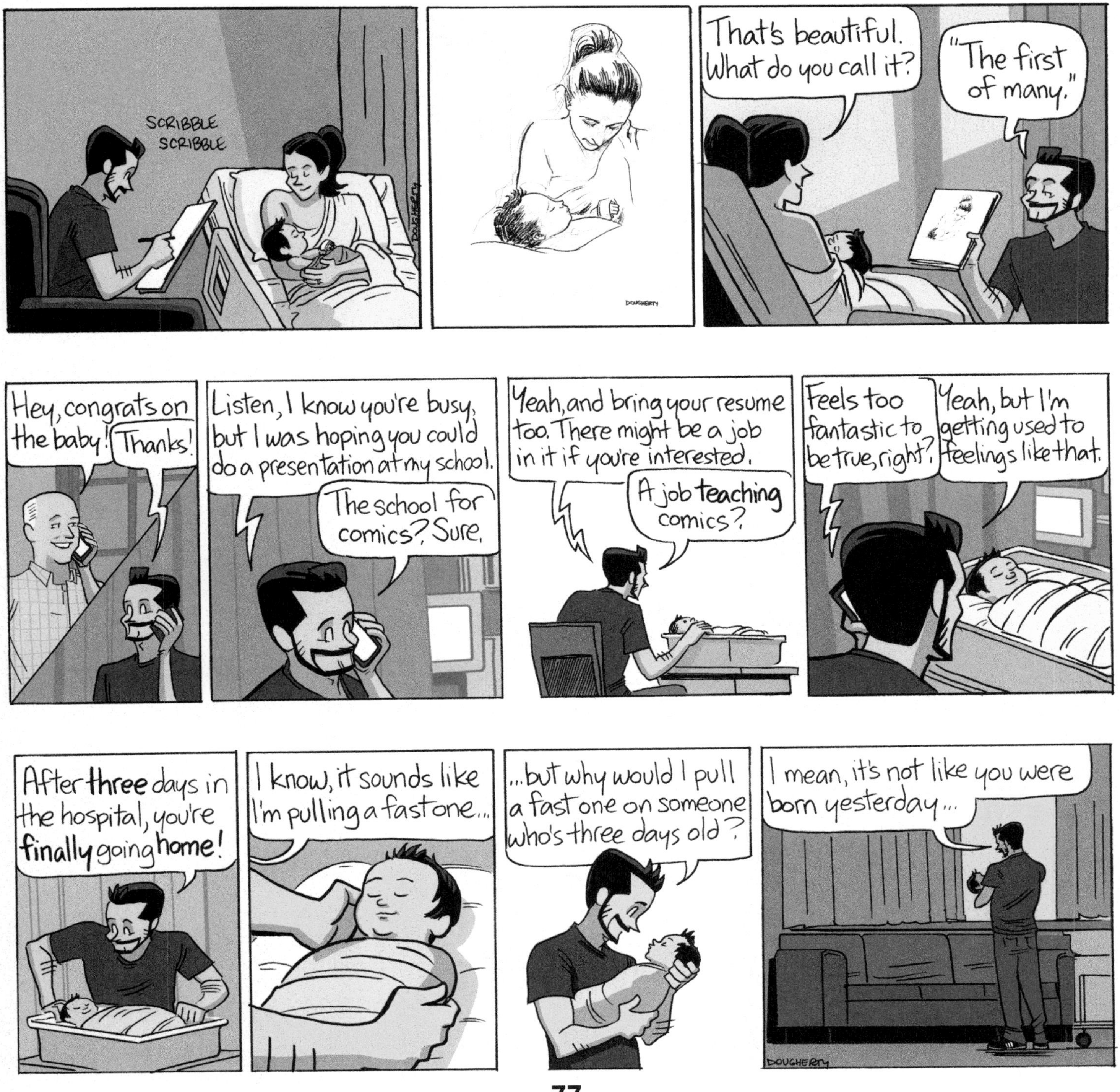
SCRIBBLE SCRIBBLE
DOUGHERTY
DOUGHERTY
That's beautiful. What do you call it?
"The first of many."
Hey, congrats on the baby!
Thanks!
Listen, I know you're busy, but I was hoping you could do a presentation at my school.
The school for comics? Sure.
Yeah, and bring your resume too. There might be a job in it if you're interested.
A job teaching comics?
Feels too fantastic to be true, right?
Yeah, but I'm getting used to feelings like that.
After three days in the hospital, you're finally going home!
I know, it sounds like I'm pulling a fast one...
...but why would I pull a fast one on someone who's three days old?
I mean, it's not like you were born yesterday...
DOUGHERTY

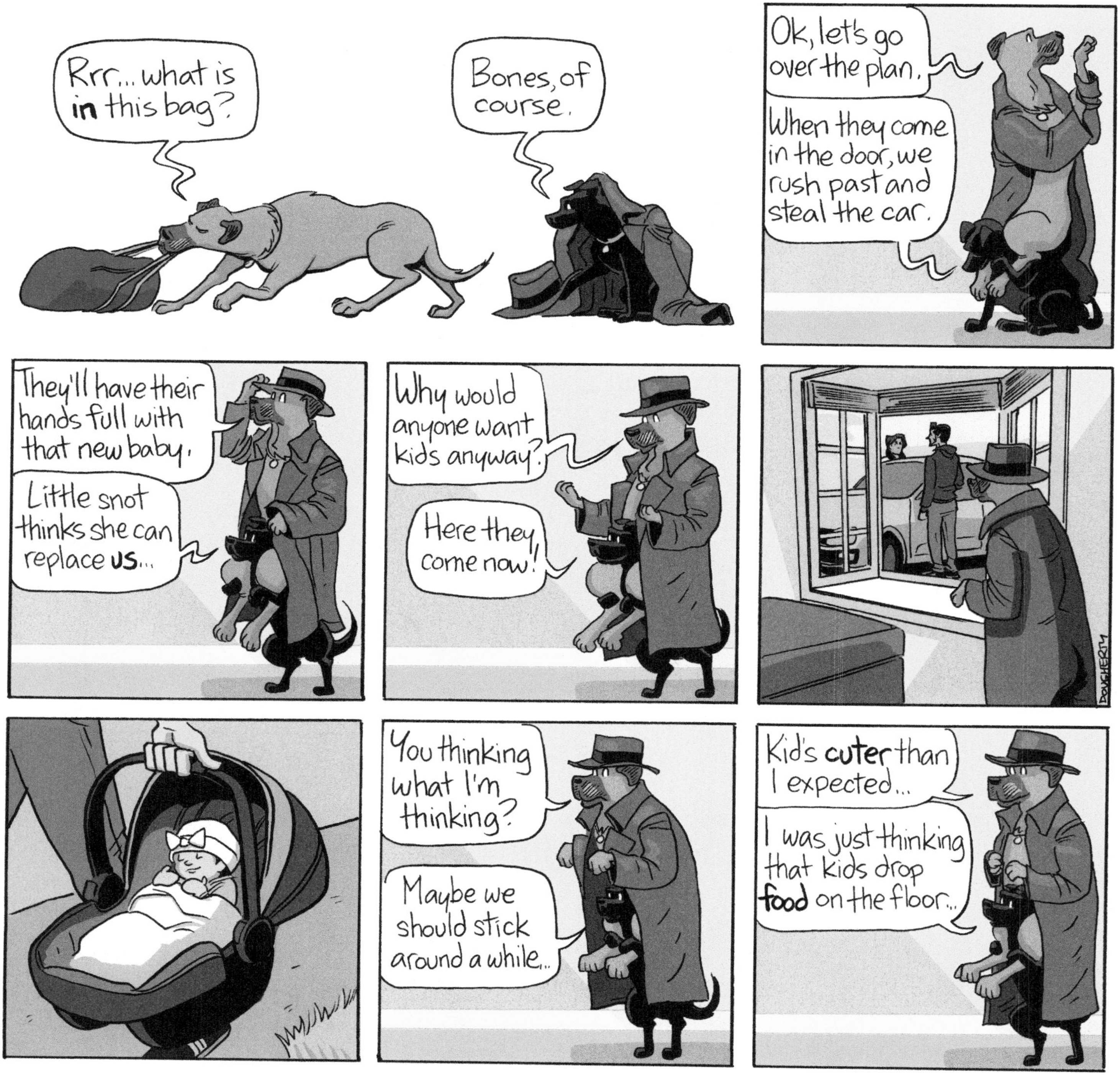

Rrr... what is **in** this bag?
Bones, of course.
Ok, let's go over the plan.
When they come in the door, we rush past and steal the car.
They'll have their hands full with that new baby.
Little snot thinks she can replace **us**...
Why would anyone want kids anyway?
Here they come now!
DOUGHERTY
You thinking what I'm thinking?
Maybe we should stick around a while...
Kid's **cuter** than I expected...
I was just thinking that kids drop **food** on the floor...

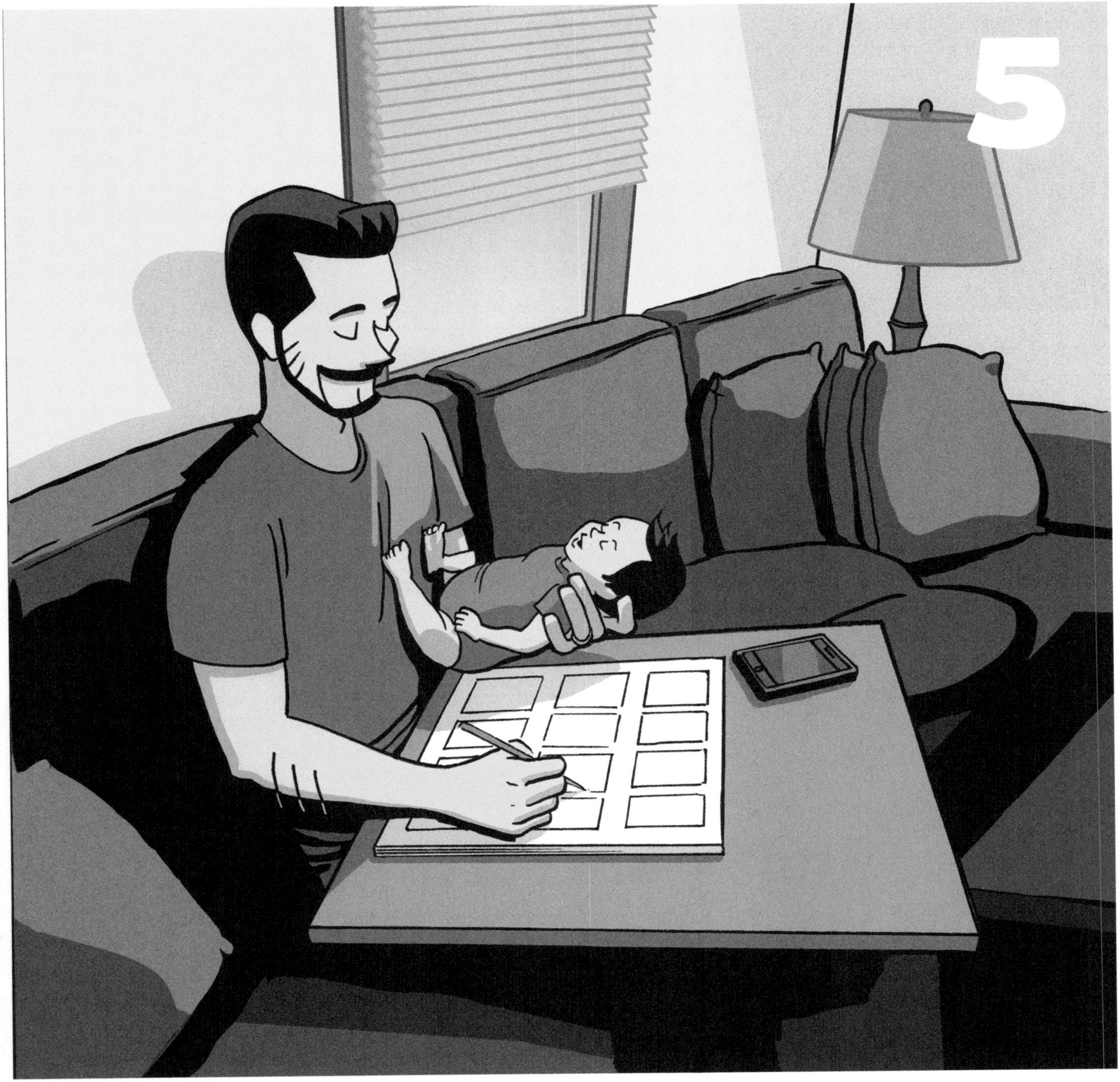
5

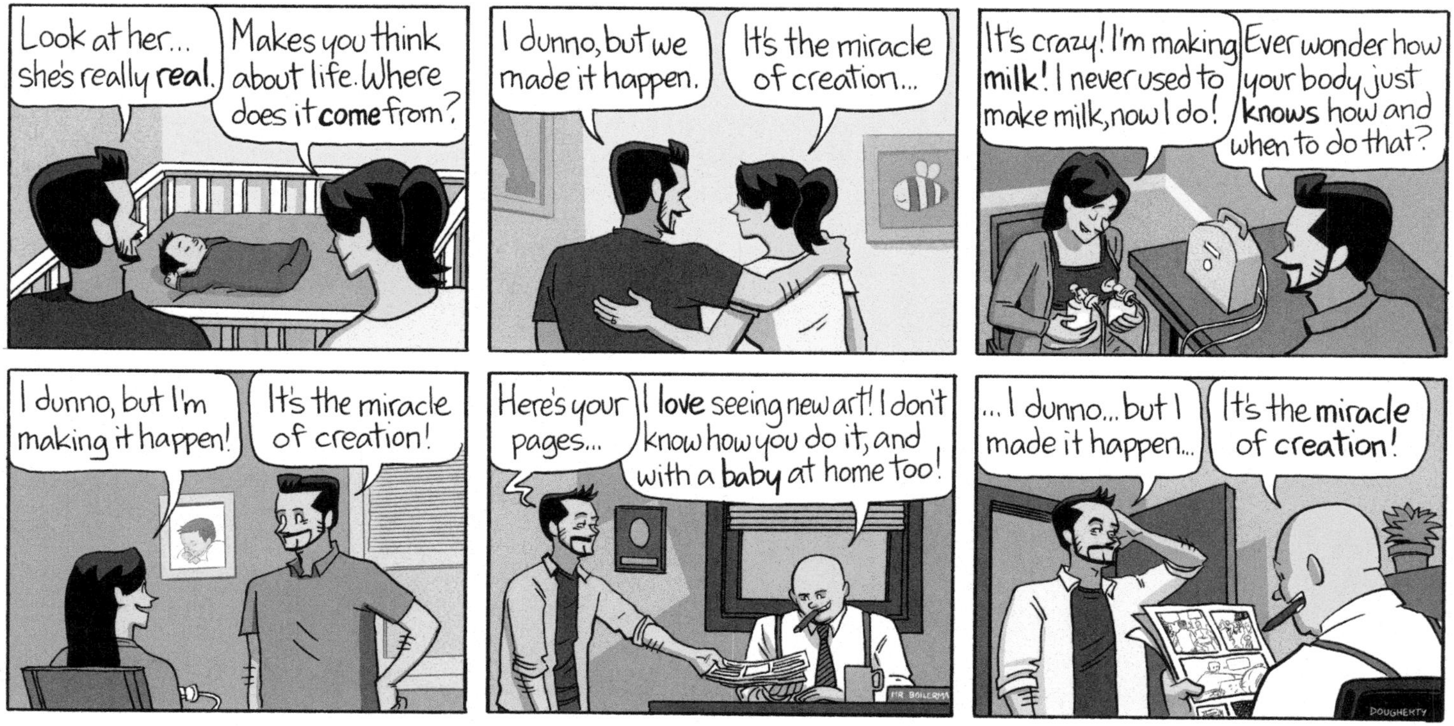
Look at her... she's really **real**.
Makes you think about life. Where does it **come** from?
I dunno, but we made it happen.
It's the miracle of creation...
It's crazy! I'm making **milk**! I never used to make milk, now I do!
Ever wonder how your body just **knows** how and when to do that?
I dunno, but I'm making it happen!
It's the miracle of creation!
Here's your pages...
I **love** seeing new art! I don't know how you do it, and with a **baby** at home too!
...I dunno... but I made it happen...
It's the **miracle** of **creation**!
DOUGHERTY

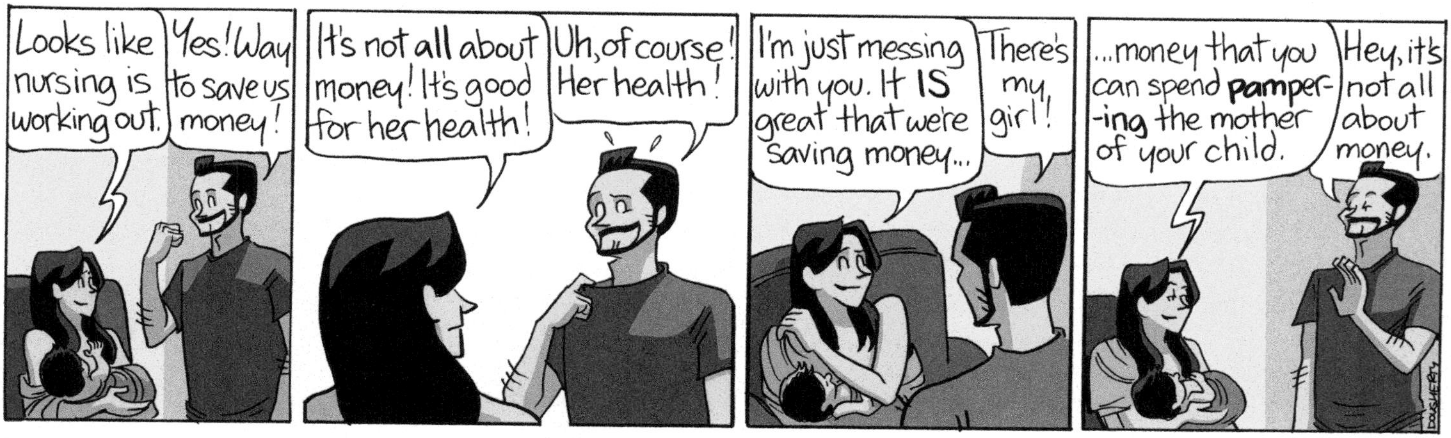
Looks like nursing is working out.
Yes! Way to save us money!
It's not **all** about money! It's good for her health!
Uh, of course! Her health!
I'm just messing with you. It **IS** great that we're saving money...
There's my girl!
...money that you can spend **pamper-ing** the mother of your child.
Hey, it's not all about money.

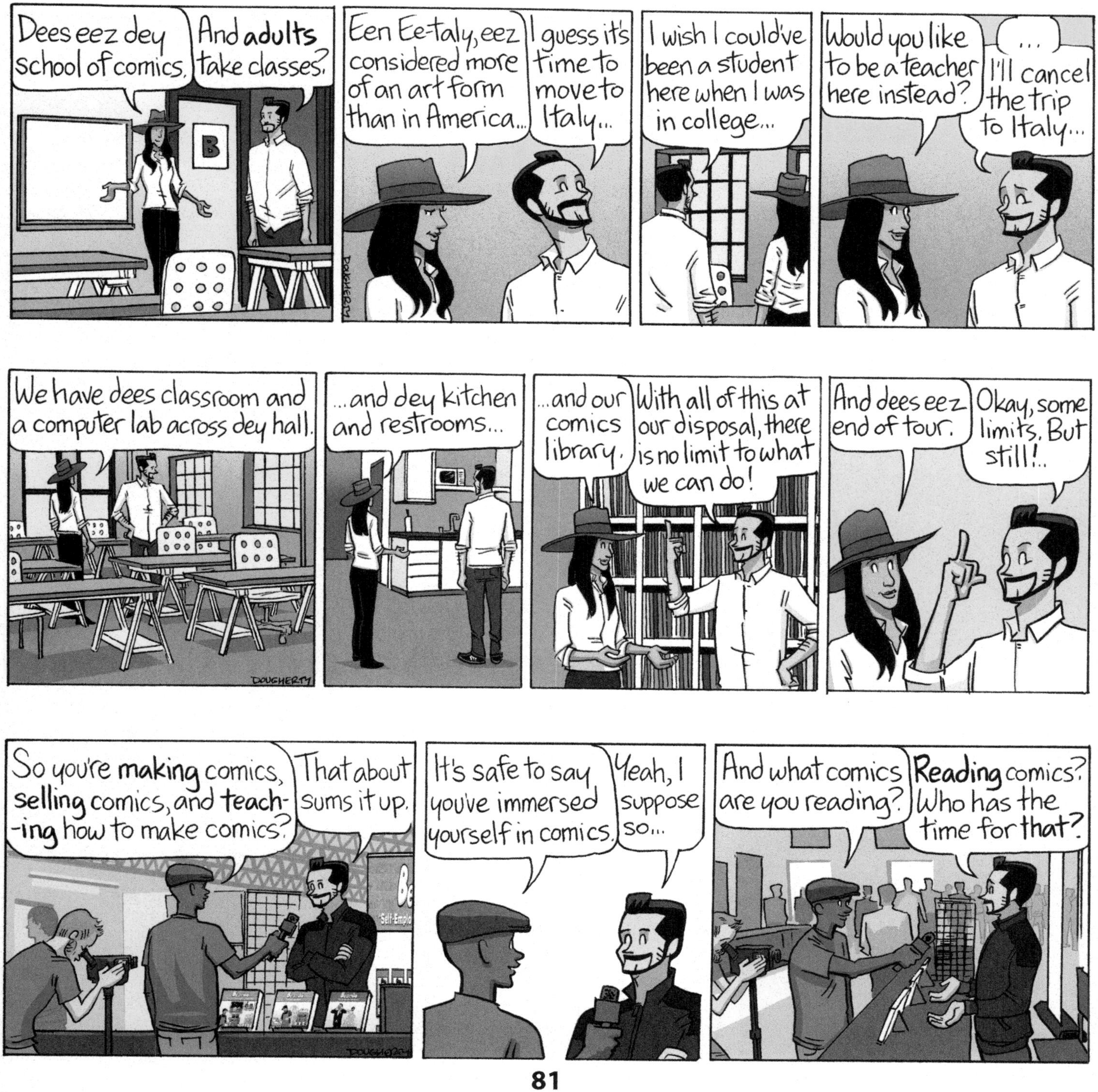
Dees eez dey school of comics.
And adults take classes?
Een Ee-taly, eez considered more of an art form than in America...
I guess it's time to move to Italy...
DOUGHERTY
I wish I could've been a student here when I was in college...
Would you like to be a teacher here instead?
...
I'll cancel the trip to Italy...
We have dees classroom and a computer lab across dey hall.
DOUGHERTY
...and dey kitchen and restrooms...
...and our comics library.
With all of this at our disposal, there is no limit to what we can do!
And dees eez end of tour.
Okay, some limits. But still!..
So you're making comics, selling comics, and teach-ing how to make comics?
That about sums it up.
DOUGHERTY
It's safe to say you've immersed yourself in comics.
Yeah, I suppose so...
And what comics are you reading?
Reading comics? Who has the time for that?

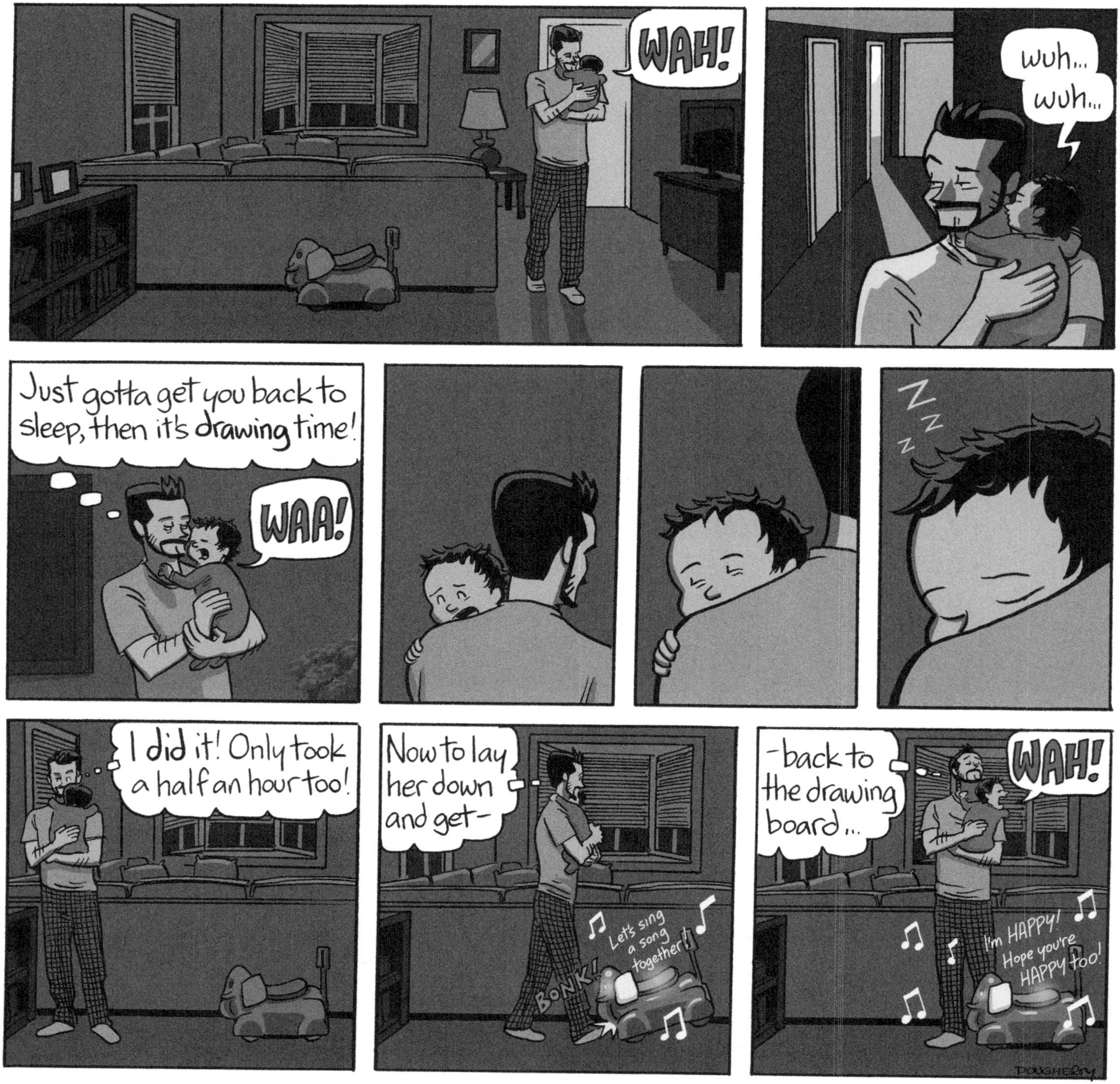
WAH!
wuh... wuh...
Just gotta get you back to sleep, then it's drawing time!
WAA!
Z Z Z
I did it! Only took a half an hour too!
Now to lay her down and get-
BONK!
Let's sing a song together!
-back to the drawing board...
WAH!
I'm HAPPY! Hope you're HAPPY too!
DOUGHERTY

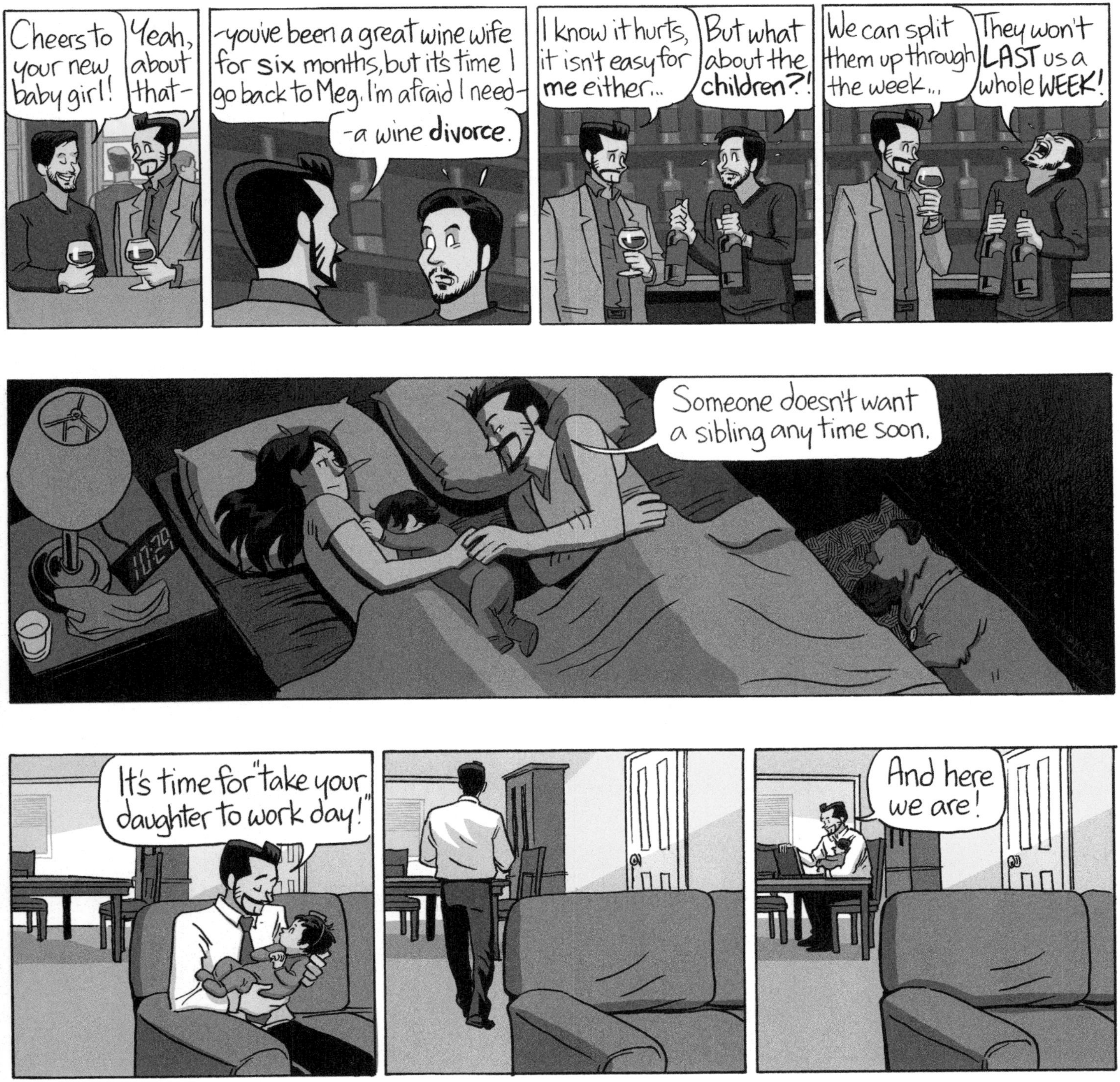
Cheers to your new baby girl!
Yeah, about that-
-you've been a great wine wife for six months, but it's time I go back to Meg. I'm afraid I need-
-a wine divorce.
I know it hurts, it isn't easy for me either...
But what about the children?!
We can split them up through the week...
They won't LAST us a whole WEEK!
Someone doesn't want a sibling any time soon.
It's time for "take your daughter to work day!"
And here we are!

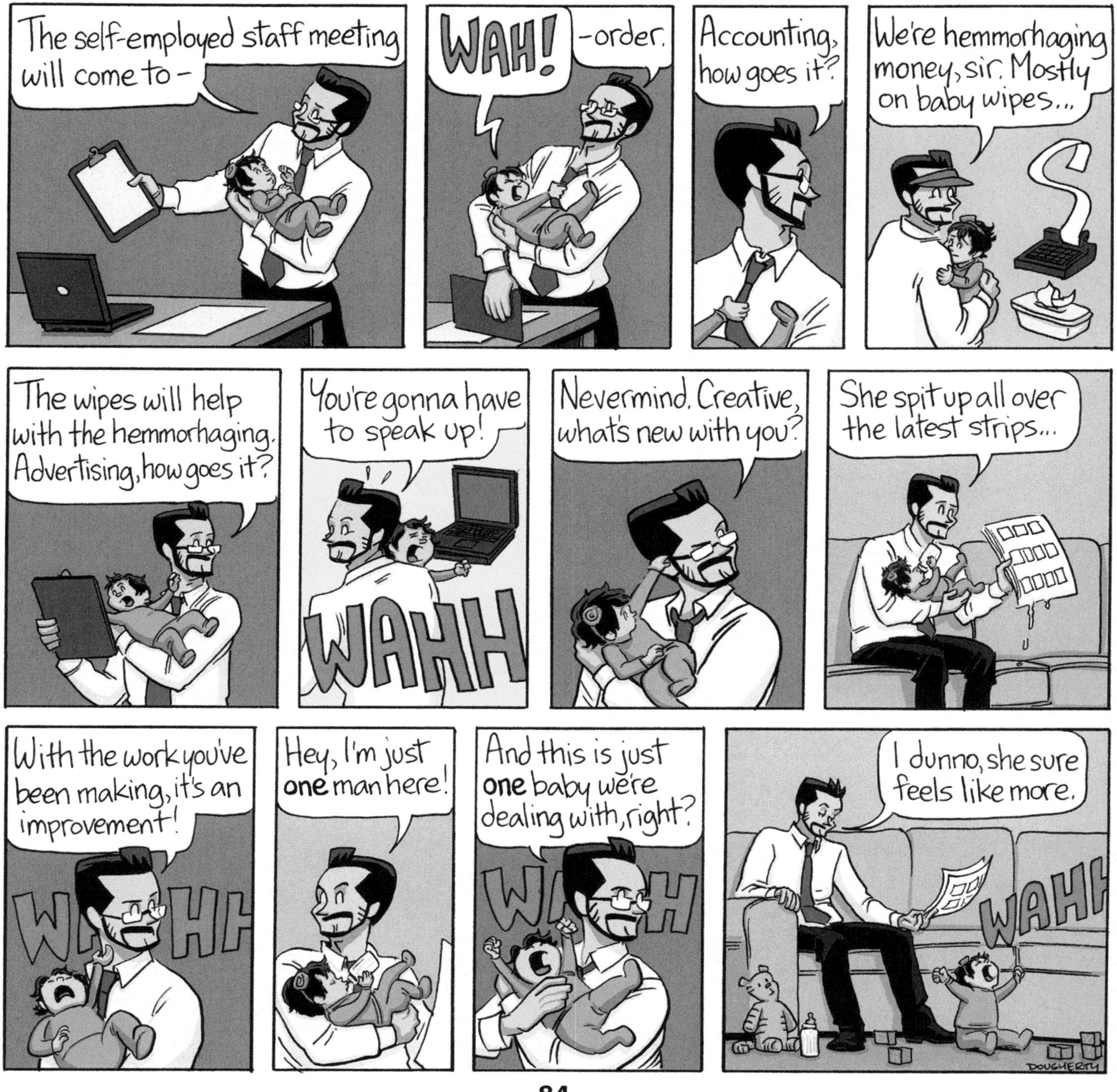
The self-employed staff meeting will come to -
WAH!
-order.
Accounting, how goes it?
We're hemmorhaging money, sir. Mostly on baby wipes...
The wipes will help with the hemmorhaging. Advertising, how goes it?
You're gonna have to speak up!
WAHH
Nevermind. Creative, what's new with you?
She spit up all over the latest strips...
With the work you've been making, it's an improvement!
Hey, I'm just **one** man here!
And this is just **one** baby we're dealing with, right?
I dunno, she sure feels like more.
WAHH
DOUGHERTY

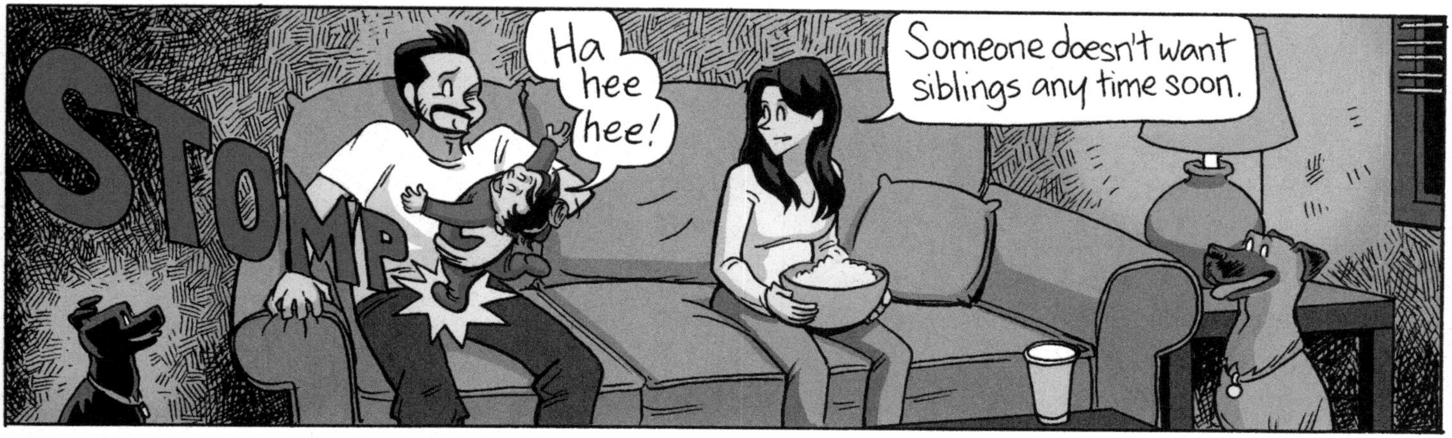
STOMP
Ha hee hee!
Someone doesn't want siblings any time soon.

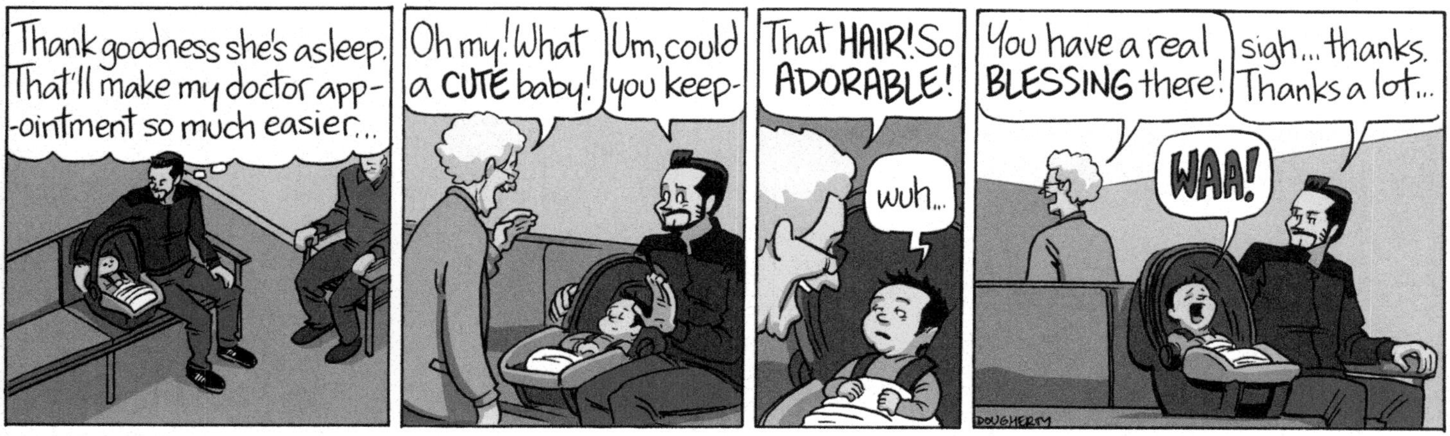
Thank goodness she's asleep. That'll make my doctor app-
-ointment so much easier...
Oh my! What a **CUTE** baby!
Um, could you keep-
That **HAIR!** So **ADORABLE!**
wuh...
You have a real **BLESSING** there!
WAA!
sigh... thanks. Thanks a lot...
DOUGHERTY

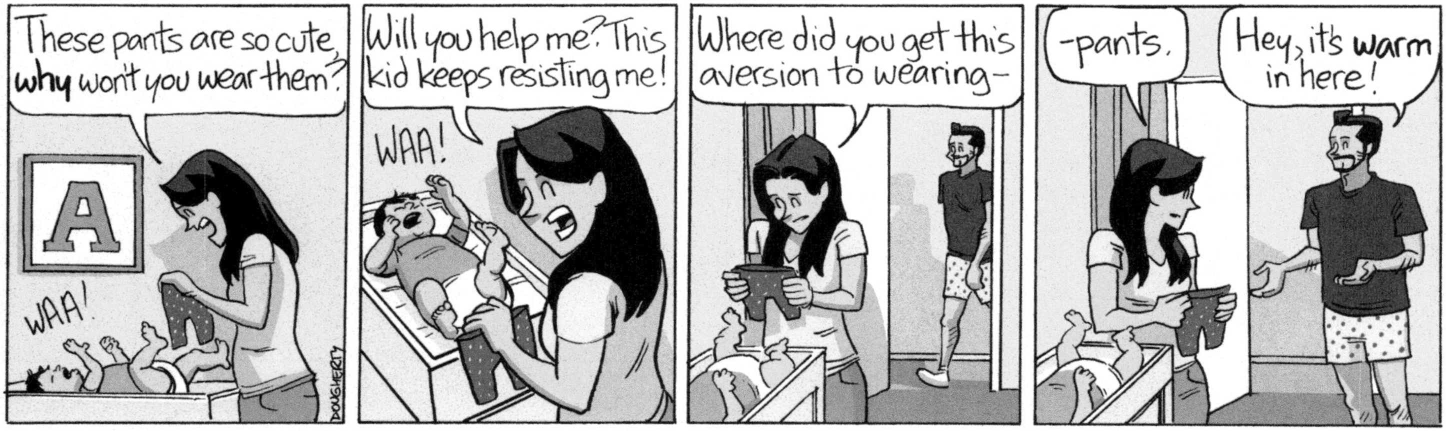
These pants are so cute, **why** won't you wear them?
WAA!
DOUGHERTY
Will you help me? This kid keeps resisting me!
WAA!
Where did you get this aversion to wearing-
-pants.
Hey, it's **warm** in here!

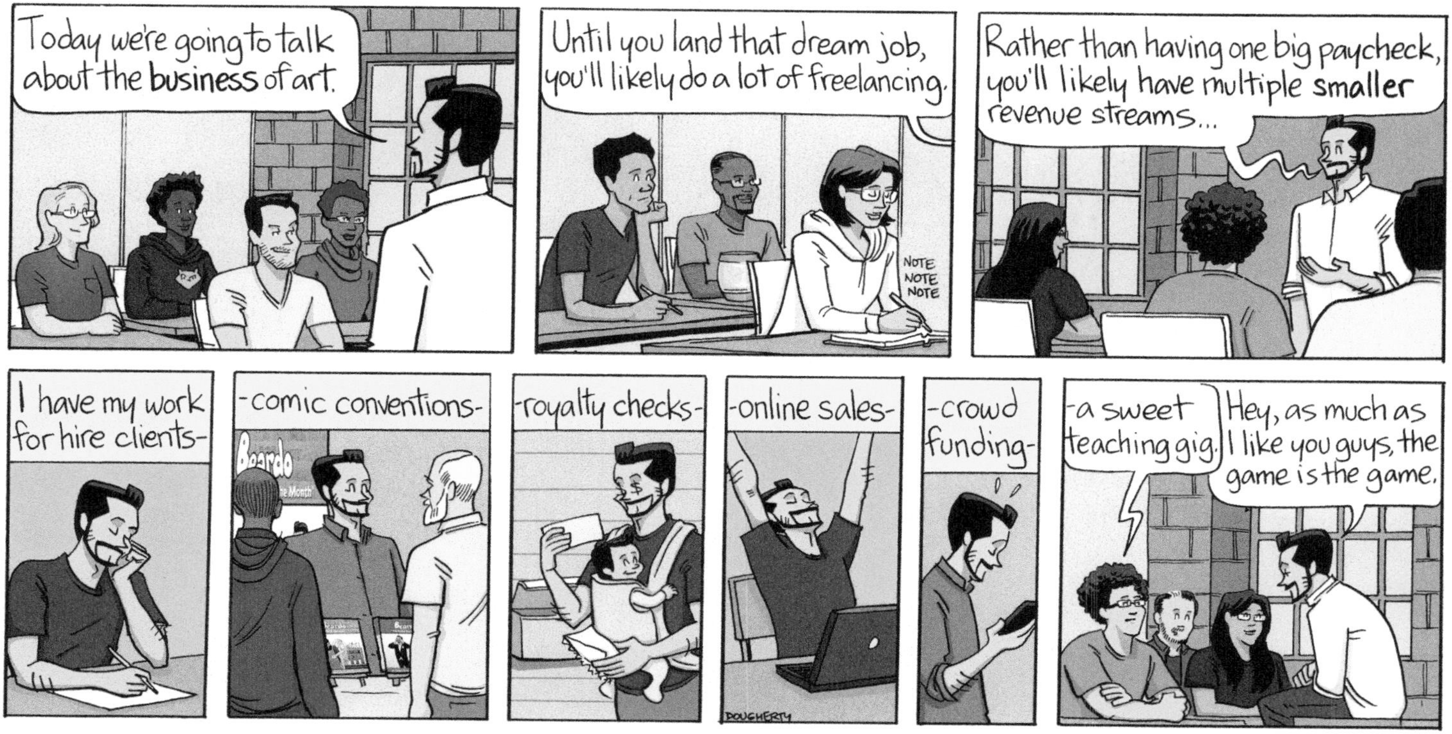
Today we're going to talk about the **business** of art.
Until you land that dream job, you'll likely do a lot of freelancing.
NOTE NOTE NOTE
Rather than having one big paycheck, you'll likely have multiple **smaller** revenue streams...
I have my work for hire clients-
-comic conventions-
Beardo
-royalty checks-
-online sales-
DOUGHERTY
-crowd funding-
-a sweet teaching gig.
Hey, as much as I like you guys, the game is the game.

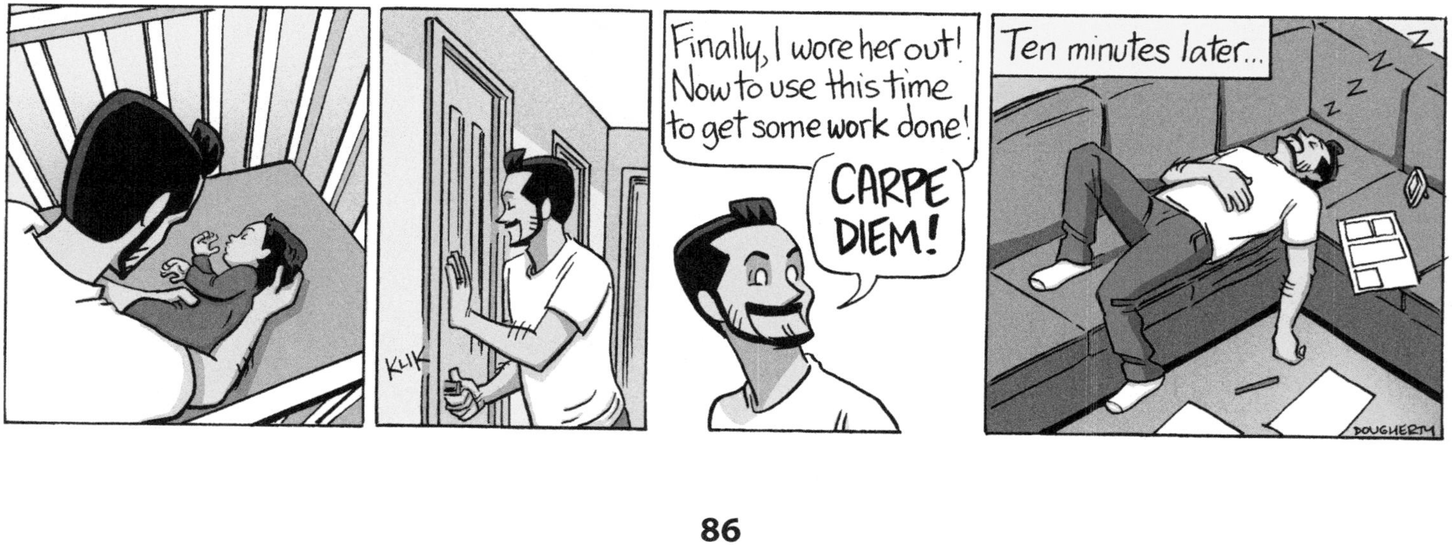
KLIK
Finally, I wore her out! Now to use this time to get some **work** done!
CARPE DIEM!
Ten minutes later...
Z Z Z
DOUGHERTY

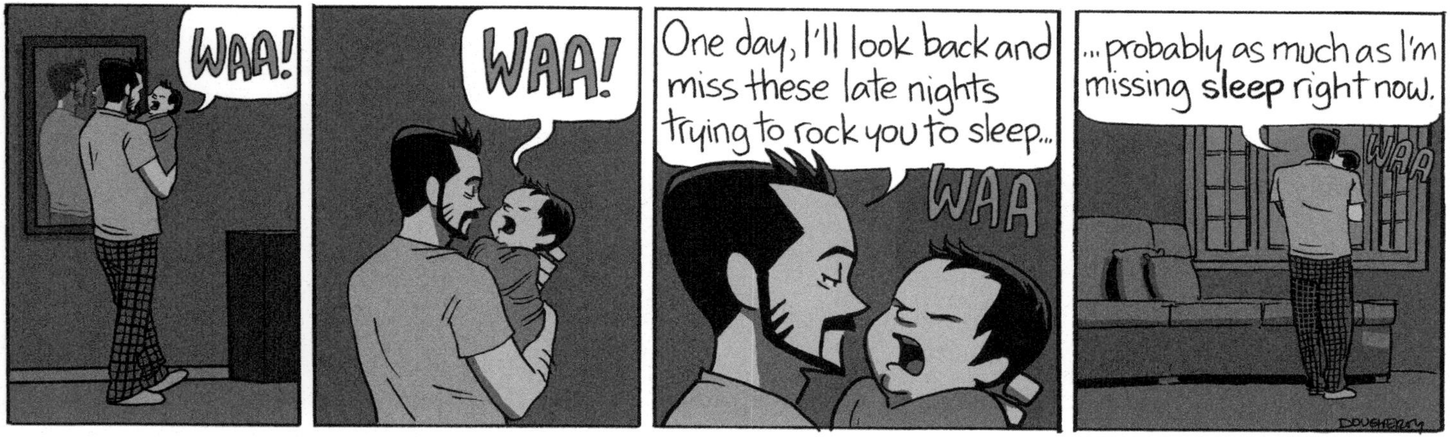
WAA!
WAA!
One day, I'll look back and miss these late nights trying to rock you to sleep...
WAA
...probably as much as I'm missing **sleep** right now.
WAA
DOUGHERTY

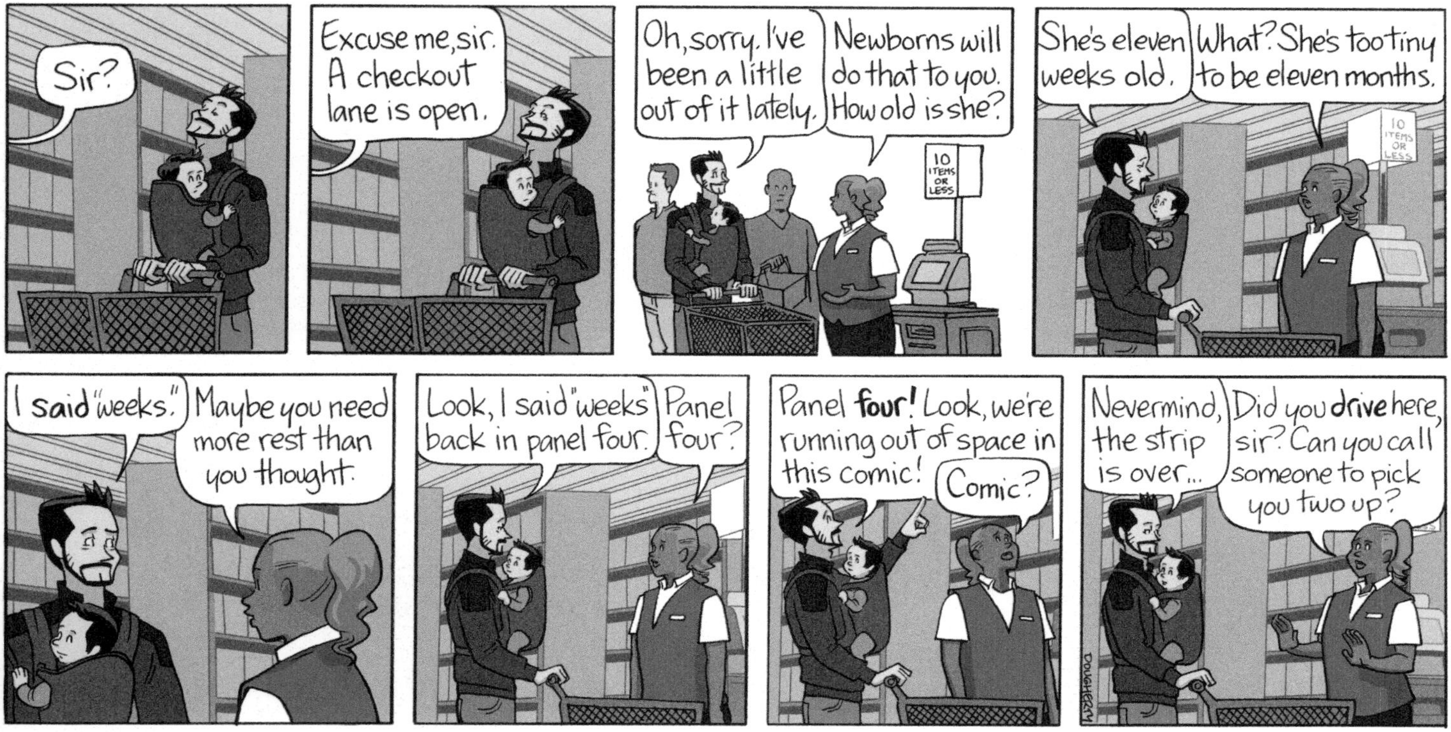
Sir?
Excuse me, sir. A checkout lane is open.
Oh, sorry. I've been a little out of it lately.
Newborns will do that to you. How old is she?
10 ITEMS OR LESS
She's eleven weeks old.
What? She's too tiny to be eleven months.
10 ITEMS OR LESS
I **said** "weeks."
Maybe you need more rest than you thought.
Look, I said "weeks" back in panel four.
Panel four?
Panel **four!** Look, we're running out of space in this comic!
Comic?
Nevermind, the strip is over...
Did you **drive** here, sir? Can you call someone to pick you two up?

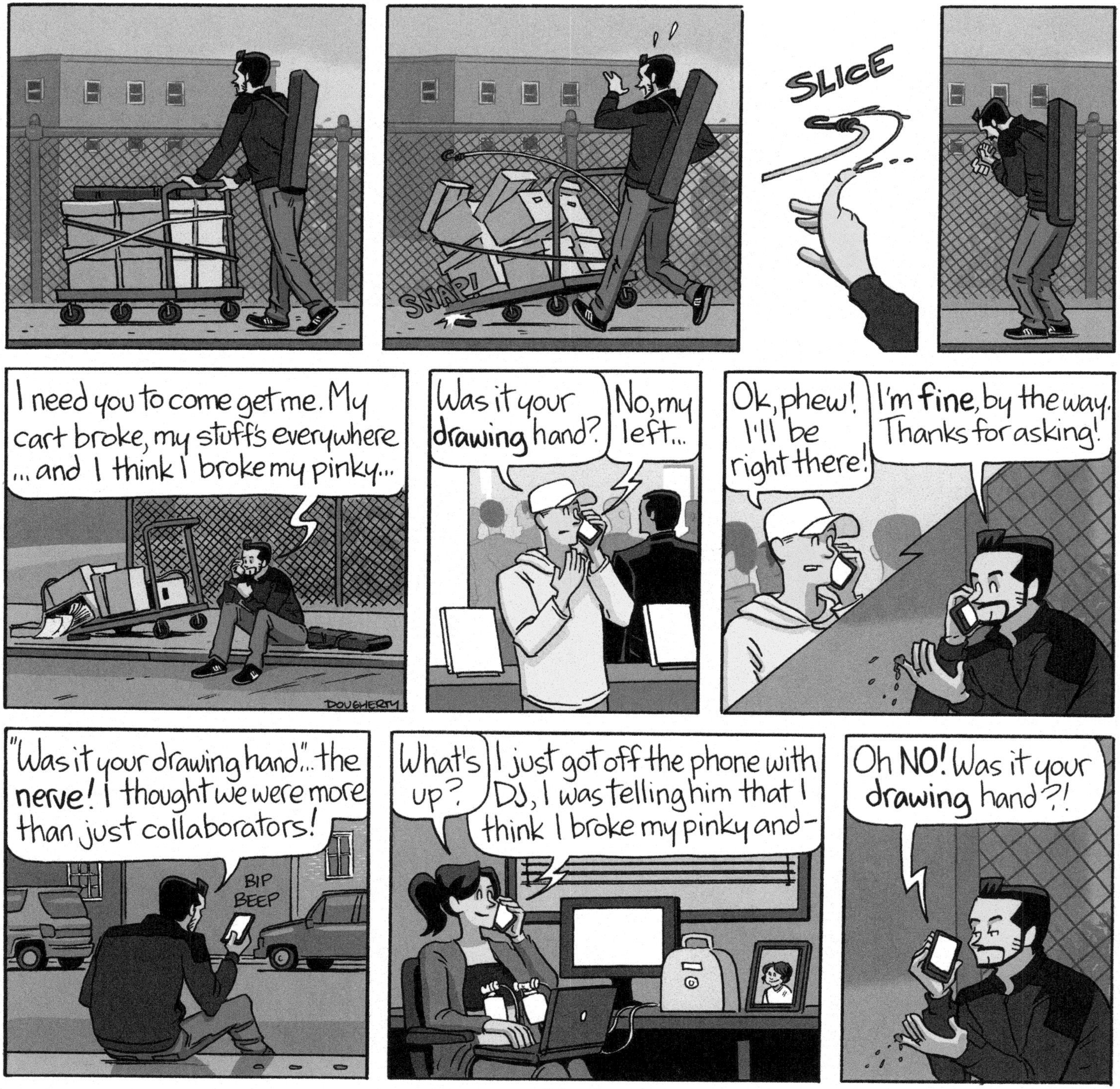
SNAP!
SLICE
I need you to come get me. My cart broke, my stuff's everywhere ... and I think I broke my pinky...
DOUGHERTY
Was it your **drawing** hand?
No, my left...
Ok, phew! I'll be right there!
I'm **fine**, by the way. Thanks for asking!
"Was it your drawing hand"... the **nerve**! I thought we were more than just collaborators!
BIP BEEP
What's up?
I just got off the phone with DJ, I was telling him that I think I broke my pinky and-
Oh **NO**! Was it your **drawing** hand?!

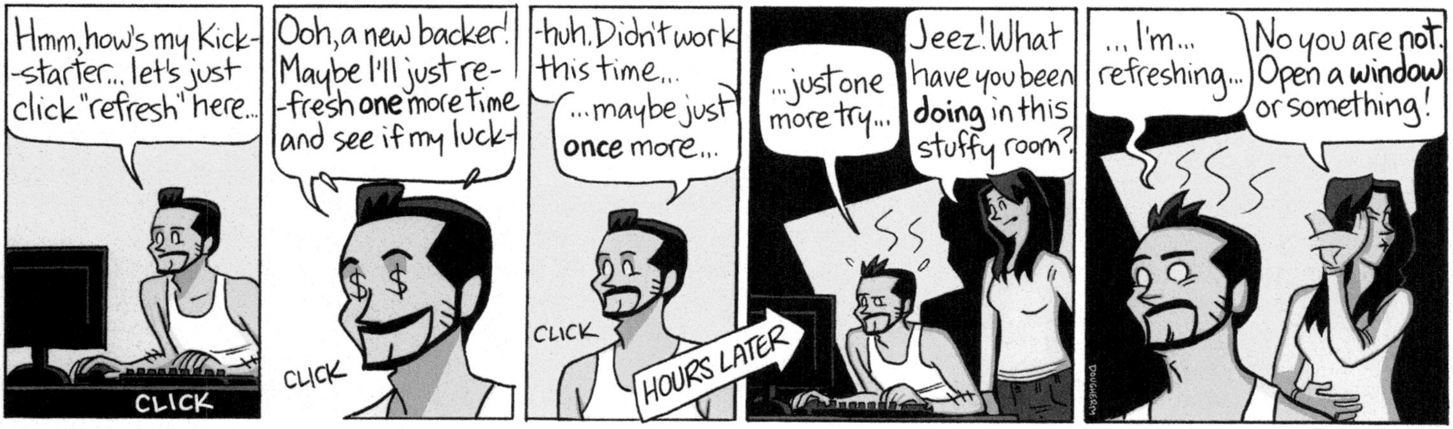
Hmm, how's my Kick- -starter... let's just click "refresh" here...
CLICK
Ooh, a new backer! Maybe I'll just re- -fresh **one** more time and see if my luck-
CLICK
-huh. Didn't work this time...
...maybe just **once** more...
CLICK
HOURS LATER
...just one more try...
Jeez! What have you been **doing** in this stuffy room?
...I'm... refreshing...
No you are **not**. Open a **window** or something!

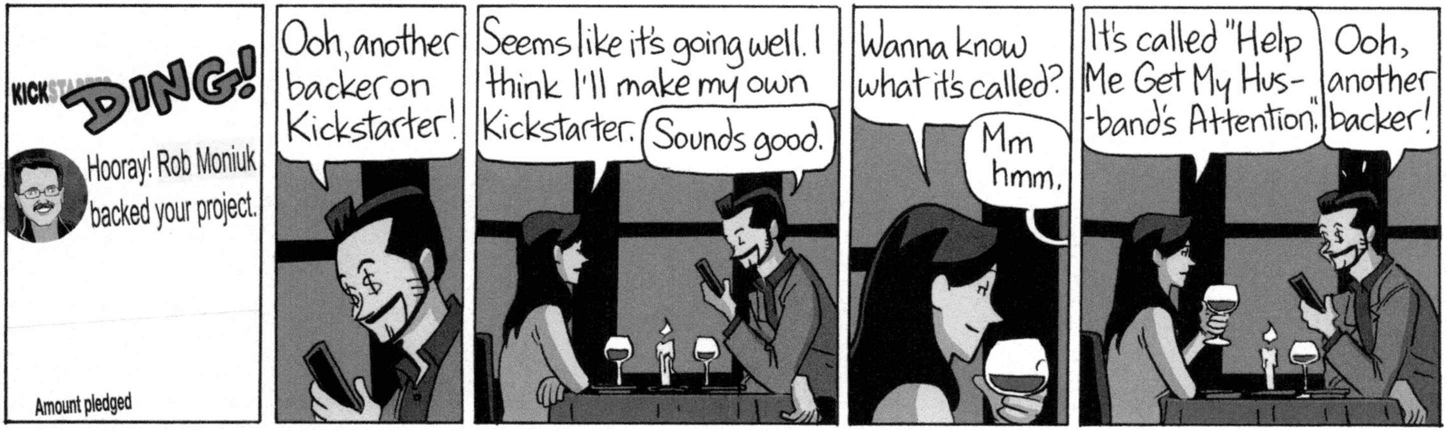
KICK
DING!
Hooray! Rob Moniuk backed your project.
Amount pledged
Ooh, another backer on Kickstarter!
Seems like it's going well. I think I'll make my own Kickstarter.
Sounds good.
Wanna know what it's called?
Mm hmm.
It's called "Help Me Get My Hus- -band's Attention".
Ooh, another backer!

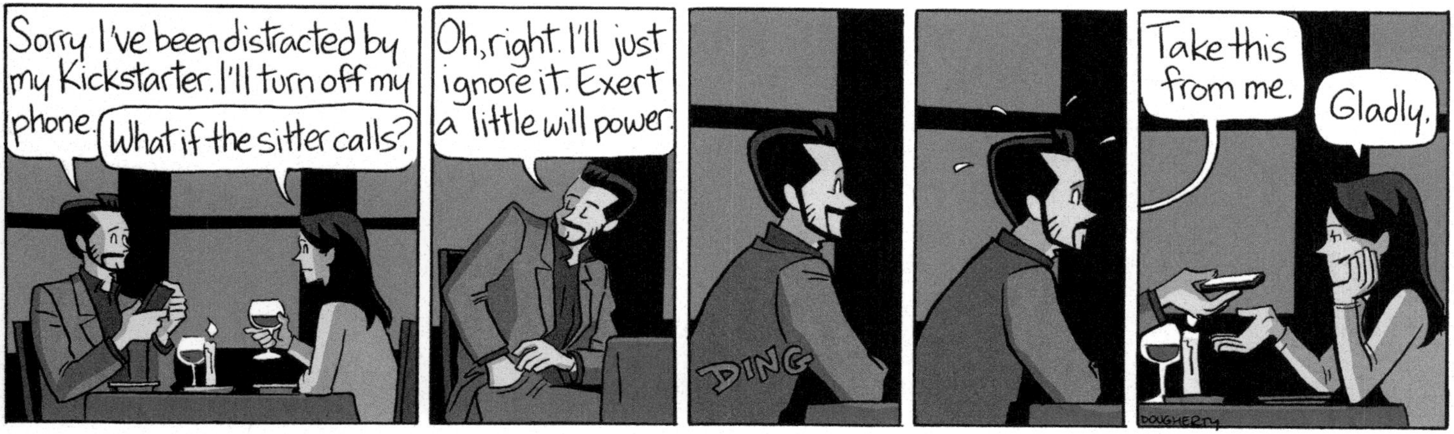
Sorry I've been distracted by my Kickstarter. I'll turn off my phone.
What if the sitter calls?
Oh, right. I'll just ignore it. Exert a little will power.
DING
Take this from me.
Gladly.

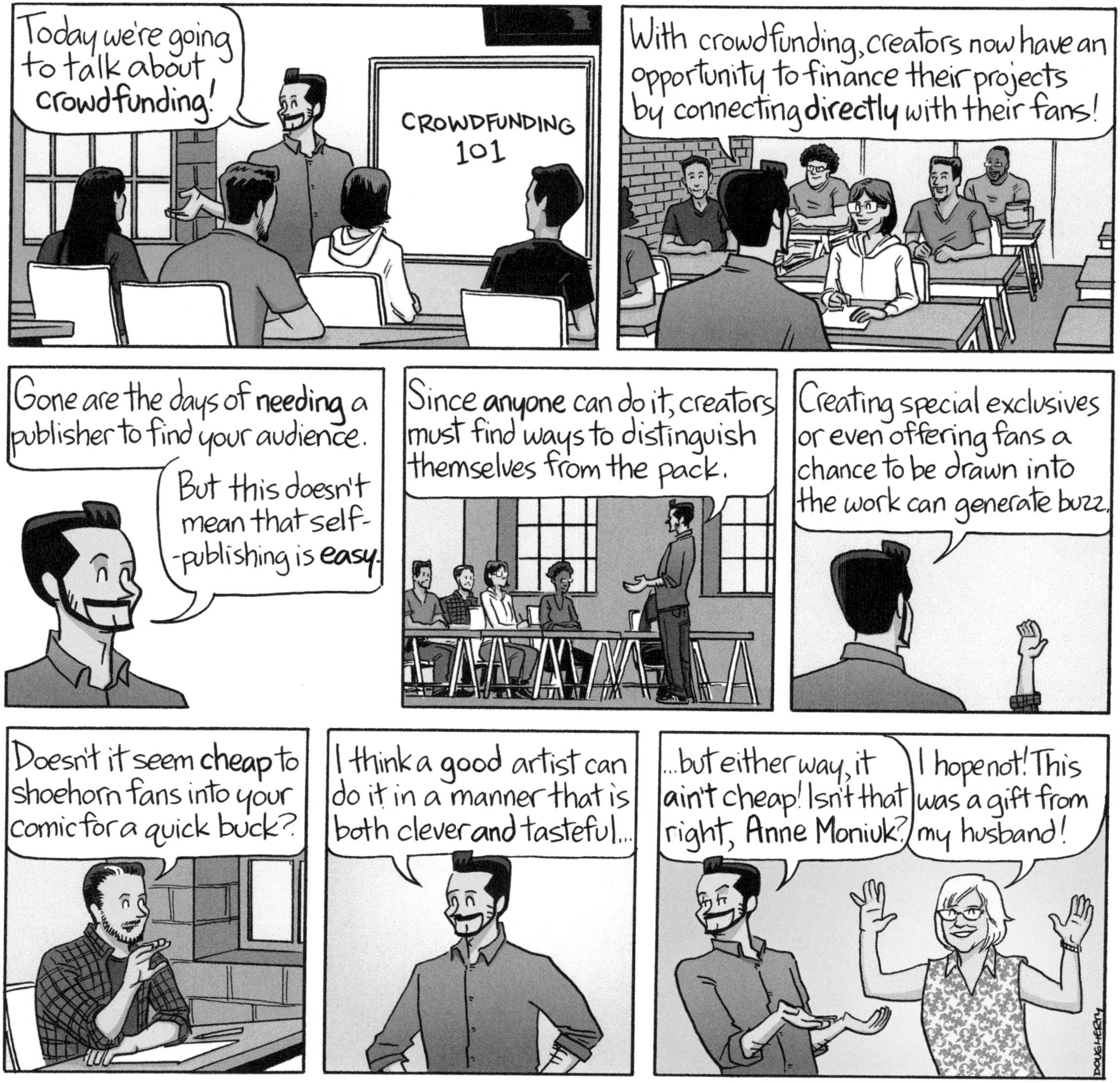
Today we're going to talk about crowdfunding!
CROWDFUNDING 101
With crowdfunding, creators now have an opportunity to finance their projects by connecting directly with their fans!
Gone are the days of needing a publisher to find your audience.
But this doesn't mean that self--publishing is easy.
Since anyone can do it, creators must find ways to distinguish themselves from the pack.
Creating special exclusives or even offering fans a chance to be drawn into the work can generate buzz.
Doesn't it seem cheap to shoehorn fans into your comic for a quick buck?
I think a good artist can do it in a manner that is both clever and tasteful...
...but either way, it ain't cheap! Isn't that right, Anne Moniuk?
I hope not! This was a gift from my husband!
DOUGHERTY

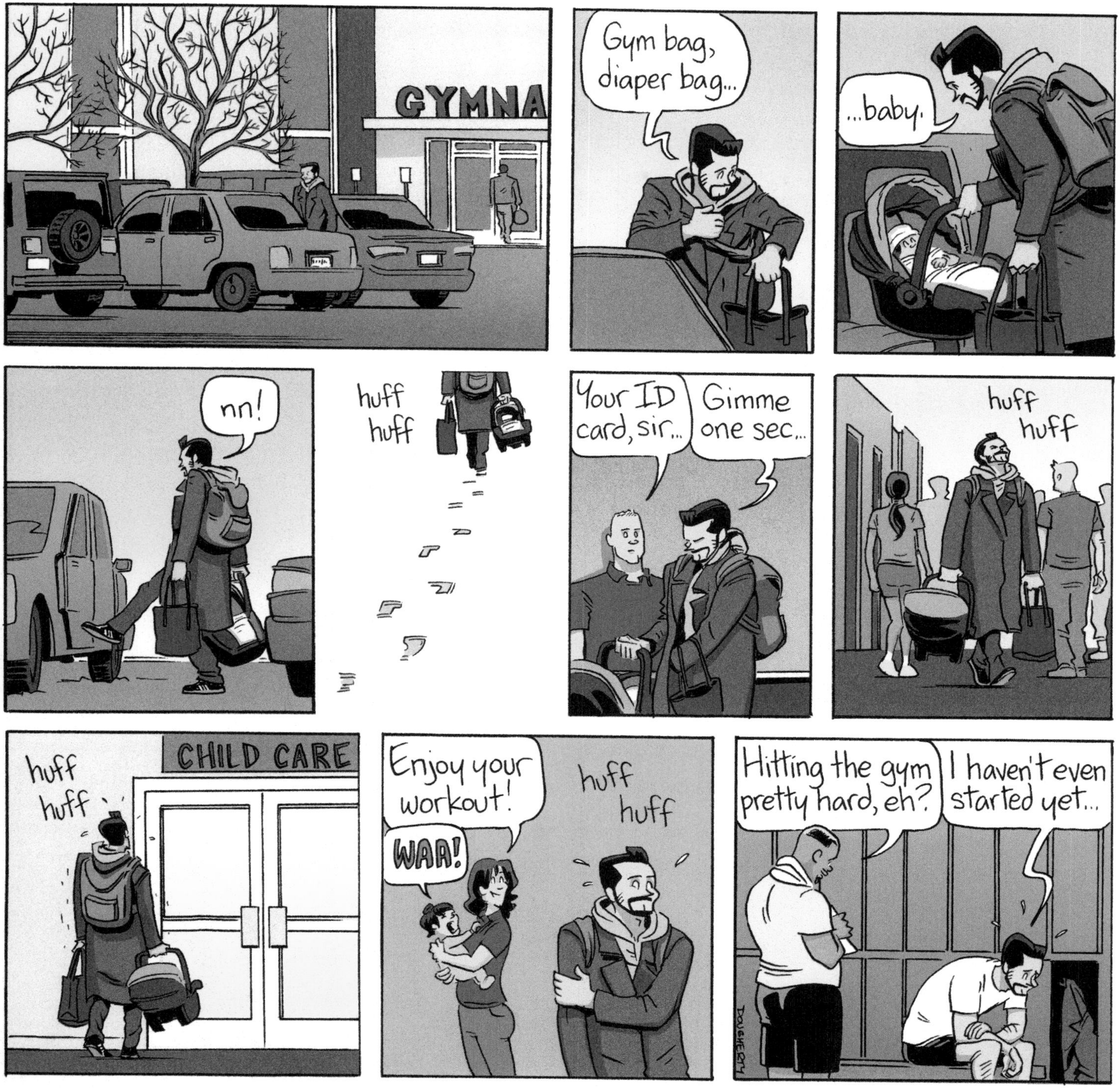
GYMNA
Gym bag, diaper bag...
...baby.
nn!
huff huff
Your ID card, sir...
Gimme one sec...
huff huff
CHILD CARE
huff huff
Enjoy your workout!
WAA!
huff huff
Hitting the gym pretty hard, eh?
I haven't even started yet...
DOUGHERTY

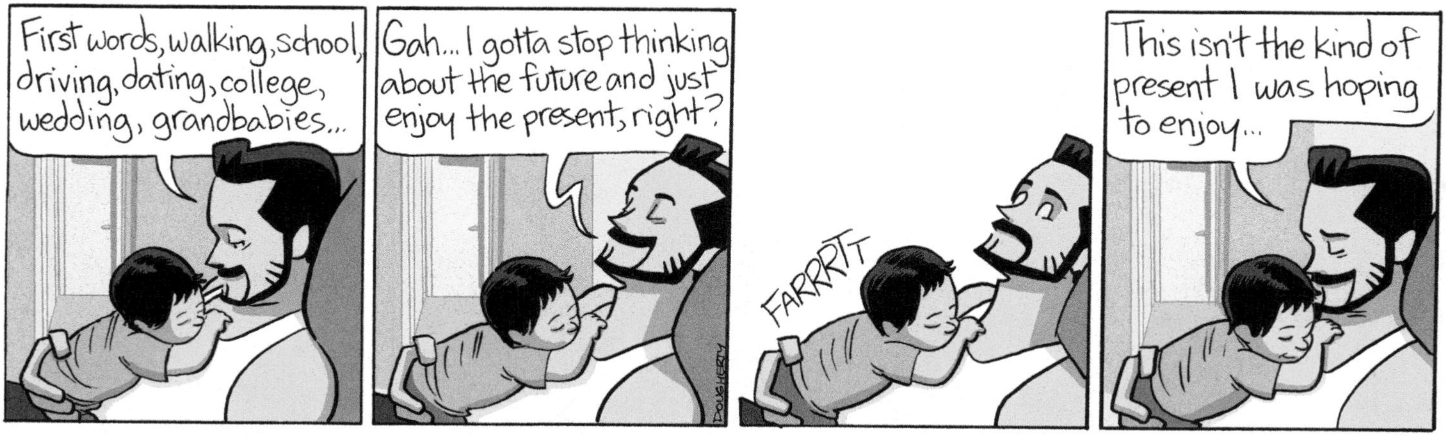
First words, walking, school, driving, dating, college, wedding, grandbabies...
Gah... I gotta stop thinking about the future and just enjoy the present, right?
DOUGHERTY
FARRRTT
This isn't the kind of present I was hoping to enjoy...

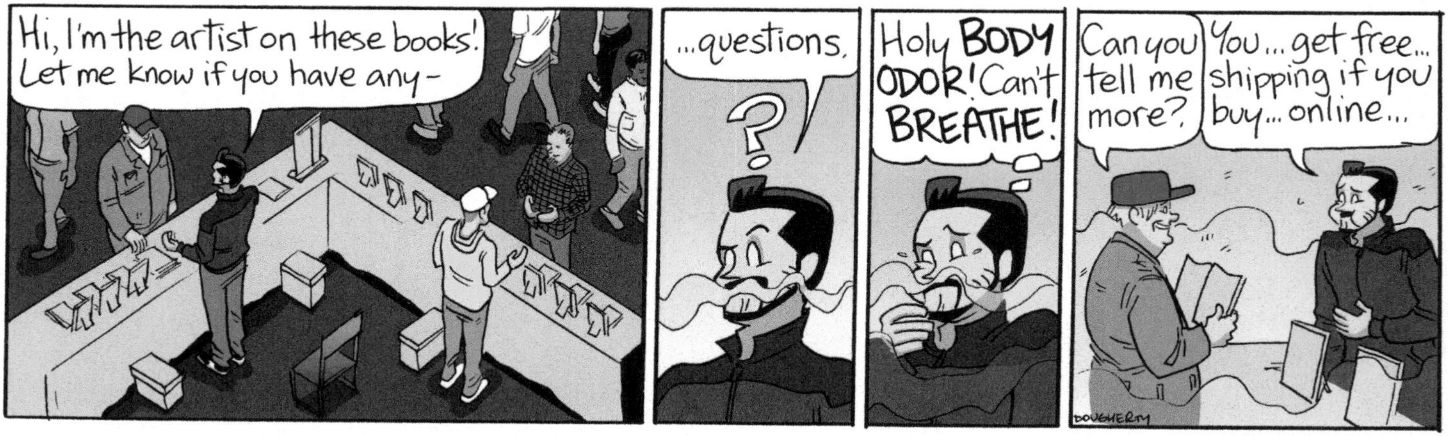
Hi, I'm the artist on these books! Let me know if you have any-
...questions.
?
Holy BODY ODOR! Can't BREATHE!
Can you tell me more?
You... get free... shipping if you buy... online...
DOUGHERTY

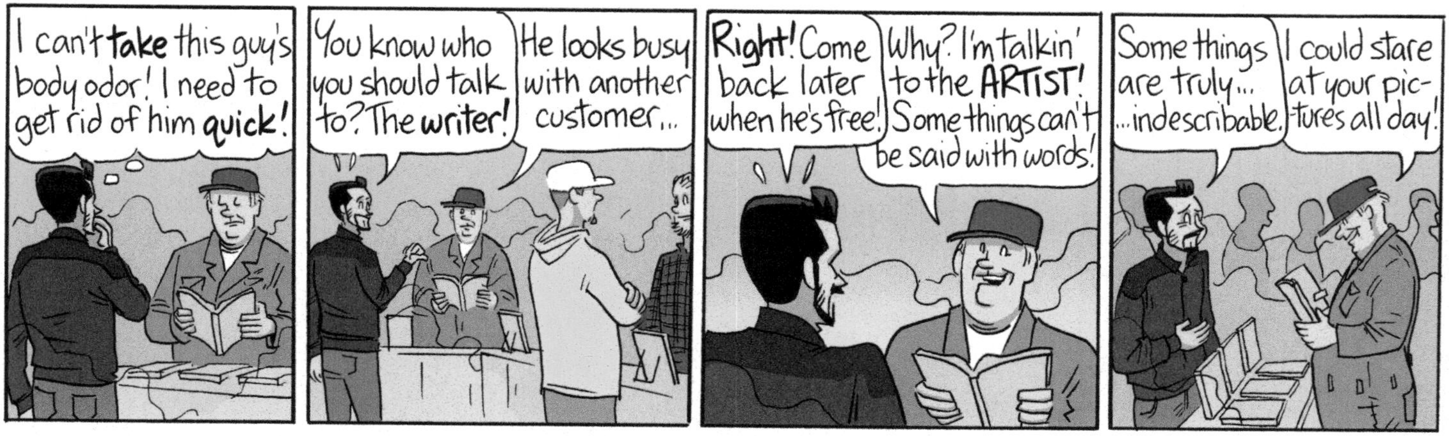
I can't take this guy's body odor! I need to get rid of him quick!
You know who you should talk to? The writer!
He looks busy with another customer...
Right! Come back later when he's free!
Why? I'm talkin' to the ARTIST! Some things can't be said with words!
Some things are truly... ...indescribable.
I could stare at your pic-tures all day!

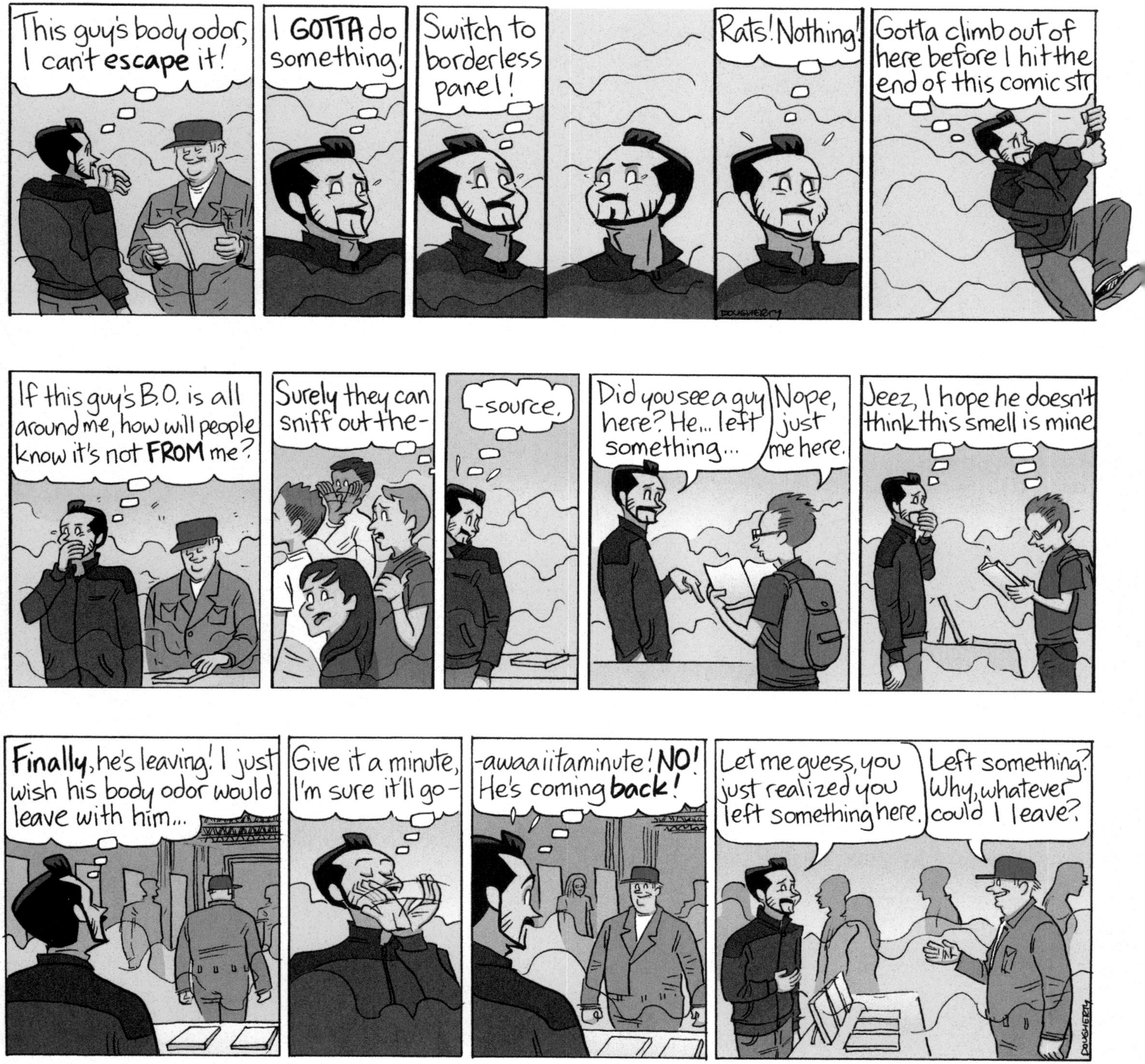
This guy's body odor, I can't escape it!
I GOTTA do something!
Switch to borderless panel!
Rats! Nothing!
Gotta climb out of here before I hit the end of this comic str
DOUGHERTY
If this guy's B.O. is all around me, how will people know it's not FROM me?
Surely they can sniff out the-
-source.
Did you see a guy here? He... left something...
Nope, just me here.
Jeez, I hope he doesn't think this smell is mine
Finally, he's leaving! I just wish his body odor would leave with him...
Give it a minute, I'm sure it'll go-
-awaaiitaminute! NO! He's coming back!
Let me guess, you just realized you left something here.
Left something? Why, whatever could I leave?
DOUGHERTY

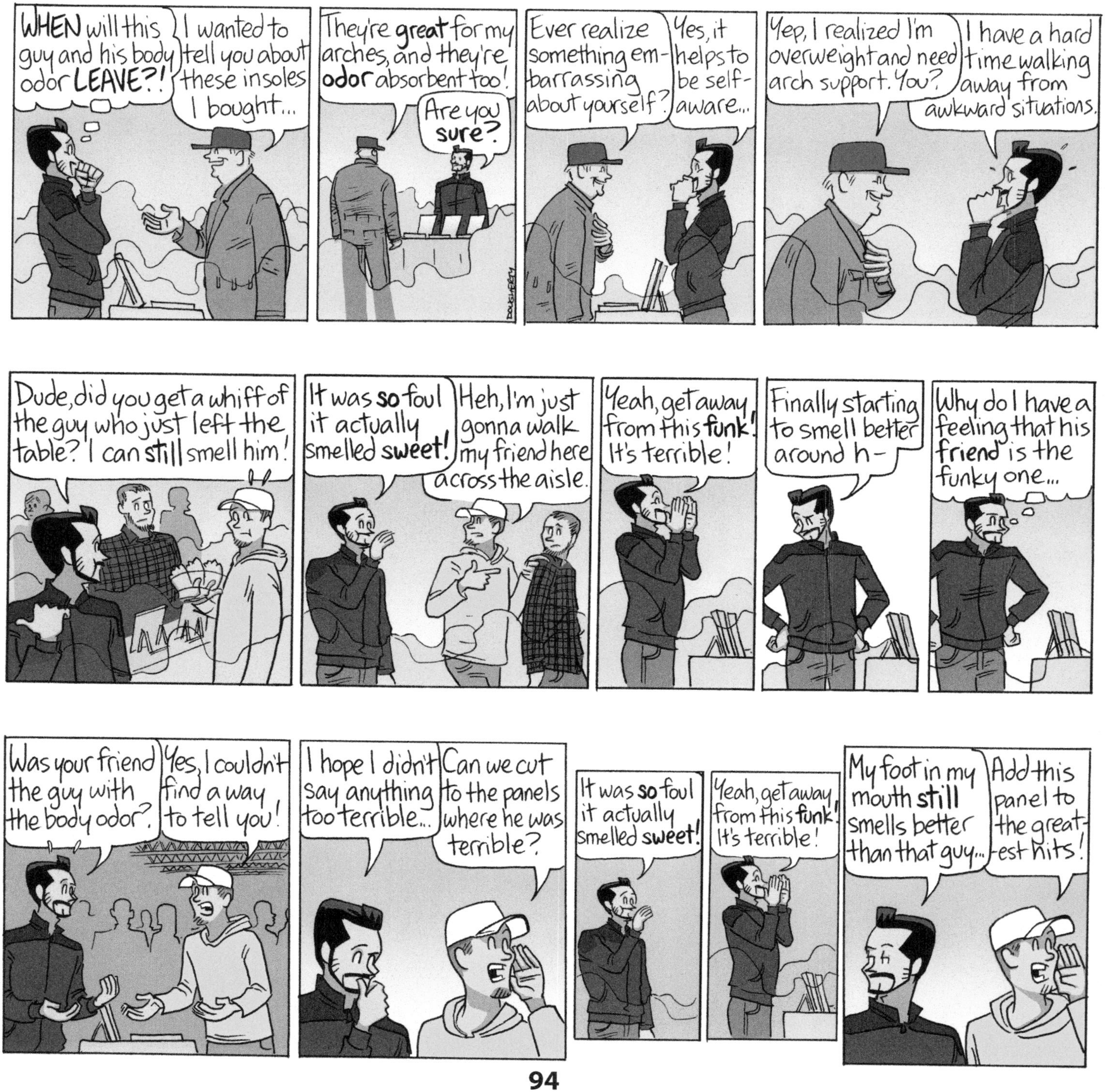
WHEN will this guy and his body odor LEAVE?!
I wanted to tell you about these insoles I bought...
They're great for my arches, and they're odor absorbent too!
Are you sure?
Ever realize something embarrassing about yourself?
Yes, it helps to be self-aware...
Yep, I realized I'm overweight and need arch support. You?
I have a hard time walking away from awkward situations.
Dude, did you get a whiff of the guy who just left the table? I can still smell him!
It was so foul it actually smelled sweet!
Heh, I'm just gonna walk my friend here across the aisle.
Yeah, get away from this funk! It's terrible!
Finally starting to smell better around h–
Why do I have a feeling that his friend is the funky one...
Was your friend the guy with the body odor?
Yes, I couldn't find a way to tell you!
I hope I didn't say anything too terrible...
Can we cut to the panels where he was terrible?
It was so foul it actually smelled sweet!
Yeah, get away from this funk! It's terrible!
My foot in my mouth still smells better than that guy...
Add this panel to the greatest hits!

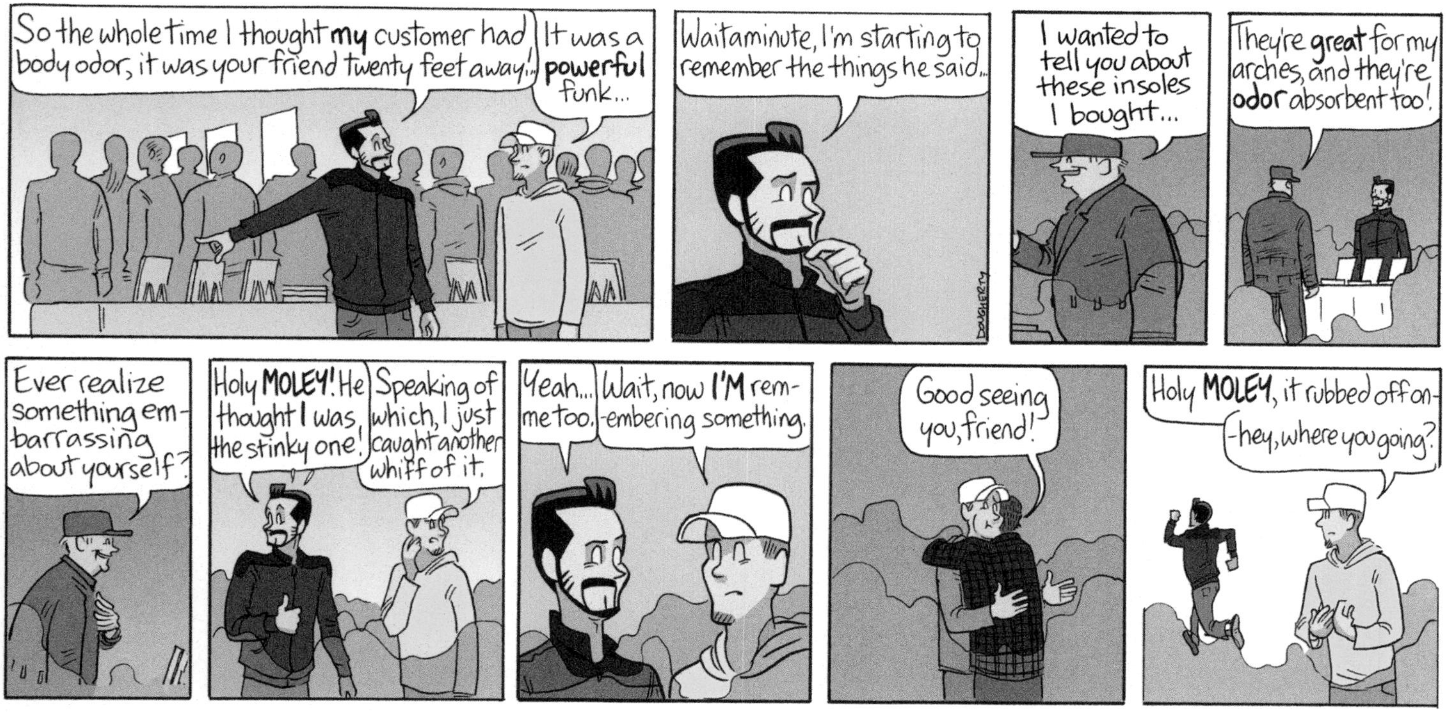
So the whole time I thought **my** customer had body odor, it was your friend twenty feet away!...
It was a **powerful** funk...
Waitaminute, I'm starting to remember the things he said...
DOUGHERTY
I wanted to tell you about these insoles I bought...
They're **great** for my arches, and they're **odor** absorbent too!
Ever realize something embarrassing about yourself?
Holy **MOLEY**! He thought **I** was the stinky one!
Speaking of which, I just caught another whiff of it.
Yeah... me too.
Wait, now **I'M** remembering something.
Good seeing you, friend!
Holy **MOLEY**, it rubbed off on-
-hey, where you going?

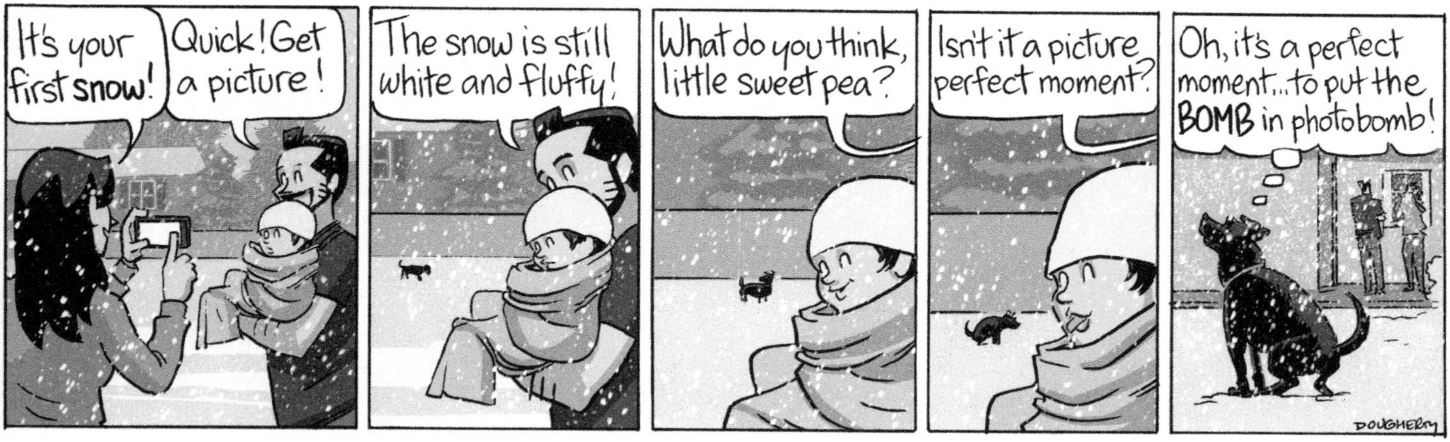
It's your first **snow**!
Quick! Get a picture!
The snow is still white and fluffy!
What do you think, little sweet pea?
Isn't it a picture perfect moment?
Oh, it's a perfect moment... to put the **BOMB** in photobomb!
DOUGHERTY

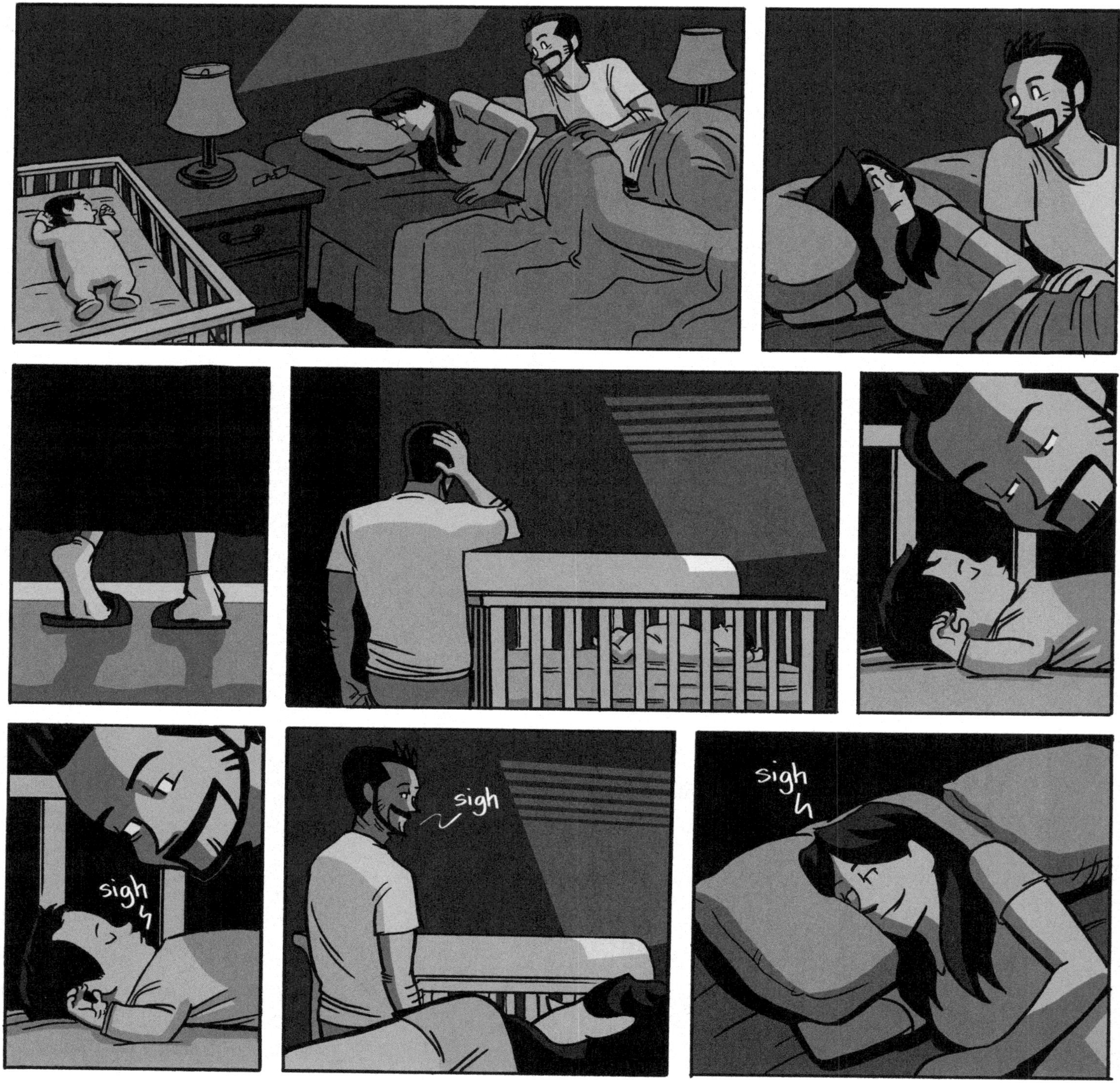
sigh
sigh
sigh

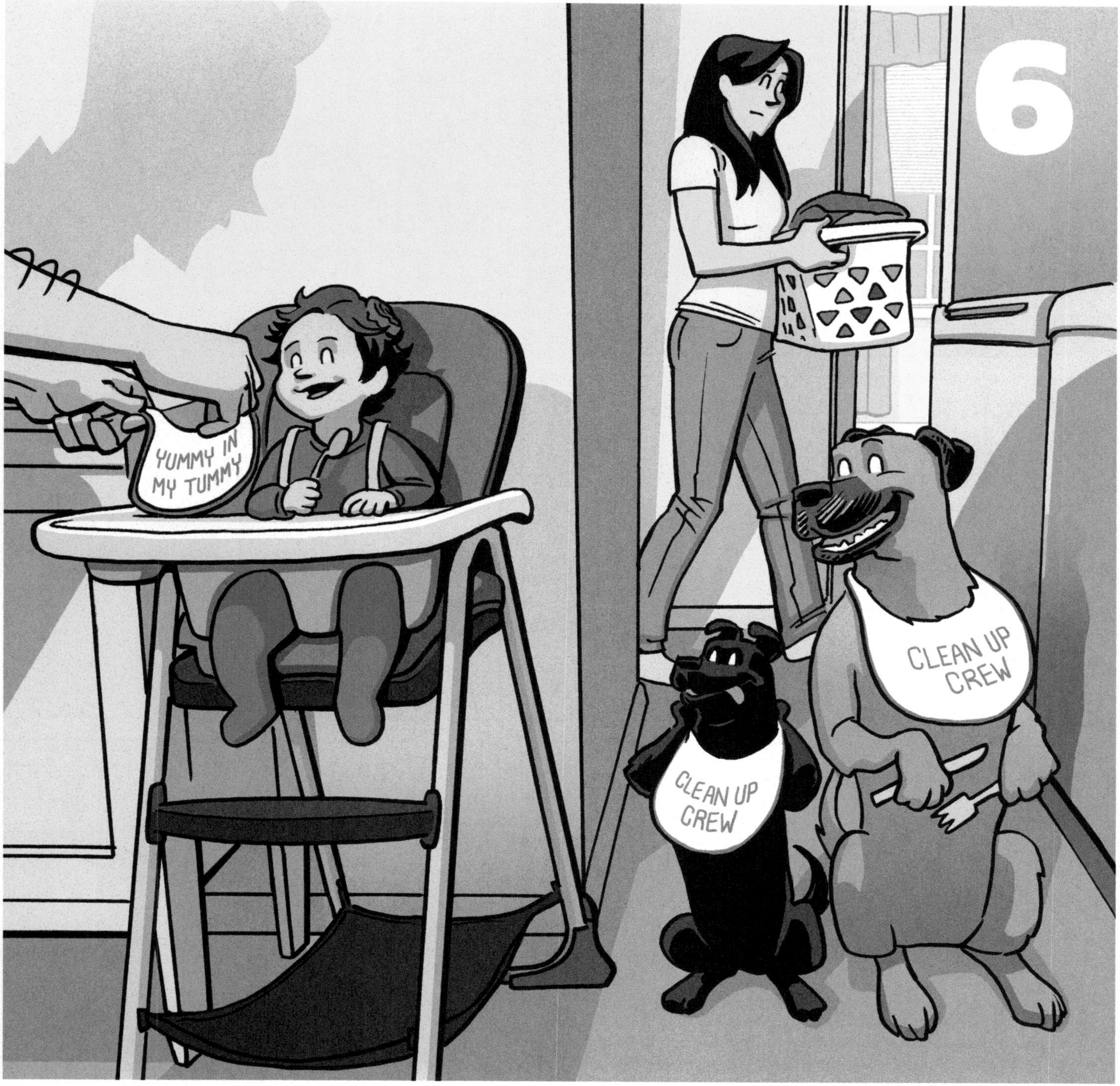
6
YUMMY IN MY TUMMY
CLEAN UP CREW
CLEAN UP CREW

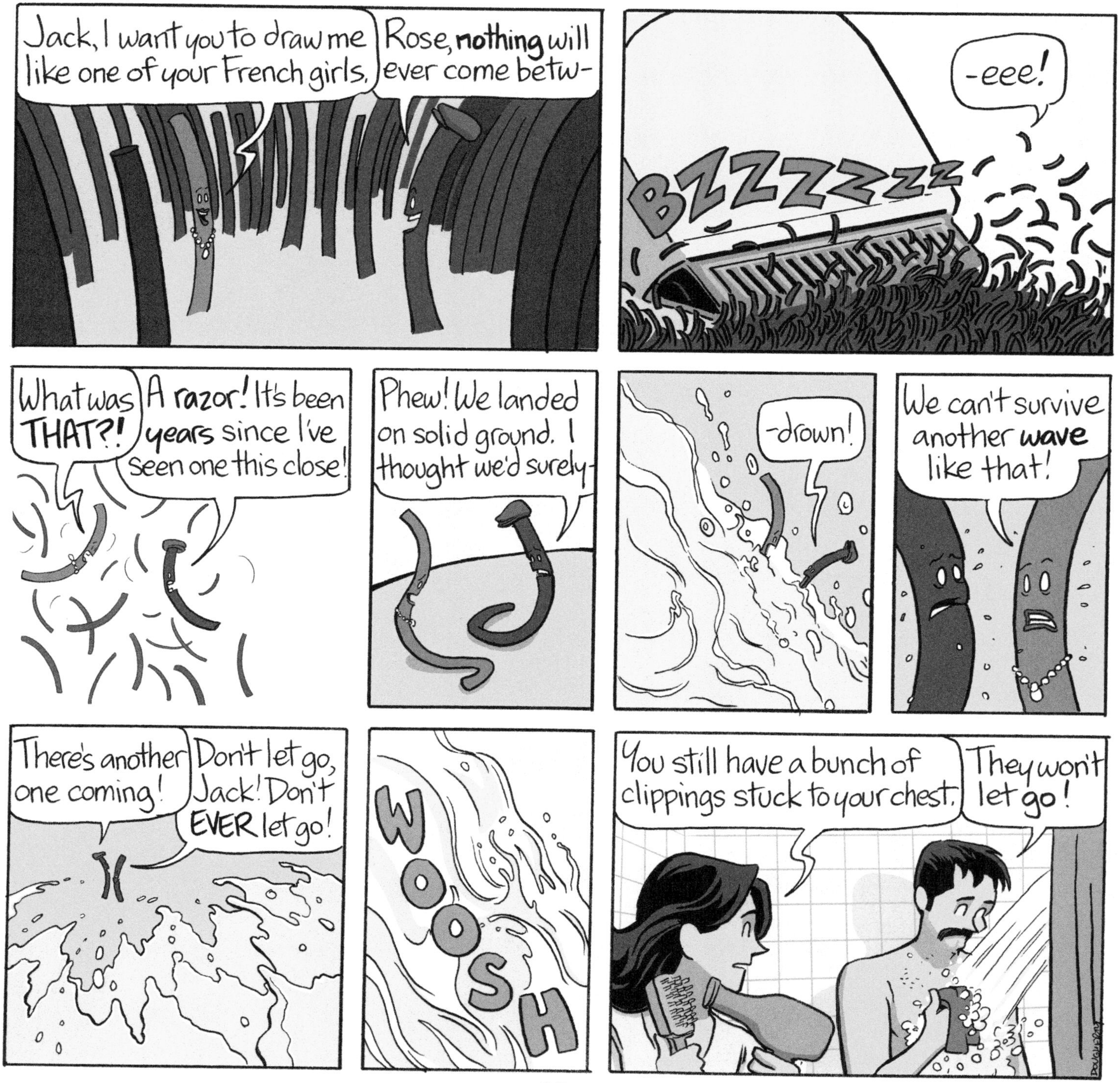
Jack, I want you to draw me like one of your French girls.
Rose, **nothing** will ever come betw-
BZZZZZZ
-eee!
What was **THAT?!**
A **razor!** It's been **years** since I've seen one this close!
Phew! We landed on solid ground. I thought we'd surely-
-drown!
We can't survive another **wave** like that!
There's another one coming!
Don't let go, Jack! Don't **EVER** let go!
WOOSH
You still have a bunch of clippings stuck to your chest.
They won't let **go**!

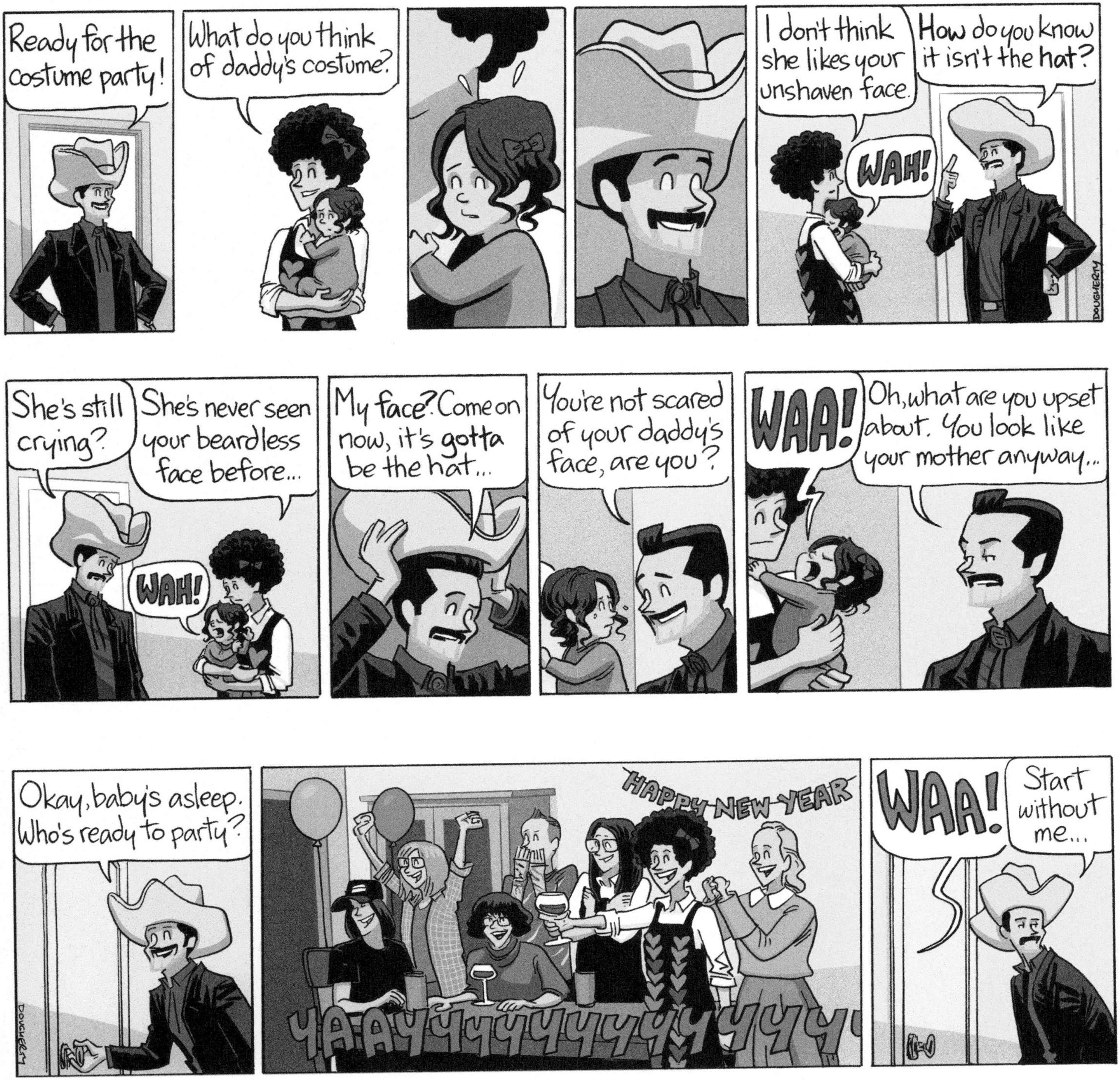
Ready for the costume party!
What do you think of daddy's costume?
I don't think she likes your unshaven face.
WAH!
How do you know it isn't the hat?
She's still crying?
She's never seen your beardless face before...
WAH!
My face? Come on now, it's gotta be the hat...
You're not scared of your daddy's face, are you?
WAA!
Oh, what are you upset about. You look like your mother anyway...
Okay, baby's asleep. Who's ready to party?
HAPPY NEW YEAR
YAAYYYYYYYYYYYYYY
WAA!
Start without me...

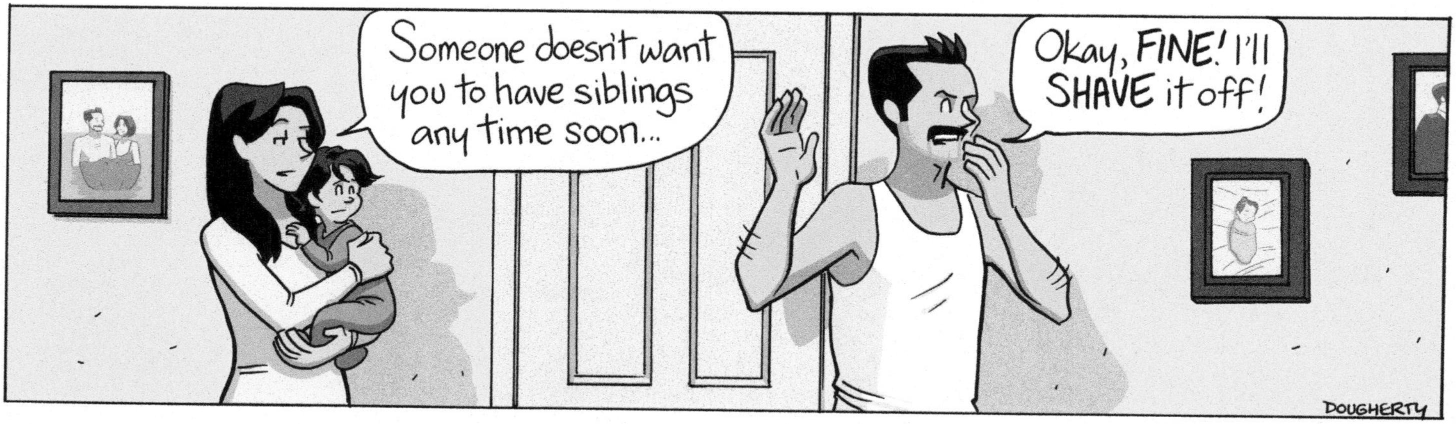
Someone doesn't want you to have siblings any time soon...
Okay, **FINE!** I'll **SHAVE** it off!
DOUGHERTY

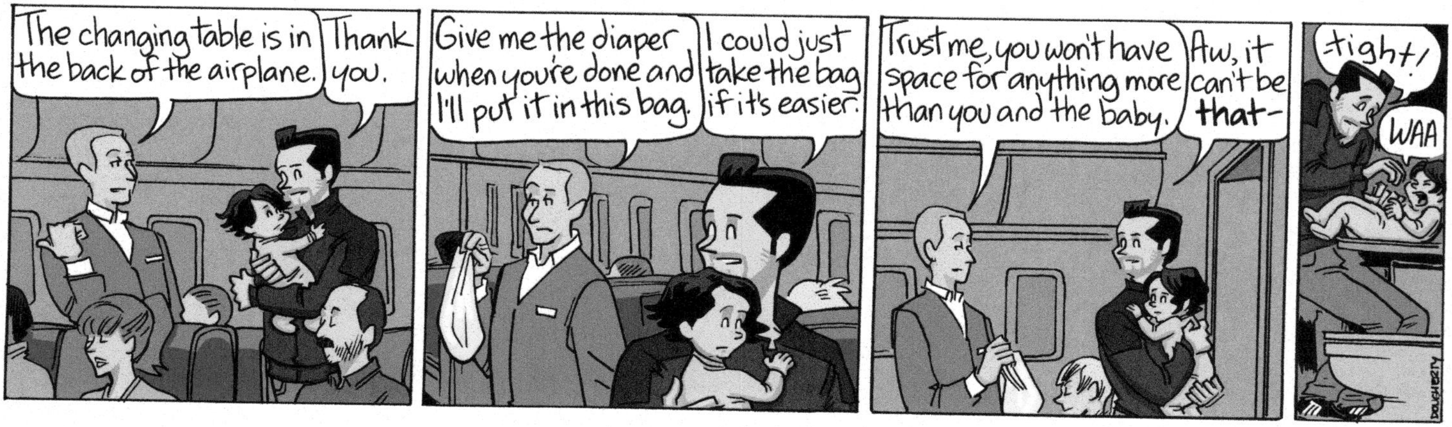
The changing table is in the back of the airplane.
Thank you.
Give me the diaper when you're done and I'll put it in this bag.
I could just take the bag if it's easier.
Trust me, you won't have space for anything more than you and the baby.
Aw, it can't be **that**-
-tight!
WAA
DOUGHERTY

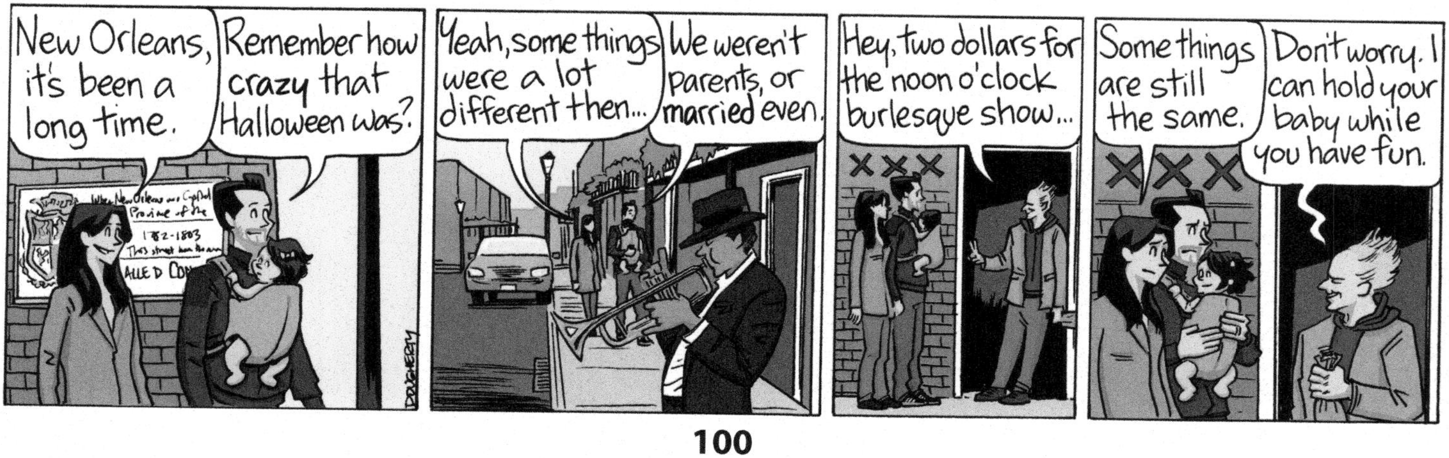
New Orleans, it's been a long time.
Remember how crazy that Halloween was?
DOUGHERTY
Yeah, some things were a lot different then...
We weren't parents, or married even.
Hey, two dollars for the noon o'clock burlesque show...
Some things are still the same.
Don't worry. I can hold your baby while you have fun.

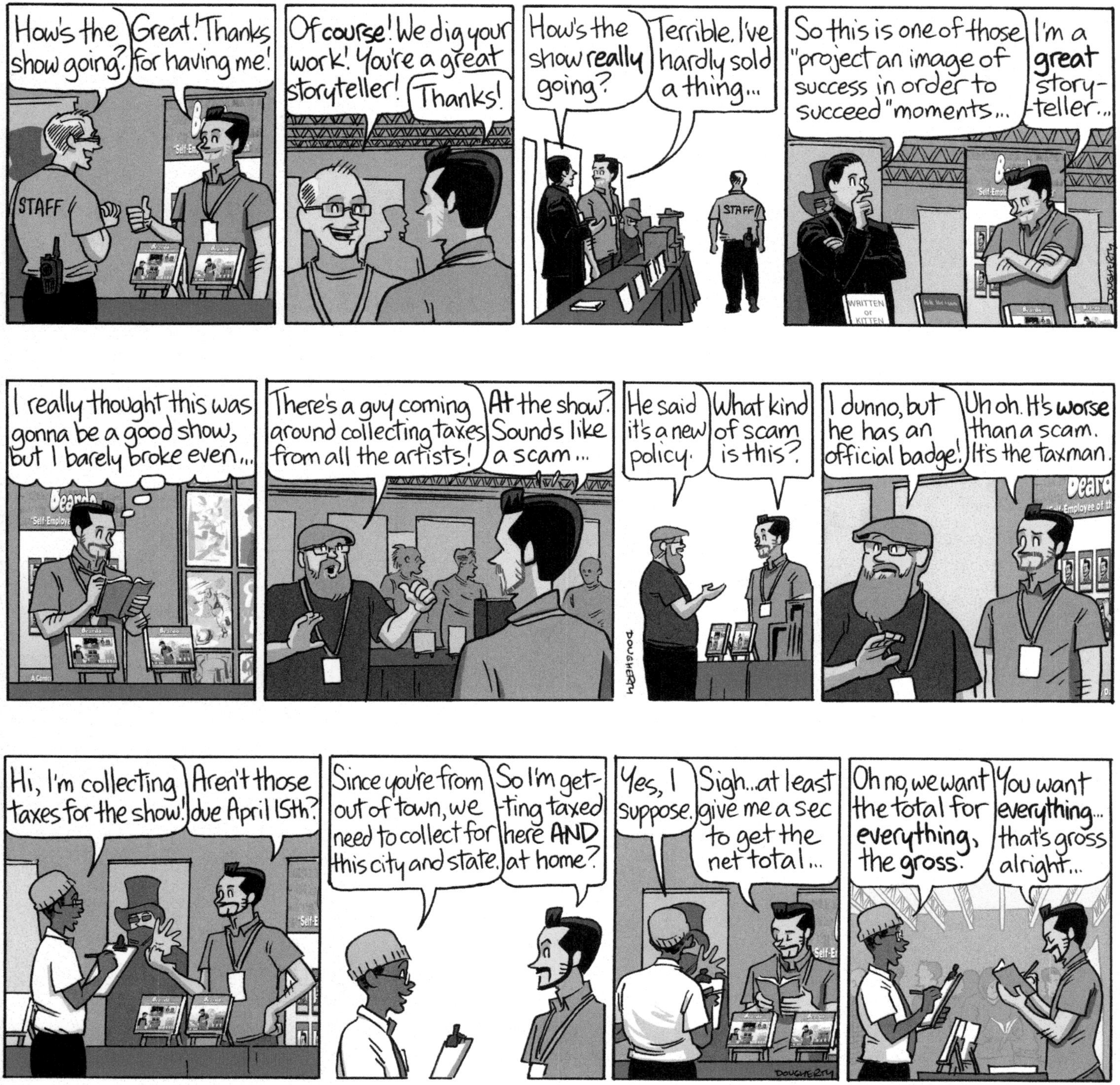
How's the show going?
Great! Thanks for having me!
STAFF
Of **course**! We dig your work! You're a great storyteller!
Thanks!
How's the show **really** going?
Terrible. I've hardly sold a thing...
STAFF
So this is one of those "project an image of success in order to succeed" moments...
I'm a **great** story-teller...
WRITTEN or KITTEN
DOUGHERTY
I really thought this was gonna be a good show, but I barely broke even...
There's a guy coming around collecting taxes from all the artists!
At the show? Sounds like a scam...
DOUGHERTY
He said it's a new policy.
What kind of scam is this?
I dunno, but he has an official badge!
Uh oh. It's **worse** than a scam. It's the taxman.
Hi, I'm collecting taxes for the show!
Aren't those due April 15th?
Since you're from out of town, we need to collect for this city and state.
So I'm get-ting taxed here **AND** at home?
Yes, I suppose.
Sigh...at least give me a sec to get the net total...
DOUGHERTY
Oh no, we want the total for **everything**, the **gross**.
You want **everything**... that's gross alright...

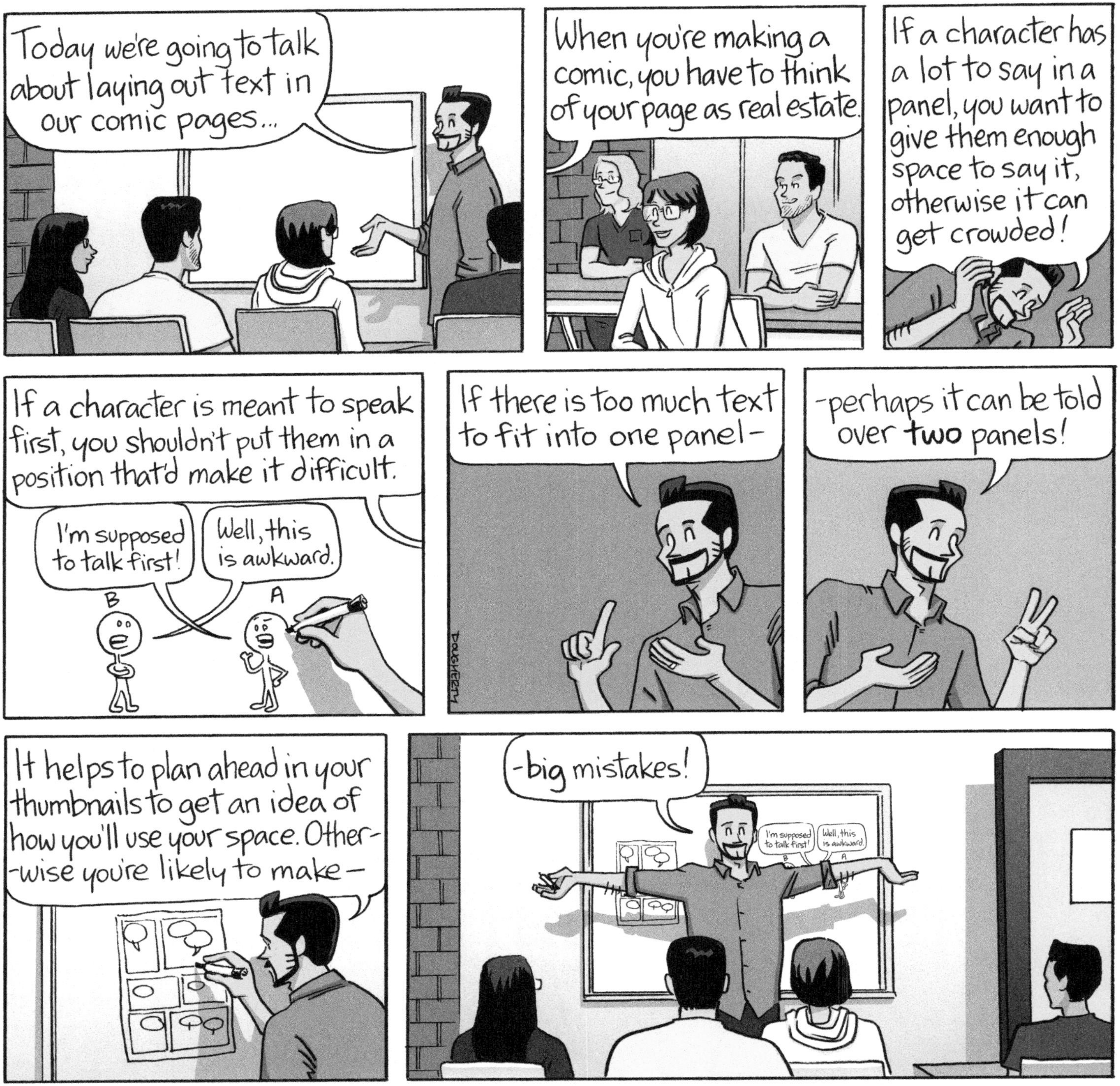

Today we're going to talk about laying out text in our comic pages...
When you're making a comic, you have to think of your page as real estate.
If a character has a lot to say in a panel, you want to give them enough space to say it, otherwise it can get crowded!
If a character is meant to speak first, you shouldn't put them in a position that'd make it difficult.
I'm supposed to talk first!
Well, this is awkward.
B
A
If there is too much text to fit into one panel-
-perhaps it can be told over **two** panels!
It helps to plan ahead in your thumbnails to get an idea of how you'll use your space. Other-
-wise you're likely to make-
-big mistakes!
I'm supposed to talk first!
Well, this is awkward.
B
A

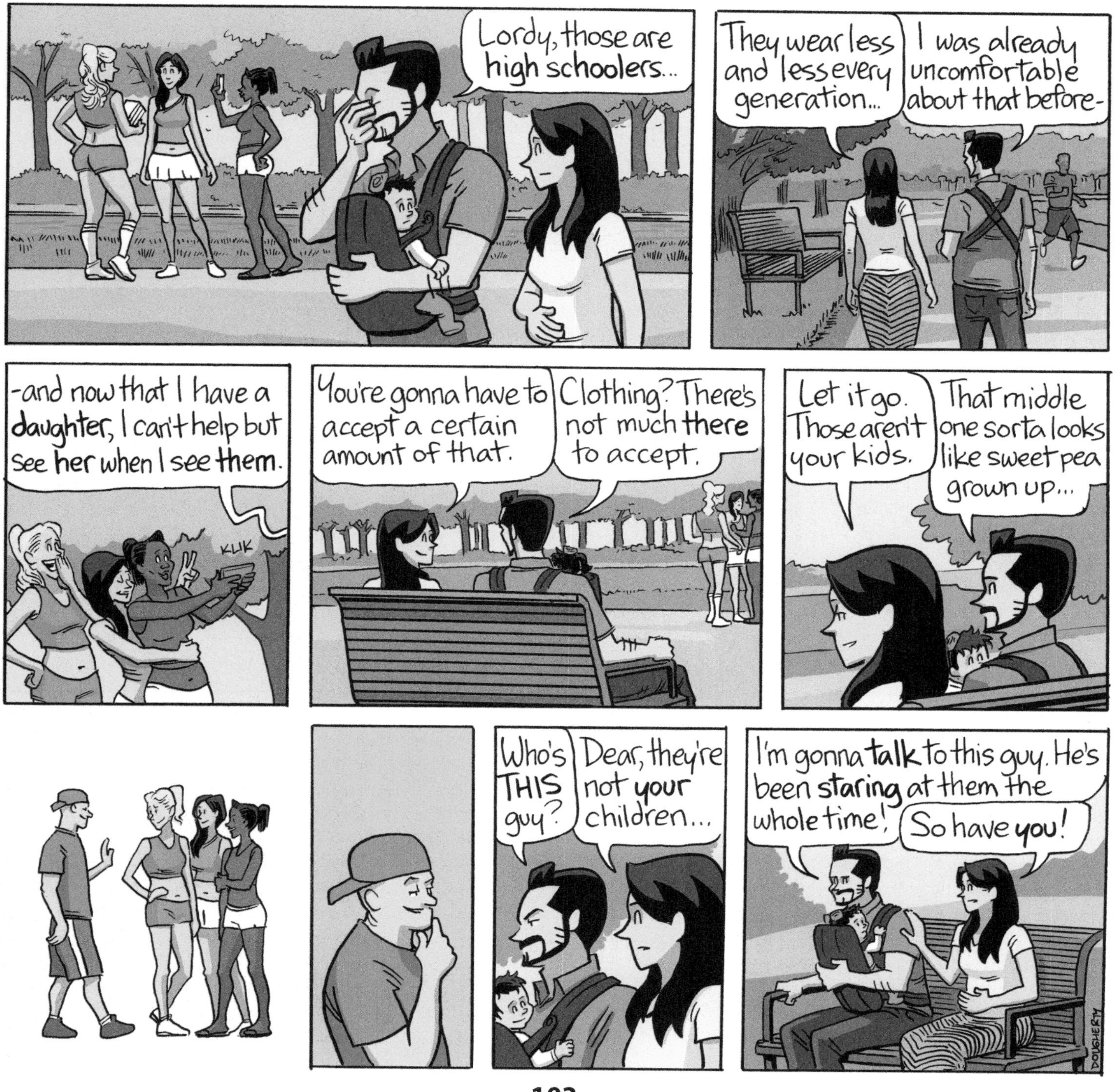
Lordy, those are high schoolers...
They wear less and less every generation...
I was already uncomfortable about that before-
-and now that I have a daughter, I can't help but see her when I see them.
KLIK
You're gonna have to accept a certain amount of that.
Clothing? There's not much there to accept.
Let it go. Those aren't your kids.
That middle one sorta looks like sweet pea grown up...
Who's THIS guy?
Dear, they're not your children...
I'm gonna talk to this guy. He's been staring at them the whole time!
So have you!
DOUGHERTY

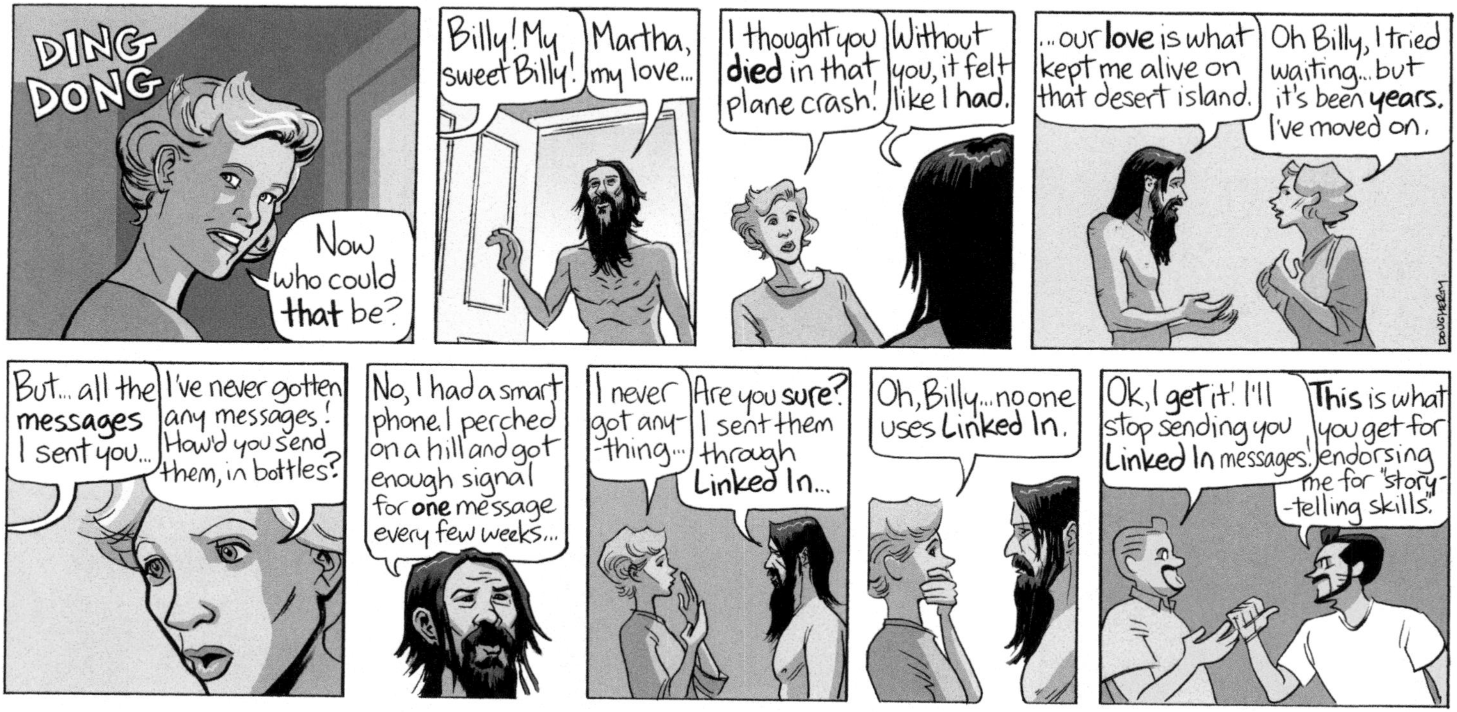
DING DONG
Now who could that be?
Billy! My sweet Billy!
Martha, my love...
I thought you died in that plane crash!
Without you, it felt like I had.
...our love is what kept me alive on that desert island.
Oh Billy, I tried waiting... but it's been years. I've moved on.
But... all the messages I sent you...
I've never gotten any messages! How'd you send them, in bottles?
No, I had a smart phone. I perched on a hill and got enough signal for one message every few weeks...
I never got any-thing...
Are you sure? I sent them through Linked In...
Oh, Billy... no one uses Linked In.
Ok, I get it! I'll stop sending you Linked In messages!
This is what you get for endorsing me for "story-telling skills."

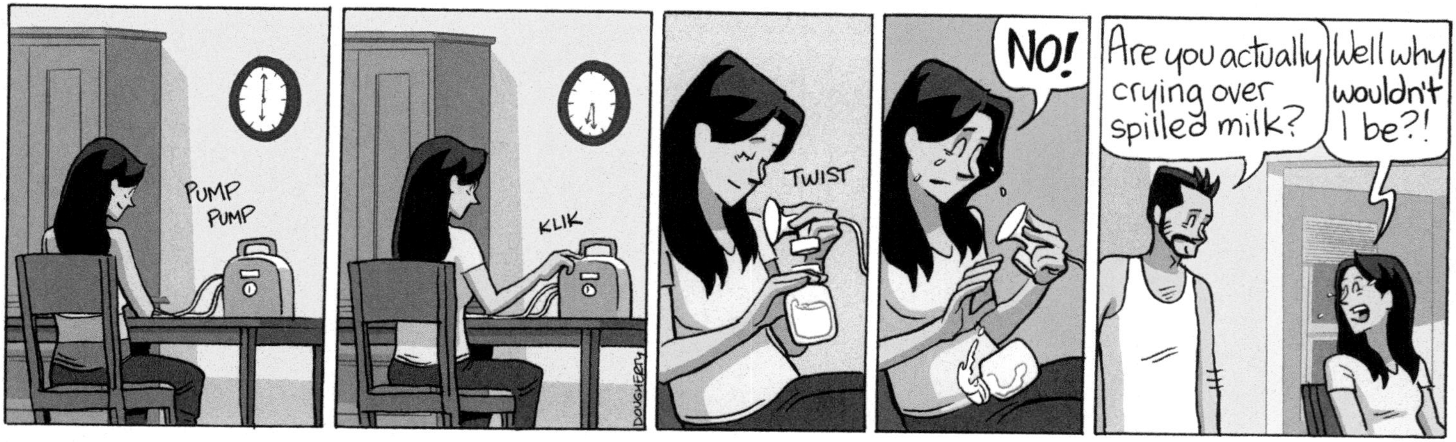
PUMP PUMP
KLIK
TWIST
NO!
Are you actually crying over spilled milk?
Well why wouldn't I be?!

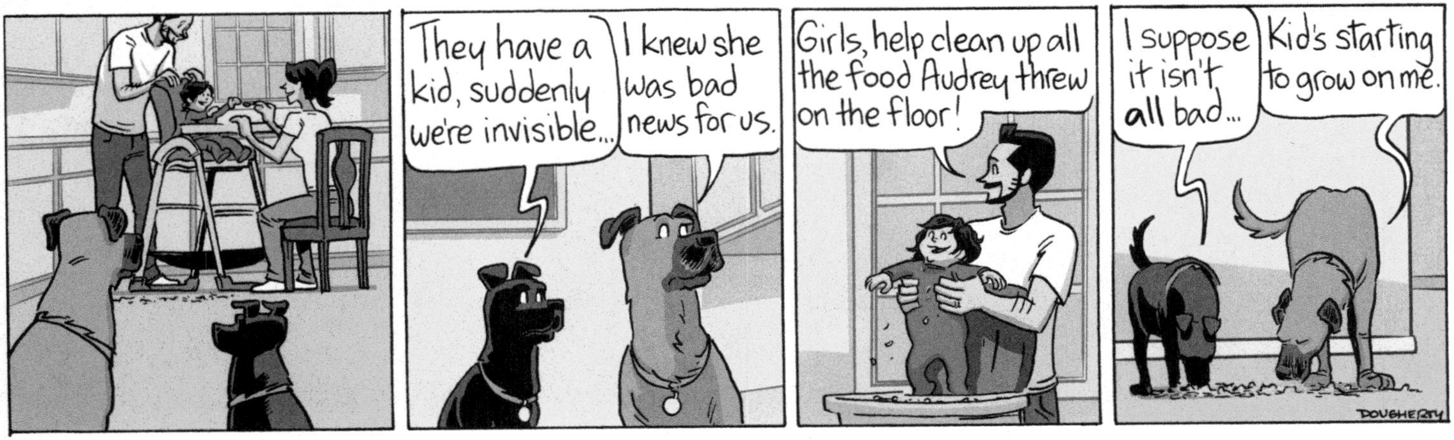

They have a kid, suddenly we're invisible...
I knew she was bad news for us.
Girls, help clean up all the food Audrey threw on the floor!
I suppose it isn't **all** bad...
Kid's starting to grow on me.
DOUGHERTY

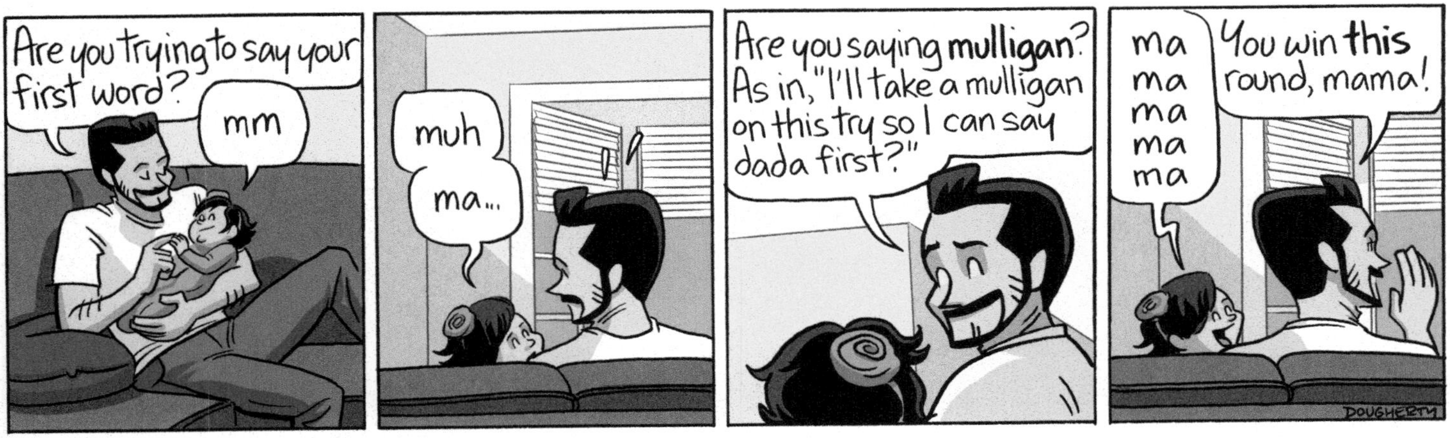

Are you trying to say your first word?
mm
muh
ma...
Are you saying **mulligan**? As in, "I'll take a mulligan on this try so I can say dada first?"
ma ma ma ma ma
You win **this** round, mama!
DOUGHERTY

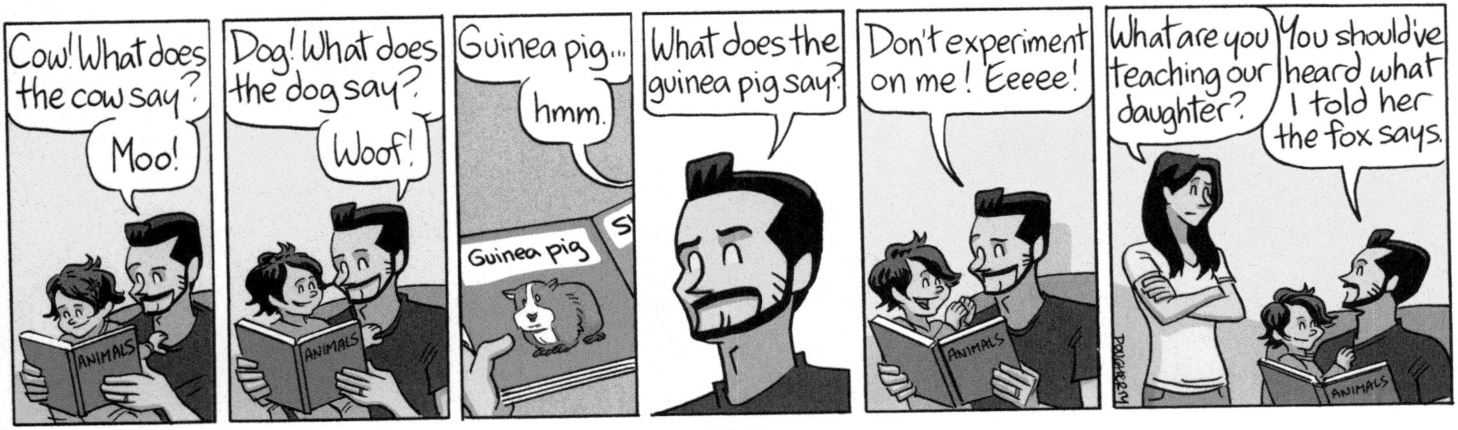

Cow! What does the cow say?
Moo!
ANIMALS
Dog! What does the dog say?
Woof!
ANIMALS
Guinea pig...
hmm.
Guinea pig
What does the guinea pig say?
Don't experiment on me! Eeeee!
ANIMALS
What are you teaching our daughter?
You should've heard what I told her the fox says.
ANIMALS
DOUGHERTY

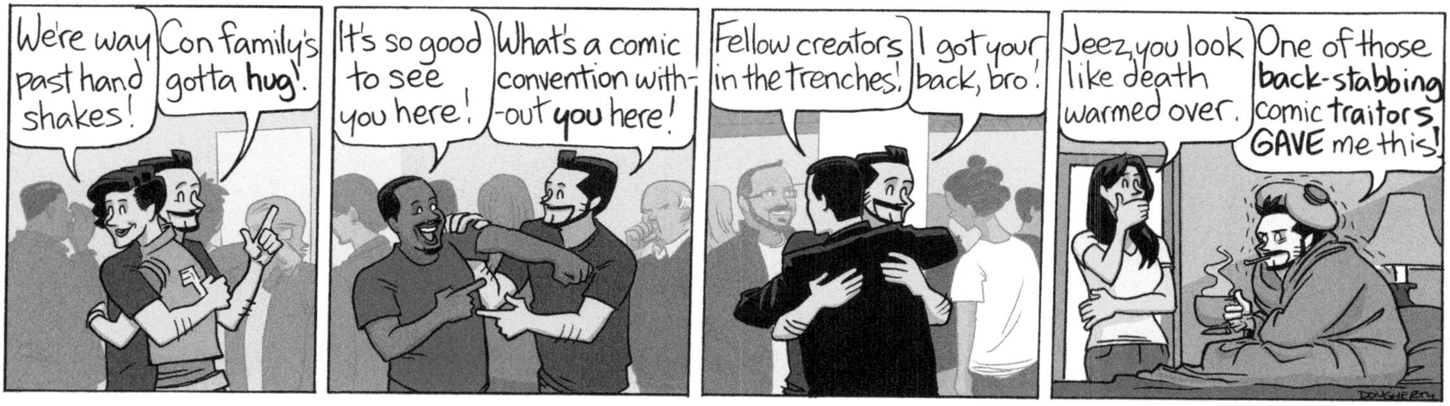
We're way past hand shakes!
Con family's gotta **hug**!
It's so good to see you here!
What's a comic convention with--out **you** here!
Fellow creators in the trenches!
I got your back, bro!
Jeez, you look like death warmed over.
One of those **back-stabbing** comic **traitors GAVE** me this!
DOUGHERTY

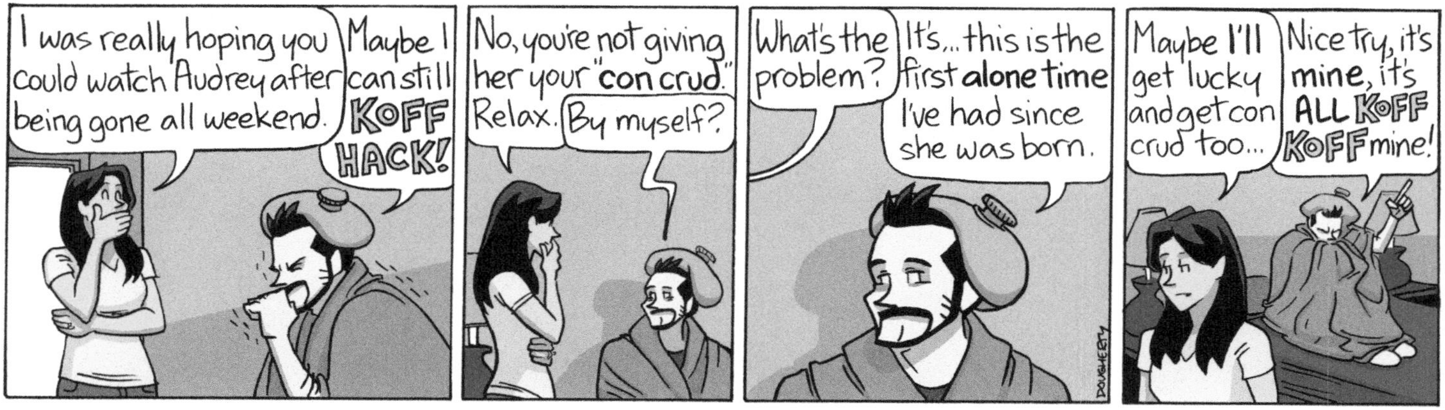
I was really hoping you could watch Audrey after being gone all weekend.
Maybe I can still KOFF HACK!
No, you're not giving her your "**con crud**." Relax.
By myself?
DOUGHERTY
What's the problem?
It's... this is the first **alone time** I've had since she was born.
Maybe **I'll** get lucky and get con crud too...
Nice try, it's **mine**, it's **ALL** KOFF KOFF mine!

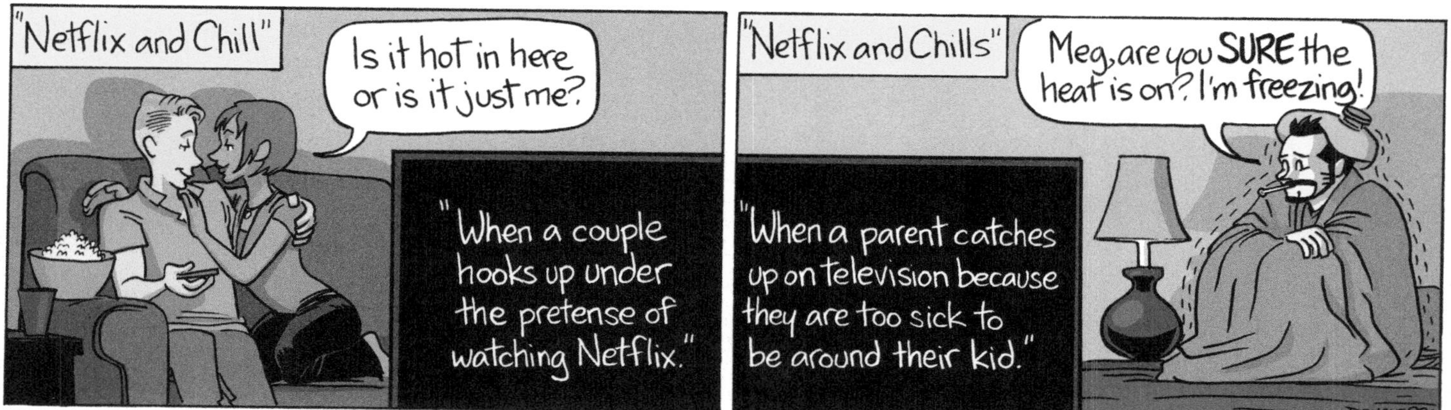
"Netflix and Chill"
Is it hot in here or is it just me?
"When a couple hooks up under the pretense of watching Netflix."
"Netflix and Chills"
Meg, are you **SURE** the heat is on? I'm freezing!
"When a parent catches up on television because they are too sick to be around their kid."
DOUGHERTY

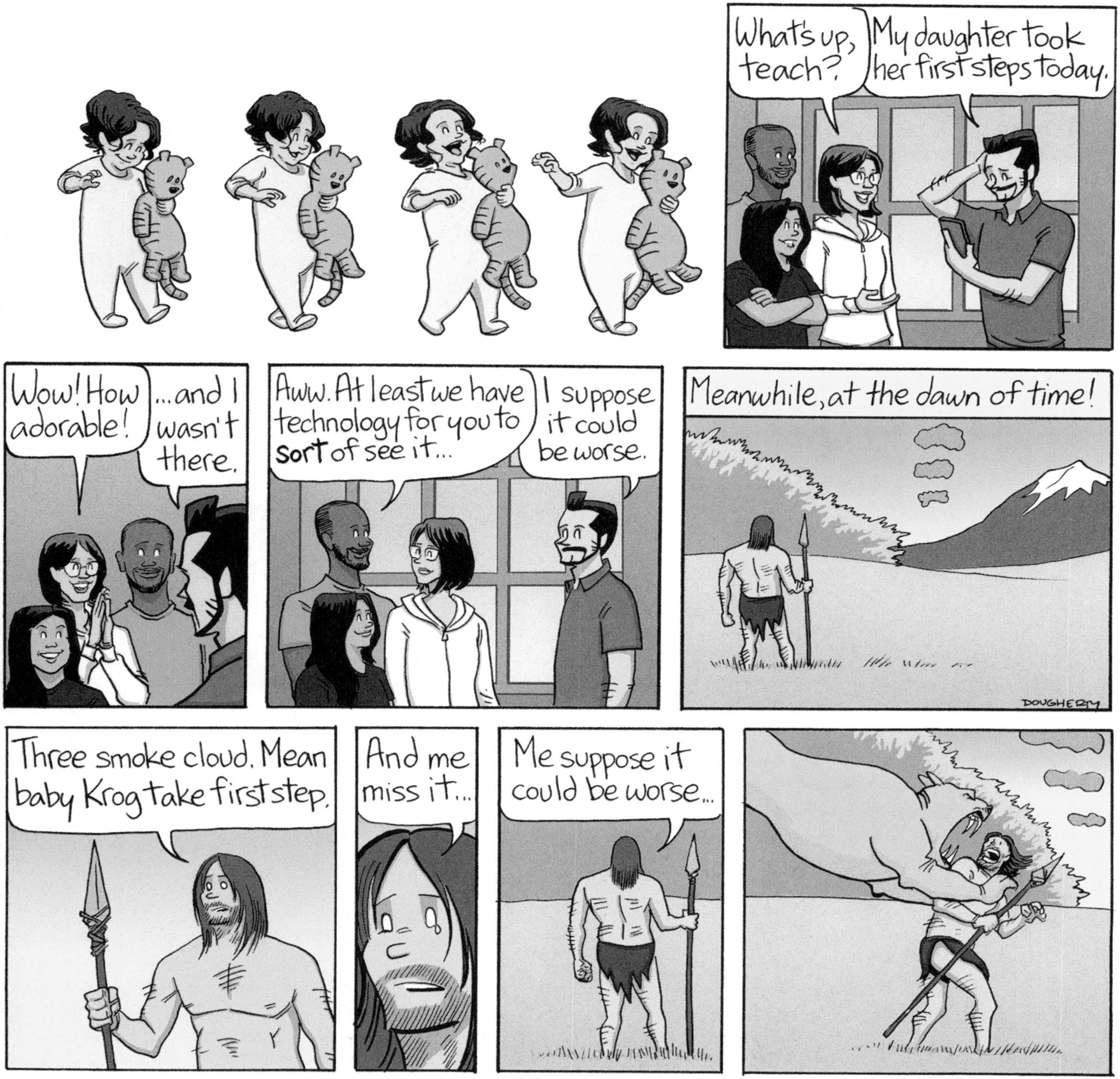
What's up, teach?
My daughter took her first steps today.
Wow! How adorable!
...and I wasn't there.
Aww. At least we have technology for you to **sort** of see it...
I suppose it could be worse.
Meanwhile, at the dawn of time!
DOUGHERTY
Three smoke cloud. Mean baby Krog take first step.
And me miss it...
Me suppose it could be worse...

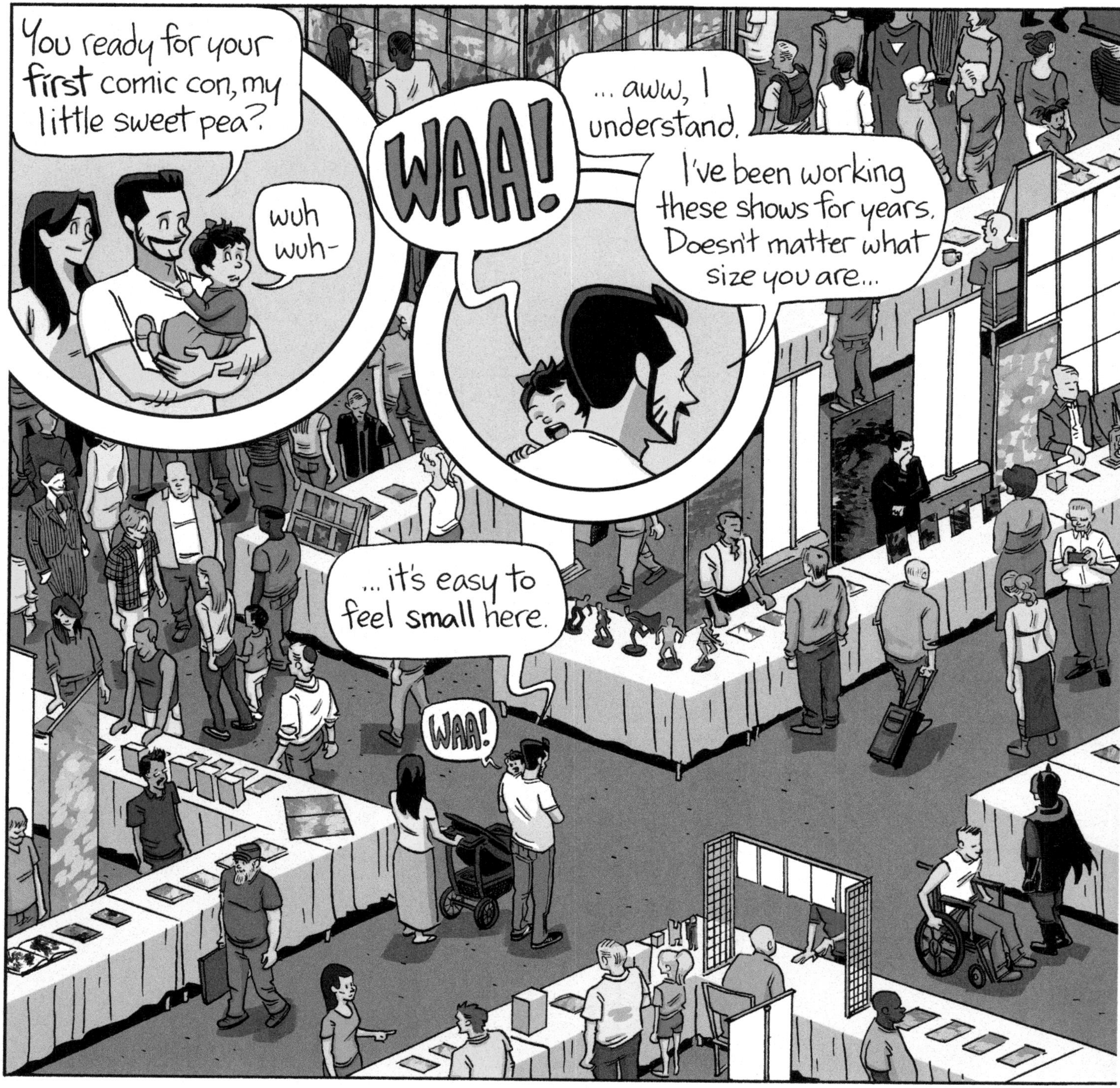
You ready for your **first** comic con, my little sweet pea?
wuh wuh-
WAA!
... aww, I understand.
I've been working these shows for years. Doesn't matter what size you are...
... it's easy to feel **small** here.
WAA!

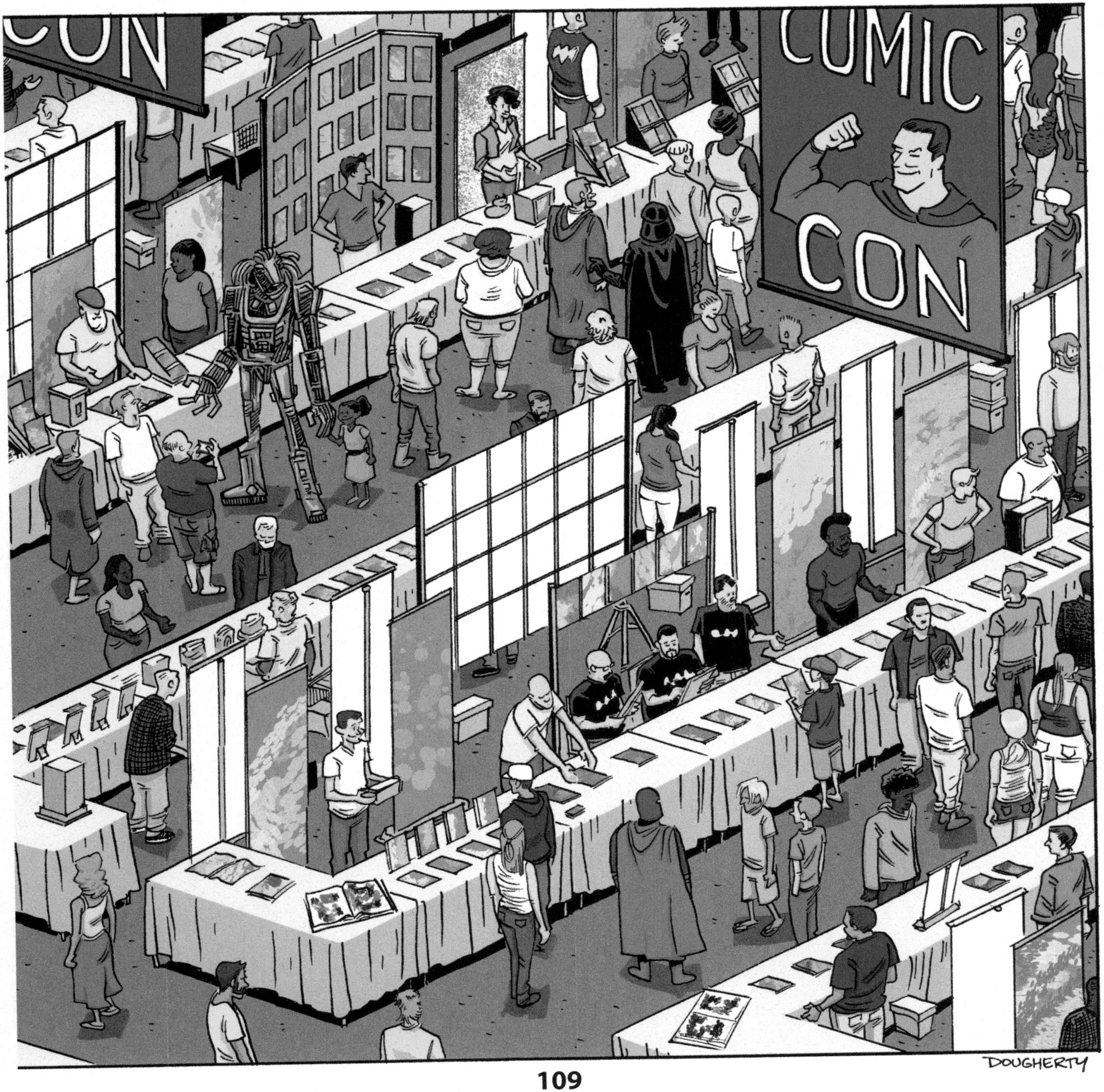
CON
COMIC
CON
DOUGHERTY

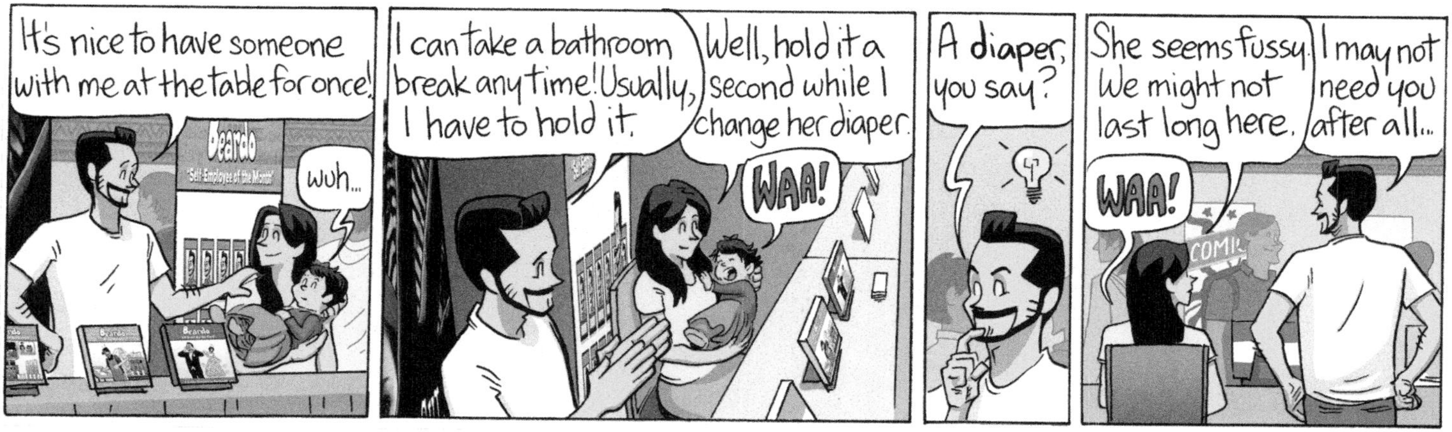
It's nice to have someone with me at the table for once!
Beardo
"Self-Employee of the Month"
wuh...
I can take a bathroom break any time! Usually, I have to hold it.
Well, hold it a second while I change her diaper.
WAA!
A **diaper**, you say?
She seems fussy. We might not last long here.
WAA!
COMIC
I may not need you after all...

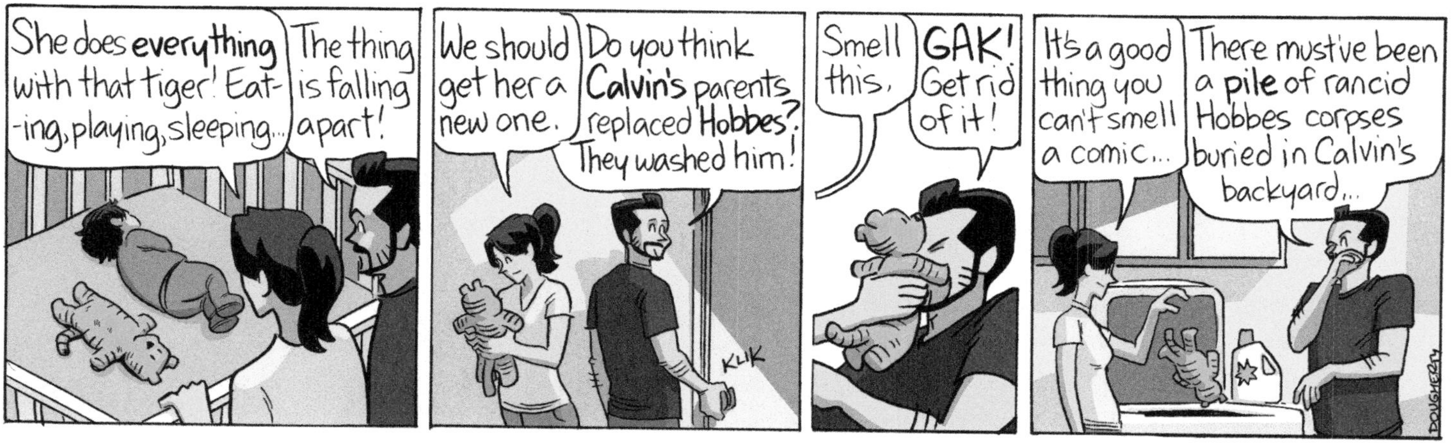
She does **everything** with that tiger! Eat-ing, playing, sleeping...
The thing is falling apart!
We should get her a new one.
Do you think **Calvin's** parents replaced **Hobbes**? They washed him!
KLIK
Smell this.
GAK! Get rid of it!
It's a good thing you can't smell a comic...
There must've been a **pile** of rancid Hobbes corpses buried in Calvin's backyard...
DOUGHERTY

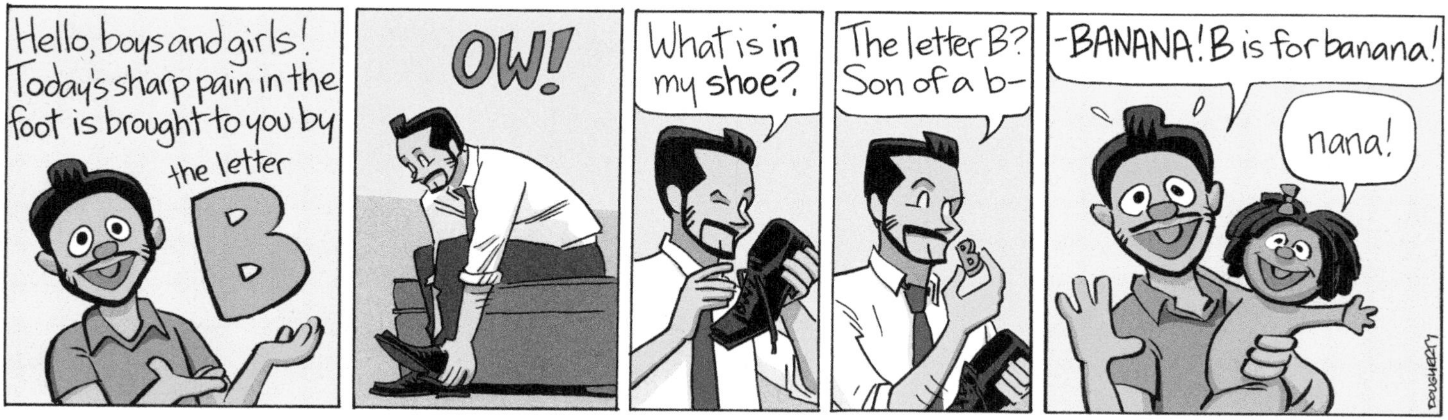
Hello, boys and girls! Today's sharp pain in the foot is brought to you by the letter
B
OW!
What is **in** my **shoe**?
The letter B? Son of a b-
-BANANA! B is for banana!
nana!
DOUGHERTY

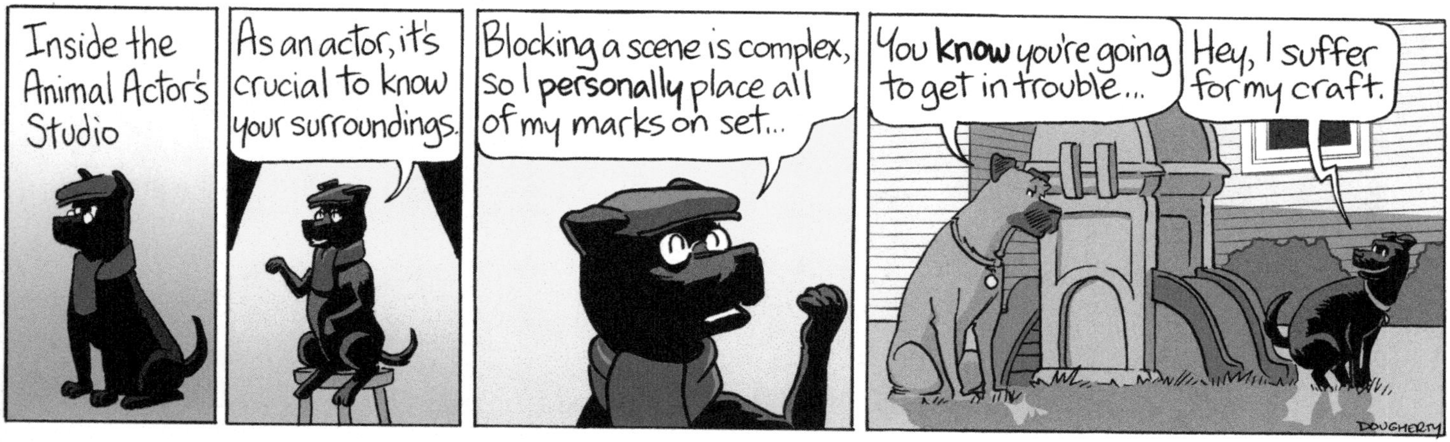
Inside the Animal Actor's Studio
As an actor, it's crucial to know your surroundings.
Blocking a scene is complex, so I **personally** place all of my marks on set...
You **know** you're going to get in trouble...
Hey, I suffer for my craft.
DOUGHERTY

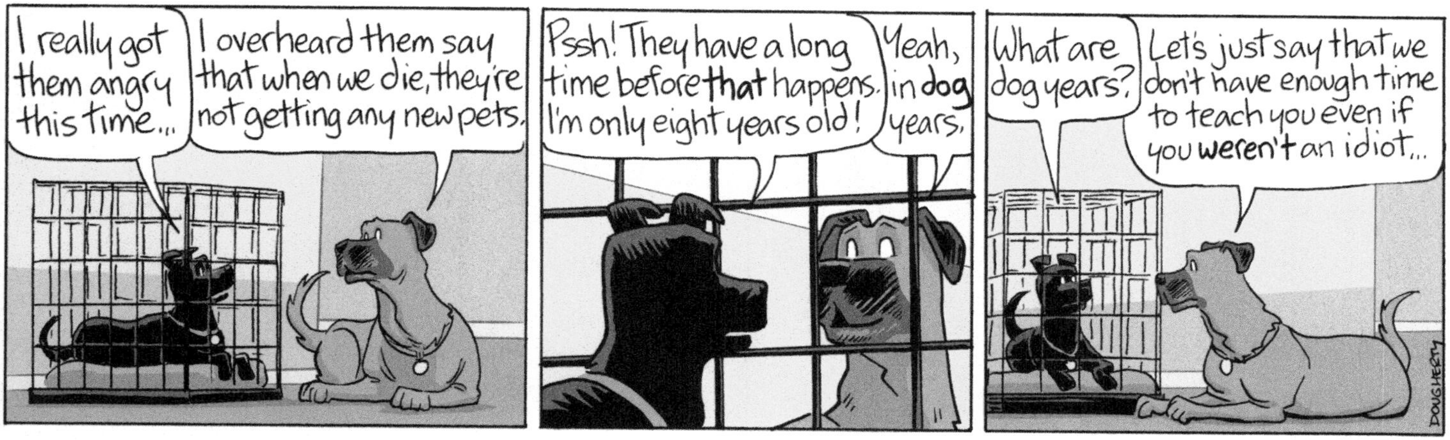
I really got them angry this time...
I overheard them say that when we die, they're not getting any new pets.
Pssh! They have a long time before **that** happens. I'm only eight years old!
Yeah, in **dog** years.
What are dog years?
Let's just say that we don't have enough time to teach you even if you **weren't** an idiot...
DOUGHERTY

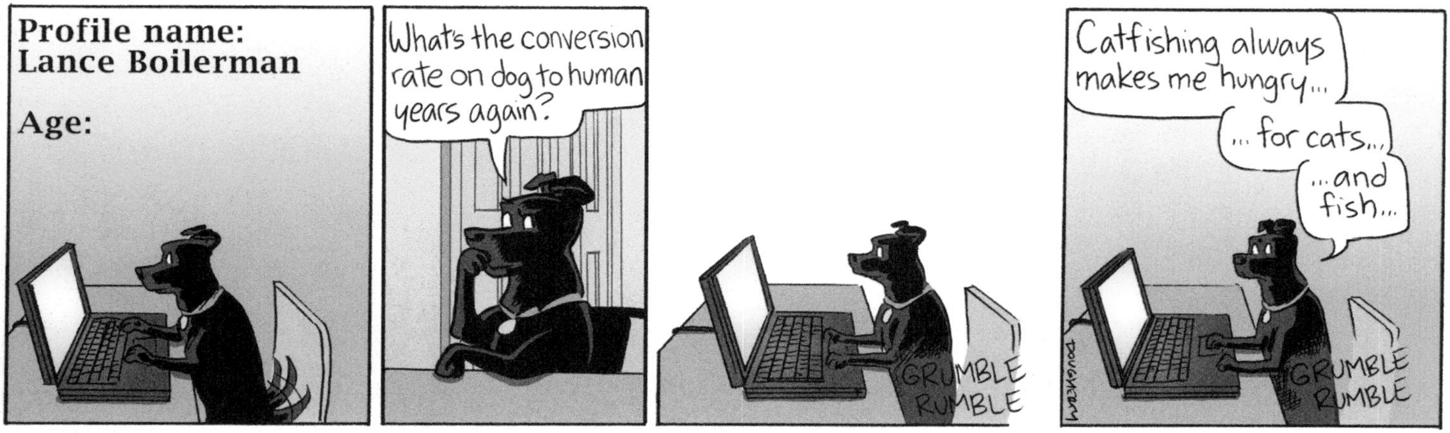
Profile name: Lance Boilerman
Age:
What's the conversion rate on dog to human years again?
GRUMBLE RUMBLE
DOUGHERTY
Catfishing always makes me hungry...
... for cats...
...and fish...
GRUMBLE RUMBLE

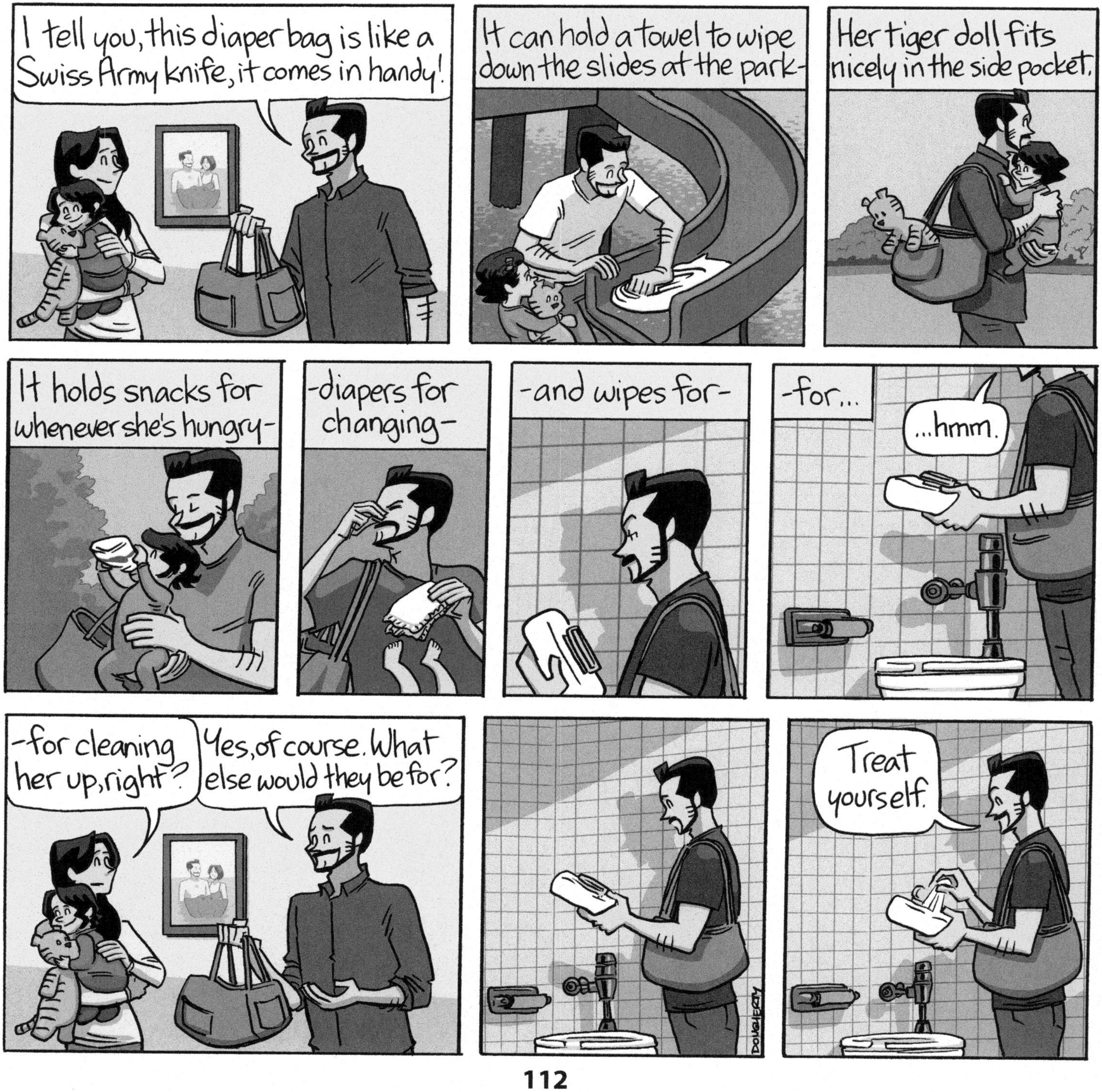
I tell you, this diaper bag is like a Swiss Army knife, it comes in handy!
It can hold a towel to wipe down the slides at the park-
Her tiger doll fits nicely in the side pocket.
It holds snacks for whenever she's hungry-
-diapers for changing-
-and wipes for-
-for...
...hmm.
-for cleaning her up, right?
Yes, of course. What else would they be for?
Treat yourself.

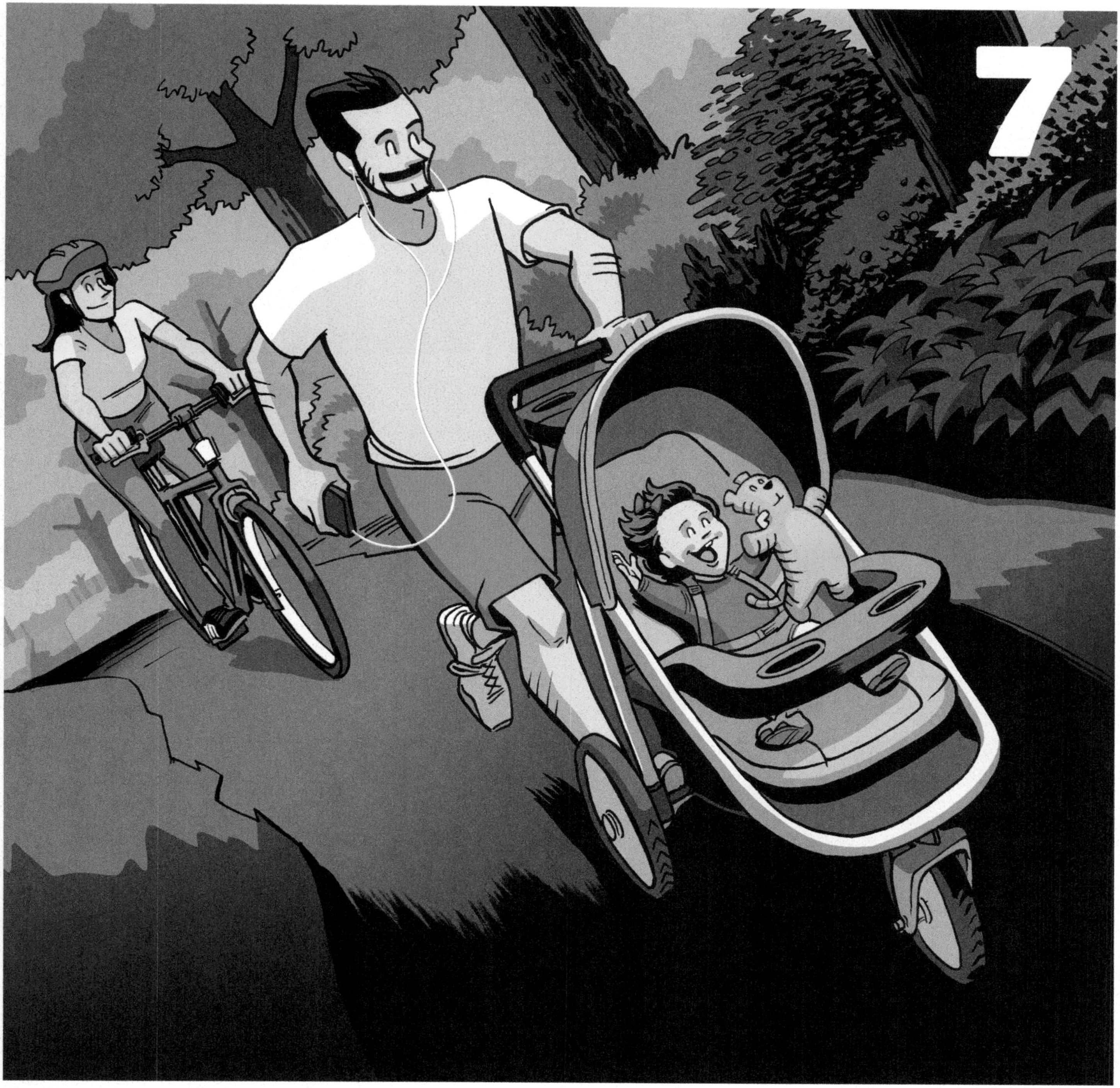
7

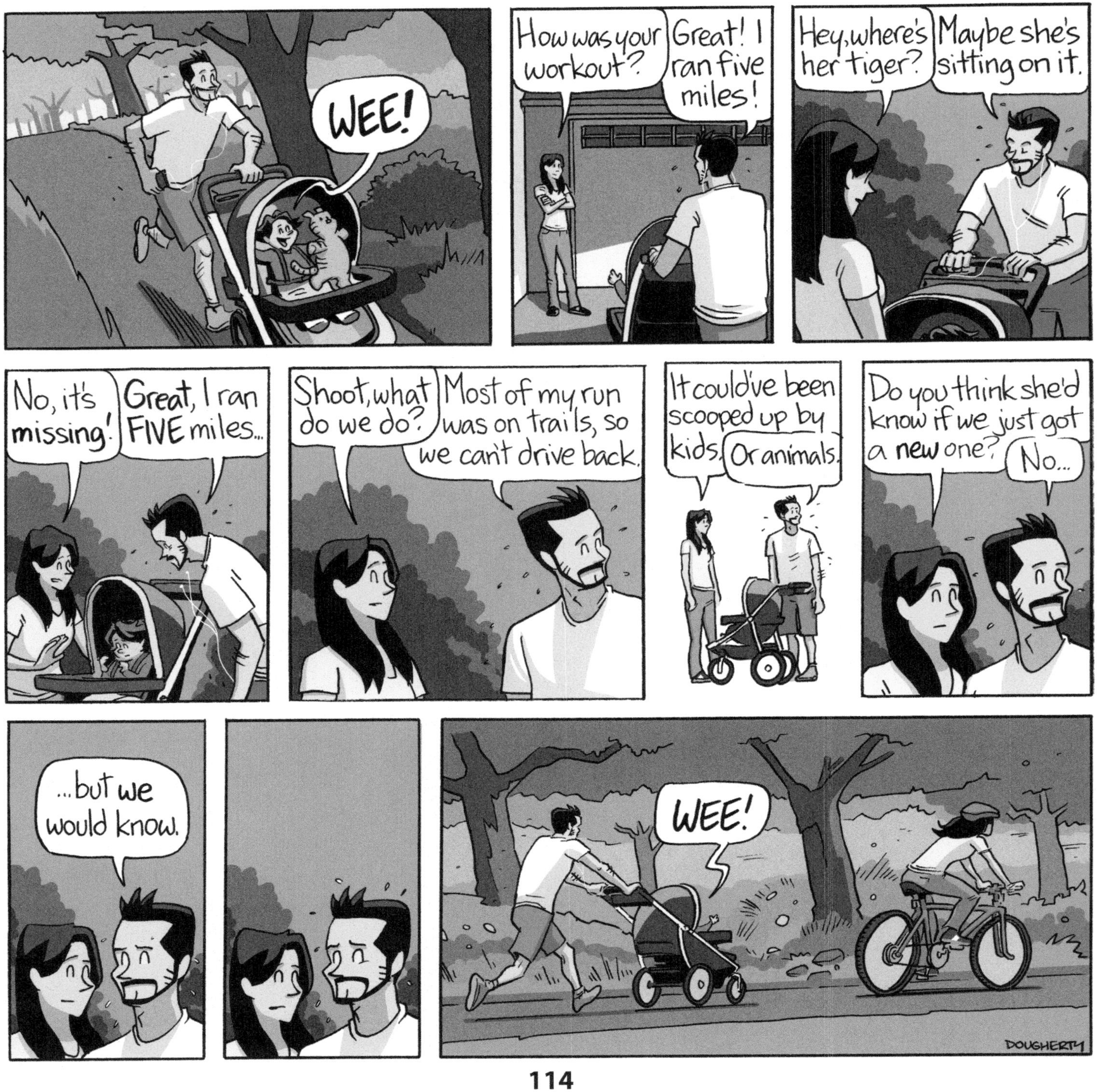
WEE!
How was your workout?
Great! I ran five miles!
Hey, where's her tiger?
Maybe she's sitting on it.
No, it's **missing**!
Great, I ran **FIVE** miles...
Shoot, what do we do?
Most of my run was on trails, so we can't drive back.
It could've been scooped up by kids.
Or animals.
Do you think she'd know if we just got a **new** one?
No...
...but **we** would know.
WEE!
DOUGHERTY

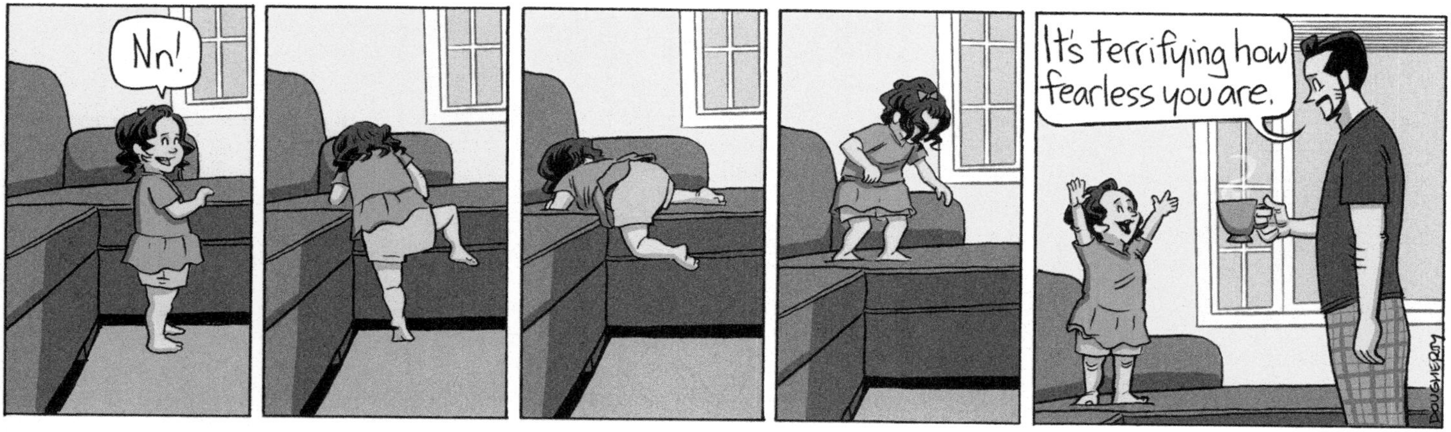
Nn!
It's terrifying how fearless you are.
DOUGHERTY

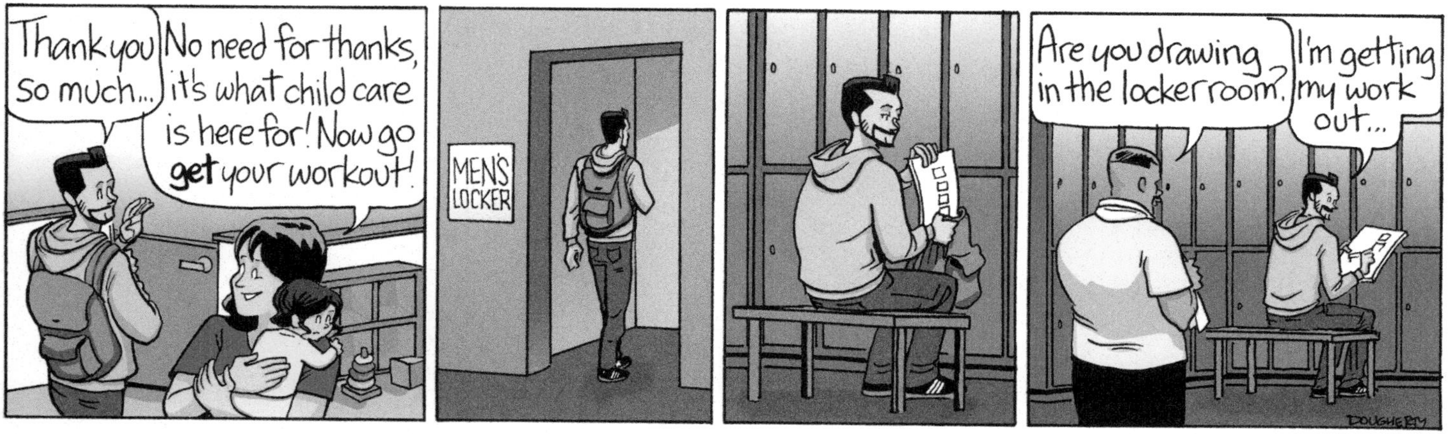
Thank you so much...
No need for thanks, it's what child care is here for! Now go **get** your workout!
MEN'S LOCKER
Are you drawing in the locker room?
I'm getting my work out...
DOUGHERTY

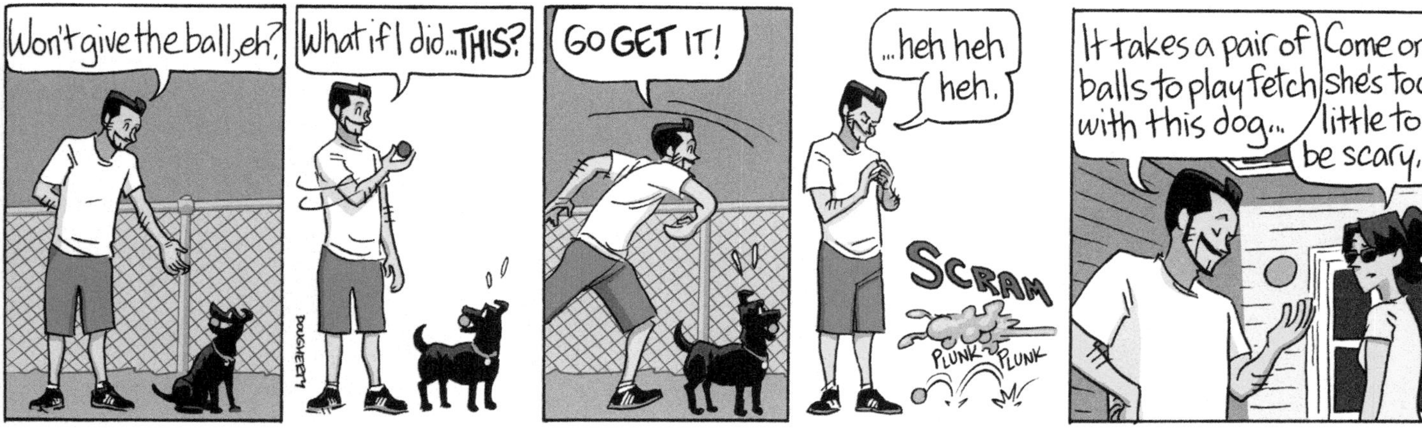
Won't give the ball, eh?
What if I did...THIS?
DOUGHERTY
GO GET IT!
...heh heh heh.
SCRAM
PLUNK
PLUNK
It takes a pair of balls to play fetch with this dog...
Come on, she's too little to be scary...

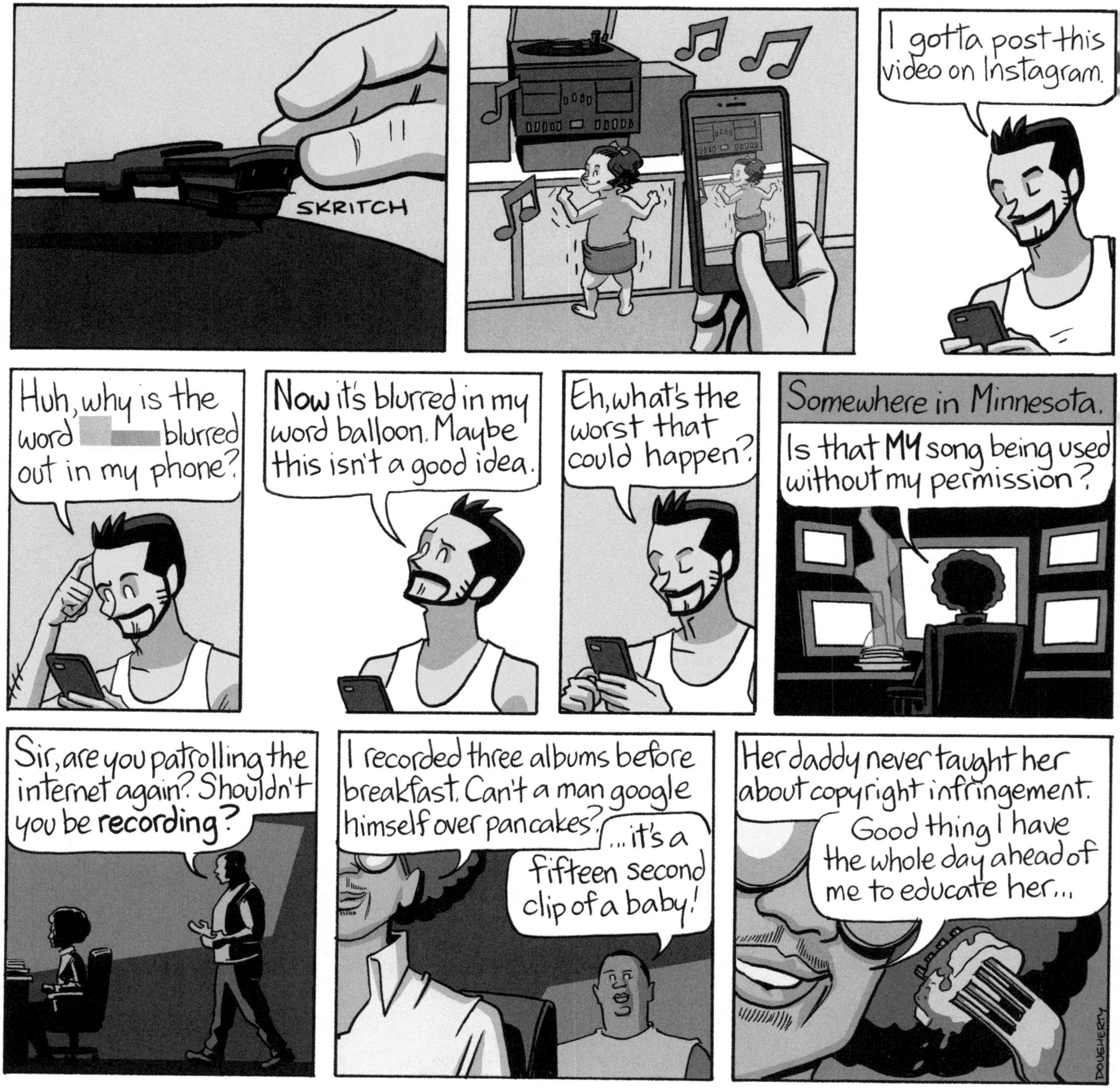
SKRITCH
I gotta post this video on Instagram.
Huh, why is the word blurred out in my phone?
Now it's blurred in my word balloon. Maybe this isn't a good idea.
Eh, what's the worst that could happen?
Somewhere in Minnesota.
Is that MY song being used without my permission?
Sir, are you patrolling the internet again? Shouldn't you be recording?
I recorded three albums before breakfast. Can't a man google himself over pancakes?
...it's a fifteen second clip of a baby!
Her daddy never taught her about copyright infringement.
Good thing I have the whole day ahead of me to educate her...
DOUGHERTY

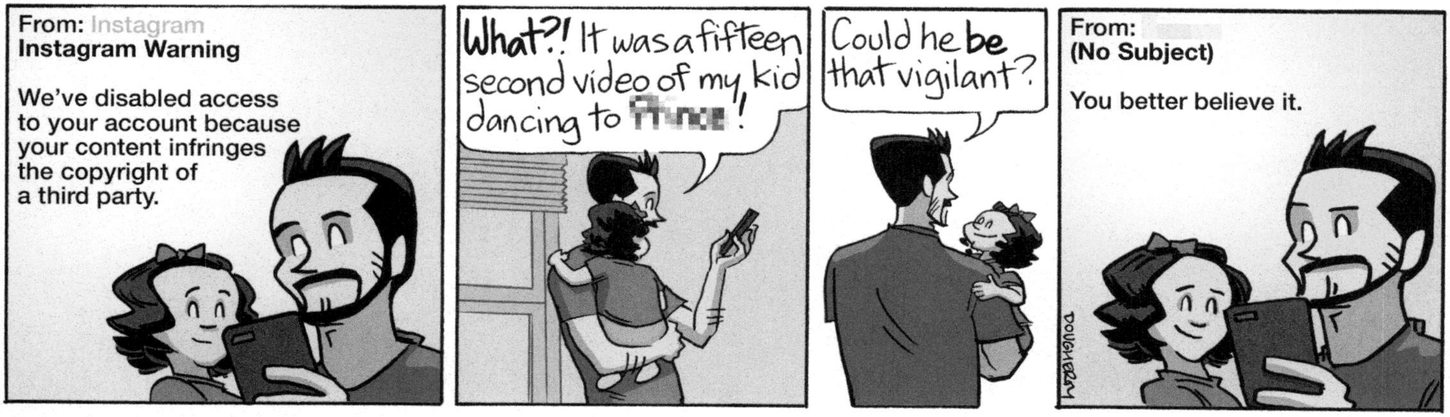
From: Instagram
Instagram Warning
We've disabled access to your account because your content infringes the copyright of a third party.
What?! It was a fifteen second video of my kid dancing to !
Could he be that vigilant?
DOUGHERTY
From:
(No Subject)
You better believe it.

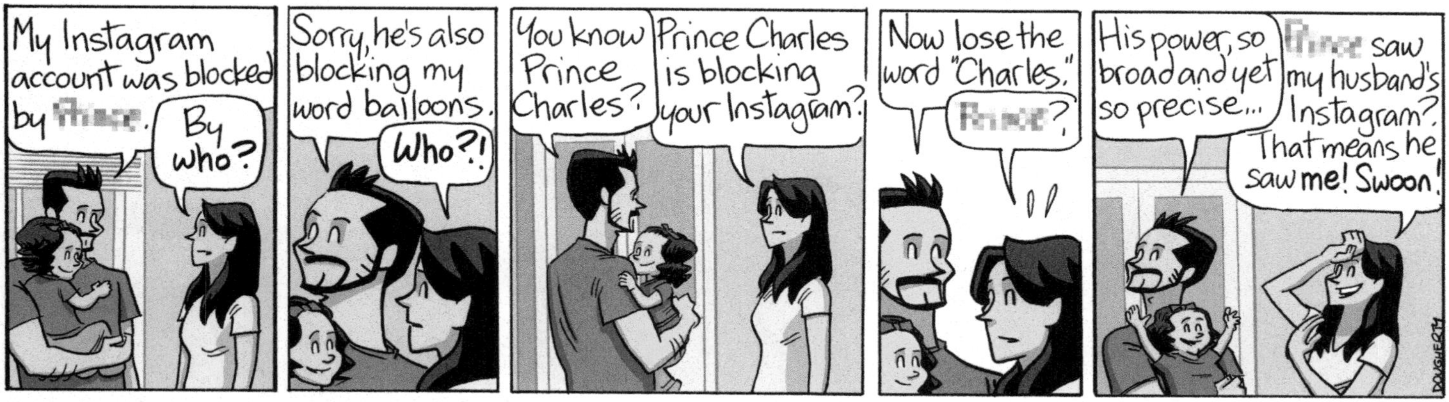
My Instagram account was blocked by .
By who?
Sorry, he's also blocking my word balloons.
Who?!
You know Prince Charles?
Prince Charles is blocking your Instagram?
Now lose the word "Charles."
?
His power, so broad and yet so precise...
saw my husband's Instagram? That means he saw me! Swoon!
DOUGHERTY

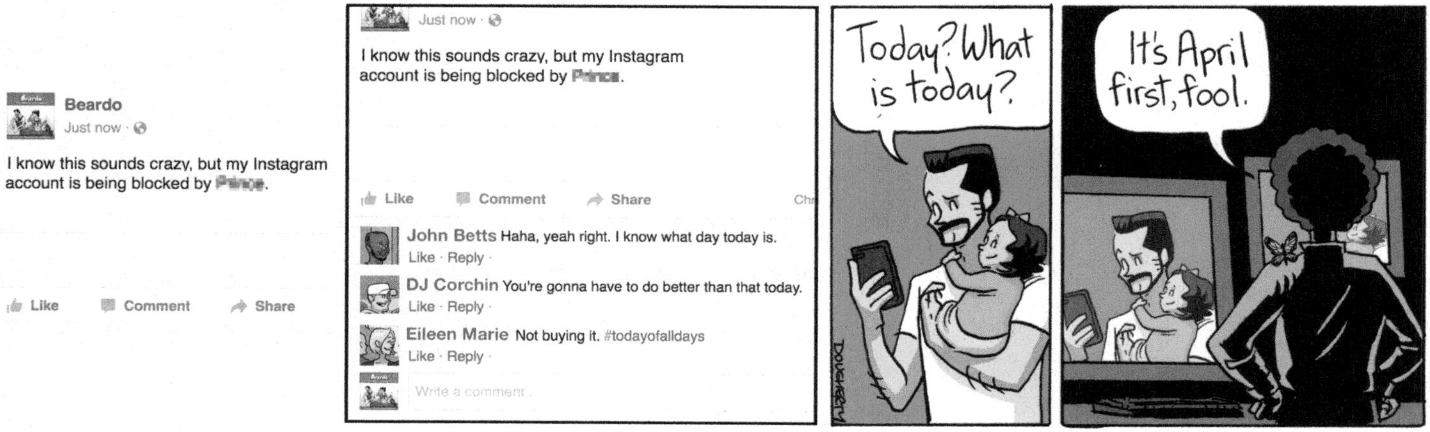
Beardo
Just now ·
I know this sounds crazy, but my Instagram account is being blocked by .
Like
Comment
Share
Just now ·
I know this sounds crazy, but my Instagram account is being blocked by .
Like
Comment
Share
John Betts Haha, yeah right. I know what day today is.
Like · Reply ·
DJ Corchin You're gonna have to do better than that today.
Like · Reply ·
Eileen Marie Not buying it. #todayofalldays
Like · Reply ·
Write a comment...
Today? What is today?
DOUGHERTY
It's April first, fool.

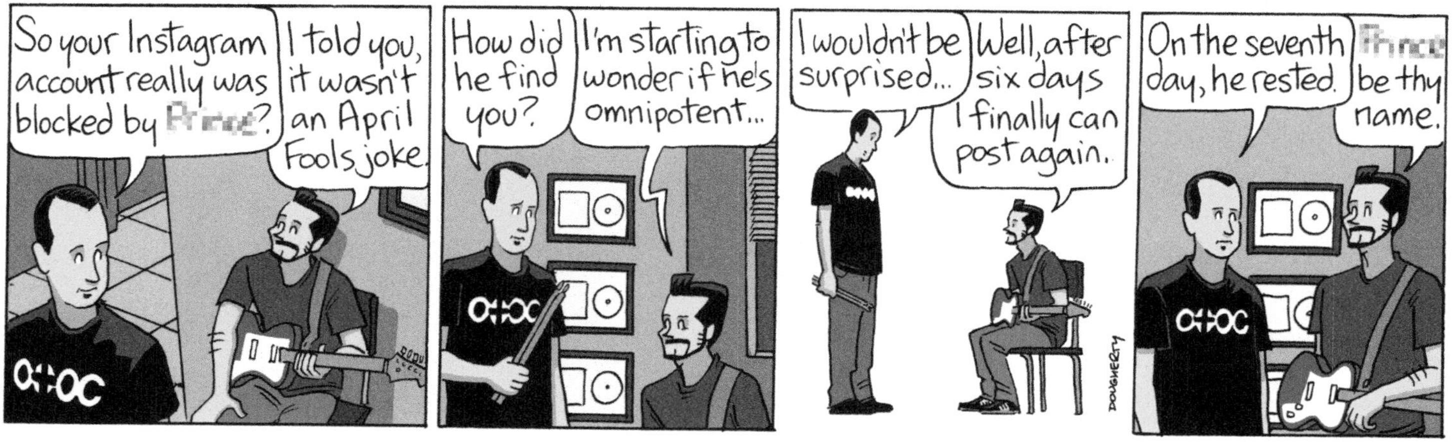
So your Instagram account really was blocked by ?
I told you, it wasn't an April Fools joke.
How did he find you?
I'm starting to wonder if he's omnipotent...
I wouldn't be surprised...
Well, after six days I finally can post again.
DOUGHERTY
On the seventh day, he rested.
be thy name.

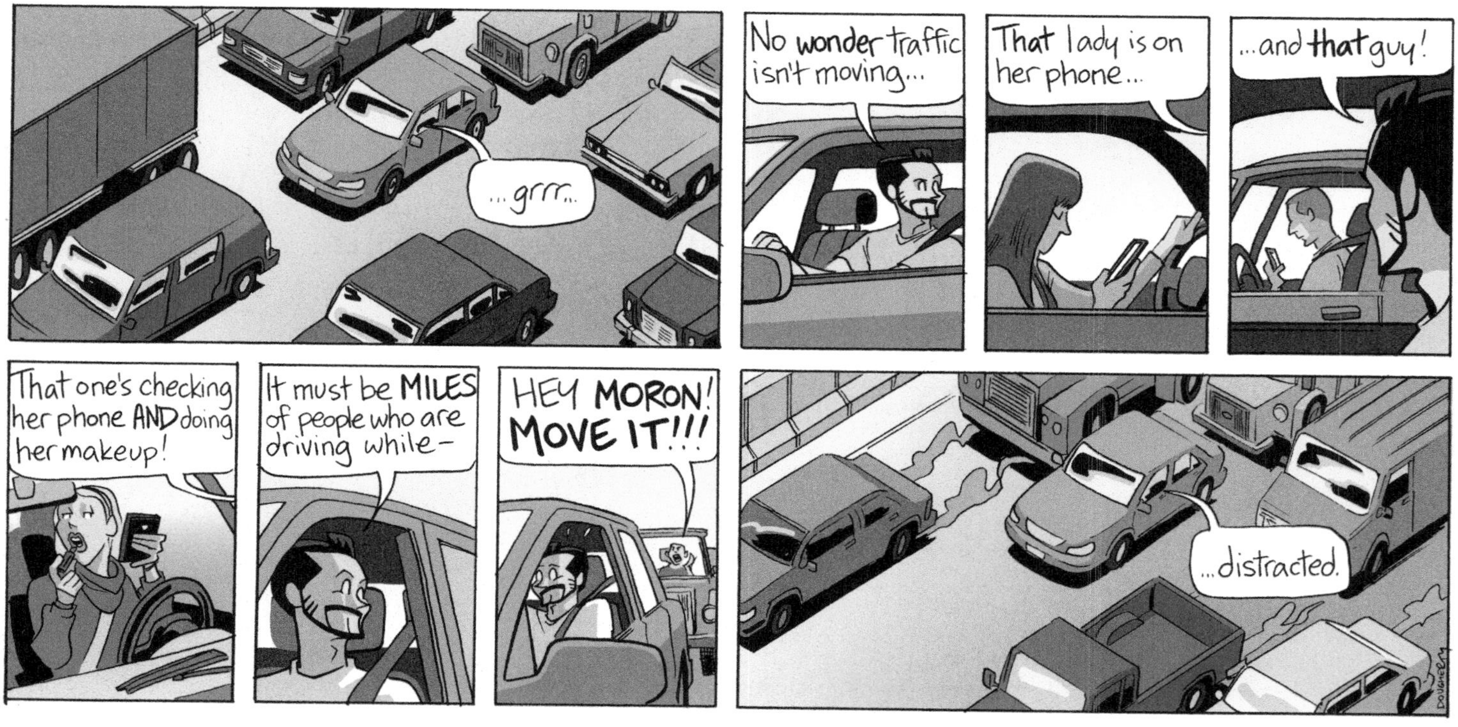
...grrr...
No wonder traffic isn't moving...
That lady is on her phone...
...and that guy!
That one's checking her phone AND doing her makeup!
It must be MILES of people who are driving while–
HEY MORON! MOVE IT!!!
...distracted.
DOUGHERTY

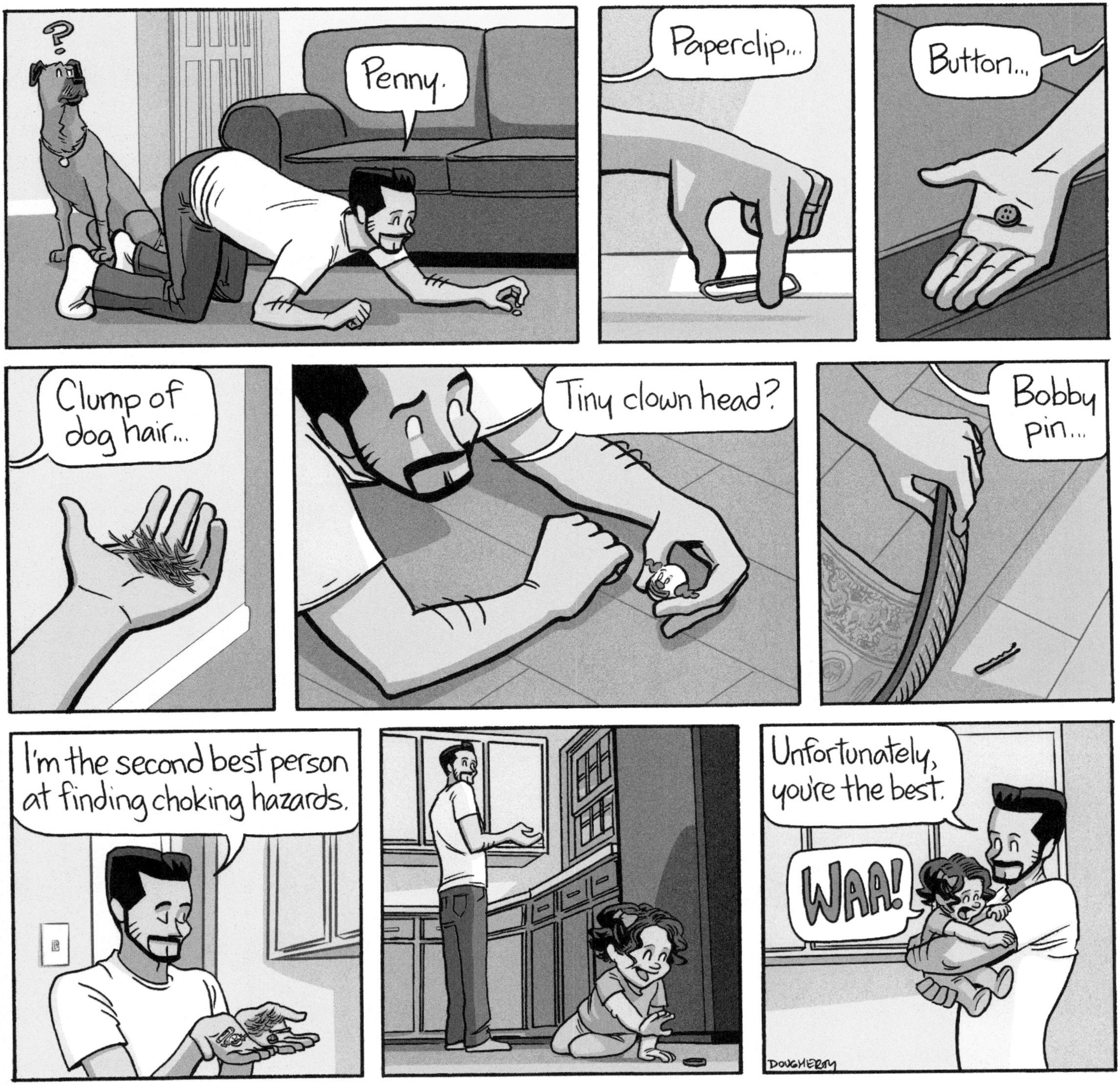
Penny.
Paperclip...
Button...
Clump of dog hair...
Tiny clown head?
Bobby pin...
I'm the second best person at finding choking hazards.
Unfortunately, you're the best.
WAA!
DOUGHERTY

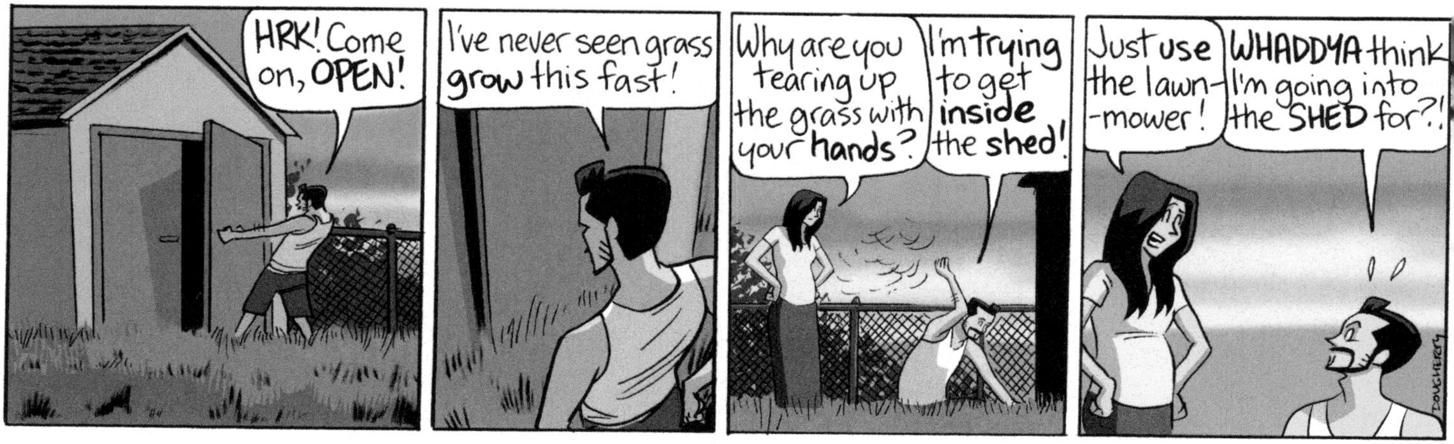
HRK! Come on, OPEN!
I've never seen grass grow this fast!
Why are you tearing up the grass with your hands?
I'm trying to get inside the shed!
Just use the lawn-mower!
WHADDYA think I'm going into the SHED for?!
DOUGHERTY

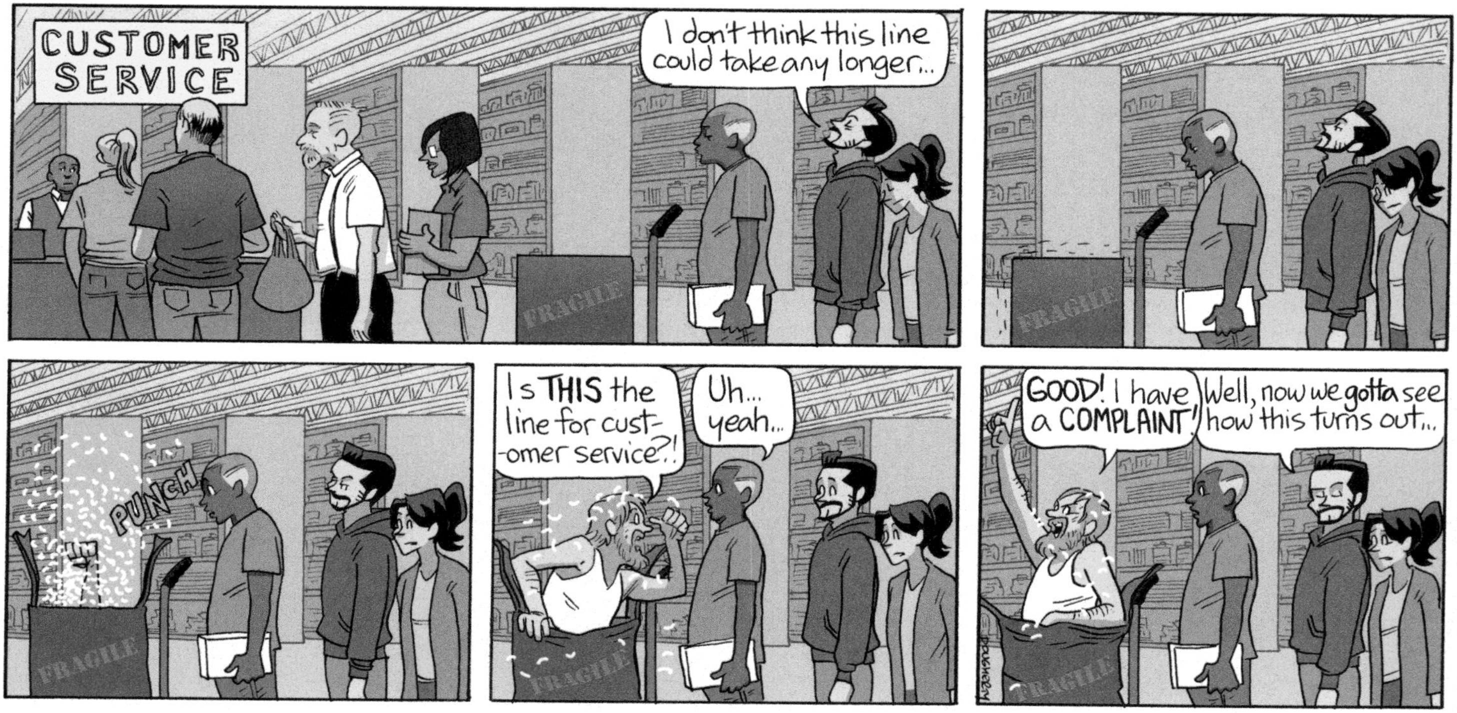
CUSTOMER SERVICE
I don't think this line could take any longer...
FRAGILE
PUNCH
FRAGILE
Is THIS the line for cust-omer service?!
Uh... yeah...
FRAGILE
GOOD! I have a COMPLAINT!
Well, now we gotta see how this turns out...
DOUGHERTY
FRAGILE

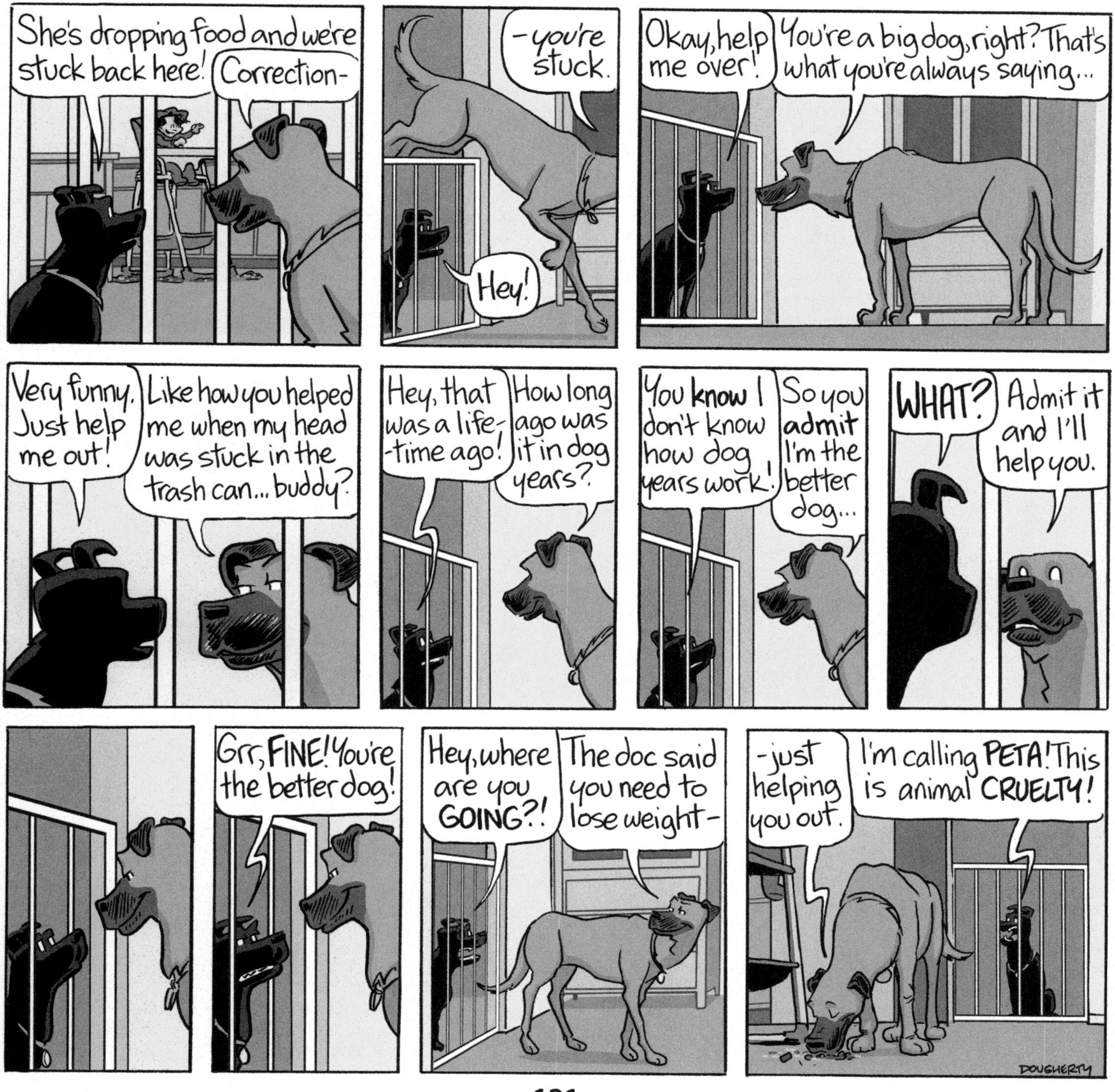

She's dropping food and we're stuck back here!
Correction-
-you're stuck.
Hey!
Okay, help me over!
You're a big dog, right? That's what you're always saying...
Very funny. Just help me out!
Like how you helped me when my head was stuck in the trash can... buddy?
Hey, that was a life-time ago!
How long ago was it in dog years?
You know I don't know how dog years work!
So you admit I'm the better dog...
WHAT?
Admit it and I'll help you.
Grr, FINE! You're the better dog!
Hey, where are you GOING?!
The doc said you need to lose weight-
-just helping you out.
I'm calling PETA! This is animal CRUELTY!
DOUGHERTY

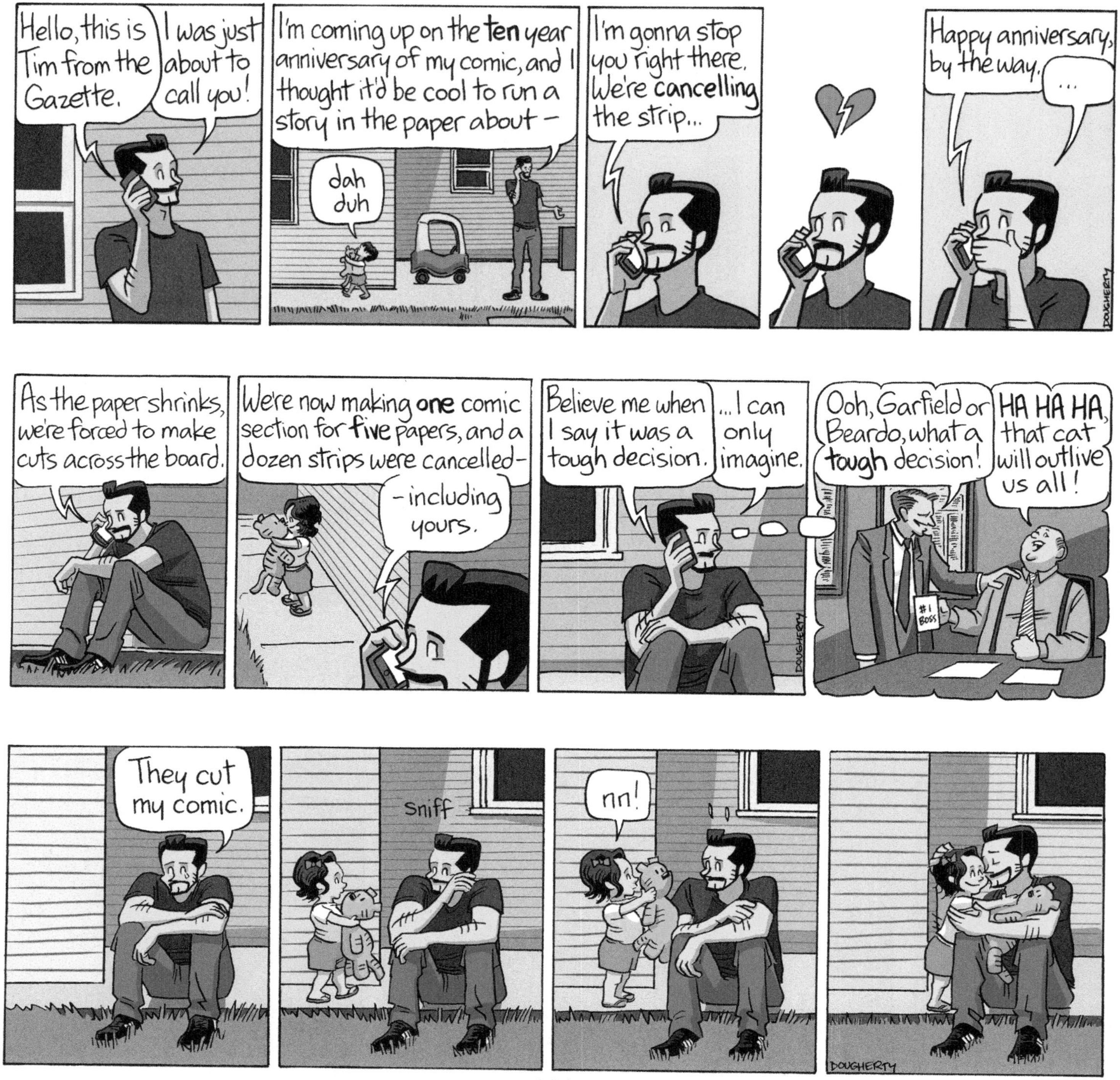
Hello, this is Tim from the Gazette.
I was just about to call you!
I'm coming up on the **ten** year anniversary of my comic, and I thought it'd be cool to run a story in the paper about –
dah duh
I'm gonna stop you right there. We're **cancelling** the strip...
Happy anniversary, by the way.
...
DOUGHERTY
As the paper shrinks, we're forced to make cuts across the board.
We're now making **one** comic section for **five** papers, and a dozen strips were cancelled–
–including yours.
Believe me when I say it was a tough decision.
...I can only imagine.
DOUGHERTY
Ooh, Garfield or Beardo, what a **tough** decision!
HA HA HA, that cat will outlive us all!
#1 BOSS
They cut my comic.
sniff
nn!
DOUGHERTY

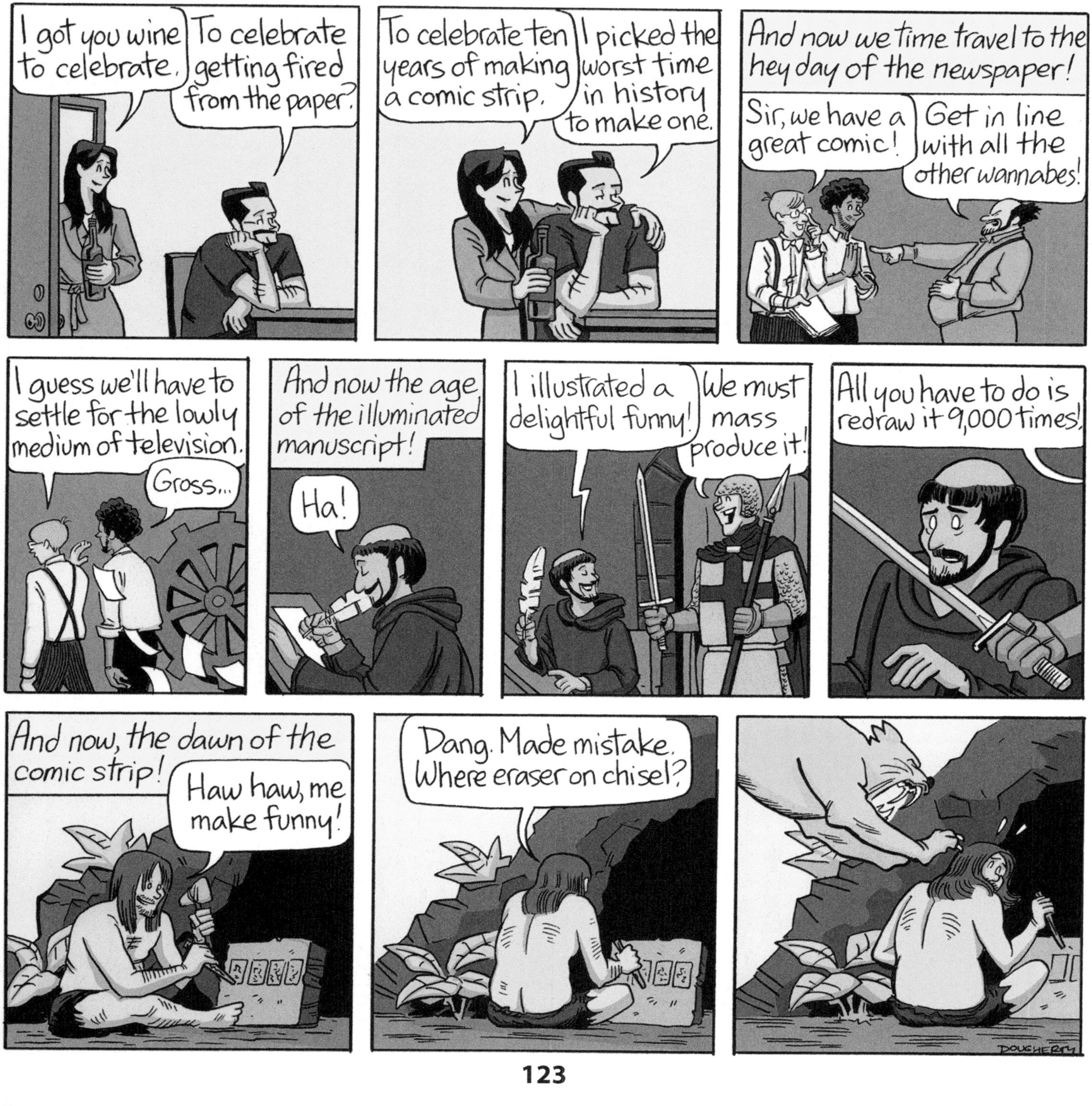
I got you wine to celebrate.
To celebrate getting fired from the paper?
To celebrate ten years of making a comic strip.
I picked the worst time in history to make one.
And now we time travel to the hey day of the newspaper!
Sir, we have a great comic!
Get in line with all the other wannabes!
I guess we'll have to settle for the lowly medium of television.
Gross...
And now the age of the illuminated manuscript!
Ha!
I illustrated a delightful funny!
We must mass produce it!
All you have to do is redraw it 9,000 times!
And now, the dawn of the comic strip!
Haw haw, me make funny!
Dang. Made mistake. Where eraser on chisel?
DOUGHERTY

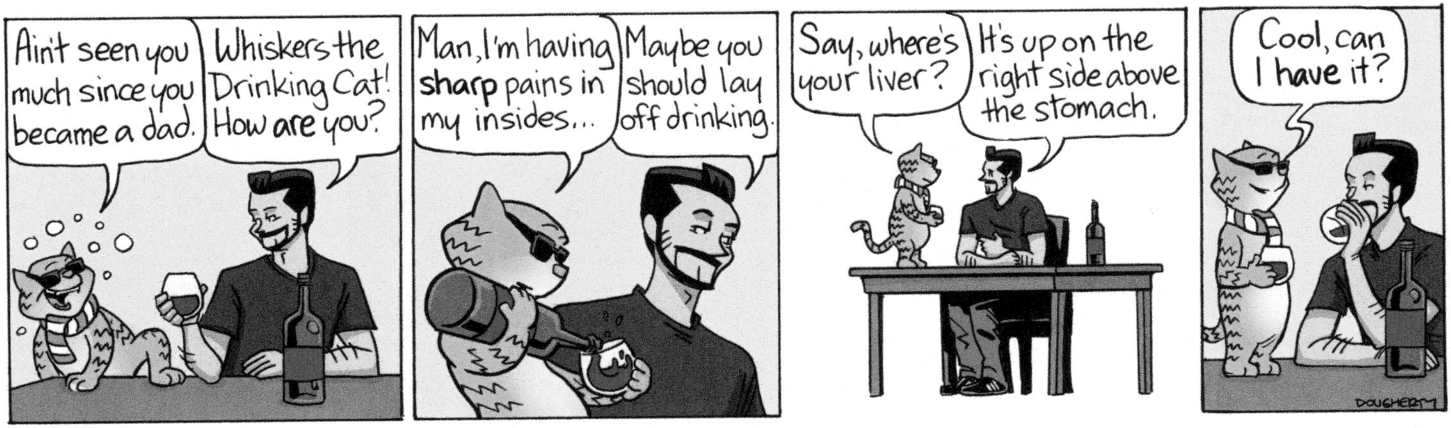

Ain't seen you much since you became a dad.
Whiskers the Drinking Cat! How **are** you?
Man, I'm having **sharp** pains in my insides...
Maybe you should lay off drinking.
Say, where's your liver?
It's up on the right side above the stomach.
Cool, can I **have** it?
DOUGHERTY

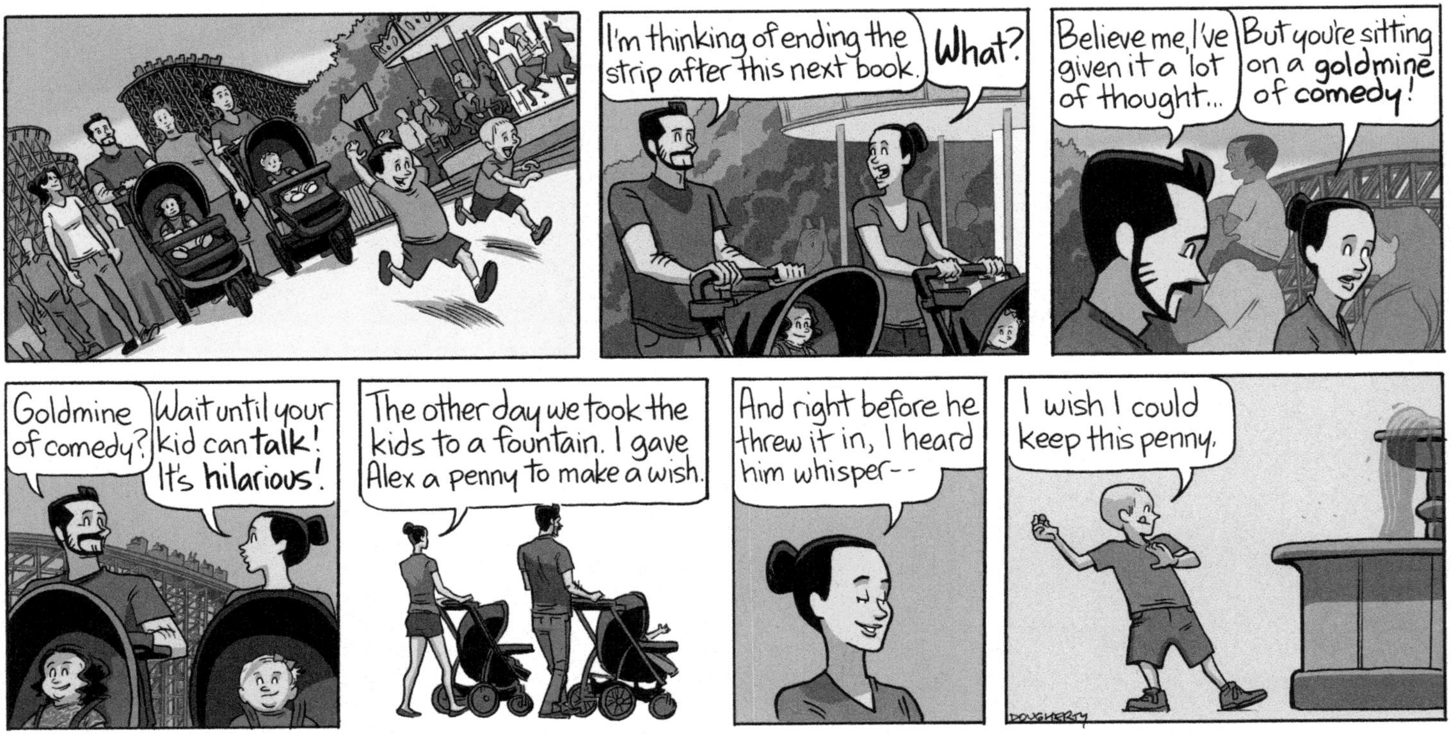

I'm thinking of ending the strip after this next book.
What?
Believe me, I've given it a lot of thought...
But you're sitting on a **goldmine** of **comedy**!
Goldmine of comedy?
Wait until your kid can **talk**! It's **hilarious**!
The other day we took the kids to a fountain. I gave Alex a penny to make a wish.
And right before he threw it in, I heard him whisper--
I wish I could keep this penny.
DOUGHERTY

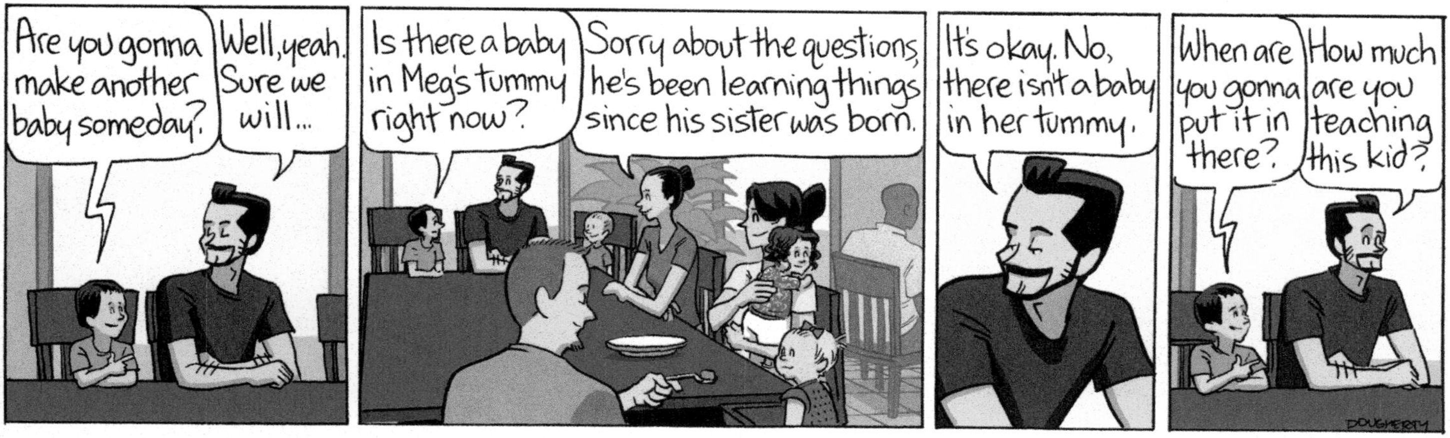
Are you gonna make another baby someday?
Well, yeah. Sure we will...
Is there a baby in Meg's tummy right now?
Sorry about the questions, he's been learning things since his sister was born.
It's okay. No, there isn't a baby in her tummy.
When are you gonna put it in there?
How much are you teaching this kid?
DOUGHERTY

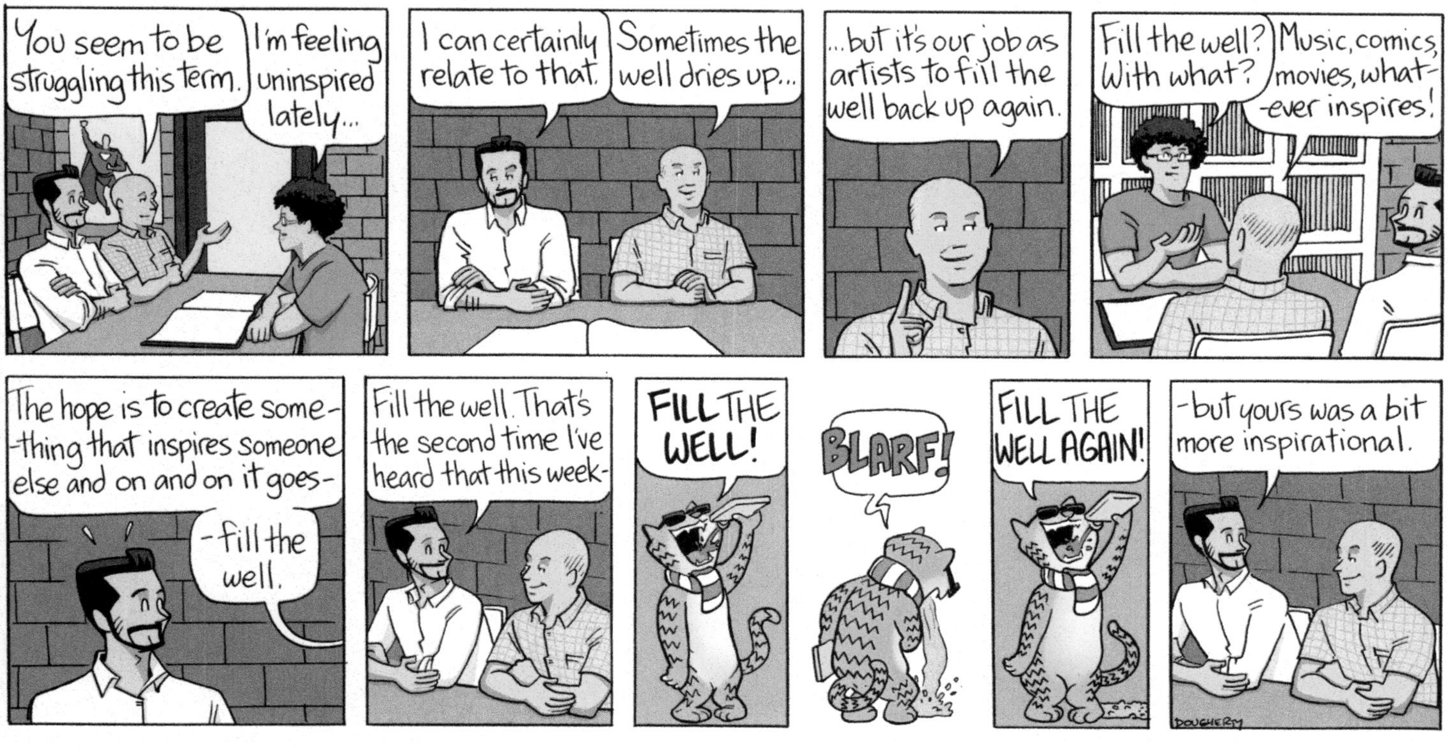
You seem to be struggling this term.
I'm feeling uninspired lately...
I can certainly relate to that.
Sometimes the well dries up...
...but it's our job as artists to fill the well back up again.
Fill the well? With what?
Music, comics, movies, what-ever inspires!
The hope is to create some-thing that inspires someone else and on and on it goes-
-fill the well.
Fill the well. That's the second time I've heard that this week-
FILL THE WELL!
BLARF!
FILL THE WELL AGAIN!
-but yours was a bit more inspirational.
DOUGHERTY

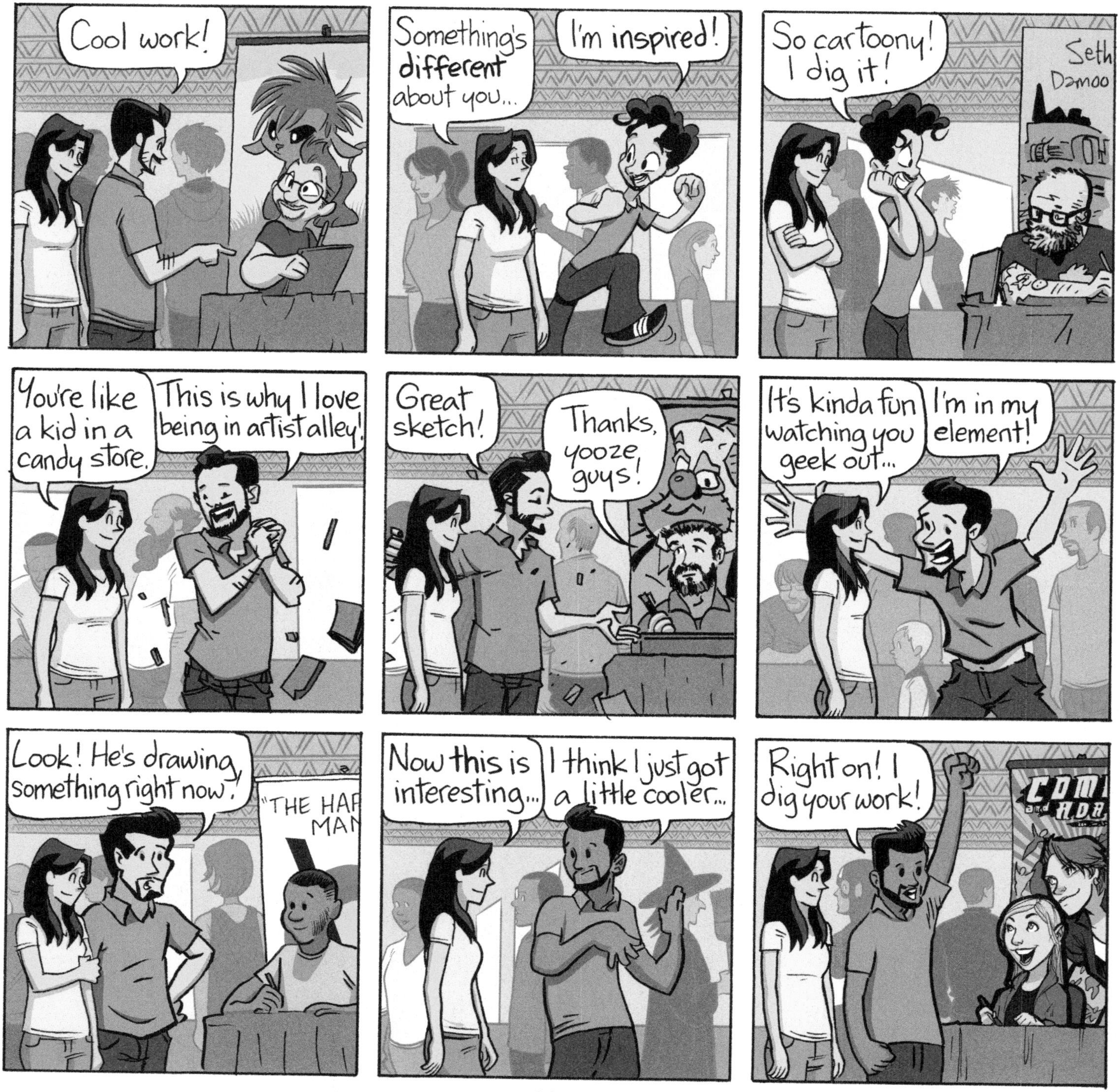
Cool work!
Something's **different** about you...
I'm **inspired**!
So cartoony! I dig it!
Seth Damoo
You're like a kid in a candy store.
This is why I love being in artist alley!
Great sketch!
Thanks, yooze guys!
It's kinda fun watching you geek out...
I'm in my element!
Look! He's drawing something right now!
"THE HA
MA
Now **this** is interesting...
I think I just got a little cooler...
Right on! I dig your work!

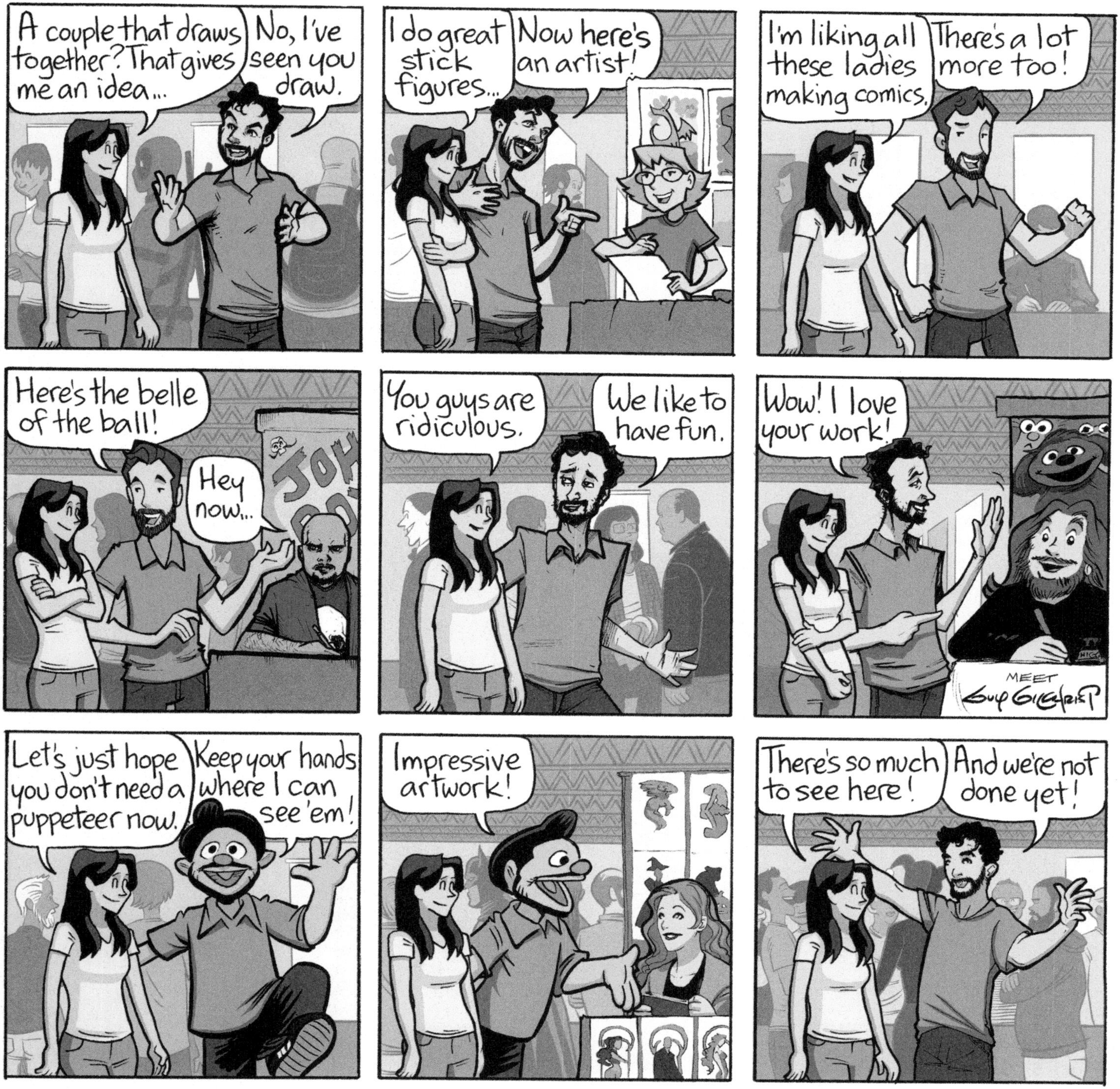
A couple that draws together? That gives me an idea...
No, I've seen you draw.
I do great stick figures...
Now here's an artist!
I'm liking all these ladies making comics.
There's a lot more too!
Here's the belle of the ball!
Hey now...
You guys are ridiculous.
We like to have fun.
Wow! I love your work!
MEET
GUY GILCHRIST
Let's just hope you don't need a puppeteer now.
Keep your hands where I can see 'em!
Impressive artwork!
There's so much to see here!
And we're not done yet!

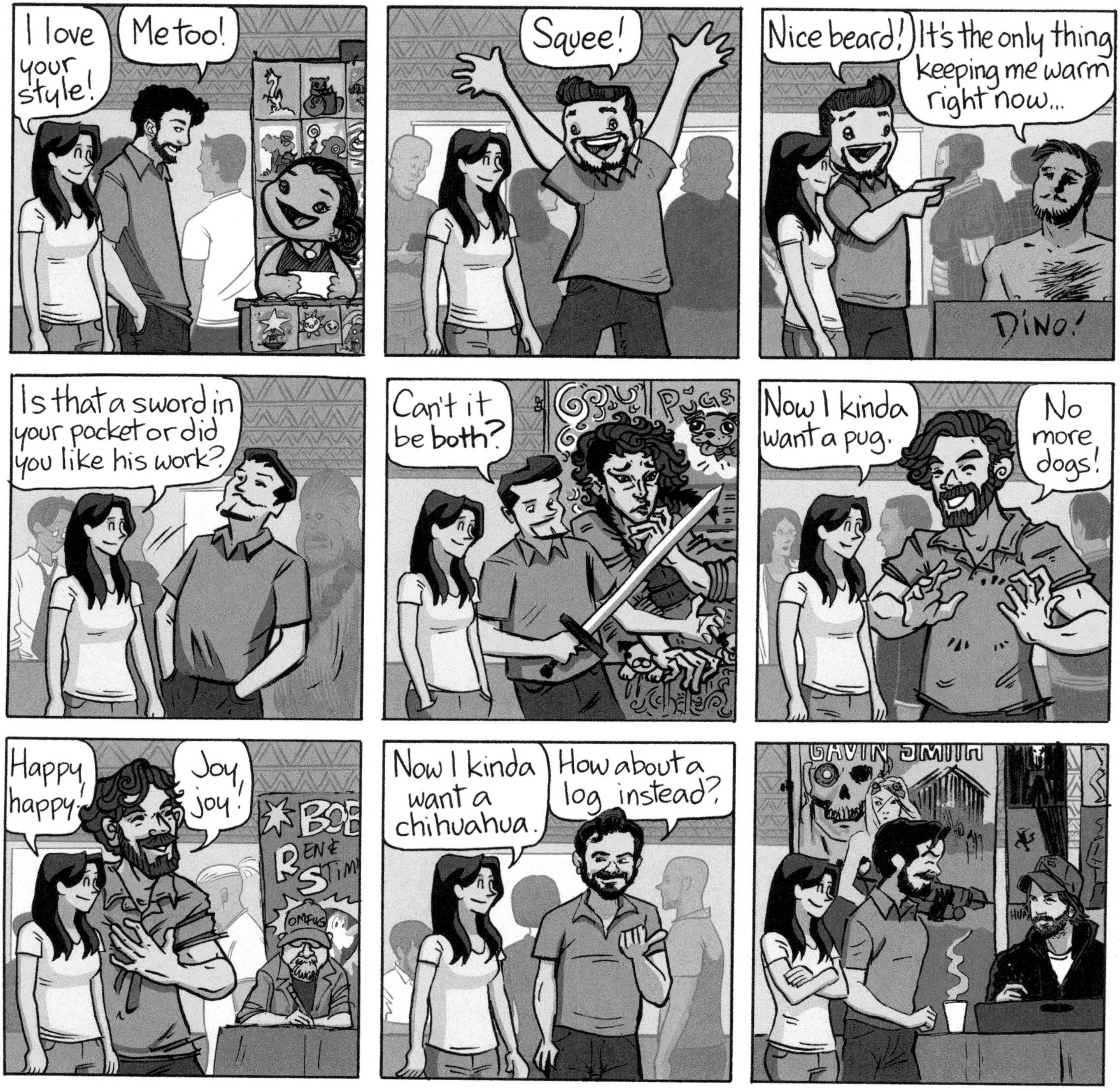
I love your style!
Me too!
Squee!
Nice beard!
It's the only thing keeping me warm right now...
DINO!
Is that a sword in your pocket or did you like his work?
Can't it be **both**?
PUGS
Now I kinda want a pug.
No more dogs!
Happy, happy!
Joy, joy!
Now I kinda want a chihuahua.
How about a log instead?

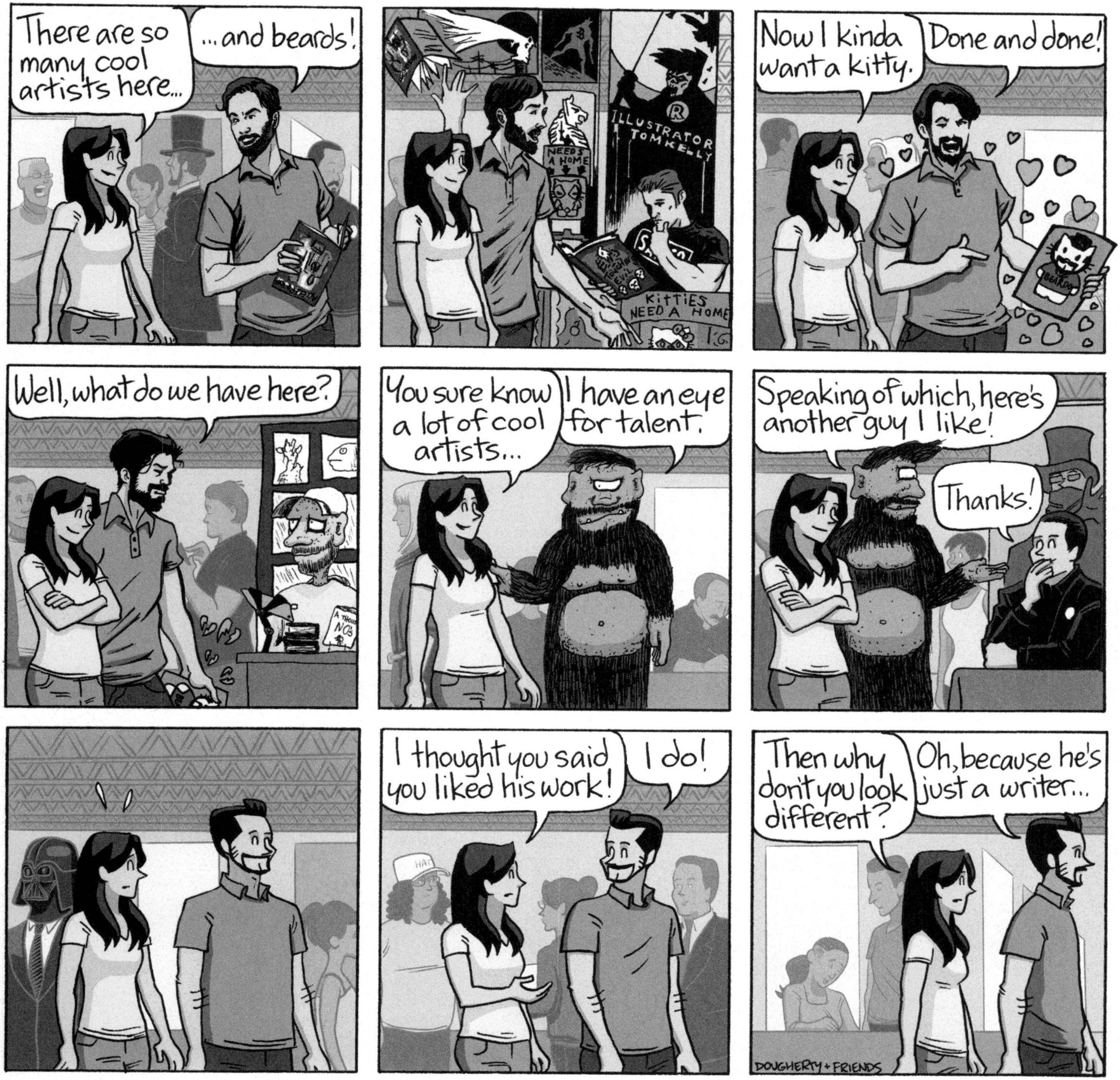
There are so many cool artists here...
...and beards!
ILLUSTRATOR TOM KELLY
NEEDS A HOME
KITTIES NEED A HOME
Now I kinda want a kitty.
Done and done!
Well, what do we have here?
You sure know a lot of cool artists...
I have an eye for talent.
Speaking of which, here's another guy I like!
Thanks!
I thought you said you liked his work!
I do!
Then why don't you look different?
Oh, because he's just a writer...
DOUGHERTY + FRIENDS

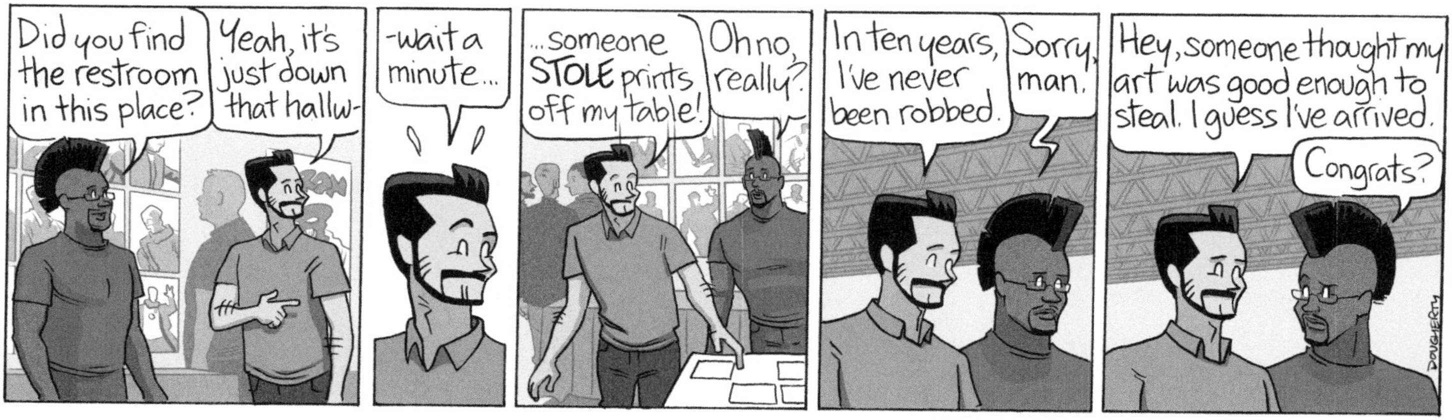
Did you find the restroom in this place?
Yeah, it's just down that hallw-
-wait a minute...
...someone STOLE prints off my table!
Oh no, really?
In ten years, I've never been robbed.
Sorry, man.
Hey, someone thought my art was good enough to steal. I guess I've arrived.
Congrats?
DOUGHERTY

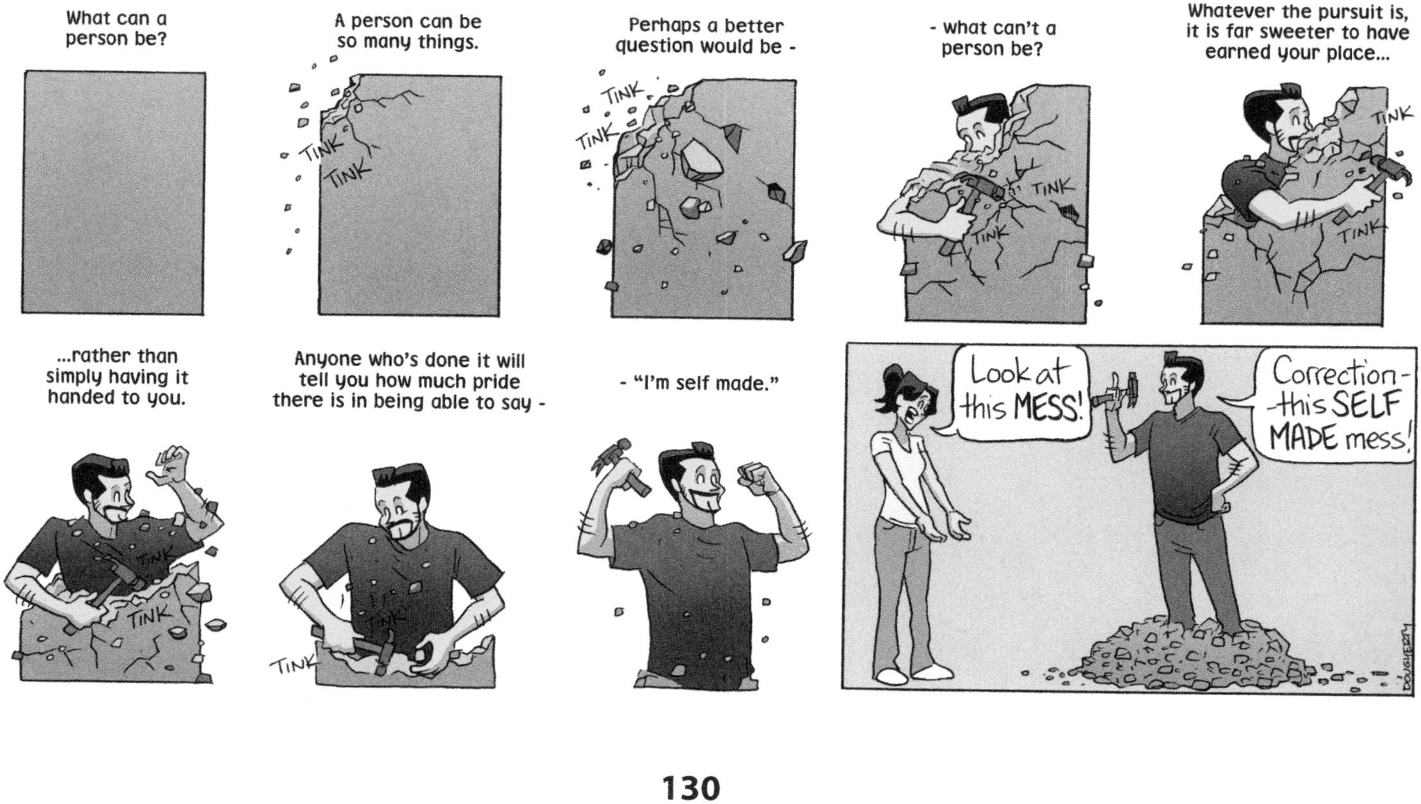
What can a person be?
A person can be so many things.
TINK
TINK
Perhaps a better question would be -
TINK
TINK
- what can't a person be?
TINK
TINK
Whatever the pursuit is, it is far sweeter to have earned your place...
TINK
TINK
...rather than simply having it handed to you.
TINK
TINK
Anyone who's done it will tell you how much pride there is in being able to say -
TINK
TINK
- "I'm self made."
Look at this MESS!
Correction - -this SELF MADE mess!
DOUGHERTY

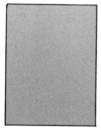

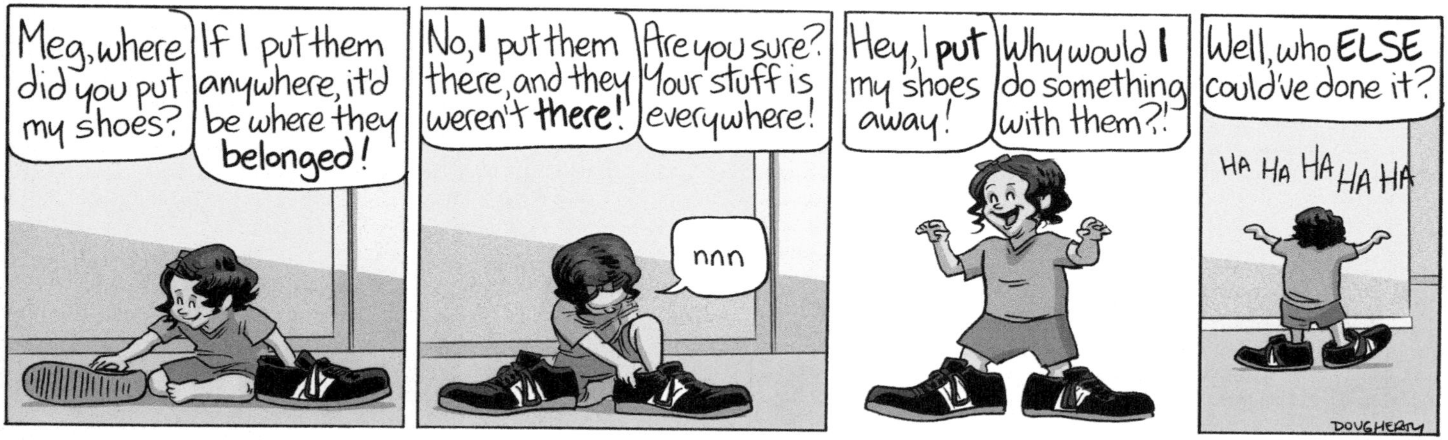
Meg, where did you put my shoes?
If I put them anywhere, it'd be where they **belonged**!
No, **I** put them there, and they weren't **there**!
nnn
Are you sure? Your stuff is everywhere!
Hey, I **put** my shoes away!
Why would **I** do something with them?!
Well, who **ELSE** could've done it?
HA HA HA HA HA
DOUGHERTY

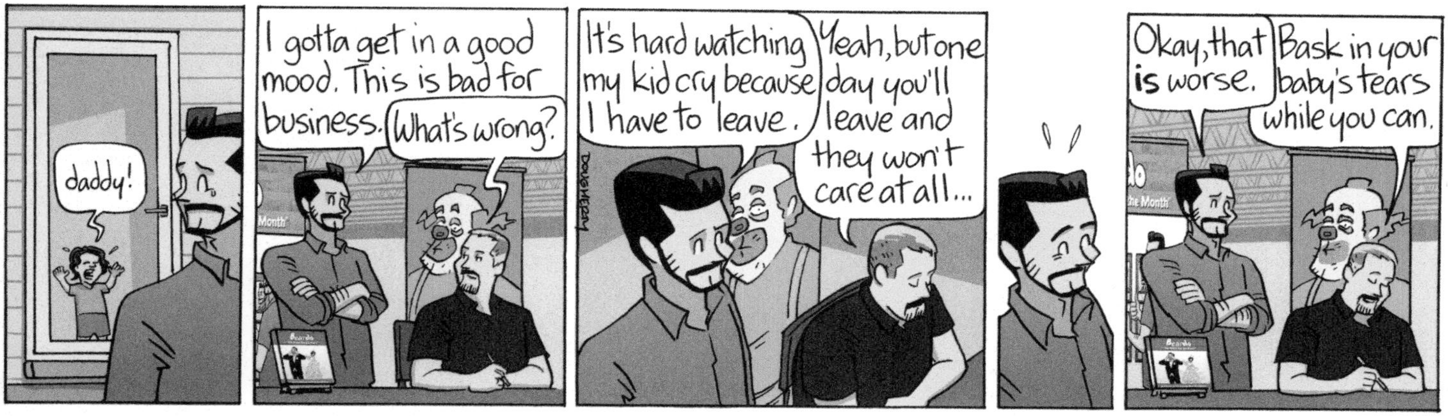
daddy!
I gotta get in a good mood. This is bad for business.
What's wrong?
DOUGHERTY
It's hard watching my kid cry because I have to leave.
Yeah, but one day you'll leave and they won't care at all...
Okay, that **is** worse.
Bask in your baby's tears while you can.

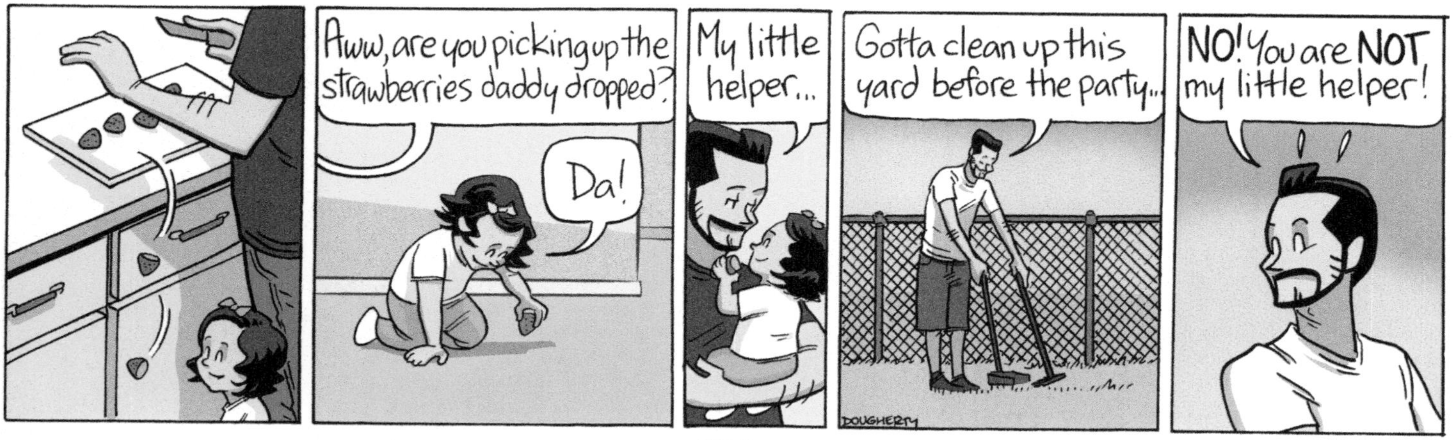
Aww, are you picking up the strawberries daddy dropped?
Da!
My little helper...
Gotta clean up this yard before the party...
DOUGHERTY
NO! You are **NOT** my little helper!

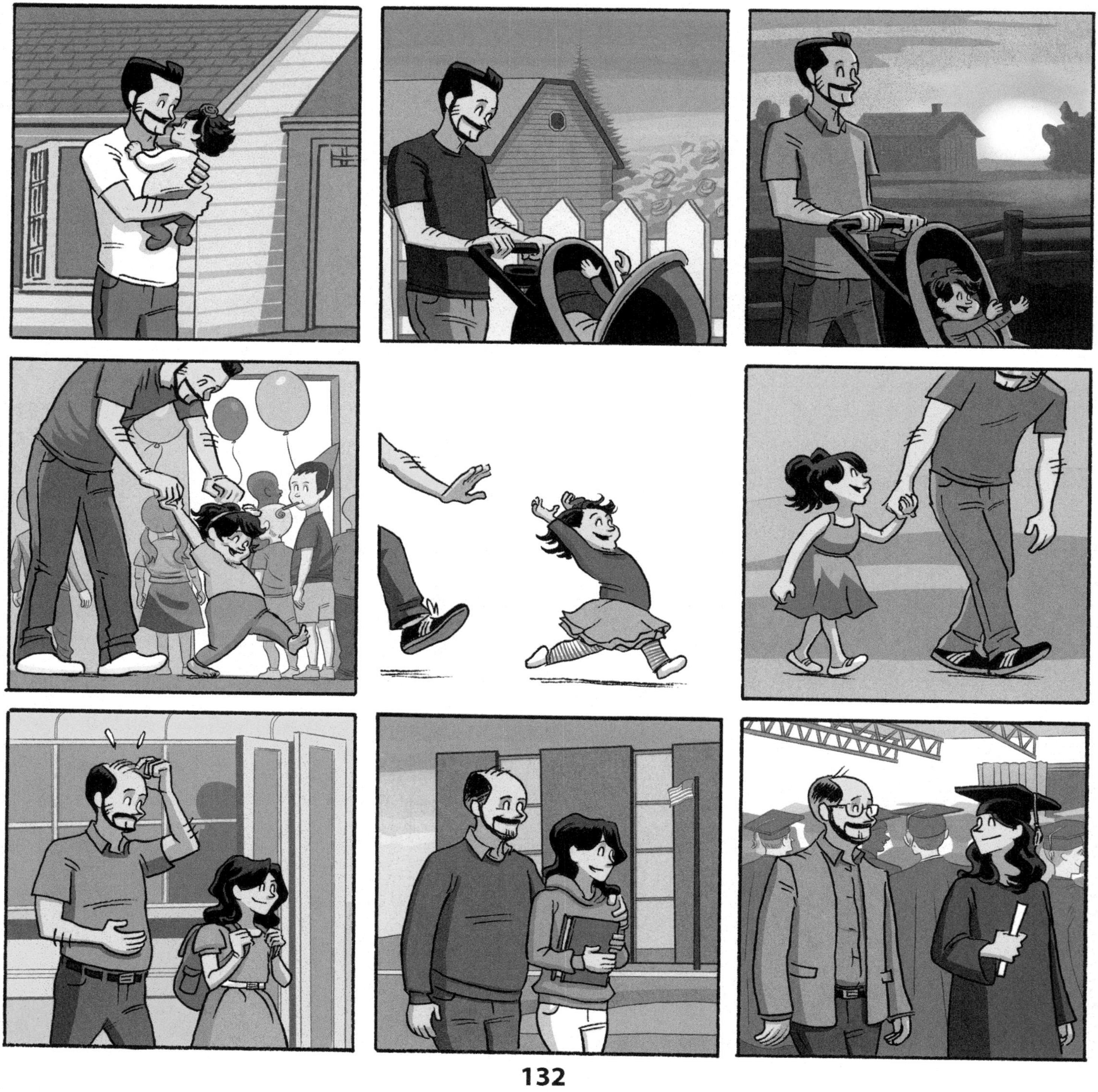

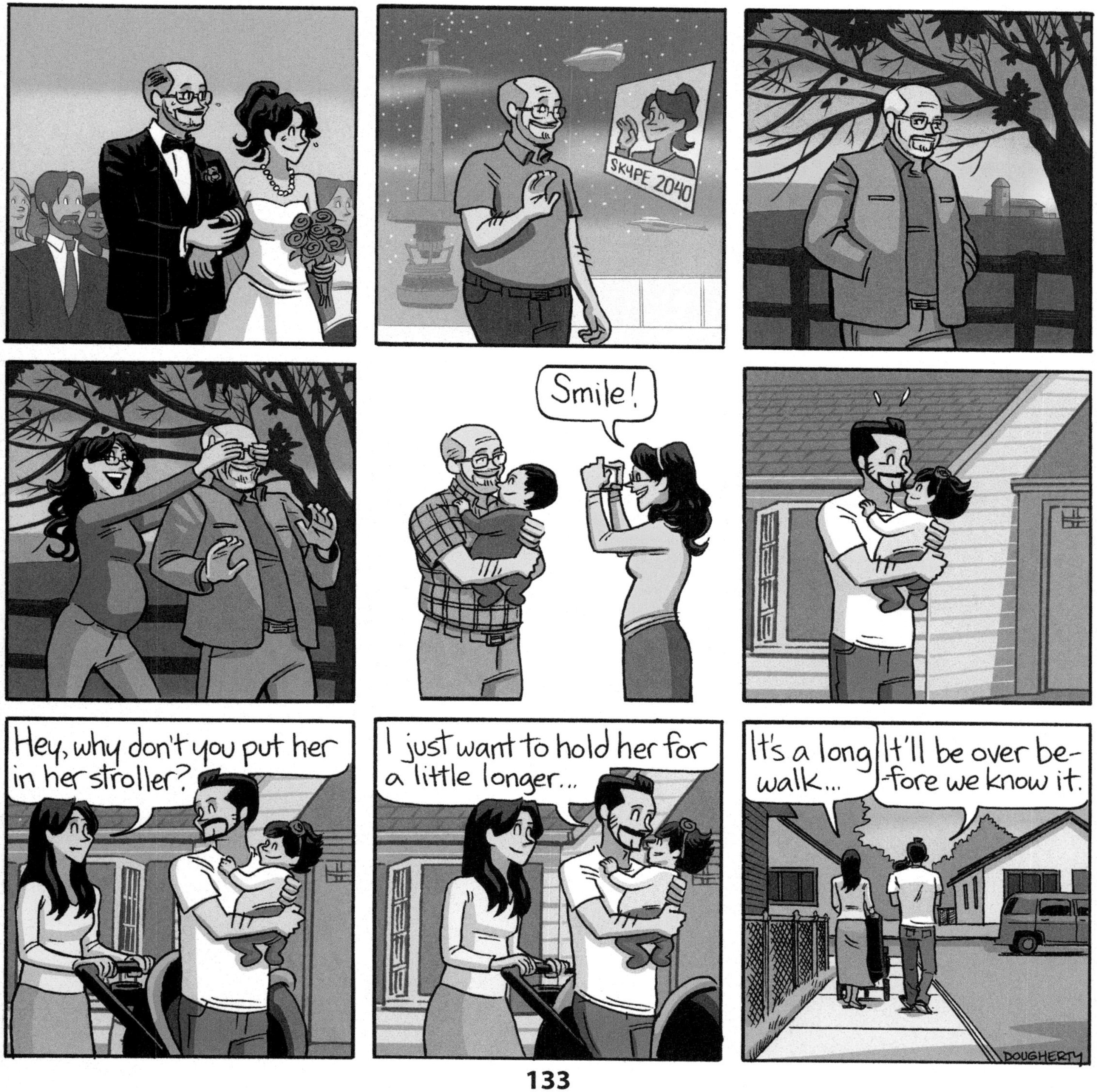
SKYPE 2040
Smile!
Hey, why don't you put her in her stroller?
I just want to hold her for a little longer...
It's a long walk...
It'll be over be-fore we know it.
DOUGHERTY

The End

Aftershave
Parting Thoughts About Beardo

It's hard to believe that it's been ten years of Beardo. I had to go back and reread the previous Aftershaves just to remind myself of where I was when all of this started. To say that my life has changed since 2006 is putting it lightly, but one thing has remained the same: at the end of each book I still feel like I have more stories to tell. In fact, I'm hungry to tell them, and I'm grateful for that hunger. Hunger is fuel as far as I'm concerned!

Despite this feeling of always wanting to do more, my days are full to the brim! If you've read this far, you know the score. I tour the comic convention circuit pretty hard (25 appearances in 2016 alone), teach how to make comics at the International School of Comics in Chicago, write and record music, write and illustrate my work *and* illustrate the work of others. It's a wonderful life if I stopped right there, but I guess I got greedy because I added a beautiful baby girl into the mix.

Well, *we* added a baby girl. Meg is not without blame for this little creature that is already growing up way too fast. Audrey Helen Dougherty was born on May 9th, 2015 and our lives have been forever changed for the better. Being her Dad means everything to me, and it's my personal mission to make sure she knows - above all else - that she is loved by her parents.

(She should probably know some other stuff too. I mean, I ain't raising no fool! And certainly not one who would use no double negative in no sentence! Go for quadruple negative or go home!)

We're still new to raising a child, and we're still learning how to juggle and balance everything that needs to be done. Part of what I want to exemplify is that with hard work and determination, you can be anything you want to be. The trouble with that is life isn't just about work. And I have a hard time accepting that. I have always struggled to relax. I am not one to live the moment as much as I'd like, and yet something has changed in me since becoming a father. I *still* struggle to relax and live in the moment, but now I desperately want to because they seem so fast and fleeting. As of this writing, she is 18 months old, and I'm afraid that if I blink I'll open my eyes to find her driving my shriveled shell of a body to a nursing home, yelling over the passing traffic, "Don't blame me, Dad! This is the best nursing home that comic money can buy!"

All of this is leading up to my big point: which is that I'm hanging up Beardo for the time being. I'm not saying that I'll never do another Beardo, but this will be the first time that I've finished a book and didn't start creating strips to plan for a follow up.

This was a decision that has been weighing on me all year, and made me really think about how I was going to end this book if it turned out to be the last one. I always had another ending in mind (I won't tell you what it is) but children have a way of changing your perspective on a lot of things, and this book is no exception. If this truly is the last book, I couldn't be happier with where I left it. And for the record, in Beardo's world Prince is still alive and well, as are most of the celebrities who passed in this awful year. (2016 can keep Castro though.)

And I'm certainly not retiring from comics! I feel like I'm just getting started, and I'm proud to say that I have a lot of new work lined up for 2017. My series *Touching Evil* will be getting the lion's share of my attention, and - if you haven't checked it out - it's now available in a deluxe limited edition hardcover thanks to a successful Kickstarter. The other work? Well, I can't speak to that just yet but I hope you'll stay tuned.

I've always been blessed with an amazing fan base for Beardo that has grown more and more with each passing book. But I learned a brand new facet as to why they (you) are amazing while I was on the road this year. I have several books on my table, and while Beardo is the most expanded series in my credentials, it's also the toughest sell. When they see one of my children's books with DJ, they're already thinking of who they're going to read it to. When they hear the premise of *Touching Evil*, they know in an instant whether or not it's the book for them. Beardo, on the other hand, is something that people need to already be reading if they're going to pick up a book, which is somewhat of a frustrating paradox! I can't really sell it to them, they're either already fans or they're moving on. Most people get their start on Beardo by reading it for free on GoComics.com or on my many social media platforms. I'm certainly not expecting every one of my hundreds of thousands of readers to actually buy a book, but I will say right now to you who bought this book: thank you. This series has lasted for ten years in what I would argue has been one of the toughest times for comic strips to exist, and it's all because you spent your hard-earned cash on something you like.

Unless you stole it, in which case I retract my thank you. Police, seize this person holding me right now! I'm a stolen book, help!

Let's keep those thank yous going by thanking one of my students who helped me immensely. Milena Deneno colored 30 pages of this book, and is a talented and upcoming artist in her own right. You can find her on Instagram at @currykitty and at facebook.com/milenadenenoart. While I'm at it, thank you to The International School of Comics for bringing me on board to such an inspiring haven for the medium that I love, and to all of my students whose drive and talent is a source of motivation for me.

My ever-growing convention family, many of whom made a cameo in this book. See if you can spot them!

The good people at ComicMix, especially Glenn Hauman, for helping me assemble and print the Beardo series.

GoComics.com for putting me in the company of my heroes.

All of the comic book retailers who dare to take on a non-superhero book by a non-major label in newspaper strip format.

Anne and Robert Moniuk for their extra support during my Kickstarter campaign.

Michael Sanow for his support and inspiration. The man truly is a dynamo and a class act to boot. And he probably won't like the special mention, but if I didn't bug him every once in a while it just wouldn't be right.

As always, my Meg. I bounce nearly all of my comics off of her first to see if they're funny or not, so if it didn't make you laugh, it's really her fault. In all seriousness though, Meg's support is the biggest reason why I've been able to do what I do. Although I can't help but laugh and agree with something Gene Ha said in our class once about how artists really get married because they would like to have a friend. Thank you for being my friend, my wife, my love and the mother of our child.

Meg, that is. Not Gene Ha.

And now for the first time ever I get to talk to my daughter Audrey in a book! To my little sweet pea, I will always be there for you no matter what, and I look forward to all of our adventures together. I know we won't always see eye to eye, but I hope that will mostly be due to the fact that I'm much taller than you and very competitive in staring contests. I apologize in advance for all of my corny dad jokes, but I promise I will bust out the top shelf super-clever humor when you're old enough. I also apologize for tormenting any future suitors you bring around, but this is just what fathers do for daughters. And bear with me if I get emotional during any and all milestones in your life, it's really your fault for being so dear to my heart.

That's all for now. I can't believe I've reached this moment. It may seem sad, but if it's any consolation at all we plan on having more children. And as my wife pointed out, it wouldn't be fair to them if Audrey was the only one featured in Beardo.

Thanks a lot, Meg.

Dan Dougherty
Chicago, IL
December 1st, 2016

"Kick Out The Jams!"

How about that jam piece, eh? Clocking in at four pages, it is officially the longest Beardo strip ever made! The crazy thing is that it could have easily been much longer, and that's because I am fortunate enough to have a very extensive "con family" to draw upon. For those unfamiliar with the term, my "con family" is comprised of the fellow creators that I've befriended while out doing comic conventions across the country. Typically we only see each other at shows, as most of us either live too far away from each other or are just putting in too much time at the drawing board to get out. The convention circuit is really the only opportunity afforded to reconnect face to face, so I do my best to make the most of my time with them. Whether it's a low-key dinner to unwind after a long day of selling to the public, or a bombastic karaoke free-for-all, the point is that we are together in this journey. It's hard leaving my wife and daughter for days at a time, but knowing that I have my "con family" waiting for me helps to ease the stress.

In that spirit, I wanted to celebrate some of my fellow artists in a big show-stopping jam piece. The idea was simple: a walk through an Artist Alley would show Beardo being so inspired by some of his comrades that their style would literally rub off on him! The format needed to have something drawn by me in each panel as a constant (cue the appearance of my partner-in-crime Meg), and then an artist would first draw themselves at their table, then draw their take on Beardo in the subsequent two panels. The piece would then be passed off to the next artist, and the process would repeat until the gag reached its end.

When I started this at Cherry Capital Comic Con in May 2016, I didn't think it would fill up so fast! I was surprised to walk away from that show with the first two pages nearly filled, and by the time Wizard World Philadelphia rolled around the following weekend I had enough artists committed to it to finish all four pages.

A huge and heartfelt thank you goes out to everyone who was generous enough to contribute to this Super Beardo strip. The following is a guide to the featured artists and where to find their work.

PAGE ONE

Jay Fosgitt is the creator of *Bodie Troll*, and *Dead Duck and Zombie Chick* (Source Point Press). He is an artist on the *My Little Pony* comics, and has done other artwork for IDW, Marvel, Image, Boom, Archie, Hasbro, Rue Morgue Magazine, and Andrews McMeel publishing, among others. Jay is a member of The National Cartoonists Society. Find him at www.jayfosgitt.com.

Seth Damoose is Michigan based artist who has illustrated the web comic *Brat-Halla* and *Spook'd* as well as the Image Comics *I HATE Gallant Girl* and *Xenoholics*. He also contributed short stories for *Bomb Queen* (Image Comics,) and short stories in the *Even More Fund Comics, Digital Webbing Presents, Nightmare World* and *Tales of Mr. Rhee*. Seth is currently working on *Savants* (Source Point Press) written by the great Gary Reed. You can find Seth at www.toocartoony.com

Tony Miello is a freelance illustrator and cartoonist. He is the creator of the comic strip *Gapo the Clown*, and has worked on comics based on the popular cable television shows *Who Wants To Be A Superhero* and *Wolfman Mac's Chiller Drive-In* and has provided art for licensed properties from Marvel, DC Comics and LucasFilm. Tony has also worked on a number of projects for Caliber Comics and is the co-founder and publisher of Rocket Ink Studios (www.rocketinkstudios.com).

Cool work!
Something's different about you...
I'm inspired!
So cartoony! I dig it!
You're like a kid in a candy store.
This is why I love being in artist alley!
Great sketch!
Thanks, yooze guys!
It's kinda fun watching you geek out...
I'm in my element!
Look! He's drawing something right now!
Now this is interesting...
I think I just got a little cooler...
Right on! I dig your work!

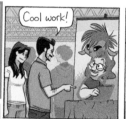

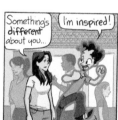

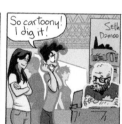

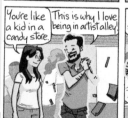

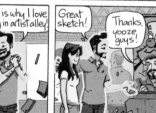

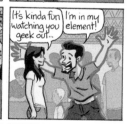

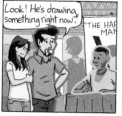

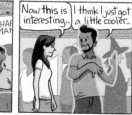

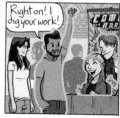

A couple that draws together? That gives me an idea...
No, I've seen you draw.
I do great stick figures...
Now here's an artist!
I'm liking all these ladies making comics.
There's a lot more too!
Here's the belle of the ball!
Hey now...
You guys are ridiculous.
We like to have fun.
Wow! I love your work!
MEET Guy Gilchrist
Let's just hope you don't need a puppeteer now.
Keep your hands where I can see 'em!
Impressive artwork!
There's so much to see here!
And we're not done yet!

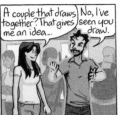

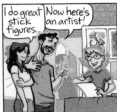

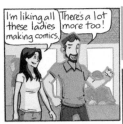

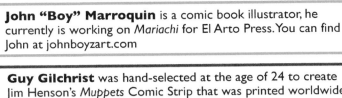

John "Boy" Marroquin is a comic book illustrator, he currently is working on *Mariachi* for El Arto Press. You can find John at johnboyzart.com

Guy Gilchrist was hand-selected at the age of 24 to create Jim Henson's *Muppets* Comic Strip that was printed worldwide in 660-plus newspapers daily from 1981 to 1986. Throughout the years, he has set his hand to such notable cartoons as *Teenage Mutant Ninja Turtles, Looney Tunes, Tom & Jerry, Fraggle Rock* and *The Pink Panther* and was instrumental in the creation of *The Muppet Babies*. Gilchrist took over the iconic *Nancy* comic strip in 1995, and is syndicated internationally in 80 countries and some 400 newspapers. *Nancy* has a viewership of 57 million readers around the world. To see more of Guy's work, go to www.guygilchristart.com

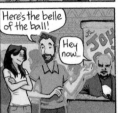

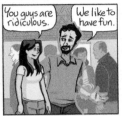

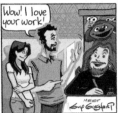

Kit Steele is an award-winning illustrator and Universal Studios gallery artist whose work exhibits her interest in Art Nouveau, Japanese animation, comics, and high fantasy illustration. Her work runs the gamut of dark and mystical to whimsical and silly. Her works can be found at: www.silvertales.storenvy.com

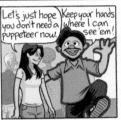

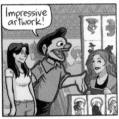

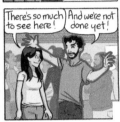

PAGE ONE CONTINUED

Victor Dandridge is a geek of infinite potential. He knows where the sidewalk ends and why the caged bird sings. He has a Green Lantern ring...and a hat. Oh yeah...and he's written some cool comics too. Bow before him. You can find Victor at www.vantageinhouse.blogspot.com

Comfort and Adam Comfort and Adam are the seven-time Harvey Award nominated husband-and-wife Action Faction responsible for the critically acclaimed series *The Uniques*, *Rainbow in the Dark*, and *The Complete Guide to Self-Publishing Comics* (Random House). They are a 100% symbiotic duo sharing the writing, pencilling, and coloring duties equally. Their long awaited return to their first series, *The Uniques*, has begun with the release of Vol. 1, and Vol. 2, with Vol. 3 soon on its heels. They will release their first weekly webcomic *Kitty Game* in 2017 with artist Corinne Roberts. Catch them at www.comfortandadam.com

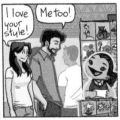

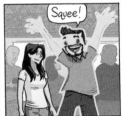

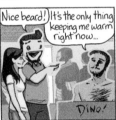

PAGE TWO

Corinne Roberts has written and illustrated *Imaginary Sea 1,2,3!* and *Out and About*. You can find more of her work at: www.corinneroberts.net

I love your style!
Me too!
Squee!
Nice beard!
It's the only thing keeping me warm right now...
DINO!
Is that a sword in your pocket or did you like his work?
Can't it be both?
PUGS
Now I kinda want a pug.
No more dogs!
Happy happy
Joy, joy!
Now I kinda want a chihuahua.
How about a log instead?

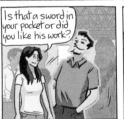

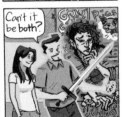

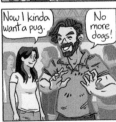

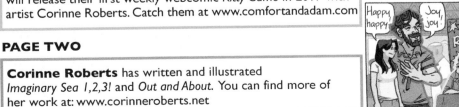

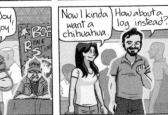

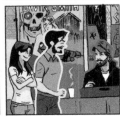

PAGE THREE

Bianca Roman-Stumpff is a painter from Orlando Florida. She loves to create artwork that is adorably random. Check out her work at http://biancaart.storenvy.com/products

Dean Haspiel is an Emmy award winner and Eisner, Harvey & Ignatz Award nominee. Dean created *Billy Dogma*, illustrated for HBO's *Bored To Death*, was a Master Artist at the Atlantic Center for the Arts, is a Yaddo fellow, a playwright, helped pioneer personal webcomics with the invention of ACT-I-VATE.com and TripCity.net, and is the co-founder of Hang Dai Editions in Brooklyn, NY. He has written and drawn many comic books, including *The Fox, Spider-Man, Batman, X-men, The Fantastic Four, Wonder Woman, Deadpool, Godzilla, Mars Attacks, Garbage Pail Kids, Creepy,* and collaborations with Harvey Pekar, Jonathan Ames, Inverna Lockpez, Jonathan Lethem, Mark Waid, and Stan Lee. Visit Dean at www.deanhaspiel.com

Ali Cantarella is a Michigan transplant turned Chicago artist, working and playing with a degree in illustration from Columbia College Chicago. When she's not working on artwork, Ali enjoys creating tasty food, biking around her beautiful city, and leaving half-drank cups of tea around her apartment. Visit Ali at www.TheWetStain.com

Bob Camp is an animator, cartoonist, comic book artist, director, and producer. His animation career started as a designer for animated series such as *ThunderCats, Silverhawks,* and later as a storyboard artist on *Tiny Toon Adventures*. Camp has been nominated for two Emmys, a Cable ACE Award, and an Annie Award for his work on *The Ren & Stimpy Show*. For more on Bob, visit www.boblabshop.com

Gavin Smith is a freelance artist living in Indianapolis. He is the artist for *The Accelerators* for Blue Juice Comics and has recently completed a story for *68* for Image. He also worked on motion comics for AT&T, the prequel comic *Charge* to the cult movie *All Superheroes Must Die,* as a cover artist for Action Lab Entertainment, and created and self-published *Human City*. He is a 2011 graduate of the Joe Kubert School. Find Gavin at www.gavinsmithcomics.com

PAGE FOUR

Tom Kelly is an award-winning comic artist who has worked for DC, Aw Yeah, Image, Marvel, Hasbro, Mattel, Topps, Fleer, Upper Deck, RCA, BMG and many more. Tom currently does a web comic *The Sword of the Savage Samurai,* as well as the children's web comic: *The Stuffed Animal Sagas*. You can find him at www.Tomkellyart.Deviantart.com and all over the Internet.

There are so many cool artists here...
...and beards!
Now I kinda want a kitty.
Done and done!
Well, what do we have here?
You sure know a lot of cool artists...
I have an eye for talent.
Speaking of which, here's another guy I like!
Thanks!
I thought you said you liked his work!
I do!
Then why don't you look different?
Oh, because he's just a writer...

DJ Corchin is an author and illustrator of many children's books. He uses his unique humor and wit to focus on socially conscious messages involving kindness and emotional awareness. A two-time winner for the International Literary Classic Awards, DJ has advocated music education through The 13th Chair, his highly popular alter ego. His award winning *I Feel...*children's series has sold over 10,000 copies worldwide and the *Band Nerds* book series over 15,000. DJ currently lives and works in Chicago. To learn more, visit www.djcorchin.com

Dirk Manning is best known as the writer/creator of *Tales of Mr. Rhee* and *Nightmare World* and *Love Stories About Death* (Devil's Due/1First Comics). Dirk is also the author of the ongoing inspirational column/book collection *Write Or Wrong: A Writer's Guide To Creating Comics* (Caliber/Bleeding Cool) and has written for the RPG company Reliquary Game Studios. More of Dirk's stories can be read in comic titles such as *Dia De Los Muertos* (Image Comics/Shadowline) and *The Legend of Oz: The Wicked West* (Aspen/Big Dog Ink) among various anthologies. Dirk can be found online at www.DirkManning.com

If this jam was as inspiring to you as it was to me, do yourself a favor and check these artists out. And tell them Beardo sent you.

Other Beardo books in the series

Volume One: The Art Degree Guarantee

Volume Two: Brew Harder!

Volume Three: 'Til Debt Do Us Part

Volume Four: Self-Employee of the Month

Also By Dan

Touching Evil Volume One: The Curse Escapes Written & Illustrated by Dan Dougherty

To order, go to beardocomics.com or djcorchin.com

Children's book collaborations with author DJ Corchin

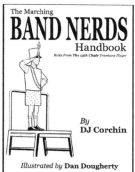
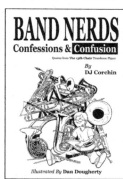

The Band Nerds Series

Sam & The Jungle Band

A Thousand No's

Thunderfeet

About the Author

Dan Dougherty is an award-winning comics creator from the suburbs of Chicago. He began his career in 2003 with his first creator-owned graphic novel *Cyclone Bill and the Tall Tales*. His most recent work has focused on the *Beardo* series and his hit supernatural thriller *Touching Evil*, which was collected into a special edition hardcover in 2016. He has illustrated dozens of comics and graphic novels, including *Bob Howard: Plumber of the Unknown, The Apocalypse Plan, Rotten, Moon Lake, Haunting Tales of Horrorbles*, and more. He has also illustrated numerous children's books with frequent collaborator DJ Corchin, including *A Thousand No's, You Got A Boogie, Sam & The Jungle Band, Thunderfeet*, and the *Band Nerds* series. Dan also teaches how to make comics at the International School of Comics in Chicago, and frequently tours the comic convention world to meet readers and find inspiration. When he isn't working in comics, Dan writes and records with his band On The Off Chance, who will be releasing their debut album in 2017.

Dan lives with his wife Meg, his daughter Audrey, and their two dogs Penny Lane and Abbey, who are both torn between feeling angry for all the attention they've lost to a baby and feeling full from all the food she drops on the floor.

About the Book

It's only appropriate that this book focuses on a baby, because this is the fifth book of the series, and - as the youngest of five - it is frequently babied and spoiled. It gets all of the attention right now while it's still fresh, much to the resentment of its fellow books. This book will have a much easier time as a child, as all of the mistakes and missteps were made on the previous books. This book will never know how hard the first book had it, and when this book is old enough the first book will be sure to never let him forget that. This book is a him, by the way. They've all been boys, except for the blue one. It's funny how life works.

As it gets older, this book will get away with more stuff than his siblings, because at this point his parents have stopped caring about enforcing every last little thing and are already dreaming of a day when they don't have to read any books. While this may seem unfair now, there will also come a time when this book envies the first book for all of its popularity, never truly understanding how hard the first book had to work for those accolades. None of the books will ever know that their father sometimes wonders if he should've stopped at one book.

This book's name is Henry. He hates it when you call him Hank, or - worse - Hanky. He is not a piece of tissue, that's absurd. He's a book.

This book will go through a goth phase, stealing makeup and clothes from the fourth book. As wild as this book's teenage years are, he will ultimately be the glue that holds the books together as they become adults, except for the second book, who isn't on speaking terms with anyone. And the third one, who is the middle child, and therefore forgettable.

CPSIA information can be obtained
at www.ICGtesting.com
Printed in the USA
FSOW04n0637040217
30386FS

9 781939 888495